Samuel Rawson Gardiner

Letters and Papers Relating to the First Dutch War

1652-1654 - Vol. 6

Samuel Rawson Gardiner

Letters and Papers Relating to the First Dutch War
1652-1654 - Vol. 6

ISBN/EAN: 9783337302528

Printed in Europe, USA, Canada, Australia, Japan

Cover: Foto ©Andreas Hilbeck / pixelio.de

More available books at **www.hansebooks.com**

LETTERS AND PAPERS

RELATING TO THE

First Dutch War

1652—1654

EDITED BY

C. T. ATKINSON

FELLOW OF EXETER COLLEGE, OXFORD
FORMERLY DEMY OF MAGDALEN COLLEGE, OXFORD

VOL. VI.

PRINTED FOR THE NAVY RECORDS SOCIETY
MDCCCCXXX

THE COUNCIL

OF THE

NAVY RECORDS SOCIETY

1930–1931

PATRON
THE KING

PRESIDENT
SIR FREDERIC G. KENYON, G.B.E., K.C.B., F.B.A., D.LITT., LL.D.

VICE-PRESIDENTS

JELLICOE, ADMIRAL OF THE FLEET, EARL, G.C.B., O.M., G.C.V.O., LL.D.
MURRAY, SIR OSWYN A. R., K.C.B.

RICHMOND, ADMIRAL SIR HERBERT W., K.C.B.
TANNER, J. R., LITT.D.

COUNCILLORS

ASTON, MAJOR-GENERAL SIR GEORGE G., K.C.B., R.M.
ATKINSON, C. T.
BRINDLEY, H. H., F.S.A.
BROWNING, ADMIRAL SIR MONTAGUE, G.C.B., G.C.M.G.
CALLENDER, PROFESSOR G. A. R., F.S.A.
DARTMOUTH, THE EARL OF, P.C., K.C.B.
DESART, THE EARL OF, P.C., K.P., K.C.B.
FAYLE, C. E.
FULLER, ADMIRAL SIR CYRIL T. M., K.C.B., C.M.G., D.S.O.
HOPE, ADMIRAL SIR GEORGE P. W., K.C.B., K.C.M.G.
LITTLE, REAR-ADMIRAL C. J. C., C.B.
NORRIS, VICE-ADMIRAL DAVID T., C.B., C.M.G.
OWEN, LIEUT.-COMMANDER J. H., R.N.

PUREY-CUST, ADMIRAL SIR HERBERT E., K.B.E., C.B.
RODD, SIR RENNELL, P.C., G.C.B., G.C.M.G., G.C.V.O., M.P.
ROSE, PROFESSOR J. HOLLAND, LITT.D.
ROUSE, W. H. D., LITT.D., F.R.G.S., M.R.A.S.
SMITH, ADMIRAL SIR AUBREY C. H., K.B.E., C.B., M.V.O.
TAYLOR, CAPTAIN A. H., O.B.E., R.N.
THURSFIELD, CAPTAIN H. G., R.N.
TUNSTALL, W. C. B.
VANDERVELL, COMMANDER H., R.N.V.R.
WEBB, ADMIRAL SIR RICHARD, K.C.M.G., C.B.
WHITE, CAPTAIN JOHN BELL, C.B.E., R.N.R.

SECRETARY
W. G. PERRIN, O.B.E., Admiralty, S.W.

HON. TREASURER
SIR W. GRAHAM GREENE, K.C.B.

THE COUNCIL of the NAVY RECORDS SOCIETY wish it to be distinctly understood that they are not answerable for any opinions or observations that may appear in the Society's publications. For these the responsibility rests entirely with the Editors of the several works.

PREFACE

THE unduly long interval which has elapsed since the appearance of the previous volume of this collection requires both explanation and some apology to any members of the Society who for any reason may have wished to see the Dutch War papers completed. The explanation is, briefly, the war, but for which Volume VI should have been ready in 1915. Moreover, besides involving a five years' postponement of the work I had in hand, the war left me for various reasons with very little spare time at my disposal and, as members of the Society know, one of its results has been a considerable reduction in the Society's output. With several volumes of much greater interest and importance to be fitted into the reduced programme, it was not till three or four years ago that it came to be realised that it was high time to complete the Dutch War series, and it happened that then I found myself unusually busy with other things. It had also been decided to include in this volume the index to the whole series; its preparation has naturally taken some time, while a further delay has been caused by the necessity for investigating certain criticisms which have recently been made on the accuracy of the translations of the papers selected from the Dutch archives.

It is much to be regretted that these criticisms

should not have been made long ago, on the appearance of the earlier volumes. Had there been any suggestion then that the translations were seriously faulty, those not yet published could have been revised before more volumes were issued. However, as it would seem that the translator was not well versed in seventeenth-century Dutch nautical terminology, the Council of the Society has decided to have the translations tested by someone who possesses the necessary qualifications. It was at first hoped to include the errata in the present volume, but Captain A. C. Dewar, R.N., who has very kindly undertaken to compare the translations with the transcripts, finds that although the errors are not numerous, nor, on the whole, very serious, the work is likely to take some time. It is therefore proposed to issue the errata later on in loose sheets, rather than still further delay this volume by waiting till all the errata are ready. The translated documents in this volume Captain Dewar has already examined and corrected, and I am very grateful to him for his help.

This collection has only included documents dealing with the main theatre of war, the North Sea and the Channel. No documents concerned with affairs in the Mediterranean were included among those collected by Dr. Gardiner and handed over to me, as they would presumably have been had it been his intention to include them. The operations 'up the Straits,' though in themselves very interesting, form a quite separate and subordinate episode, which exercised so little influence over the main course of the war that they may well be left to be treated separately, probably as a section in another volume of *The Naval Miscellany*. There is the less reason for

PREFACE

their inclusion in this collection in that many papers, throwing considerable light on the doings of Appleton, Badiley, and Galen, have recently been published in the *Calendar of State Papers, Venetian*, edited by Mr. A. B. Hinds. These papers also contain many interesting letters from Paulucci, the Venetian representative in London, which are concerned with the war in home waters. Though hardly authoritative, as they contain many inaccurate and doubtful statements and represent rather current rumour and the general belief than actual facts, they should certainly be consulted by anyone interested in the Dutch wars.

In conclusion, I should like to thank the Secretary of the Society, to whose assistance over this volume I am much indebted. He has, in particular, himself checked the transcripts of the English papers at the Public Record Office, and has in many other ways given invaluable help, which I am very glad to acknowledge.

C. T. A.

September 1930.

CONTENTS

OF

THE SIXTH VOLUME

PART XIII

THE LAST WINTER

	PAGE
1213. August $\frac{10}{20}$, 1653.—De With to States General[1]	23
1214. August $\frac{11}{21}$, 1653.—A Letter from the Hague	24
1215. $\frac{\text{August } 23}{\text{September 2}}$, 1653.—De With to S.G.	27
1216. $\frac{\text{August } 26}{\text{September 5}}$, 1653.—Nieuport to Beverning	29
1217. $\frac{\text{August } 26}{\text{September 5}}$, 1653.—Navy Victuallers to Navy Commissioners[2]	29
1218. $\frac{\text{August } 26}{\text{September 5}}$, 1653.—Beverning and van der Perre to S.G.	31
1219. $\frac{\text{August } 27}{\text{September 6}}$, 1653.—Lawson to Monck	32
1220. $\frac{\text{August } 27}{\text{September 6}}$, 1653.—Welch to Downing	37
1221. $\frac{\text{August } 29}{\text{September 8}}$, 1653.—Benson to Thurloe	39
1222. $\frac{\text{August } 30}{\text{September 9}}$, 1653.—De With to S.G.	39
1223. $\frac{\text{August } 30}{\text{September 9}}$, 1653.—Bradshaw to Thurloe	41
1224. September $\frac{1}{11}$, 1653.—N.C. to Admiralty Commissioners[3]	43
1225. September $\frac{2}{12}$, 1653.—Proceedings of Council of State[4]	44
1226. September $\frac{2}{12}$, 1653.—Orders for Captain Wm. Hill	44
1227. September $\frac{2}{12}$, 1653.—A Letter .. from Holland	45
1228. September $\frac{2}{12}$, 1653.—A Letter .. from the Hague	47

[1] Afterwards S.G.   [2] Afterwards N.C.
[3] Afterwards A.C.   [4] Afterwards C.o.S.

		PAGE
1229. September $\frac{3}{13}$, 1653.—List of Ships		49
1230. September $\frac{4}{14}$, 1653.—De With to S.G.		53
1231. September $\frac{6}{16}$, 1653.—Knowlinge to N.C.		55
1232. September $\frac{6}{16}$, 1653.—Bourne to A.C.		56
1233. September $\frac{7}{17}$, 1653.—Orders by de With		58
1234. September $\frac{8}{18}$, 1653.—Pointer to N.C.		60
1235. September $\frac{9}{19}$, 1653.—De With to S.G.		61
1236. September $\frac{10}{20}$, 1653.—Committee of Council to S.G.		63
1237. September $\frac{10}{20}$, 1653.—Victuallers to A.C.		68
1238. September $\frac{13}{23}$, 1653.—Proceedings of C.o.S.		70
1239. September $\frac{13}{23}$, 1653.—Beverning and van de Perre to S.G.		70
1240. September $\frac{13}{23}$, 1653.—Van de Perre to de Bruyne		72
1241. September $\frac{13}{23}$, 1653.—A.C. to N.C.		72
1242. September $\frac{18}{28}$, 1653.—Monck to Willoughby		73
1243. September $\frac{10}{20}$, 1653.—N.C. to C.o.S.		74
1244. September $\frac{10}{20}$, 1653.—Decision of Court Martial		75
1245. September $\frac{10}{20}$, 1653.—De With to S.G.		76
1246. September $\frac{20}{30}$, 1653.—Bradshaw to C.o.S.		78
1247. September $\frac{20}{30}$, 1653.—Blake to Moulton		79
1248. $\frac{\text{September 22}}{\text{October 2}}$, 1653.—N.C. to A.C.		80
1249. $\frac{\text{September 26}}{\text{October 6}}$, 1653.—Bourne to A.C.		82
1250. $\frac{\text{September 26}}{\text{October 6}}$, 1653.—Harman to A.C.		84
1251. $\frac{\text{September 27}}{\text{October 7}}$, 1653.—Bourne to A.C.		85
1252. $\frac{\text{September 29}}{\text{October 9}}$, 1653.—Bourne to N.C.		87
1253. $\frac{\text{September 29}}{\text{October 9}}$, 1653.—Instructions of C.o.S.		89
1254. $\frac{\text{September 30}}{\text{October 10}}$, 1653.—Hutchinson and Pett to A.C.		93
1255. $\frac{\text{September 30}}{\text{October 10}}$, 1653.—Committee of Council to S.G.		94
1256. October $\frac{1}{11}$, 1653.—Hayward to C.o.S.		98
1257. October $\frac{2}{12}$, 1653.—Bourne to A.C.		100
1258. October $\frac{4}{14}$, 1653.—Myngs to A.C.		104
1259. October $\frac{4}{14}$, 1653.—Commissions by Blake and Monck		104
1260. October $\frac{5}{15}$, 1653.—Order of A.C.		106
1261. October $\frac{5}{15}$, 1653.—Pett to A.C.		107
1262. October $\frac{6}{16}$, 1653.—De With to S.G.		109
1263. October $\frac{7}{17}$, 1653.—Bisdommer to Beverning		112
1264. October $\frac{7}{17}$, 1653.—Advertisements from London		113
1265. October $\frac{8}{18}$, 1653.—Bourne to A.C.		114
1266. October $\frac{12}{22}$, 1653.—Order of A.C.		116
1267. October $\frac{15}{25}$, 1653.—Decisions of Council		117

CONTENTS

xiii

		PAGE
1268. October $\frac{16}{20}$, 1653.—De With to S.G.	.	119
1269. October $\frac{17}{27}$, 1653.—Ruijter to S.G.	.	122
1270. October $\frac{19}{20}$, 1653.—De With to S.G.	.	124
1271. October $\frac{21}{31}$, 1653.—Bourne to A.C.	.	128
1272. $\frac{\text{October 26}}{\text{November 5}}$, 1653.—De With to S.G.	.	130
1272A. $\frac{\text{October 26}}{\text{November 6}}$, 1653.—Mayor of Colchester to Lieut. of Tower	.	132
1273. $\frac{\text{October 28}}{\text{November 7}}$, 1653.—Additional Article of War	.	133
1274. $\frac{\text{October 28}}{\text{November 7}}$, 1653.—A Letter of Intelligence	.	134
1275. $\frac{\text{October 31}}{\text{November 10}}$, 1653.—Orders of A.C.	.	136
1276. Aug. 31 to Nov. 1, 1653.—Ruijter's Journal	.	136
1277. November $\frac{2}{12}$, 1653.—Wassenaer to S.G.	.	158
1278. November $\frac{3}{13}$, 1653.—De With to S.G.	.	161
1279. November $\frac{4}{14}$, 1653.—A Letter from the Hague	.	164
1280. November $\frac{4}{14}$, 1653.—De With to Beverning	.	165
1281. November $\frac{4}{14}$, 1653.—Beverning to de With	.	166
1282. November $\frac{5}{15}$, 1653.—Wassenaer to S.G.	.	166
1283. November $\frac{6}{16}$, 1653.—Bourne to A.C.	.	168
1284. November $\frac{7}{17}$, 1653.—Wassenaer to S.G.	.	170
1285. November $\frac{10}{20}$, 1653.—Bourne to A.C.	.	172
1286. November $\frac{10}{20}$, 1653.—List of ships cast away	.	175
1287. November $\frac{11}{21}$, 1653.—Letter from Portsmouth	.	176
1288. November $\frac{12}{22}$, 1653.—Monck to C.o.S.	.	176
1288A. November $\frac{12}{22}$, 1653.—List of Ships in the Hope	.	177
1289. November $\frac{14}{24}$, 1653.—Hatsell to N.C.	.	178
1290. November $\frac{17}{27}$, 1653.—Monck to A.C.	.	180
1291. November $\frac{18}{28}$, 1653.—A Letter from Holland	.	182
1292. November $\frac{19}{29}$, 1653.—Monck to A.C.	.	183
1293. November $\frac{19}{29}$, 1653.—Warrant by Monck	.	186
1294. $\frac{\text{November 22}}{\text{December 2}}$, 1653.—Bourne to A.C.	.	186
1295. $\frac{\text{November 28}}{\text{December 8}}$, 1653.—Monck to A.C.	.	187
1296. December $\frac{2}{12}$, 1653.—Proceedings of C.o.S.	.	189
1297. December $\frac{3}{13}$, 1653.—Monck to A.C.	.	189
1298. December $\frac{5}{15}$, 1653.—Ruijter to S.G.	.	190
1299. December $\frac{16}{26}$, 1653.—Instructions by Generals	.	191
1300. December $\frac{16}{26}$, 1653.—Monck to C.o.S.	.	195
1301. December $\frac{16}{26}$, 1653.—Poortmans to Blackborne	.	196
1302. December $\frac{17}{27}$, 1653.—Order by the Generals	.	197
1303. December $\frac{17}{27}$, 1653.—A List of the Winter Guard	.	199
1304. $\frac{\text{December 26}}{\text{January 5}}$, 165$\frac{3}{4}$.—Report of Fleet Committee	.	202
1305. $\frac{\text{December 29}}{\text{January 8}}$, 165$\frac{3}{4}$.—Monck and Penn to Generals	.	203

CONTENTS

		PAGE
1306.	December 29 1653 / January 8, 1654.—N.C. to A.C.	205
1307.	Undated.—T. Taylor to A.C.	206
1308.	January 2/12, 1654.—Myngs to A.C.	208
1309.	January 3/13, 1654.—Monck and Penn to A.C.	209
1310.	January 3/13, 1654.—Foster to A.C.	210
1311.	January 5/15, 1654.—A Letter . . . from the Hague	216
1312.	January 5/15, 1654.—Disbrowe and Blake to Protector	217
1313.	January 6/16, 1654.—Monck and Penn to Generals	218
1314.	January 9/19, 1654.—Penn to A.C.	219
1315.	January 16/26, 1654.—Poortmans to Blackborne	220
1316.	January 20/30, 1654.—Penn to Generals	221
1317.	January 16-20 / 26-30, 1654.—Fragments of Journal	222
1318.	January 24 / February 3, 1654.—Pack to A.C.	225
1319.	January 25 / February 4, 1654.—Blake and Penn to A.C.	226
1320.	January 30 / February 9, 1654.—Blake and Penn to A.C.	226
1321.	January 31 / February 10, 1654.—Heaton to Blackborne	227
1322.	February 3/13, 1654.—Beverning to S.G.	228
1323.	February 4/14, 1654.—Wettewang to A.C.	229
1324.	February 5/15, 1654.—Blake and Penn to A.C.	230
1325.	February 6/16, 1654.—Petitions to Protector	232
1326.	February 14/24, 1654.—Blake and Penn to A.C.	235
1327.	February 15/25, 1654.—F. Willoughby to A.C.	238
1328.	February 16/26, 1654.—Porter to N.C.	239
1329.	February 17/27, 1654.—Blake and Penn to A.C.	241
1330.	February 22 / March 2, 1654.—E. Alkin to Blackborne	242
1331.	February 25 / March 7, 1654.—Blake and Penn to A.C.	243
1332.	February 27 / March 9, 1654.—E. Alkin to Blackborne	244
1333.	March 3/13, 1654.—A Letter of Intelligence	245
1334.	March 4/14, 1654.—Blake and Penn to A.C.	246
1335.	March 10/20, 1654.—An intercepted letter	247
1336.	March 14/24, 1654.—Blake and Penn to A.C.	247
1337.	March 18/28, 1654.—Commissioners for Sick and Wounded	248
1338.	March 18/28, 1654.—Blake and Penn to A.C.	249
1339.	April 13/23, 1654.—Mill to A.C.	251
1340.	April 14/24, 1654.—Sacheverell to A.C.	252
1341.	April 17/27, 1654.—Burton to A.C.	254
1342.	April 17/27, 1654.—Smyth to A.C.	256
1343.	April 17/27, 1654.—Stayner to A.C.	258
1344.	April 21 / May 1, 1654.—Proceedings of C.o.S.	259
1345.	April 25 / May 5, 1654.—Proceedings of C.o.S.	260

THE
FIRST DUTCH WAR

PART XIII

INTRODUCTORY

A. THE LAST WINTER.

THE last 'Part' of these papers ended with the departure on August $\frac{24}{3+}$ of a squadron of about forty sail under Rear-Admiral Lawson to resume the blockade of the Dutch coast which Monck had been forced to raise after the battle of the Texel. Lawson describes his movements in a long letter of $\frac{\text{Aug. 27}}{\text{Sept. 6}}$ from off the Texel (No. 1219), but his account does not come from the pen of a ready writer and is none too lucid. He seems to have picked up a fair number of prizes, mostly vessels trying to get home without waiting for a convoy (*cf.* No. 1228), but he encountered much bad weather and had some difficulty in keeping his squadron together. Several of his ships had been taken to sea after a somewhat perfunctory refit and were not really seaworthy. Bourne's invaluable series of letters from Harwich afford ample evidence as to the 'shaken' state of many of the ships and the great difficulties of repairing them for want of stores and, above all, of money (*cf.* No. 1224). Indeed, though Monck was able to leave Aldborough Bay on $\frac{\text{Aug. 29}}{\text{Sept. 8}}$ with a reinforcement of eighteen ships and met Lawson two days later (No. 1234), a council of 'flag officers,' which met that evening, decided that the 'great ships' and the merchantmen should 'go in,' leaving only a few frigates on the Dutch coast. Apparently one reason for this decision was that Monck had just missed meeting de With and bringing him to action. De With had sailed on Sept. $\tfrac{1}{11}$ (*cf.* No. 1227) for the coast of Norway with the double errand of escorting the outward-bound ' trade ' out of the reach of danger of interception and of bringing home the large number of vessels, 'Straitsmen,' East India 'return ships' and some West Indies traders as well as ships from the Baltic (*cf.* Nos. 1214, 1220 and 1235), which had been collecting in the shelter of the Norwegian ports to await an opportunity of a safe return home. De With puts his charge of outward-bound merchant ships at 340 and his escorting warships at forty-three (*cf.* No. 1230), and it may be wondered that Monck, whose squadron when united to Lawson's was over sixty strong, did not proceed Northward in search of de With and his charge. Encumbered with so large and important a convoy, de With, whose squadron by his own account was none too well equipped (*cf.* No. 1222), would have found himself in a difficult position.

No very definite account of the reasons for this decision is included in these papers, though it is clear that Monck's squadron was in no condition to keep the seas for any length of time or to stand the buffeting of an equinoctial gale in the North Sea. Much may be gleaned, however, from the long paper addressed by the Committee of the Council of the Admiralty to the States-General (No. 1255). This urges very strongly the advisability of copying the English and laying up the bulk of the ships during the stormy months of winter, so as to be better able to fit a large fleet out in the spring. It is here pointed out that the more ships are kept at sea during the winter the harder it will be to have them ready for service in the spring, when there will be more work for them to do. To keep a large fleet at sea during the winter is costly and dangerous, exhausting to the crews, consumes large quantities of stores and is hard to justify on the score of any object. There is nothing much to attack in the North Sea during the winter, while for the protection of Dutch trade the best plan is not to assemble large fleets of merchantmen, and so provide the enemy with an attractive quarry, but to let the ships come home singly or in small parties. If this is done the English are very unlikely to bring their fleet out for so small a prospect of gain. This document should be compared with Monck's letter of $\frac{\text{Nov. 28}}{\text{Dec. 8}}$ (No. 1295), in which he lays special stress on the importance of having the 'summer fleet' out before the Dutch, one of the chiefest advantages of which will be to block them up in their harbours before they can deal with us in similar fashion. It may be taken then that the policy adopted by the English was deliberate, and that a long view was being taken, the greater ultimate advantage being preferred to the lesser immediate gain. Still, it may be questioned whether, if Monck had known half as much about de With's fleet as these papers disclose, he would not have accepted the risks of a North Sea gale and pursued de With towards the Sound. Scouting, and what one may call 'cruiser-work,' was very much in its infancy, as has been shown in earlier 'Parts,' and to this de With, who was fully aware (*cf.* Nos. 1215 and 1222) of the risks he was running in carrying out his instructions, largely owed his escape.

De With's proceedings on this voyage are fully set out in a series of his letters (Nos. 1230, 1235, 1245, 1262, 1267, 1270, 1272, 1278, 1280, 1282), which is supplemented by Ruijter's Journal (No. 1276). It is not necessary here to detail his movements, but it is fairly clear that he was far from happy over the errand entrusted to him, put to sea with considerable and well-grounded misgivings, and was quite pessimistic as to his prospects in the event of a battle. With so small a force, he asks, what can he possibly effect? (No. 1222, *cf*. 1245). His ships were under-manned (No. 1236) and short of ammunition (No. 1215), they were not victualled beyond the middle of November (No. 1236), so that as early as Oct. $\frac{8}{18}$ he had to put his crews on short rations (No. 1262), while Ruijter speaks with some horror (No. 1267) of the greater number of the men being reduced to drinking water and having only two meals a day. De With speaks of the men as suffering from hunger and being very discontented (No. 1272), and the general tone of his letters is one of anxiety, almost of despondency. He was in such a hurry to be back (No. 1267) that he would not wait for all the homeward bound ships to join him (*cf.* No. 1291), and although two reinforcing squadrons (No. 1263) had joined him on Oct. $\frac{14}{24}$ and $\frac{18}{28}$ respectively (No. 1268), so that he had over seventy warships, they also were no better off for provisions. By $^{\text{Oct. 24}}_{\text{Nov. 3}}$ he was back off the Texel, very anxious to get into harbour without further delay (No. 1268, *cf.* 1270).

That his anxiety was well warranted is evident from the narratives of the storm which caught him and his fleet outside the Texel on $^{\text{Oct. 28}}_{\text{Nov. 7}}$ and continued to rage for several days. It is described by Ruijter (No. 1276), more fully by Wassenaer (No. 1277), and at some length by de With himself (No. 1278). The damage done was enormous: de With himself speaks of twenty-seven sail as dismasted, one has a list of fifteen vessels lost (No. 1286) mostly with all hands, and it is clear that the fleet was practically put completely out of action. De With was only too glad to get inside the Texel with what was left of his fleet, ' shattered or otherwise,' and he himself informed the States-General ' we cannot hold out at sea any longer.' The losses which his fleet had suffered seem to have at last convinced the States-General of the unwisdom of exposing the fleet at sea any longer (No. 1280), and, as one ' Letter of Intelligence ' (No. 1279) explains, ' fighting with the sea, the winter and the tempest, *remotis Anglis* ' had proved a doubtfully desirable policy. It is interesting to notice that the Zealanders ' who are used to sail and trade more in the winter than in the summer ' are said to have been largely responsible for this policy. It has been suggested by Dr. Gardiner (*Commonwealth and Protectorate*, Vol. III. p. 60) that ' only lack of provisions prevented the ships of the States from making a dash at the mouth of the Thames and sinking vessels to block up the river in support of the negotiations for peace.' This statement seems to be based only on the not very solid authority of a Letter of Intelligence from the Hague (No. 1274),[1] but it is clear from De With's letters

[1] Dr. Tanner, who adopts the same view in the *Cambridge Modern History* (Vol. IV. p. 476), seems merely to be following

that, even if this project may for a moment have been entertained (*cf.* No. 1272), its execution was completely beyond the capacity of his squadron. The voyage to Norway and back had been quite as much as it could undertake with any prospect of success; indeed, the Dutch had been lucky that the storm which shattered de With's fleet had not caught it a few days earlier with the convoy of merchantmen still at sea. It may be true, as Dr. Gardiner says (*ibid.*), that 'the English fleet was in no condition to make its former mastery felt,' but these documents (especially Nos. 1255 and 1295) show that if the English fleet was not actively exercising its hard-won 'command of the sea' during the autumn and winter months this was deliberately done, not because the Dutch were in effective condition to dispute it. Rather it was felt to be better to make sure of re-asserting that command decisively in the next spring. Dr. Tanner, too, has spoken (*Cambridge Modern History*, Vol. IV. p. 478) of Tromp's final effort as having 'set the Channel free.' This is hardly borne out by these documents. One finds Dutch traders bound for France and for the Indies taking advantage of De With's escort as far as the Skaw on their way 'Northabout' (No. 1230), one meets a few Dutch warships plying at the mouth of the Channel (No. 1289) and hears of cruisers being detached to look out for them (No. 1290), and of some prizes being captured (*cf.* No. 1321). Some captures of Dutch merchantmen in the Channel are also recorded, one lot being taken by Myngs off Dieppe (No. 1258) and others by Penn in February 1654 (No. 1317 and 1326), but it would seem (*cf.* No. 1340) that for all practical purposes the Channel was closed to Dutch trade until the acceptance by the United Provinces of Cromwell's terms re-opened it to their ships (*cf.* No. 1333).

Actually, the Channel seems to have been systematically and effectively patrolled by English ships during the winter. Monck, after deciding to send the 'great ships' into port and to pay off most of the hired merchantmen (No. 1268), seems to have collected a squadron of

Dr. Gardiner, and his acceptance of this view is hardly to be cited as an independent corroboration.

about sixty sail at the Hope (Nos. 1264 and 1281). It is at least probable, therefore, that had the Dutch fleet been in a condition to attempt the raid on 'the river' suggested in No. 1274, it might have found itself confronted with a force of about equal strength and quite as capable of undertaking active operations. Certainly when, early in December, Monck moved from the Hope to the Channel (No. 1281) his squadron seems to have been efficient enough to establish a quite systematic and effective patrol of the Channel. Part of the time the whole squadron appears to have been out plying between Beachy Head and the Isle of Wight and the opposite French coast (*cf.* No. 1300), but as a rule some cruisers were out patrolling, the main body being at St. Helen's in readiness to come out should the wind go into the East, 'for the better intercepting of any ships that wind may bring from the coast of Holland' (No. 1305). One may perhaps see in this the idea ultimately developed into Howe's system of open blockade: the main body was not exposed to the buffetings of the winter gales, and the few 'nimble frigates' who were at sea proved enough to discharge such work as there was to do. In January Monck went up to London (No. 1314), leaving the fleet in the Channel under Penn, who along with 'Disbrowe' (Desborough) had been joined with Blake and Monck as Generals at Sea (Dec. $\frac{2}{12}$), Lawson becoming Vice-Admiral in Penn's place. Blake was sufficiently recovered in health to be able to take command again in January, though rumours had been prevalent in October that he would not go to sea again (No. 1264). One finds Blake and Penn making several short cruises in the Channel during January and February (Nos. 1316 and 1317) and picking up several prizes (No. 1326). During this period the main trouble in the Channel seems to have come from Frenchmen, privateers or, as they are described, 'Brest pirates' (No. 1338). Lundy is mentioned as a point to be specially watched (No. 1336), and it is evident that reprisals were vigorously levied on French trade. One reads, for example, of the capture of several Frenchmen by Mill of the *Falmouth* (No. 1339), but the incident

INTRODUCTORY 7

which seems to have given most satisfaction was the capture by the *Constant Warwick* of the notorious pirate Beach and his ship the *Royal James* (No. 1339, *cf.* Nos. 1321 and 1326). The general impression to be gathered is one of some very efficient cruiser work and of the effective protection of our trade. But while English activities were mainly concentrated in the Channel, the North Sea was not neglected. One hears of small squadrons being employed in the North Sea to harass Dutch trade (No. 1293), and there are good accounts (Nos. 1308 and 1310) from Myngs of the *Elizabeth* and Foster of the *Phœnix* of their voyage to Gothenburg with the ambassador Whitelocke (*cf.* Gardiner, *Commonwealth and Protectorate*, Vol. III. pp. 73 ff) and of their encounters *en route* with the Dutch. Rather before this one has had details of the arrangements to protect the incoming Hamburg ships (No. 1246), whose safe arrival is warmly welcomed (No. 1256), especially as it had been feared that de With might intercept them (*ibid.*). These vessels were bringing much-needed supplies of ammunition, masts and other naval stores from the Baltic, and Bradshaw's letters from Hamburg dealing with his efforts to procure these commodities are of considerable interest (Nos. 1223 and 1246). The arrival of the convoy ' doth make all good again ' it is reported (No. 1264). About the last incident recorded in these documents is the capture in April of a richly-laden East Indiaman of 900 tons by Stainer of the *Plymouth* and Smith of the *Tarrenton* (Nos. 1342 and 1343). There is also an interesting complaint from Wettewang of the *Sparrow* (No. 1325) of the difficulties of escorting the Newcastle colliers who ' will not keep together so that it is impossible to secure them.'

In the main, however, the letters dealing with administrative matters exceed in importance and interest those relating to movements. The main object of the authorities was to secure that as large and efficient a fleet as possible should be ready early in the spring if peace had not previously been concluded. On this topic the series of letters from Bourne at Harwich is quite invaluable. One hears of the shortage of every kind of stores (Nos. 1249, 1252,

1257), of want of carpenters and other skilled artisans (Nos. 1252 and 1257), of seamen clamouring for their arrears of pay (No. 1265), of their disorderly and riotous conduct. Bourne writes of the urgent need for troops to assist in maintaining discipline (No. 1257), and Pett at Chatham was equally insistent in his demands for a troop of horse (No. 1261). Bourne expresses his surprise at the dismantling of the Harwich garrison ' at this season . . . whereas there never was so much use of it since it was appointed.' Want of money to pay the men their long over-due wages was not the only cause of their disorders. Bourne writes of the ' base tippling houses which do so much debauch the seamen,' while Hatsell at Plymouth found himself compelled to quarter men ' in tippling houses . . . to their great detriment ' (No. 1289), and urged that it would be better to hire a house in which to lodge them. Bourne went to the length of ' banishing strong waters ' (No. 1285), and with the aid of the troops succeeded in securing several of the ringleaders in the mutinies. Four of the *Assurance's* men, who had been ' chiefly active in raising that evil spirit among them,' found themselves lodged in Landguard Fort and were ' remaining there seemingly sorrowful.' But he writes mournfully of the seamen as being ' sensible neither of what is the public or their own interest but are below the beasts that perish ' (No. 1285). He writes of Harwich as ' very nasty and sickly . . . something like a prison to me ' (No. 1251), but he was evidently an energetic and resourceful official who did his best to grapple with a really difficult task.

Want of money, want of stores—Hatsell complains bitterly of the difficulty of obtaining hemp and cordage (No. 1289)—the disorders and riotous conduct of the seamen, a great want (No. 1315) of ' chirurgeons,' all these were substantial difficulties but the want of men was perhaps even more serious. The taking off of the embargo on the departure of merchantmen may have been a necessity on economic grounds, but it was clearly a source of much trouble to those responsible for manning the fleet. Monck writes of it as a great mistake (No. 1290, *cf.* 1297) and it is pointed out that ' a general liberty to merchants' men going to sea ' will make it extremely hard to man the summer fleet (No. 1329) and that an embargo is absolutely necessary (No. 1331). The competition of ' private ships ' for men is also noted (No. 1340), and recourse as usual had to be had to shipping soldiers (No. 1336). One hears the usual criticisms of the inefficiency of the press agents in shipping boys and old men (No. 1283), and there are many complaints from the victuallers (cf. No. 1326).

Of the measures taken by the Council of State to remedy abuses and improve matters generally one gets a few glimpses. There is a long set of instructions issued for the care of the sick and wounded (No. 1253), to look after whom special commissioners were appointed, possibly (cf. No. 1240) with the idea of relieving the overworked Navy Commissioners. In this connection two letters from ' Parliament Joan ' (Elizabeth Alkin) are of considerable interest (Nos. 1330 and 1332), while the Instructions issued by the Generals at Sea in December (No. 1299) are important as a stiffening up of the ordinances and as a means to the improvement of discipline, while it may be wondered whether the Additional Article to the Laws of War (No. 1273) was in any way the result of Bourne's representations. Among other points of some interest the return of the merchant ships to their owners may be noted (No. 1218), together with the announcement (No. 1304) that if merchant ships were employed again the authorities will appoint their captains: the ' owner-captain ' was notoriously not above taking over good care of his own ship. Tactical matters figure but infrequently, though in No. 1260 there is a reference to the order issued in February 1653 for the division of the fleet into three squadrons.

Administrative difficulties were by no means confined to this side of the North Sea. De With's letters are full of evidence of those under which the Dutch laboured. His lack of provisions has been already mentioned, but he was also short of stores and supplies (No. 1262), while the Dutch, like their enemies, were in great need of men (No. 1236), being quite unable to man their ships. De

Ruijter's Journal shows how low was the proportion of men to guns carried, only three to four per gun in some cases. There is a long description of the pitiful condition of the Dutch (No. 1236), possibly a highly coloured and exaggerated picture, but even allowing for some overstatement it shows the Dutch as having reached 'a climax of embarrassment and distress.' Want of funds is insisted upon (*cf.* No. 1255) as a main cause of administrative inefficiency. This in turn was partly due to the blows from which Dutch trade was suffering: with a greatly reduced volume of commerce coming in and out, with their merchant ships waiting for peace before they put out (No. 1333), Dutch finances naturally declined. That the Dutch had been more damaged than they had at first admitted in the last encounter between Monck and Tromp seems clear from a comparison of several accounts (Nos. 1213, 1215 and 1228), even without de With's testimony, and though one reads of great endeavours by the Dutch to have a large fleet at sea early in March (No. 1331, *cf.* No. 1291), to achieve this was even harder for them than for the English. One hears of them wanting to discharge more ships during the winter, but being afraid to let the crews go lest they should never get them back (No. 1291), but the Letter of Intelligence of March $\frac{1}{18}$ (No. 1333) suggests that even so the Dutch fleet was hardly in a position to put up much of a fight. The English, on the other hand, had quite a substantial fleet collecting in the Channel. As early as the last week of February Blake and Penn were calling in the cruising ships to rejoin the main body (No. 1331, *cf.* 1334), and the superior readiness of the English for the renewal of active hostilities may at any rate be inferred from the acceptance by the Dutch of the greater part of Cromwell's demands. As Dr. Gardiner puts it (*Commonwealth and Protectorate*, Vol. III. p. 67), peace, if to England 'a relief from the burdens and anxieties of war,' was 'a necessity to the United Provinces.'

B. GENERAL CONCLUSIONS.

The war, whose conclusion was formally proclaimed by the heralds on $^{\text{April 26}}_{\text{May 6}}$ (*cf.* No. 1345), presents many points of interest. It is one of the few examples of a purely naval war in which neither side ever attempted or even contemplated any land operations. It was in a sense the first great naval war between two fairly equally matched powers since the ocean-going and sea-keeping ship, built and designed for war, had come into existence. Neither Elizabeth's war with Spain nor the maritime part of the longer but somewhat intermittent struggle of Spain against her revolted provinces in the Netherlands can quite be described in those terms, even if, as Sir Julian Corbett has shown, the Spanish Navy had before 1603 become far more capable of contending with that of England than it had been in 1588. In the first Anglo-Dutch War one has an example of a war waged by navies organised on professional lines, in which the armed merchantmen were being very definitely relegated to a subordinate part. That this development was more pronounced in England than in the United Provinces must be admitted: it was one of the main causes of the greater success achieved by English arms. In the Elizabethan Navy professional elements of a quite rudimentary character can be detected, that the brunt of the fighting against the Armada had been borne by the Queen's ships is—or should be—a platitude, but since the conclusion of peace with Spain there had been a progressive development in the warship, coupled with an increasing differentiation between the Navy and the mercantile marine, not only in material but also in personnel, even if the differentiation was not as yet rigid and the line of demarcation quite indistinct. The Commonwealth, too, had done much to develop and improve naval administration: though credit must be given to James I and Charles I, as well as to Buckingham and Northumberland, for their endeavours in this direction. Admittedly they had not achieved much, but they had paved the way towards much that the Commonwealth did achieve.

The documents contained in these volumes have contained many references to administrative matters, mainly, it is true, to administrative deficiencies and shortcomings, to difficulties in manning, provisioning and equipping ships, to want of stores and supplies, to want of discipline and order, but the picture of what was amiss must not obscure that of the things which did not go wrong. After all, it is about deficiencies and shortcomings, about what needs to be put right, not about what is working smoothly and does not require readjusting, that administrators and their subordinates, naval, military and civilian alike, mainly correspond. It may be claimed that these volumes have supplied ample proof of what Dr. Gardiner outlined in his Introduction to Part II of these documents (*q.v.*) about the general superiority of the English administration over that of their opponents. Tromp, Ruijter and de With all testify in no unmeasured terms how terribly the Dutch admirals were hampered and handicapped by the manifold shortcomings of the Dutch administration, with its unspeakably cumbrous division between the five separate Boards of Admiralty, quite apart from the additional complication of the Directors (*cf.* Vol. I. p. 56) who provided another competing and overlapping authority. The English had their troubles, but the United Provinces suffered worse things by far, and if England's naval activities and achievements were severely limited by administrative shortcomings, still the second main cause of English success is to be found in the superiority of her administration and in the superior centralisation and vigour of her executive.

A third cause of English success is to be found in the geographical relation of the two countries, especially when considered in connection with their economic condition and their respective dependence upon overseas commerce. Since the last volume of these papers was published the North Sea has been the scene of a far greater and more vital struggle than that to which these

INTRODUCTORY

volumes have been devoted. The strategical position of the British Isles in relation to the sea-borne trade of the countries on the farther side of the North Sea was conclusively illustrated between 1914 and 1918, and though for various reasons things worked out very differently then, there is still a substantial resemblance between the two wars. Except for her important Baltic trade all Holland's overseas commerce, like that of Germany, had to run the gauntlet of the Channel or to take the long and difficult 'Northabout' route, in which it had the British Isles on its flank. In 1914 the German merchant marine disappeared off the ocean within a few days of the outbreak of war, never to reappear till after peace was signed: between May 1652 and April 1654 the Dutch were by no means precluded from carrying on their overseas trade, and Ruijter in the summer of 1652 and Tromp in that autumn were both successful in escorting large and valuable outward-bound convoys down the Channel. Tromp, in the following February, managed, with much difficulty and considerable loss, to bring back up the Channel a vast fleet of homeward-bound merchantmen, but to all intents and purposes after February 1653 the Channel was closed to the Dutch. In the North Sea they fared better, and the chief event recorded in the present volume is de With's success in escorting home the valuable fleet of vessels which had for some time been collecting in the friendly Scandinavian ports, but the importance of his achievement lies largely in the fact that between the battles of the Gabbard and the Texel the English had 'held the Dutch coast as it were besieged,' and that de With had to risk a good deal to bring his convoy in. Even the route to the Baltic was flanked by English ports, and though it was not under the same necessity of passing within reach of the British Isles as were East and West Indiamen and 'Straitsmen' using the 'Northabout' route, it was by no means free from loss and danger of interruption.

England's trade, on the other hand, was far less exposed to Dutch attack. That with Germany and the Baltic only had to pass within near reach of Dutch ports.

The Southern and Western harbours, from Portsmouth and Southampton round by Plymouth to Bristol and the not yet very important Liverpool, were effectively covered from direct attack. Vessels from the 'Straits' and from the Indies were not in serious danger of being intercepted, and one does not hear half as much in these volumes of the necessity for escorting ' the trade ' on the English side. To reach London, of course, vessels had to come up Channel and pass through the Straits of Dover on their way round to ' the river,' but in doing so they had a friendly shore close at hand. Indeed, French privateers, Barbary and other pirates and Dunkirkers were probably responsible for more captures in the Western approaches to the Channel than were the Dutch, whether State's ships or private ships.

In the relative economic condition of the two countries England, a primarily agricultural country, self-supporting and largely self-sufficing, was far less vulnerable at sea than the great trading communities of the United Provinces. Bacon has written of the 'ticklish and brittle state of the greatness of Spain,' whose ' treasure dependeth on the Indies ' and so was ' at the mercy of such as be masters at sea.' The same applies with even more force to the Dutch. It is an old saying that Amsterdam was 'built upon herrings,' and the importance of the fisheries to Dutch prosperity is hard to exaggerate. To be denied access to North Sea fishing-grounds would be a blow almost as serious as the cessation of that carrying trade which was the other great foundation of the commercial greatness of the United Provinces. Situated at the mouth of the greatest of all Germany's waterways, the Rhine, the Dutch were the natural carriers of German manufactures, and it was largely through Holland that Germany in the seventeenth century imported the products of the East and West Indies. On these products again Dutch industry and manufactures largely depended. In natural products the Provinces were not rich : they had no metals and no timber, and without imports of raw materials from the Indies Dutch manufacturers would in large measure be crippled. A country which contains within its own boundaries large supplies of raw materials is bound to be less injured, even by a total stoppage in war of its overseas trade, than one whose function is in the main that of carrier and importer. Should war drive the trade of Germany into other temporarily safer channels, the Dutch had no guarantee that it would return to them with peace. The United Provinces were therefore more vulnerable at sea than their enemies, increasingly valuable and important as English overseas trade had by this time become. It is difficult to form any exact estimate of the mercantile marine of the two countries, or of their respective losses, but it may be asserted with some assurance that, relatively, England had far more to attack and exposed less. The United Provinces depended on their commerce and could far less afford to have it suspended or damaged, while, though extensive captures of English merchantmen would make both the war and the Commonwealth government unpopular with a class which on the whole favoured them, our overseas trade was as yet of less than vital importance and, as already mentioned, it was hard for the Dutch to get at most of our trade or to undertake a blockade of our ports. Even after Dungeness Tromp was not able to do much. This was doubtless because he was preoccupied with the defence of a convoy of great size and value and could not afford to detach many vessels to attack English trade.

Security of her merchant ships being thus of essential importance to Holland, it is interesting to see that, insistent as Tromp was (*cf.* IV. 206) on the principle that the destruction or neutralisation of the enemy's fleet was the best means for protecting commerce, there were times, as in May 1653, when even he had to subordinate the seeking out of the enemy's fleet to the more urgent necessity of escorting a large outward 'trade' clear of the main danger zone. If in the opening phases of the war the Dutch were the quicker to appreciate the importance of bringing the enemy's fleet to action (*cf.* I. 338), this may be attributed partly to the fact that the English had more immediate and obvious quarries in the herring-fleet and in the Dutch Indiamen. Blake's action in June 1652 in sailing North to attack Dutch commerce need not be so emphatically condemned as it has been in some quarters. He can hardly be credited with having realized that the best way to bring a hostile fleet to battle is to make for some vulnerable point it is bound to defend, but Tromp's original intention was to go North at once in pursuit of Blake (I. 338); it was only as an after-thought that he turned against Ayscue and the weak detachment in the Downs. This move was largely inspired by a desire to retake the prizes recently captured by Ayscue from a ' Portugal convoy ' (*cf.* I. 345), and was partly due to the winds being unfavourable for proceeding in pursuit of Blake. The exposure of Ayscue to Tromp was a serious blunder, a violation of that principle of concentration on which Tromp more than once laid great emphasis (*cf.* V. 152), but it was more venial than those errors which led to the gratuitous and unnecessary defeat off Dungeness.

This defeat is not so much an example of following wrong principles as of basing one's plans on unsound data and an over-optimistic estimate of the situation. The error of believing that the Kentish Knock had been a more decisive defeat for the Dutch than was really the case may be attributed in some slight measure to Blake himself (*cf.* III. 20), but the main blame for the defeat must attach to the Council of State. The reorganisation after Dungeness, which has been described at length in the Introduction to Part VIII., may be reckoned the turning-point of the war inasmuch as it was then that Monck was appointed one of the ' Generals at Sea.' To attribute to this professional soldier the developments in tactics which undoubtedly took place in the spring of 1653, and bore fruit in the battles of the Gabbard and the Texel, seems on the whole warranted. The point has been discussed at length already, and there is no need to repeat the arguments. But Monck seems equally with Tromp to have emphasised the importance of concentration (*cf.* Nos. 959 and 963) and of bringing the enemy to battle. In the weeks preceding the Gabbard it was

INTRODUCTORY

Monck rather than Tromp who was the more eager to seek out the enemy (*cf.* V. 2), but with the art of scouting so much in its infancy (*cf.* V. 5), seeking out the enemy in the North Sea was not particularly well calculated to bring on a battle. One does not meet the phrase 'bad visibility' in the narratives given in these volumes, but the condition so described in modern terms existed in those days, and traces of it may be found in these papers. It is perhaps strange that Monck should not have appreciated the advantages to be gained by taking post in the near neighbourhood of the Texel and waiting for his quarry to come to him there. Still, if Monck's influence is to be given the chief responsibility for the better direction of England's efforts in 1653, Blake seems to have been capable of learning from his failures. It is clear that after returning from the North Sea in August 1652 he went down Channel to look for Ruijter with the definite object of forcing battle on him (II. 165), and though he missed him, mainly by bad scouting, he does seem to have profited by this to adopt rather more careful methods for finding Tromp on the latter's return up Channel in February 1653. One account, indeed—not, it is true, of any special authority (No. 858)—declares that Blake's arrangements were such that 'we could not have missed him' (Tromp). When again in command in the Channel in the following February (1654), he seems to have been distinctly more systematic over patrolling.

Of the importance of the battle which began off Portland and finished near Cape Grisnez as the first approach to a definite victory, enough has already been said.[1] Tromp saved most of his convoy and prevented the English victory from being absolutely decisive, as but for his skill and seamanship it might well have been, but the tide had turned there and the Gabbard saw the English definitely in the ascendant. Even Tromp's last battle could not reverse that verdict. His death was a heavy price to pay for the merely temporary relaxation of the English blockade, for, as shown in Part XII. (*cf.* Vol. V. p. 182), Lawson was able to resume it within

[1] *Cf.* Introduction to Part IX.

three weeks of the battle. No doubt the re-established blockade was soon abandoned, but this decision was taken for reasons in which the battle of the Texel is not as much as mentioned (*v.s.* p. 2), even if the damages sustained by many of the English ships in that battle contributed substantially to the administrative difficulties on which the decision was mainly based. Even so, Tromp's last battle can hardly be claimed as a strategic victory for the Dutch. As pointed out above (p. 3) de With's letters are not those of one who is anxious to risk another engagement or who entertains any hopes as to the outcome of such an encounter. Possibly Ruijter might have adopted a more optimistic tone had he been in command, but, even if allowance be made for any personal element in de With's appreciation of the situation, the evidence on the Dutch side as to conditions in the autumn of 1653 is against the idea that Tromp's supreme effort had really altered the strategical situation.

On the vexed question of the tactics of the war a good deal has already been said in the Introductions to the different Parts (*e.g.* Vols. IV. 17-18, 209-210, V. 8-9, 167-168). Any attempt to sum up all the evidence and arrive at anything like definite conclusions is at once met by the difficulty which lies in the character of so much of the evidence. It is essential to avoid reading too much into the use of words and phrases which came in later times to have a more definite and particular meaning than they had in the minds of those who used them.[1]

There are plenty of phrases which it would be quite easy to interpret as definite evidences for the 'line ahead' if one were inclined to seek for anything which can be

---

[1] One may perhaps draw a comparison with the misconceptions or over-emphatic conclusions which have so often been drawn from the use in the seventeenth century of the word 'Cabinet.' There are writers who have tended to give to this phrase an altogether too definite and rigid meaning, and whose views on the development of the 'keystone of the arch of the British constitution' are largely vitiated by the undue burden they place on words probably used in a quite loose way, with no approach to a scientific or exact terminology.

made to support such a view. One has, for example, Gibson's remark that Tromp's was 'the headmost ship of the fleet' (I. p. 9), or the statement from *The Perfect Account* (III. 107) that Blake 'drew out' his fleet at Dungeness, or that in *Mercurius Politicus* (II. 121) that in Ayscue's fight with Ruijter off Plymouth the enemy 'charged us one after the other in order.' It is equally possible to find a great many passages which point—or at any rate seem to point—as definitely in the opposite direction if one is seeking confirmation for the opposite theory. What must be remembered, however, is that the negative argument can be pressed too far—what is not mentioned did not necessarily not exist. Formations and tactical methods are matters to which comparatively few contemporaries usually devote much attention. There is a tendency to take such things for granted, rather than to go out of one's way to explain them. Writers of contemporary accounts were writing not for the benefit of posterity but for the information of their friends, to whom the things that puzzle later ages were usually familiar. Their personal experiences, the losses on both sides, the results of the battle rather than the methods by which those results were reached, are what occupy the majority of them. One may, perhaps, be allowed to cite the analogy of much of the evidence for the operations of the War of 1914-1918. To anyone starting to examine the evidence, official as well as unofficial, for the infantry tactics employed in the campaign of Mons and the Marne and Aisne—to take one example only—without an exact knowledge of the British infantry tactics of 1914 and of the training manual for that arm, the accounts of that campaign would be largely unintelligible or misleading. Not only would it be hard to describe the normal methods, even important changes are sometimes allowed to pass unnoticed. The discovery that concealment from artillery fire was more important than an extensive 'field of fire' for the rifle, so that with the high standard of musketry training possessed by the original 'B.E.F.' a much shorter 'field of fire' than had previously been considered necessary was quite sufficient, is ignored in the average battalion War Diary. These and similar things are more often occasionally commented upon in private records, but those were for the most part written by professional soldiers, many of them careful students of war, to whom such points were of real interest and the utmost importance. This analogy is not to be pressed too far, but it does afford additional reason for not being in too great a hurry to be over-positive either way.

One important piece of evidence has come to light since Volumes IV. and V. of this collection were published. It is to be found in Mr. C. R. Boxer's carefully edited *Tromp's Journal* for the year 1639 (Cambridge University Press, 1930). Here one has definite evidence from two authorities (*cf.* pp. 37-39, 45 *n.*, 209-210) for the use by Tromp of a line formation. That this by itself constitutes a claim on the part of Tromp to be the inventor and only begetter of the 'line ahead' Mr. Boxer does not assert. It does, however, suggest that the idea of bringing ships into action in succession was already familiar: how otherwise the best use was to be made of an armament disposed on the broadside system it is difficult to see. Still, from the occasional use of a linear formation for a squadron—and Dutch tactics do not seem to have progressed beyond the adoption of a squadronal organisation for their fleets (*cf.* Vol. I. p. 321)—to the definite adoption of a linear formation as a tactical system it is a far cry. As has been argued elsewhere in these volumes (IV. 18, IV. 209 and V. 8, *cf.* N.R.S., Vol. XXIX. pp. 92-98), the issue shortly after the battle of Portland of definite instructions prescribing the adoption of a linear formation is the all-important factor. With these in existence, vague references to the 'excellent order' of the English fleet (No. 1074) acquire an importance they would not otherwise possess, while definite statements in newsletters or similar authorities which (*cf.* No. 1080) do not of themselves carry much weight require to be seriously considered. That the First Anglo-Dutch War does mark a very definite stage in the development of naval tactics may be taken as well established, as may also the theory that this development is to be closely connected with the influence of the soldier-admirals whom the 'New Model' Army lent to the Navy.

The large part played by these soldier-admirals makes it the more remarkable that this war should be, as already mentioned, purely naval without any military action on either side. With England in possession of so large and efficient an army, and probably stronger relatively to the other armies of Europe than she has ever been, it might have been expected that some use might have been made of the 'New Model' to complete the victories gained by the fleet, by attacks on the harbours in which the defeated Dutch had taken refuge (*cf.* V. p. 155). Difficulties of navigation may well have deterred the English from an attempt on any point among the intricate network of islands, channels and shoals at the mouths of the Rhine, Meuse and Scheldt. The Texel presented a less formidable proposition, and the ships in refuge there might have been served as Abercromby in 1799 served the relics of the fleets defeated two years earlier by Duncan at Camperdown. But the difficulties of collecting transports for an expeditionary force would probably have been insuperable: as it was, the maritime resources of England were being drained dry. On the difficulties in obtaining enough sailors there is little need to enlarge. Actually the 'New Model' was being fairly extensively used to fill the gaps in the crews of the warships, and even its soldiers could not do double work, their own on land and that of the missing mariners at sea. Moreover, before the battle of the Texel England's 'command of the sea' was hardly sufficiently well-established to warrant any such venture. Monck's blockade of the Dutch ports exerted pressure enough to bring Tromp out to sea without the very risky expedient of tempting him out by an overseas military expedition. After the Texel it was too late in the year to think of anything of the sort. Thus, if the object of gaining 'command of the sea' be defined as 'securing to one's self the control of the ocean waterways for the use of one's military expeditions and trade, and denying the use of them for the same purposes to one's enemies,' the First Anglo-Dutch War stands out as a struggle in which only half these purposes were involved. There was no question of preventing a Dutch invasion of England, there was no question of using our troops to do what our ships could not do and follow up our defeated enemies into their places of refuge, there were not even, as in the Second War, any operations far afield against the hostile colonies: the attack and defence of trade was the ultimate object of the contending navies, and it was with this ultimate end in view that both sides came to appreciate and practise the principle that the defeat of the enemy's fighting forces is the sure and only means to the effective attainment of that end.

1213. *August 10/20th*, 1653.—*DE WITH TO STATES GENERAL*[1]

[Archives of the Hague.[2] Translated.]

Noble and Powerful Lords,—My Lords,—I beg respectfully to make the following report to your Lordships. All possible efforts are being made by the Lords Delegates of the States here to get the State's fleet ready, and I have not failed to lend a helping hand everywhere. I beg to assure your Lordships that the said fleet has suffered considerably more damage than reported by some people. After the store-schedules had been delivered in, I ordered the captains whose ships required fresh masts or had shot-holes under water to be filled up to sail into the Balg, where more can be done in one day than in three off the Scheldt or in the Moscovy Roads. Also, my Lords, with the approval of my Lords Delegates of the States, I have granted two days' leave for

[1] Hereafter abbreviated 'S.G.'
[2] Hereafter abbreviated 'A.o.H.'

the men of one watch from each ship to go and refresh on shore on the Island of Texel. Measures had been taken to prevent desertion by guarding the ferries. But I have been informed to my regret, that before the said leave was granted several sailors and soldiers had left their ships without the consent of their officers; I have therefore recalled the leave to go ashore. I also see with pleasure, my Lords, from their H.M.'s resolution of the $\frac{4}{14}$th Instant, that the chief command of the State's fleet is conferred upon me till further orders; I shall hope to express my gratitude by faithful service, and to thank your Lordships for the same directly I arrive, &c., &c.

(Signed) WITTE CORN: DE WITH.

<small>Done on board the ship *'t huijs te Swieten*, lying off the Nieuw Diep, the $\frac{19}{20}$th August, 1653.</small>

1214. *August* $\frac{11th}{21st}$, 1653.—*A LETTER FROM THE HAGUE*

[Clar. MS. 46, fol. 170.]

Hague, $\frac{11}{21}$ August, 1653.

The 15. hereof the deputies of Amsterdam acquainted the States General with some advertisements they had received by the way of Aleppo out of the East Indies, that the Dutch there had lately taken two English East India ships richly laden, with a gallion of Portugal, and withal besieged a carack of Portugal and blocked up Goa.

The 16. Vice Admiral Evertse and Commodore de Ruyter, being come from the Texel, made report to the Assembly of the States General, that to their knowledge there was but eight or nine of our ships missing in the last fight, whereof they are sure that three was sunk, and one taken, and that of the English a great many were shattered and made unserviceable, and eighteen or nineteen of them sunk, burnt or blown up, complaining of the slight usage they received of Vice Admiral de Witte when they came to him at the Texel, under whom both of them declared they had no inclination to serve, in special Vice-Admiral Evertse offered to give up his commission, saying that he had served and fought long enough to have no thanks but blame for his pains, both of them averring that it was impossible for either of them to remove into other ships, when their own were made unserviceable. Evertse in particular complained of a certain Lord of the Briel who having been aboard his ship had written to the Committee of the States of Holland that it was not in any such bad condition that he had any need to come in, but might have kept the sea, which he said was a base untruth, and the writer of it was an idiot and unfit to execute the charge he had. And de Ruyter complained of the smallness of our ships, one of the English being as he saith sufficient to fight with eight of them, and professing he will go no more to sea, unless our fleet may be strengthened with with [sic] greater and abler ships and that this State take the King of Great Britain by the hand.

 This State is much perplexed what person that may be acceptable to the seamen they shall appoint to be successor to Trump. The States of Holland labour much to persuade Monsieur Beverweert to accept of it, who hath hitherto excused himself. In the meantime the States

General have sent order [1] to Vice-Admiral de Witt to command the fleet by provision which is to stay at the Texel until the ships that have need of reparation may be fit to take the sea, for which purpose there are store of shipwrights sent for from all places.

The 17. hereof the States General have received advice from the Admiralty of Amsterdam, that three East India Holland ships homewards bound were come in to Bergen in Norway, and five more into the Sound with eighteen Straitsmen, and some others that come from France and elsewhere to the number of forty-two in all, and are thinking of the best means to convey these ships safe home. By this and other intelligence from the Indies the value of the adventures in the East India Company is raised thirty in the 100.

Upon the 19. the States General (upon report of a committee of their number appointed for examination of that business) have cleared Vice-Admiral Evertse and Commodore de Ruyter's carriage in the last sea-fight declaring their approbation thereof, with assurance of their favour towards them in all occasions wherein they may witness their respect to either of them, and it is believed that de Ruyter shall be sent out with forty of the least damaged ships of the fleet to convey homeward the East India ships and others that lie at Bergen and the Sound, which employment is not given to de Witte, by reason that in the year 1644 he being in the Sound with some ships of this State gave some distaste to the King of Denmark, nor is it thought fit to employ Evertse, lest de Witte should take jealousy of it, that his competitor should be sent out in the first

[1] *Cf.* No. 1213.

action of moment that falls out after the death
of Admiral Trump so as it is conceived that
de Ruyter may be employed therein with least
envy.

[Endorsed :] Newes from the Hague.
21 August 1653.

1215. $\frac{Aug.\ 23rd}{Sept.\ 2nd}$, 1653.—*DE WITH TO S.G.*

[A.o.H. Translated.]

Noble and Powerful Lords,—My Lords,—
I think it my duty to inform your Lordships that
since we came in to the Texel on the $\frac{1st}{11th}$ August,
with the State's fleet (most of the ships being
in a very disabled condition, as I have already
reported in previous letters), we have not been
standing still, but have sent schedules of the stores
required by the several ships to all the respective
Boards to which they belong, by express to avoid
delay; and on the $\frac{20}{30}$ August, in consequence
of the zealous efforts made by my Lords the
Delegates of the States, assisted and furthered by
my own, we had made such progress that sixteen
ships, such as they are,[1] were ready and in a
position to put to sea; but they have up till the
present been prevented by a contrary wind and
rough weather. The instructions for our present
voyage have just come to hand to-night from my
Lords Delegates of the States here. We have
had a continuance of this rough weather and
contrary wind up to to-day, and I shall not fail to

---

[1] This phrase, which de With uses several times, seems to give
the number at the time of writing, but to imply that the number
would vary from time to time as more ships joined.

carry out my instructions and put to sea with the first favourable wind, as soon as the pilots can bring us out, taking with us the twenty-two or twenty-three merchant-ships that have put in here from the Meuse and the Goereesche Gat. I must not omit, moreover, to inform your Lordships that divers kinds of ammunition and stores thereto, owing to deficiencies in the supplies to the ships, have been taken from the small ships ordered to sail with the State's fleet; so that we shall find very little ammunition with which to furnish the ships under our command in case of need, which will necessarily be a very serious inconvenience in case of an engagement. I therefore humbly beg that this inconvenience may be avoided by your Lordships sending us timely succours, so that when our ships get into action they shall not be obliged to seek a way of escape. Further, I beg to submit to your Lordships' consideration whether it is not in the highest degree desirable for the ships remaining here to put out to join us, as soon as they shall be ready in fair numbers, the more especially as we shall be putting to sea (God amend it) under their H.M.'s orders with a very small body of ships (which is an unusual thing, and we would gladly see it otherwise, since our division is still most eager to get fitted out) because this would the better ensure the safety of the State, and the great stake for which we are being sent out.

As the homeward-bound ships might easily miss us between Flekkefiord and the coast of Jutland, if the weather were rough or misty, they will be able to get tidings of us and learn where we are to be found, just South of the Hook of Skagen, a mile out from the shore; and word should be sent to the incoming ships to be prepared for this, and to endeavour to get news of us there, &c., &c.

(Signed) WITTE CORN: DE WITH.

Done on board the ship *'t huijs te Swieten*, lying a little way inside the shoals of the Texel, the $\frac{23rd\ Aug.}{2nd\ Sept.}$, 1653.

1216. $\frac{Aug.\ 26}{Sept.\ 5}th$, 1653.—*NIEUPORT TO BEVERNING*

[Thurloe State Papers, i. 448.]

My Lord,—De Witt, De Ruyter and Peter Floris are ready in the Texel to go out to sea with the fleet. Suycken told me to-day, that there was a fleet of thirty ships come in safe through the Channel. This week there are arrived in the Moege[1] at least forty herring-ships well laden.

Hague, Sept. 5th, N.S.

1217. $\frac{Aug.\ 26}{Sept.\ 5}th$, *NAVY VICTUALLERS TO NAVY COMMISSIONERS*

[[2] S.P. 18, xxxix, 86.]

Gentlemen,—We have considered your order from the Commissioners of the Admiralty and Navy and the abstract of the General's letter of the 20th present, and do conceive that before the expiration of the victuals now in the fleet a proportion of 10,000 men's victualling 28 days may be got in a readiness either at Chatham or Quinborough to give the fleet a further supply, but then the State's declaration must immediately be perfected with a distribution unto the several ports, and therein we desire that such care may be

[1] i.e. Meuse.
[2] The P.R.O. reference given in the earlier volumes as 'S.P. Dom.' or 'S.P. Dom. Commonwealth' is now S.P. 18.

taken for this port of London as may sufficiently answer what may be further demanded for the supply of the ships, and to make good what is already issued over and above former contracts, as also to accommodate this supply now desired which will be about 2500 men's victualls six months. And for the more certain dispatch of what is before proposed we humbly consider it very requisite that the empty cask now with the fleet may be forthwith sent into this port, and the rather because our great issues from hence [and] the little returns unto this day, have so emptied the stores thereof as that we shall have scarce enough to answer the winter service without it.

We are very much troubled to consider unto what extremity we are driven in order to the winter's supply, and that for want of a timely declaration, we having not above a month's time to make ready that with three months is scarce sufficient to perform, the which we have often signified, and yet it is not sensibly minded.

In case the State shall resolve to have this supply aforesaid put into a fitting readiness then we desire that convenient shipping may be provided to take in the beer and other provisions, the whole quantity of stowage importing near 3000 tons.

And we do apprehend it will be no disservice to the State if the beer were daily sent out in sufficient ships unto the fleet at sea to be taken in as occasion shall require, the drier provisions being of lesser consequence as to stowage may be dispatched unto them upon all emergencies, and according to such advice as shall be given from the General from time to time, and so the fleet kept at sea, or at least the ships intended for the winter guard without coming so soon into port, care being taken to put the greatest quantity of provisions aboard such ships as are intended for the winter service.

We remain,
Your affectionate friends and servants,
THO. ALDERN.
WILLIAM BEALE.
D. GAUDEN.
RIC. PREICE.

Victualling Office,
26th Aug. 1653.

1218. $\frac{Aug. 26}{Sept. 5}th$, 1653.—*BEVERNING AND VAN DER PERRE TO S.G.*

[Thurloe State Papers, i. 440.]

High and Mighty Lords,—The commissioners, who have been with the fleet from the Council of State, do affirm as yet that there was but one frigate and one fireship lost in the last engagement and that the whole fleet will be out again very suddenly under the command of General Monck and that 46 or 48 are already gone for the coast of Holland under the command of Rear-Admiral Lawson, which is undoubtedly held for certain here, and will be better known to your High and Mighty Lordships than to us. Whether it be so or not, it is certain that 42 or 44 of the said ships that were in the last encounter, are restored to the merchants, of whom they were hired, much torn and damnified, without any reparation or satisfaction, being most of those which according to our former information were brought into Harwich ; and the fleet of the State's here, wherewith they intend to manage their business, doth consist of 140 ships of war ; and they do still build new ones.

We have with much grief and sorrow understood the late mischance, which God hath caused to send to our States in the loss of the courageous sea-commander, but we have not had particular notice of the occasion and manner of his death. The great and eminent virtues of courage, conduct and of a poised moderation, which all the world doth willingly acknowledge to have been in him, and commend him for, are notwithstanding eclipsed and overcast with some reports of temerity, as if he had carelessly put himself in danger, where necessity did not require it, standing too naked upon the stern, where General Monck coming might easily have seen and known him; and thereupon did cause all his musketeers to discharge all together for which he had caused them to stand ready. Moreover it is said here that the sterns of the English ships have several thick cables hung about them, which are musket-proof, so that no one musket-bullet can hurt those that have them before them, which ours have not; whether it be so or not, we know not.

Westminster, Aug. 26th / Sept. 5th.

1219. Aug. 27th / Sept. 6th, 1653.—*LAWSON TO MONCK*

[S.P. 18, xxxix, 85.]

Right Honourable,—The 21st instant at night when we put off from our own shore had some of our officers together by whom was resolved what I here send Your Honr. The 22nd at ten of the clock forenoon had the shoaling of the fourteens of the Texel, it begun to blow hard and rain, the wind south west. I called the officers together to have their judgments concerning what had passed, which they approved of. Before they could get on board their ships again it proved very stormy, so laid our ships' heads to the northward in our mainsails, and laid all that day and the night in our mainsails and mizzens.

The 23rd in the forenoon one of the merchant ships bound for Hamburg set his fore course, put out his ensign and bore away, so I gave the signal to the convoys to bear after, which they did, but the commander of the Paul was not aboard hereat; all his orders were sent by Captain Haward,[1] commander of the Gilliflower, who had not weather after that to convoy them, so I set the galley and hoy (attending this ship) to look for the Paul, and acquainted him with it, but she could not find her, so we fired a gun at the Seven Brothers being a little in the wind of us, who bore under our stern, which we called to, to bear after the Gillyflower for Hambrough, which she did. The Paul afterwards had notice, so that I think there be five of our ships gone for the Elne,[2] the same named in the result of the officers the 21st instant, that night we parted from them, the wind west and be [by] North; supposed ourselves north-west from the Flye[3] thirteen or fourteen leagues. That night we laid most in our main course, this ship making much water not enduring her fore course; kept one pump constantly going, and baling forward on the ship being stoked[4] most of our powder is spoiled.

The 24th blew fresh showers and gusty weather, see most of our ships but had lost company of some, set our fore course laid north west with the stem, towards noon proved better weather, set our main topsail, the wind came to the west north west and north west and by west. We came by

---

[1] sic. Hayward, cf. No. 1256.   [2] Sic. ? Elbe.   [3] Vlie.
[4] i.e. 'stoaked,' when the water cannot get to the well; cf. Manwaring's *Seaman's Dictionary*, N.R.S. LVI. p. 237.

the Centurion which was at anchor, yards and top masts down. Made no signal to her to weigh, not knowing whether her masts or yards were defective. Towards night stood to the westward, it blew hard that night, carried a pair of sails; the next morning the wind came to the west again.

The 25th at 6 in the morning bore up our ship to the northward, laid north north west and sometimes north west; at eleven of the clock Captain Saunders in the Ruby came under our stern and told us that he had spoke with an Ostender which told him that upon Bergen reef he was in company with a fleet of Dutch merchant ships come from the Sound, and that he believed they were about where we then plied.

At 12 o'clock see some sails, set our maintopsail afterwards our foretopsail; chased them, the Ruby, Foresight and some others came up with some of them, but they outsailed us, and most of the merchant ships—the frigates seized some five or six, and sunk two, they were laden with salt, from St. Uves[1] in Partingale. This day the Centurion came into our company, but feared to carry sail, his lower masts are so bad. The Foresight with carrying sail on a sudden had eight foot water in hold, the water within one strake of his gun deck, was forced to strike all his sails amain, being close by several of the Dutch flutes which then got away. He got his frigate freed with pumping and baling at eight or nine o'clock at night, but most of his powder and provisions are spoiled. This night the wind came to the N.W. and by W., and north west, so plied to the westward. A buss that the Centurion had taken told us that the 24th at 4 in the afternoon he see forty sail of Dutch merchant ships five or six leagues in

[1] Setubul in Portugal.

the wind of us. The best intelligence we have at present is this, the Ostender captain Captain Saunders spoke was bound for Hull came from Cottenburg¹; told him that the five East India ships of Dutch that was at Bergen are now at Copenhagen in the Sound, and that there is twenty sail of the King of Denmark ships ride at anchor before Copenhagen; that the East India ships are to stay till the fleet of men of war come to convoy them.

Captain Saunders in the Ruby has taken a galliot that came from Greenland which had spoke a pilot boat since he came upon the coast that told him there was thirty sail of men of war at the Fly² ready to sail, and ten at the Texel now making ready—this is ten days since.

Yesternight the Success spoke four Swedes, and one Ostender came from the Sound which told him that the five East India ships are at Copenhagen, and that they unlade their goods there and that some [of] it to be sent home in small vessels, othersome disposed there, and that there is four East India ships more at Bergen with some other ships.

Here is enclosed the examination of a master of a buss that the Centurion took, and some Dutch letters. Our frigate was close in with the Fly the 20th instant, and their hath been no weather to go in with the shore since. Indeed we had much to do to keep off the shore, and it is a great mercy the winds have been variable. I am afraid if we had been forced to anchor it would have gone ill with some of us, they were in with the Texel; also that day see twenty-five or seven and twenty sail of men of war ride where De With ride two or three days before the last engagement. This day pretty clear, see the Texel, lay driving in sight

¹ Gothenburg. ² The Vlie.

thereof most part of the day, getting our ships together which were to the leeward, at 3 in the afternoon stood off with an easy sail, the wind north west and by west.

This day called the officers together when several things were considered and debated, the results whereupon is here enclosed, by which Your Honour will know our present condition and motion, there are many complaints, and several ships have received damage since we come on this coast, some in masts, some in hull, some their sails blown away; the Tiger hath most of a suit of sails split to pieces; this day to make the Victory the worse, the Dolphin merchant ship came thwart her hawse, has broke her head and sprung her bowsprit.

Yesternight I sent the Ruby and Pelican to ply to the north eastward to look for the rest of the ships and frigates to let them know that, God willing, we intended to be ten leagues west of the Texel, the 30th inst., according to instruction, in order to conjunction with Y^r. Hon^r., and this night I have ordered the Tiger to ply in that station to acquaint all she meets withal of our motion.

The last three frigates and the first six never see one another yet, neither is there two of them that keeps together. We are twenty leagues to the northward of the Vly; see only the Centurion which is with us, his lower masts is not to trust to; dare not carry sail if it blow hard. The Pelican and Ruby as before hinted, but I think as they are scattered they annoy the enemy in their trade, the most for that they have no convoy with them that trade as yet. I beseech Y^r. Honour pardon my not presenting an account sooner, but the weather hath been so bad, and having no ketch but this one that attends the Unicorn, could not do it before with convenience ; begging Y^r. Honour's acceptance of the presentation of my most humble and bounden service, craving leave to subscribe myself,

R^t. Honble.
Your most humble and real servant,
Jo. LAWSON.

Aboard the State's
Ship George,
West north west
of the Texel, 27th August
1653.

For the R^t. Honble. Lt. General Monck.
General of the Commonwealth of England's
Navy.

1220. $\frac{Aug. 27th}{Sept. 6th}$, 1653.—*WELCH TO DOWNING*

[S.P. 18, xxxix, 87.]

Hon^d. Sir,—Here being arrived a ship from Norway I thought it good to acquaint you with the intelligence which the master tells me, that at Vleckfort,[1] a place in Norway about seven leagues benorth the Nasse, arrived about three weeks since nine Dutch East India ships, the place being a good harbour but of no strength. They landed their guns and planted them upon the shore for their defence.

At Vleckery,[2] about fifteen leagues by East the Nasse, there is also eleven rich ships from the Straits and at Bergen eighteen and two Dutch men of war, in one of which is the corpse of Van Galen, slain in the Straits, and in many other

[1] i.e. Flekkefiord, which is about 25 (English) miles N. by W. of the Naze.
[2] Probably Flekker, an island at the mouth of the entry into Kristiansand, about 50 (English) miles E. of the Naze.

ports in Norway as this man reports near 120 sail of Holland's merchantmen. But those East India and Straits ships aforementioned being ships of force, and having well refreshed themselves with fresh victuals, resolved to sail homeward about ten days since, being about forty in number, and to that end those from Bergen and them at Vleckery were ordered to sail for Vleckfort to meet the East India ships, and so to sail away for Holland, and as this master informed me, who see both the ships at Vleckfort and those at Bergen, that those in Bergen [1] prepared to sail when he came away, and that the masters and captains of the ships had taken an oath to be faithful one to another, and did give out that they would not care for twenty or thirty men of war of the English, and that they would fire their ships before yield(ing).

I have acquainted the Commissioners with this intelligence who I believe will advise some of your Council of it. I wish the fleet had notice of it, that either they might meet with them upon the Holland coast, or between that and Norway, and that care might be taken that the Dutch claw not the English coast aboard, and slip between the Texel and Yarmouth.

    Yr. very humble servant,
        Wm. Welch.

Leith,
27 Aug. 1653.

For the Honble. George Downinge, Esq.,
  Scout Master General, of ye Admir:
      These.
   Whitehall.

[1] Defaced.

1221. $\frac{Aug. 29th}{Sept. 8th}$, 1653.—*BENSON TO THURLOE*

[Thurloe State Papers, i. 443.]

Sir,—That which this week hath produced is only with reference to the Hollanders: fifty of their Eastland ships being come from Amsterdam into these seas, ten whereof are here, the rest being gone for Konigsburg and Riga; also six of their French fleet, which are laden here wholly with corn, ready to sail for the Sound with the first wind. They are resolved to take the opportunity of the open seas, and not to stay in the Sound for the expected convoy, fearing our ships may come again upon their coasts. The same course as many as can get speedily laden are resolved to take, so that if any of our frigates be upon their coasts they cannot miss abundance of prizes, being ships of great burden and no strength, not one in twenty who useth this trade as hath a gun in them. . . .

Dantzick, Aug. 29th.

1222. $\frac{Aug. 30th}{Sept. 9th}$, 1653.—*DE WITH TO S.G.*

[A.o.H. Translated.]

High and Mighty Lords,—My Lords,—I think it my duty humbly to inform your H.M. that, on the $\frac{26}{5}$th $\frac{August}{September}$ we received tidings from divers quarters that the enemy had taken up a position with about forty ships off Texel and the Vlie, and I think my Lords the Delegates of the States here have already written to report this to your H.M. On receiving this news, on the $\frac{27}{6}$th $\frac{August}{September}$, I dispatched four vessels to reconnoitre at sea between Texel and the Vlie. Up to the present

I have received no intelligence. We are lying directly off the Shallows, to enable us to put to sea with twenty-eight ships, such as they are,[1] directly orders arrive ; and if this is to be done, I leave your H.M. to decide what advantage we shall get over the enemy. Nevertheless, I shall not fail to make every effort and to do my duty. The preparations on the rest of the State's ships here are going forward very slowly ; and it is to be wished that in these anxious times more zeal was displayed by those concerned. Ammunition and stores thereto, as I wrote in a previous letter, are very deficient in some of the ships, although we shall probably have orders to go to sea with a small force, where eighty to ninety ships were required before, and then (God amend it) we fared ill enough. I am therefore very sore troubled about the slowness of the equipment, and would submit to consideration whether the rich treasure, on account of which we are sent out, is not being put to great risk. But I shall not fail to persevere in faithful service, in so much as that will avail ; but I can clearly see that our enemy's force will be increasing every day and that (God amend it) we, meanwhile, are making but little progress. I have noticed, also, that when I bring the slowness of the preparations home to the right quarter, it is taken amiss by some people.

And I have thought it my duty to bring all the above to the knowledge of your H.M., &c., &c.

(Signed) Witte Corn: de With.

Done at the Helder,
 the 30/9th August/September, 1653.

[1] Cf. No. 1215.

1223. *Aug. 30th / Sept. 9th*, 1653.—*BRADSHAW TO THURLOE*
[Thurloe State Papers, i. 444.]

Sir,—The post hath failed this week, yet we hope not taken but only hindered by tempestuous weather. By the enclosed to the Council you will see what quantities of powder, shots and masts is ready to go with this convoy of four ships of war. Now that I see the Council's order, I am troubled this business was not sooner thought upon, but I shall do what's possible to effect the needful, but being this proportion of powder is all that at present can be got here and in parts near about (excepting about 500 more which I have a promise of to be delivered within five weeks) I cannot rely upon more, yet I doubt not that by one means or other to get a larger proportion ere long. I will remove every stone for it and advise you weekly. Yesterday the powder should have been put on board the two ships with masts, but when the holds were opened, there came such a moist damp from the masts having lain long in the water, as would have spoiled all the powder, had it been put upon the masts. I sent to the men of war to see if they would have taken it in amongst them, but they could not : in which strait, there being not a ship or vessel here but what were freighted by the merchants, that no time might be lost I have made use of one of the merchant's smallest ships of 100 and 10 tons and have promised him the like freights the merchants were to have given, being 160 l. st. for the whole burthen of the ship, the merchants to have the use of what room can be spared and to shift for the rest of their goods as they can, so as now the powder shall all be laden in a new lightship, and God willing, within three days, if the wind come fair, they shall all be ready to set sail. The convoyers want masts, which some of them are setting, but they will lose no time, and steer directly to the squadron under Captain Lawson at the Texel, that being their order, and if those ships be gone of the coasts, then to make the best of their way for England. The merchants make all possible haste to have the benefit of his convoy, having great store of very useful commodities to return, but if the wind and weather serve, the convoy shall not stay here. Here's but little of such sort of shot as the Council ordered for, but ball of 20 lb. and of 12 lb. I could now have a good quantity and of 6 lb. weight: if you must have only for D.[1] cannon, whole culverin and D.[1] culverin, then I must send for such sorts to Sweden whence all shot comes hither. It may be shipped to Lubeck and come by land passage as cheap as it can be bought here. I will write by next post for it, that no time be lost, that so if possible, I may get another proportion of powder and shot to send with these masts, and another convoy before the frosts shut up this river. I this day charge my bills on the Commissioners for £6000 in full of the £10,000 the powder, masts and shot, which I shall now send, and what I have contracted for and hope to get will require more money, therefore pray cause a further letter of credit sent me from the Commissioners, their last limiting me only to £10,000; and allow that you will take care the bills I charge be duly paid by them, that no prejudice or disparagement ensue.

Hamburgh, Aug. 30th, 1653.

[1] *I.e.* demi.

1224. *Sept.* 1st/11th, 1653.—*NAVY COMMISSIONERS TO ADMIRALTY COMMISSIONERS*[1]

[S.P. 18, xl. 6.]

Right Honble.,—About two months since we sent an estimate to you of the charge of this summer's fleet wherein it appeared there would be £1,115,000 0s. 0d. requisite to be paid between this and the last of December, without including the second rate ships intended to be built, or the winter guard. Since which time there hath been another engagement at sea whereby much prejudice hath been done to the hulls and tackle of the ships, which have both drained the stores and added much charge. Notwithstanding all this, finding no considerable provision made for money we conceived it necessary for us to lay before Your Honours the daily clamours for want thereof, the vast and unreasonable charges the State is at in the price of commodities, besides the disreputation the State lies under, in having our contract broken, and credits laid low, whereas if your debts were paid and money were seasonably provided we might save you twenty in the hundred in price of commodity; and it is not imaginable what the advantage is in payment of mariners at their first coming into harbour, for whereas every 1000 men in your own ships that have been nine months out at sea £10,800 would pay them off, if they lie but one month unpaid it will cost the State £13,000 and if in merchants' ships about £14,000 which is £300 interest for £100 a year.

Being desirous to discharge our own duty we have presented these things to your serious consideration, hoping there will be some more

[1] Hereafter abbreviated 'N.C.' and 'A.C.' respectively.

effectual means used than our former representations have thereto procured.

We are, &c.,
E. Hopkins,
Fr. Willoughby.

Navy Office,
　this 1st of September, 1653.
　　R. Hutchinson.

1225. *Sept.* ²ⁿᵈ/₁₂ₜₕ, 1653.—*PROCEEDINGS OF COUNCIL OF STATE* [1]

[S.P. 18, xl. 10.]

Friday, 2 Sept. 1653.
At the Counsell of State at Whitehall.

Ordered.—That the number of ships for the next winter guard shall be eighty.

Jo. Thurloe,
Secretary.

1226. *Sept.* ²ⁿᵈ/₁₂ₜₕ, 1653.—*ORDERS* [2] *FOR CAPTAIN WM. HILL*

[S.P. 18, xl. 11.]

You are upon sight hereof, wind and weather permitting, to set sail with the ship under your command [3] in company with the Bristol and seventeen frigates more and to ply off of Heligoland till the 18th of this month, during which time you are to observe such instructions and directions as you shall receive from Captain Roger Martin, commander of the Bristol frigate whom I have appointed to command you and the rest of

---

[1] Hereafter abbreviated 'C.o.S.'
[2] These appear to have been issued by Monck, who had his flag in the Resolution, as No. 1242 shows.
[3] Worcester.

the ships above mentioned. You are to be very careful during your continuance in that station not to give chase any further than to return again by night into the body of the squadron, that so upon any emergency of service you may not be separated; and if you shall be found wilfully to offend herein you shall not only be cashiered from your employment, but suffer the loss of your wages for the time you have served. After expiration of the time limited for this service you are to expect further orders from the said Captain Martin for your disposal. But in regard he is not at present in the fleet, you are hereby authorised to take charge of the said squadron and to make use of his instructions for your direction in this service as fully as if they were directed by yourself, until you shall meet with him, and then you are to deliver them up to him with such other instructions as are herewith given you, and this shall warrant your so doing.

Given under my hand and seal on board the Resolution on the 2nd Sept., 1653.

To Capt. William Hill,
 Commander of the Worcester.

A true copy.
 The like to the rest of the captains of that squadron except the last clause beginning
 But in regard ...

1227. *Sept. $\frac{2nd}{12th}$, 1653.—A LETTER OF INTELLIGENCE FROM HOLLAND*

[Thurloe State Papers, i. 447.]

Yesterday being Thursday the Dutch fleet of men of war sailed out of the Texell with a fair wind, being some sixty in number of the ablest ships in this country, who convoyed with them some four or five hundred merchant-ships for Eastland and other places, and 'tis hoped that they being so strong, the spy boats not having discovered more English upon this coast than forty-two, that, if ever, the English will be now beaten, if they be met with.

De Witt and de Ruyter are commanders of this fleet and the Heer Van Opdam goes not to sea before the whole body of the fleet be ready; nor is Jan Evertsen in this fleet, his son being by his wounds so ill, that they expect death every hour. Here are a fleet of ships, who impatient to wait so long for a convoy, have ventured to come from the Sound.[1] The report is they were seventy or eighty sail in all but a spy-boat hath brought news, that he saw the English take twenty-six of them, which causeth our merchants to look blank. In this fleet is come the Leopard, formerly taken from Captain Appleton in the Straits. 'Tis pity the Dutch should have such a ship. She was missing two days. I was in hope she had been retaken. . . .

Of the imprisoned captains six are declared to be innocent, viz. Captain Skipp, Captain Bayners, Captain Hecke, Captain Jan Adriaen, Captain Adrian Cornelys, and the captain of the ship called the Garden of Holland, but nine captains are still prisoners, of which three lay bound hand and foot, and the provost, the hangman, and three assistants are gone to the ship Captain von Campen, to do execution upon them.

Sept. $\frac{2}{12}$.

---

[1] Probably those mentioned in No. 1220 as about to sail without convoy.

1228. Sept. 2nd/12th, 1653.—*A LETTER OF INTELLIGENCE FROM THE HAGUE*

[Thurloe State Papers, i. 448.]

I have received yours of 19/29 of Aug. and of 26 Aug./5 Sept. both of them together. How many were exactly killed in the last fight is very hard to be known. The thirty or forty ships which they feigned to have failed in their duties, have not one man slain, for their ships were not able to sustain the brunt of the English. How many men de Ruyter had slain on board is to be seen in his printed letter which he writ. Jan Everts hath not properly said how many he had slain, but his ill-wishers do say, he had very few. De Witt had but four or five. On board Tromp's ship likewise there were but three or four slain. Every captain in particular doth all ways to make men believe he had several slain and wounded and many shot between wind and water, but the State doth take no delight to take an account of all this, that so they may not discourage the soldiers and mariners. At the most there cannot have been above 400 or 500 slain; but by reports there is commonly a great many wounded, and that number is well three times greater. The Commissioners of this State in England write nothing of their negociation, or of peace, but only concerning their prisoners. In private letters they write to have sent a confiding person to several harbours and ports, to inform themselves of the dead and wounded of the English: he hath informed them, that in such a place there were 300 wounded, in such a place 700, in another place 500, and at least 1200 slain, &c., &c., uti quisque suum vult esse, ita est. Here upon the sea-shore from Heyden as far as Huysduynen men have here a sad spectacle to see, from day to day several dead bodies do arise which undoubtedly are those that were slain in the last engagement. There is order given by the State for the burying of them. There have already two or three hundred of them been buried, but men are made to believe that they are English. . . .

They have here very much flattered themselves, by reason they did absolutely believe and conclude, that they had driven the English home; and the ships in the Sound believing that also, set sail from thence for their own country without any convoy, as believing the English to be gone home; and in the meantime a good many of them are taken, they speak here of twenty-five. Behold a bad effect of flattery.

The Vice-Admiral de Witt was ready to go out to sea with thirty ships, the wind being good, but they do fear that he dare not, and in the meantime they are still equipping. But the people doth still believe, that this State doth not use so much diligence and vigor as they ought, for say they, why is it that the English can be sooner ready, presupposing that the English were more damnified than ours: and so the poor magistrates or States of Holland are blamed by the people. Behold a second ill effect of flattery.

But the truth is, the English have better ships, more power or money. The people here (chiefly the Zealanders) who did boast that they alone would drive home the English, being ignorant of this ground, did build castles in the air, and did frame to themselves maxims which have prejudiced and will prejudice this State. The wise men know it well enough but they dare not speak it.

THE LAST WINTER

Holland begins to refuse the payment of the companies of the land army and to employ that money to the use of the fleet. . . .

Just now comes news from the Helder, that the Vice-Admiral de Witte was set sail with forty-nine ships of war, conducting a fleet out of the Vlie of at least 500 merchant ships for the Sound : at least this is published to be so.

Sept. 12th N.S.

1229. *Sept.* $\frac{3rd}{13th}$, 1653.—*LIST OF SHIPS* [1]

[S.P. 18, lviii. 35.]

Ships' Names	Commanders	Men	Guns
Sovereign	—	600	100
Resolution	John Bourne	550	88
Triumph	Lionel Lane	350	62
James	William Penn	360	66
George	John Lawson	350	58
Andrew	George Dakins	360	56
Victory	John Stoakes	300	60
Unicorn	Wm. Goodson	300	58
Vanguard	Joseph Jordan	300	56
Swiftsure	—	300	56
Rainbow	Peter Strong	300	58
Paragon	Rich. Badiley	262	52
Speaker	Sam. Howatt	300	56
Fairfax	—	300	58
Worcester	Will Hill	220	50
Essex	Wm. Brandley	250	56
Laurel	Rich. Newbery	200	48
Kentish	Jacob Reynolds	180	50
Lyon	John Lambert	220	50
Sussex	Roger Cuttance	180	46

[1] This list cannot be that of the winter guard (*cf.* No. 1225) as it contains nearly 120 names and includes all the larger ships which were to be laid up during the winter. It should be compared with the list given as Appendix I. to the Introduction to Part XI. (*cf.* Vol. V.) and with No. 1303 in this volume.

Ships' Names	Commanders	Men	Guns
Centurion	Walter Wood	200	42
Entrance	Rob. Tucker	200	43
Diamond	Tho. Harman	180	42
Newcastle	Nath. Cobham	160	42
Adventure	Rob. Nixon	160	40
Great President	Fran. Parke	180	42
Bristol	Roger Marten	180	46
Ruby	Robert Sanders	180	42
Portland	Edw. Blagg	180	46
Hampshire	Robert Blake	180	36
Assistance	Willm. Crispin	180	44
Foresight	Rich. Stayner	180	42
Portsmouth	Rob. Durnford	180	42
Advice	Jeremy Smith	180	42
Sapphire	Nich. Heaton	170	38
Phœnix	Owen Coxe	150	36
Elizabeth	Cristoph. Mynns	150	36
Nonsuch	Tho. Penrose	170	40
Tiger	Gabriel Sanders	170	40
Assurance	Phil. Holland	160	36
Dragon	John Seaman	160	38
Amity	Hen. Pack	150	36
Expedition	Tho. Vallis	140	32
Constant Warwick	Rich. Potter	140	32
Guinny F	Edw. Curtis	150	34
Reserve	Rob. Clarke	180	44
Pelican	Peter Mootham	180	40
Providence	John Pidner	140	33
Nightingale	John Humphreys	90	24
Mermaid	John King	100	26
Pearl	James Cadman	97	29
Primrose	John Sherwin	90	24
Swan	Tho. Wilkes	80	22
Drake	Rob. Clarke	90	12
Merlin	Geo. Crapnell	90	12
Martin	Willm. Vesey	90	12
Greyhound	Tho. Bunn	90	12
Tenth Whelp	David Dove	60	18
Warwick	Willm. Godfrey	90	12
Cygnet	—	80	12
Little President	Tho. Sparling	80	12

Ships' Names	Commanders	Men	Guns
Nichodemas	Willm. Ledgant	50	10
Paradox	Rog. Jones	60	16
Truelove	Rob. Vessey	30	12
Mayflower	—	90	20
Weymouth	Rob. Wilkinson	80	—
Sparrow	John Wetwang	60	16
Hard Kitch	Rich. Pittock	30	12
Lilly	Isaias Blowfield	50	12
Wren	—	50	10
Horsey Down Shallop	Willm. Smithson	50	—
Deptford Shallop	—	50	—
Henrietta—pinnace	—	25	7
Prizes:			
Convertine	Anth. Joyne	210	44
Beare	Fran. Kirby	200	46
Welcome	Tho. Bennett	200	40
Discovery	Tho. Marriott	180	40
Marmaduke	—— Grove	160	42
Success	Willm. Kendall	150	38
Gillyflower	John Hayward	120	32
Raven	Robert Taylor	140	38
Princess Marie	Seth Holley	170	38
Stork	Roger Harman	180	—
Violet	Hen. Southwood	180	44
Crow	Tho. Thomson	140	36
Heartsease	Tho. Wright	150	36
Middleburgh	Tho. Witheridge	120	32
Arms of Holland	Fran. Harditch	120	34
Advantage	Edw. Thomson	100	26
Fortune	Anth. Archer	100	32
Paul	Ant. Spatehurst	120	28
Tulip	Joseph Cubitt	120	32
Plover	—	100	26
Mary Prize	Hen. Maddison	120	37
Dolphin	Rob. Davy	120	30
Hound	Jonathan Hide	120	36
Duchess	Rich. Suffield	90	24
Swift	Edw. Barrett	130	34
Peter	John Littlejohn	100	32

Ships' Names	Commanders	Men	Guns
Hector	John Smith	100	30
Recovery	Fran. Allen	90	26
Bryer	Rob. Sansum	90	26
Waterhound	Giles Shelley	120	32
Satisfaction	Michael Nutton	100	32
Marigold	Hum. Felstead	100	30
Falcon Flyboat	Barth. Yates	80	28
Samson	Rob. Plumleigh	120	32
Sophia	Rob. Kirby	160	38
Cock	John Edwin	140	36
Great Charity	James Terry	130	36
Little Charity	Wm. Whithorne	150	32
Black Raven	Sam. Dickinson	150	38
Rosebush	Val. Tatnel	130	24
Mathias	Philip Gethings	150	38
Westergate	Sam. Hankes	140	34
Half Moon	Barth. Ketcher	110	30
Katherine	Willoughby Harman	130	36
Pelican prize	John Symons	120	34
Elias	Edw. Mordcock	140	36
Cardiff	Rob. Story	130	36
Falmouth	—— Jeffreys	100	28
Convert	—	120	32
Church Prize swam in Portland bought for the State by G. D.	—	30	5
Fox	—	—	—
Redheart Pincke	Ro. Thorpe	—	—
Fire Ships :			
Foxe	—— Cornelius	30	10
Fortune	Hump. Morris	30	10
Wildman	—	—	—
Falcon	—— Coxe	30	10
Renown	James Salmon	30	10
Victuallers :			
Adam and Eve	—	100	20
Concord	—	—	—
Hope	—	—	—

THE LAST WINTER

Ships' Names	Commanders	Men	Guns
Mary Flyboat	—	30	12
Sun	Symon Orton	—	12
Augustine	—	—	27
Hulks for careening:			
Eagle at Chatham.			
Fellowship, at Deptford.			
A new hulk built at Portsmouth.			
The Ostrich at Portsmouth.			

Endorsed :
    The new list made the 8th Sept., 1653.

1230. *Sept. $\frac{4th}{14}$, 1653.—DE WITH TO S.G.*
    [**A.o.H.** Translated.]

Noble and Powerful Lords,—My Lords,—I have to inform your Lordships that on the $\frac{1st}{11th}$ instant we sailed out of the Texel with forty-three warships, as far as I know at present, and about forty merchantmen ; in the afternoon of the same day we came off the Vlie, where we fell in with over three hundred merchant-ships, which we took under our protection, and then set our course for the Jutish reef, the wind being S.S.W. On the $\frac{3rd}{13th}$ instant, we found that about thirty ships from France and Spain had sailed to the westward and outside of our fleet, without letting us know ; with the view of fulfilling my instructions I sent a ship of war to them to act as convoy. On the morning of the $\frac{4}{14}$th we found ourselves on the south edge of the Jutish reef, without having seen anything of the enemy since we sailed (in (*sic*)) out of the Texel. I enclose herewith a copy of my second letter to Mijnheer Keyser at Copenhagen, and beg to submit the same for your Lordships' information. I would further beg to submit once more to your Lordships' consideration, whether it would not be advisable for the ships, which we were obliged to leave lying in the Texel, as they were then unready to sail, to join us with the least possible delay, sailing in a body for the greater security. And in protecting the treasure we have been sent out to ensure, and in convoying it home in the safest way, we shall not fail to acquit ourselves on all occasions as good and experienced sailors and soldiers.

Herewith, &c., &c.

(Signed) WITTE CORN: DE WITH.

<small>Done on board the ship *'t huijs te Swieten*, between the coast of Norway and Jutland, the $\frac{4}{14}$th September, 1653.</small>

Enclosure. Sept. $\frac{4}{14}$th, De Witt to Keyser.

[A.o.H. Translated.]

My Lord,—I have to inform you that we have this 14th passed Jutland Shoal and making every effort to convoy the East and North shipping with all possible security to off the Skaw Riff. I have written the 30th August, 6th, 8th, and 12th September to Bergen, Norway [to instruct all] that the ships of our State lying there shall proceed as speedily as possible to Flekkefiord there to be convoyed home. Where I now am also sending letters by express to the captains lying in Flekkefiord with orders that on sight of same with wind and weather as speedily as possible got together shall likewise put to sea and can find us off the Skaw Riff; there not finding us, as speedily as possible come and find us between the Hook of the Skaw

THE LAST WINTER

and Kleine Helms. I request that with all speed orders be drawn up [bidding] East Indiamen return ships and others straightway off Copenhagen to be sent as speedily as possible between the Kleine Helms and the Skaw Riff which positions I have chosen as the most convenient and the safest rendezvous. I dare say 50 per cent safer than between Jutland Riff and the Naze where through contrary winds, mist or bad weather, we can easily be lost. When the said ships are come to the rendezvous I intend to convoy them home with all possible security in accordance with the orders of their H.M. My Lord, I request that you will send me an answer as speedily as possible, we being in strength exactly 42 ships of war.

[W. C. DE WITH.]
Not signed.

Done on board the ship *'t huijs te Swieten*
Sept. $\frac{4}{14}$th, 1653.

1231. *Sept. $\frac{6}{16}$th,* 1653.—*KNOWLINGE TO N.C.*
[S.P. 18, xl. 41.]

Right Honble.,—We have been of late daily spectators not only of Dutch but of French pirates, which ride not only in Torbay very near us but lie near and before our harbour mouth, so that several of our ships bound out durst not stir. But the Lily frigate, being off the Land's End, met with a Brest man of war, a new small frigate of four guns and thirty men whom she chased from 7 in the morning to 4 at noon, and off the Start got her up and boarded her; whom the pirate resisted very stoutly until the captain and lieut. and three more were slain and six or seven much wounded. The Lily had seven or eight men wounded but not mortal.

The prize was brought into Torbay about five or six days since, and is expected in to our harbour next opportunity.

About the same time there was brought into our harbour by a private man of war a Dutch ship of about 200 tons laden with French salt, which probably will be prize, which is all this place affords for present.

    Do humbly crave leave and remain
        Y^r servant to be commanded,
                STEPH. KNOWLINGE.

1232. *Sept. $\frac{6th}{16}$, 1653.—BOURNE TO A.C.*
[S.P. 18, xl. 42.]

Right Honble.,—I received yours dated the 2nd instant and have accordingly given order to the commanders of the Thomas and William,[1] Hopefull,[1] Luke[1] and Royal Defence[1] to come up into the river with all speed.

We have had the weather very tedious for rain and wind else the remnant had been gone, but if the Lord please, the Hannibal[1] and Richard and Martha[1] and Dolphin of the State's shall sail to-morrow; the rest are all gone (unless the Mary prize and the Swift), the first had one of her bows broken down to the water and lost her bowsprit, the latter lost her mainmast and proved very leak at sea. It will be the middle of the next week ere they can be ready.

When I was last with the General I received order from him for the sending away the Dolphin and Mary prize to ply about Isle [of] Wight and the Casketts, but he did not then foresee how much time the Mary prize would require to be repaired, therefore the Dolphin being ready I have sent her away with the Hannibal, &c., to the

[1] All apparently hired merchantmen: not mentioned in No. 1229.

fleet, and in the room of her shall appoint the Swift to consort with the Mary prize, and when they are ready to order them both into the Downs, and then wait your honours' commands.

They shall come out clean and victualled complete for three months. I am bold humbly to offer my thoughts that they, being ships of a reasonable good force and quality, may be of very good use to ply about the Land's End, where much mischief will be done if not prevented by some speedy course. I hope your Honours will pardon me in this (it flowing from the sense I have of the public good).

The great charge the State is at about transporting water and provisions to the fleet makes me study all means whereby the burden may be eased as much as possible and therefore here being several ships put into Harwich that came from the fleet having beer and water in them, I have caused all the men of war remaining to take in what quantity of either of them they can stow for the use of the fleet, and have discharged those ships. One ship laden with beer from Lynn being very leak having about 150 tons of beer, I have ordered to remain at Harwich until I hear further from the fleet.

As for the sick and wounded men remaining at Ipswich, Harwich, &c., I have already sent away those that are recovered, and those that are lame and not capable of service by the loss of their limbs, or otherwise, are in part sent away yesterday to London and the remainder shall come by the next opportunity. In pursuance whereof I am come hither to take an account how the whole business stands in reference to the sick and wounded that are yet here, that so I may contribute what is in my power, both for their good as also for the benefit and advantage of the State whose expense hereabouts rises high.

I purpose to send messengers to Aldborough and Southwold to take care of those that are in those towns also, and shall endeavour to discharge my duty as the Lord shall enable me in whatsoever else relates to the affairs committed to my trust, and shall hasten up as soon as I can to receive yr. Honours' commands, for I doubt the time will not be long ere there will be need of some person at Harwich to take care of your affairs, as also of a supply of stores to answer the exigencies of the service.

I crave leave to remain, &c.

N. BOURNE.

Ipswich,
6 Sept. 1653.

1233. *Sept. 7/17th*, 1653.—*ORDERS BY DE WITH*

[**A.o.H.** Translated.]

As we see every day, to our regret, that the captains make a practice of sailing at random, and do not keep company with their squadrons as they should do carefully both by day and night, paying no heed to the frequent cautions given them, therefore, to promote the service of the country, the said captains are charged once more and for the last time to remain strictly with their squadrons, and whosoever neglects this order shall be fined four Rix dollars at the first meeting, and likewise those who either by day or night sail before Vice-Admiral de Witt, without having any cause for haste.

Also, as we deem it advisable that all our ships of war should come in to us as quickly as possible, no one excepted, and that no one need wait for another, small vessels being included also in this order, therefore in the event of our flying a red flag from the mizzen-top-mast or else from the mizzen-yard, and firing a shot, whoever does not come as quickly as he can shall be fined eight Rix dollars at the first meeting, as a pledge ; and when the said signal is made, when we are in action, all our ships, both those to windward and to leeward, ahead and to the rear, shall do their best to come up with us and with the enemy as quickly as possible, and shall place themselves in suitable positions against the enemy. And the said flag shall be kept flying throughout the engagement, so that no one will have any excuse to make (unless they shall have been employed rescuing any crew or ship), with regard to the order by signal and by their instructions ; and whosoever in spite thereof shall neglect this order, which God forbid, shall be punished by death without mercy, and the attorneys are charged to keep a strict watch over everything, to keep memoranda, and to come and make reports from time to time.

Also, when we require the nearest and quickest-sailing ships of war to come up with mine as quickly as possible, to receive some order, we shall fly a national pennant to the rear of the flagstaff.

Also, when we are convoying merchantmen, and any of them get damaged so that they cannot sail, it shall be the duty of the nearest ship to take the same in tow, and to give them all possible assistance, bringing them along with the fleet, omitting nothing in their power ; and for the rest to regulate themselves according to their instructions and the signals made.

    Done on board the ship
      't huijs te Swieten,
        the $\frac{7}{17}$th September, 1653.

(Signed)   Witte Corn: de With.

1234. *Sept.* $^8_{18}$*th,* 1653.—*POINTER TO N.C.*

[S.P. 18, xl. 54.]

This is to acquaint your worships that upon Monday the 29th of August the General (about three or four of the clock in the afternoon) set sail out of Aldborough Bay with about eighteen sail of men of war.[1] We stood over for the coast of Holland. Tuesday following at night we espied about forty sail of busses to the windward of us, the Martin galley took two of them, which was all that was taken. Towards morning we met with Rear-Admiral Lawson. All day Wednesday we stood for the Texel,[2] till towards the evening. A frigate then brought intelligence that De Witt with his fleet was gone this Tuesday morning towards Norway. A council of the flag officers was then presently called, and resolved that all the great ships and the merchant men should go in, and only that some frigates should be left behind to scout upon the Holland's coast; we presently tacked about for the coast of England. The next day the wind proved contrary to us and great tempestuous weather which lasted for four days and nights—we were not a little afraid of our ship which before was much leaky. But it hath pleased the Lord to preserve us, and we with the fleet ordered to go in are now lying off of Yarmouth about seven leagues, expecting a fair wind to carry us up to the river.

We hear of no great damage the fleet hath received in the storm save only the Newcastle frigate spent her mainmast, who is ordered to go to Yarmouth.

[1] *Cf.* No. 1210 (Vol. V) for their names.   [2] Tessel.

I have not else at present to acquaint your worships only that in sincerity of heart I desire to approve myself, &c.

THO. POINTER.

From on board
the Resolution,
8 Sept. 1653.

Endorsed—
These for the Rt. Worship the Commissioners of the Navy at the [   ] Office on Tower Hill
London.

1235. *Sept.* $\frac{9}{19}th$, 1653.—*DE WITH TO S.G.*

[**A.o.H.** Translated.]

Noble and Powerful Lords,—My Lords,—I think it my duty respectfully to inform your Lordships as follows :—that after my last letter of the $\frac{4}{14}$th instant, when we had passed the Jutish reef, on the $\frac{7}{17}$th, we were under the Skagen reef, and here the traders for the North parted company from us, not one of them having suffered any injury from the enemy ; we were obliged by a contrary wind and rough weather to anchor there with the greater part of the Baltic ships, the remainder having got into the Katte-water ahead of us. We were then informed by a letter from Mijnheer Keyser that the three last East-India return-ships,[1] and some vessels from the Straits and West Indies, had come into Bergen in Norway on the $\frac{24th\ Aug.}{3rd\ Sept.}$ and were still lying there on the $\frac{30th\ August}{9th\ September}$. I sent off an express to Bergen immediately on receipt of the said letter, requesting and charging the said ships to come without loss of time to between the Hook of

[1] *I.e.* homeward bound.

Skagen (the Skaw) and de Kleine Helms, nearest the latter. I had also previously sent a similar notice to Flekkefiord, and had likewise informed Mijnheer Keyser of our arrival, requesting that the East-India return-ships lying off Copenhagen might be sent to us at the rendezvous, with any victuals to be provided for the ships expected from Norway. I also learnt from Mijnheer Keyser's letter that these five East-India return-ships were to be conveyed to us at the rendezvous by thirteen or fourteen warships belonging to the King [1]; I therefore replied that, if such were to be the case, I hoped they would remain till we sail from here on our homeward journey, the more especially as I was directed by my instructions to wait for the ships from Bergen in Norway. And I hope that the warships we left lying in Texel, still incomplete, will be made ready and will join us without delay, the better to enable us to ensure the safety of this rich treasure, and I trust, with this long continuance of south wind, that they are well under weigh. I took the precaution, on my departure, of informing my Lords Delegates of the States at the Helder of where I had appointed the rendezvous for the greater certainty; and was told in reply that I must use all my experience in seamanship to ensure that the ships do not have to seek us up and down but shall find us at the rendezvous. I have also determined to send notices to the masters of ships belonging to our country lying in Flekkefiord, Maerdon,[2] Langesund, Soonwater and Svinshad, to be ready in Oxö within six to eight days, and to come and join us as quickly as possible,

[1] of Denmark.
[2] Probably Maërdo, which lies a little east of Flekker. This seems more likely than Mandal.

and that I purpose at my coming to provide them with convoy. Further, my Lords, I am most anxious (with all respect) to be informed of the enemy's position at sea, and whether they continue to hold themselves off between the Texel and the Vlie; which intelligence, coming in time, will help our decisions and be of great service to the State.

My Lords, I shall not fail on all occasions to use all my knowledge of seamanship and warfare in the service of our country, and to conduct myself as a faithful servant of your Lordships.

(Signed) WITTE CORN: DE WITH.

Done on board the ship 't huijs te Swieten, between the Hook of Skagen (the Skaw) and the Helms, in the evening of the $\frac{9}{10}$ September, 1653.

1236. *Sept. $\frac{10}{20}$th, 1653.*—*COMMITTEE OF COUNCIL TO S.G.*

[A.o.H. Translated.]

High and Mighty Lords,—We received to-day your H.M.'s dispatch of the $\frac{3rd}{13th}$ of this current month, requiring our views on the sending of a few quick-sailing frigates into the Mediterranean to keep a look-out on the English. After having discussed the question we feel obliged respectfully to reply to your H.M. that, for brevity's sake we beg to refer to our recommendations on this same subject, sent to your H.M. with our letter of the date above-mentioned, in which we stated that it was necessary to protect the Mediterranean with ships of war belonging to this country, but that, owing to lack of means, it was impossible for us to contribute anything thereto. And we take this opportunity of adding that, in consequence of what we have heretofore advised your H.M. relative to our difficulties, our means are now so terribly reduced that to-day, on the report made to us by our Receiver General, we have ordered our naval agent, after satisfying the claims of the carpenters and labourers engaged in fitting out and preparing the ships of war and fireships lying off this town, to pay them all off excepting a few, and thus bring the work to a standstill ; we have also ordered the clerks, charged with payments to individuals, to stop all payments to officers, their wives or attorneys, and to distribute the little that can be supplied them (which from our whole income will not provide a fourth part of what is necessary) amongst the most indigent and needy of the sailors only, and these also will have to go unpaid before long, if we are obliged to pay the interest on the gross sums we have been forced to borrow to the holders of the bonds, and to enable us to do this, all orders for payments granted by us, even to common workpeople, for amounts under 100 gulden, will have to be suspended. All our powers and means are now exhausted, we are deprived of our ordinary income, and left unprovided with what we have been so often solemnly promised to receive, to our ruin under the burdens which we took upon us in our desire to do our best for the country ; and now that matters have reached a climax, the work has to be stopped, nothing remains to us, and our loyal desire to do good service is powerless to act. On this subject we have always protested, and shall never cease doing so. And we and the Lords here present have been almost in despair how to arrange matters for the best (having been unassisted for so long), and we have therefore resolved to write to all those who are absent, summoning them, that we may take counsel together what to do for the sake of the country and to improve our own position; in the which we have to consider not only the burden that is at present crushing us with its weight, incurred in purchasing goods from numbers of honest men, and in employing the blood, sweat and toil of our fellow-citizens, for which we are unable to pay, but also more especially the difficulties it involves not only to our Board and persons but to the public also, such as our inability to pay the officers and sailors who have already come in, and the others who are daily to be expected from the Mediterranean; the providing of stores that will necessarily be consumed very shortly in the serious and fierce encounter with the English that seems close at hand, whilst our stores of all kinds are exhausted; and, even if everything falls out in the best way (which God grant), part of the ships of war (none of which, without exception are victualled for longer than till the middle of November) will be coming in at the end of next month, and must be sent to sea again before the approaching winter season to oppose the enemy and provide for the protection of commerce; we have to consider moreover how to satisfy the heavy claims of the crews who have been serving for a high monthly wage; whilst the ships that are brought in ought to be paid off, and the goodwill of their crews retained, lest they be driven by disgust and vexation at delayed payments to take refuge with our adversaries, who would gladly receive them and treat them well. We can do nothing for our part but simply represent to your H.M. the difficulties that have arisen from want of means, which (with all reverence) can only be averted by immediately furnishing considerable sums of money in proportion to the requirements of the several Boards of Admiralty, and especially our Board ; and we are of opinion (under correction) that the same should be issued before any statement or accounts are given in (which nevertheless we are always ready to do), on account of the urgency of the situation ; otherwise the time that yet remains will be spent in manifold and wearisome discussions, as (God amend it) some of the time has already been spent ; while, to all appearance, even if these discussions had relieved us of our burdens, there is nothing to look forward to but that the glory and fame of this country on the seas, which, by God's grace, has hitherto prospered and flourished in the sight of all the surrounding nations, like a burning torch, will be untimely overturned and extinguished, leaving nothing behind but a foul smoke ; and then the pitiful question will arise, how it has come about, and we shall at the same time have the most painful discussions [as to whether] perhaps the country has been steadily defying this government, and whether every one is willing and able to prove the efforts he has made and his honest zeal with regard to all measures proposed to obviate such a disaster, when the course of events shewed what was to be anticipated, and which proposals were made opportunely and in good time ; there will be no remedy then for the disaster already suffered, nor any means of recalling the lost opportunity of retaining our status and position. As far as regards ourselves, we recognize it without anxiety, and we can appeal without fear to what is known to your H.M. And we can therefore await, with an easy conscience and without perturbation, whatever continued and persistent dilatoriness in the adoption of necessary measures may perchance bring forth ; but, nevertheless, in so much as we have the honour to participate in the Government, and possess a thorough knowledge of what is wanting to remedy this state of affairs, we have been anxious to do our duty to the utmost by faithfully representing what we see close at hand and what is committed to our care, very humbly begging your H.M. in this behalf once more, that, arranging with your H.M.'s usual wisdom and zeal for the conduct of affairs in this present juncture, when time presses, your H.M. will be pleased to contrive and devise some ready means of remedying a state of things, which, as far as we are concerned, has reached a climax of embarrassment and distress, and also to provide what is necessary at the present moment having regard to the end of the year and the approach of the winter season. And this last ought now (under correction) to be taken into consideration, that it may afterwards be carried into effect; otherwise it looks as though the ships of war and fire-ships, belonging and returned to this port, will be obliged to remain lying outside the harbour, including all those who ought to come inside by reason of damages by storm and from the enemy. Besides, we have grave doubts whether all our ships lying in the Texel will be able to put to sea, owing to deficiency of men, for almost all the musketeers engaged have been removed from the said ships by your H.M.'s Delegates, and only a very few returned in their stead, which necessitated part of their crews serving as such to supply the places of musketeers wanting on board the ships that put out under Vice-Admiral Witte; which has greatly increased the burden and charges of this Board, by reason of the difference of the pay of soldiers and sailors. Every effort has been made here, but unsuccessfully, on account of the lack of men, and the matter must now be allowed to drop for want of money, unless what is wanting is supplied by your H.M.'s order, or otherwise several of the ships will be obliged either to remain lying there or to put to sea much under-manned. But we cannot say exactly what is required on this account, because we have received no statement of the number of soldiers removed or returned; and also, by reason of the bad weather, we have not received any reports from our agents there for some days, with regard to the condition of the ships, details of which have been supplied to your H.M.'s Delegates. And, in the hope we have satisfied your H.M. with regard to the advice required of us, and discharged what appeared to us our duty on receiving the report made by our Delegates on their return from the Hague, and on finding to-day the situation of affairs here, we commit the whole of the rest of the business entirely to your H.M.'s care, &c., &c.

   (Signed) SIMON VAN ALTEREN.
Your H.M.'s very humble servants
the Committee of the Council for Admiralty,
and by their command.
   (Signed) DAVD. DE WILD.

Amsterdam, the 19/29th September, 1653.

1237. *Sept.* 19/29*th*, 1653.—*VICTUALLERS TO A.C.*

[S.P. 18, xl. 60.]

Rt. Honble.,—We having jointly considered the proposal you were pleased to make yesterday unto some of us, viz. That if the State declared for so many men six months for the winter and summer's guard as that their provision of victualling should amount unto £195,000. That then our payments should be £30,000 presently by way of imprest and the rest by £15,000 per mensem for eleven months, beginning the first of October, and so in proportion for a greater or lesser number of men. Do humbly return this our answer. That considering your Honours' readiness to do what the emergent occasions of the public will at this present admit we shall therefore willingly submit to this your proposal (though far short of what our contract according to your interpretation of it would afford us) only with this small variation that the monthly payments may be ten and £16,500 per mensem beginning as above. But then we humbly intreat that our payments may be certainly affixed upon some good receipt where we may have punctual payment, and thereby may be in some measure enabled to carry on your service and our credits the better supported when we shall make use thereof which will be very considerable to serve so great a bulk of provisions.

And that the respective proportions of victuals for this winter and next summer's guard may be distributed by affixing the number of men to the several ports as the State shall judge most conducing to the public.

The formalities of certifying and ordering the payments, we humbly crave leave to offer to your consideration and humbly desire to be heard as to those things which concern the better and more speedy securing of our provisions and the regular issues and expense thereof,

Craving leave to remain, &c.

NATH. ANDREWES.
THO. HERNE.   WILLIAM BEALE.
T. GAUDEN.   RIC. PREICE.

Victualling Office,
10th Sept. 1653.

1238. *Sept.* 12th/22nd, 1653.—*PROCEEDINGS OF C.o.S.*

[S.P. 18, xl. 64.]

Monday, the 12th Sept. 1653.
At the Council of State at White-Hall.

The Council having taken into consideration what number of men are to be provided with victuals for the next winter and summer's guard do resolve and declare that the provision of victuals be made for 36,000 men to be employed in the next winter and summer's guard for six months, to begin from the 1st day of October, and to end the first day of April, and it is hereby referred to the Commissioners for the Admiralty to send for the victuallers of the Navy and to confer with them concerning the making of the said provisions, and to acquaint the Council with what they shall do herein.

That it be referred to the Commissioners for the Admiralty to give order for the making of a dry dock in the States Yard at Woolwich and to give order for the payment of such money as shall be disbursed in the doing thereof.

1239. *Sept.* 13th/23rd, 1653.—*BEVERNING AND VAN DE PERRE TO S.G.*

[Thurloe State Papers, i. 477.]

My Lords,—We have received your High and Mighty Lordships' resolutions of the 11th, 12th, 18th, 24th, and 25th of last month. We shall govern ourselves according to the contents thereof, humbly desiring, that your Lordships would be pleased to approve, that notwithstanding the strict narrow watch kept over the prisoners here and the prohibition of this State, yet we have made a shift to transport 192 prisoners for the Flemish coast, who were most of them in the country and were bringing up to London against the winter. The prisoners at Chelsea, the Mews and at Colchester, as elsewhere, do suffer an unspeakable deal of misery, lying upon straw, without anything to cover them and in the open air, which we are once more necessitated to represent to your Lordships, to perform the bitter desperate complaints, that are made to us daily. The last week there only died twenty-four at Chelsea, and this week there were seventeen buried in one day. There are 400 sick amongst them, of which there are 200 in great danger. When we complain of these hardships to some lords here upon occasion, they make answer, that their men in our country are far worse used and have but 3d. a day allowed them, whereas ours have 6d. We have endeavoured to make a provisional exchange of fifty or sixty of ours against as many of theirs in Holland and Zealand, that so we may get off our best seamen, but as yet we are not agreed, by reason the general of the prisoners doth stand precisely to exchange an officer for officer, mariner against mariner, with distinction of men of war and merchantmen, but we shall endeavour to act further herein and to do as well as we can.

The great ships of the fleet of this State are come into the river as far as Rochester, where they are to lie all this winter and that eight of the ships of the fleet lie before Yarmouth, much damnified and without masts. We do by our next intend to give your High and Mighty Lordships a particular account of the condition of their fleet. In the meantime,

High and Mighty Lords,
Your Lordships' most humble servants,
BEVERNING, VAN DE PERRE.

Westminster, Sept. 23rd N.S.

1240. Sept. ¹³ᵗʰ⁄₂₃ᵣd, 1653.—*VAN DE PERRE TO JOHN DE BRUYNE, raedt pensionary of the States of Zealand*

[Thurloe State Papers, i. 484.]

My Lord,—Since my last the fleet of this state hath been seen upon the coast of this country and is since come to Solebay, Yarmouth and Harwich, having left forty frigates before the Texell. Those ships, that are come in, are said not to be much damnified through the tempest, which was exceeding violent, but that they will go out to sea again very speedily to join with those ships before the Texell, which is to be their rendezvous; and for this purpose they press great store of watermen and other fresh water soldiers. In the said tempestuous weather there was one frigate cast away upon the West coast, and four upon the Irish. The sickness amongst the prisoners at Chelsea increaseth daily. Captain Stellinswerf died here in the Mews on Tuesday last, and was buried by the rest of the captains, and some of our family, who accompanied his body to the grave. And although that a strict watch is kept at both the said prisons, to keep them from getting out; yet several steal out and escape in the night, as also by daytime who come to us for relief to carry them over.

Westminster, Sept. 23rd N.S.

1241. Sept. ¹³ᵗʰ⁄₂₃ᵣd, 1653.—*A.C. TO N.C.*

[B.M. Add. MS. 9304, fol. 79.]

13th September, 1653.
By the Commissioners for the Admiralty and Navy.

Upon consideration and treaty this day had with the Victuallers of the Navy for victualling 37,000 men which the Council have declared shall be employed for six months in this winter and next summer's service, and the Victuallers having agreed to accept of payment for the same, which at viid. ¾ a man per diem amounts to £200,725 in manner following, viz., £30,225 in hand by way of imprest, and the remainder by £15,500 per mensem, the first payment to begin the first of October next without prejudice to their general contract made with the State. It is ordered that the Commissioners for the navy do proceed to perfect the said agreement for victualling the said 37,000 men, and to make out bills of imprest unto them for the said imprest and monthly payments accordingly.

    Jo. Carew,
     Nath. Rich,
   Ed. Salmon,
     Will Burton,
      John Disbrowe,
  Tho. Kelsey.

1242. *Sept.* $\frac{18}{28}$*th*, 1653.—*MONCK TO WILLOUGHBY*

[S.P. 18, xl. 79.]

Sir,—Intending by the first opportunity of wind and weather to send in the greatest ships for Chatham, having disposed of the rest of the ships into the river, Harwich and Portsmouth to be refitted, and ply in the Channel according to orders, I do desire that so many of them as shall come into Stokes Bay or the Spithead and the captains of them making their repair to you to be supplied with what they want, may not be suffered to come into Portsmouth Harbour with their ships but ride in the road before the town, and having their victuals and other provisions sent off to them except it shall appear to you their condition is such that of necessity they must come into the harbour to be refitted. Your care herein is much desired, the service of the State requiring a considerable number of ships for guard thereof very speedily.

If any of those ships that shall come into the harbour to be refitted have been out any considerable time I think you may do well to give notice thereof to the Commissioners of the Admiralty, that their men may be paid off, yet so as may stand with the good of the service.

Yr. very assured friend,

GEORGE MONCK.

Resolution in
  Alborough road,
    the 18th Sept. 1653.

1243. *Sept. $\frac{19}{29}$th, 1653.—N.C. TO C.o.S.*

[S.P. 18, xl. 64.]

Right Honble.,—Finding the business of our office so much increased, we made application to the Commissioners of the Admiralty to take off that part lately imposed on us, relating to sick and wounded men, the widows and impotent parents of such as are slain in the service, and of prisoners, which to be done as it ought is business sufficient to take up our time.

But besides the prejudice that comes through our want of time seriously to attend this business, it's a great disservice to have the lamentable cry of such persons in the ears of seamen, who by multitudes have recourse to our office.

Now understanding from the Commissioners of the Admiralty that they have made report to your Honrs. of several persons with instructions to manage that affair, we humbly entreat your

speedy settlement thereof, which will accommodate the service and assist employment and encourage,
>Your Honours' real servants,
>E. HOPKINS,
>THO. SMITH,
>ROB. THOMSON,
>FR. WILLOUGHBY.

Navy Office,
the 19th Sept. 1653.

1244. *Sept. 19th, 1653.—DECISION OF COURT MARTIAL*

[A.o.H. Translated.]

The members of the Naval Council of War, now sitting at the Helder, by the appointment of their Lordships the Delegates of their H.M. the States General, to decide on the cases of unofficer-like conduct and disobedience on the part of several of the captains and commanding officers of the State's warships of this country, reported to have occurred in the last engagement with the English, in the presence of his Lordship Heer Halewijn, nominated by their H.M. to preside over the said Council of War, having seen the indictments, criminal charges and accusations brought forward by Advocate-Fiscal de Bije, and his assistant Thimeus Faber, against Lieutenant Henrick Hay, together with the papers and answers put in by the said lieutenant to prove his innocence, the said Council of War having examined all the documents, heard the evidence on all sides and carefully considered every point material to the case, giving sentence in the name, and on behalf, of their H.M. the States General of these United Provinces, condemn the lieutenant aforesaid to be keelhauled three times with a halter round his neck, and sentence him then to the house of correction for twenty years at hard labour, and order him to pay the costs and expenses of the action. Disallowing the indictment and charge brought against the accused by the said Fiscal, for reasons moving the said Council of War thereto.

Done in the Council Chamber at the Helder, the $\frac{19}{20}$th September, in the year 1653. We say hard labour for twenty years in the house of correction.

(Signed)

A. HALEWIJN. GILLIS JANSEN. JAN POUWELZY.
B. RUSSELL.   D. VIJGH.
  1653.   1653.
HENDRICK DE RAET. E. GOMES. A. J. VAN NES.
  1653.   E. MEIJER.
W. D. ZAAN.

1245. *Sept.* $\frac{19}{29}$th, 1653.—*DE WITH TO S.G.*

[A.o.H. Translated.]

Noble and Powerful Lords,—My Lords,—I think it my duty humbly to submit to your Lordships the following report. I wrote last to report our proceedings to your Lordships on the $\frac{5}{15}$th and $\frac{10}{20}$th of this month, begging, amongst other things, that the State's ships which we left lying in the Texel still not ready, when we sailed out on the $\frac{1st}{11th}$ instant, might be sent in a body to join us at the rendezvous as quickly as possible, with a view of better securing the safety of the rich treasure we were sent out to fetch. On the $\frac{14}{24}$th instant I learnt from Hendrick Scholte, master of a Dantzig boat that sailed from London on the $\tfrac{6}{16}$th instant, that before he left that place one hundred ships had sailed for the coast of Holland to blockade the rivers; whilst, on the other hand, our force consists of forty-four ships, such as they are. I have previously sent your Lordships a statement of the number of guns and men they carry, and the length of time for which they are victualled; and I do not hesitate to say, that, unless further reinforcements are sent us from home, the treasure, for which we are now lying on the watch, and the State's fleet under our command, will run a great risk, as I leave your Lordships to judge. I should never have supposed that so great a treasure would be hazarded with so small a force, with which, in our opinion, the welfare or adversity of our country is so closely bound up. Our experience and achievements on divers occasions heretofore, when the numbers of the enemy's fleet and ours have been equal, are of course well known to your Lordships; and I do not hesitate to say that if the materials and stores for the ships still lying in the Texel not ready, had been forthcoming in proper time, they would have been able to put to sea with us; and now they have had plenty of time again, so that dilatoriness is growing into a hard and fast rule with us, and the English, who have learnt dexterity from us, now always get the wind of us in every thing, and are always ready before us. I shall not ask your Lordships to send me word where to bring the State's fleet in, after we have performed the convoy; but shall act in this matter in accordance with circumstances, favourable and otherwise. We are waiting very patiently, expecting to see the ships from the Sound every hour, and shall then at the first opportunity join the rest of the ships in

Flekkefiord, so as to proceed on our journey from that place with them and the others. I must repeat my anxiety to be informed of the position of the enemy off our coast, &c., &c.

(Signed) WITTE CORN: DE WITH.

Done on board the ship *'t huijs te Swieten*, the $^{20}_{30}$th September, 1653.

1246. *Sept.* $^{20}_{30}$*th*, 1653.—*BRADSHAW TO C.o.S.*

[Thurloe State Papers, i. 491.]

Sir,—The convoy with the powder, masts and merchant ships are (I doubt) still in the river, except they got out to sea this day. It's now above ten days since they had their dispatch, and all means possible have been used to get them to sea, but the winds have still been contrary: they are as low in the river as they can be, waiting the first opportunity. The 15th current came an express to the convoy from Captain Hill of the Worster [sic] frigate, to let them know that our fleet were drawn towards our own coast, and that he with fourteen more frigates would stay for them twelve or fifteen leagues to the norwest of Heligoland, the island in the mouth of this river. Since the return of that messenger I have received intelligence, that the States of Holland, having notice of these provisions and the merchant ships, have ordered twelve men of war to lie in wait for them, as they come forth, of which I have given Captain Howard[1] notice, and have sent out a boat with a letter to Captain Hill, to give him notice thereof, if possible to meet with him, that he may draw to the island with those frigates, lest these ships should fall into the enemy's hands before they can join with the frigates. By letters from

---

[1] *Sic*. Probably Hayward. *Cf.* Nos. 1219 and 1256.

the Sound we have it, that de Witt will out thence with their East India ships, such merchant ships as are ready, and some say that the Dane will lend him some of his great ships, but I believe not that: they hear the body of our fleet is drawn home by the last foul weather, so they will out with the first wind. It is also said that the Dutch will come forth with thirty or forty sail, to meet their de Witte from the Sound, but that you may know as well as we here. I shall still lay out for more powder, but as in my last and my former I writ you, except I have a further supply of money, I cannot effect what the Council orders. . . .

                Your humble servant,
                      R. BRADSHAW.

[Hamburg.]

1247. *Sept. 20/30th*, 1653.—*BLAKE TO MOULTON*

[S.P. 18, xl. 95.]

Capt. Moulton,—I have sent for your harbour along with Captain Young [1] in the Worcester, the Sapphire frigate and three men of war called the Dolphin, Princess Maria and Arms of Holland. The two first I desire you to see cleaned and revictualled with all expedition, and the latter to be taken in hand, I having writ to the Council desiring their approbation for continuing them in lieu of so many merchant ships.

There is money due to all of them for short allowances—I desire you will see them paid as you shall see fit, that no discouragement may be put upon them. I should gladly have seen you here had your health permitted.

---

[1] *Sic.* In the two lists given in this Part (Nos. 1229 and 1303) as well as in Nos. 1226 and 1246 Wm. Hill appears as in command of the Worcester. Young's name does not appear in either list.

I have no more at present but to tell you that I am, &c.

Rob. Blake.

Resolution,
Sept. 20, 1653.

The Laurel likewise comes in whom I would have you stay till further order.

1248. $\frac{Sept.22}{Oct.\frac{1}{2}}nd$, 1653.—*N.C. TO A.C.*

[S.P. 18, xl. 109.]

Rt. Honble.,—We have often represented (in discharge of duties and trust) our apprehension for a reasonable supply of stores for the Navy, and have not neglected to put those which were concerned in mind of such provision of money as was necessary for carrying on a work of so great import, as by many of our letters transmitted to that Board may appear.

We have also improved the utmost of our care and diligence in laying hold upon all opportunities presented, and within our power, for gathering in what hemp, cordage and masts were attainable, though in the former part of the year the want of punctual performance of what we engaged for to the merchants in matter of payment was some discouragement to them to adventure upon that trade in these times of so much hazard.

We have, as we conceive, in stores about 300 tons of hemp and cordage, and contracts made for 1300 tons more, having since we received your order upon the 20th present made an addition to what we had formerly of near 300 tons which is all we can yet attain, though we are ready according to our direction to give encouragement by some addition of price, if we find the Service may be advantaged thereby, which yet we discern not.

We do understand besides what is already engaged to us, there is a considerable quantity expected from Hamburg which we shall lay in for, and if it arrive in safety may somewhat add to our supply.

We cannot therefore but in faithfulness express our thoughts that it is of exceeding great concernment that a strong convoy be ordered for the security of those ships in which the welfare of our affairs under God is much concerned.

It is in our thoughts as soon as we are assured what may be had from Hamburg to fall in with some merchants to make provision this winter for a further supply of hemp at Riga or Quinsborough,[1] &c., which may be here at first of the spring and be helpful to the next summer's provision.

Our thoughts are not less exercised how a competent supply of masts may be attained, and indeed the difficulty now seems greater than in the former. We have acquainted you with six ships bound for Gothenburg upon that account. Three are expected from New England, two more we intend thither this winter, and some small supply may probably be had from Scotland, but allowance far short of our desire and what your occasions may require, especially if any of these should fall into the enemy's hands. And therefore we humbly conceive also that it is no small concernment that such strength do lie upon the coast of Norway, that that passage be secured so far as may be, the convoy designed for those ships being too weak to engage with any considerable strength of the enemy who doubtless will improve their utmost endeavour to prevent these supplies.

We are informed this morning of two ships bound from Norway with masts taken by the

[1] *I.e.* Königsberg.

enemy whereby may easily be discerned in what
hazard all the supplies expected are, if we maintain
not a prevailing strength in those seas, which we
leave to your consideration, and remain, &c.,

                          Rob. Thomson,
                          Fr. Willoughby,
                          E. Hopkins.

Navy Office,
  22 Sept. 1653.

[*Minuted by A.C.*]

Report to the Council of State matter of fact as to the loss of the two ships mentioned as above, and whether they shall think fit to order any ships to ply upon or towards that coast, in relation to the protection of whatsoever ships with masts are expected from thence, considering the great want of materials of that kind, which is too probable.

1249. Sept. 26/Oct. 6*th*, 1653.—*BOURNE TO A.C.*

[S.P. 18, xl. 119.]

Rt. Honble.,—Since my coming upon this place I have been able to do little in order to the business I came about, the weather proving very bad this day past; I shall at present give your Honours an account of those ships and frigates that are in this port, viz. Newcastle, Centurion, Convertine, Expedition, Constant Warwick, Mermaid, Middleboro', Raven and Concord which are all that belong to the State sent in from the General.

Here is also the Swift and Mary prize ready to receive your orders. The Guinea frigate, Richard and Martha, Hannibal and some others are in the

Rolling Grounds, and have orders to sail to Portsmouth and the river of Thames.

As for these that are appointed to be fitted here, I shall fall upon something preparatory thereunto in the morning, also I have made a particular survey of them and endeavour the speedy repairing of them.

But I perceive by the little I have observed already that divers of them are much defective in their hulls, and all the store of masts we have will but very hardly afford two mainmasts, one for the Newcastle, the other for the Centurion, and what our occasion may be hereafter we are not able to supply any great masts. The hulk appointed for this place will be very much wanted here the beginning of the next week : as for other stores I doubt not but the vessel that laded them is by this time dispatched at Deptford and ready to come away.

It is a principal part of my care how to order the business relating to the paying of the seamen, but I am apt to conclude (as to my own apprehensions) that it is no way advisable to pay them till they be completely fitted and ready to sail, for I find a good part already gone to London, and other places.

I hope I shall not need to mind your Honours, about the troop of horse, and an order to the Governor of Landguard Fort that he take particular care for a convenient guard for this town, without which there will be no living here, or keeping up any face of authority. The letter to the Mayor and magistrates of this town is not yet come, to require them to put forth their power in suppressing the excessive number of base tippling houses which do so much debauch the seamen. I am not yet ripe to give your Honours an account of the houses you ordered me to treat about, but you shall suddenly receive something concerning the same.

I am here purely in obedience to your Honours' command out of a ready spirit to do service in any capacity or place—although I cannot but acknowledge I find it irksome in several particulars, but I desire to be anything and in any condition where the Lord is pleased to cast me, and while I remain here I shall obey your command with cheerfulness, and give me leave to mind you of that which I hope you are very sensible of (viz.) of the business of masts.

I shall not add further to your troubles at present, but remain, &c.

N. BOURNE.

Harwich,
26 Sept. 1653.

1250. $\frac{Sept.\ 26}{Oct.\ 6}th$, 1653.—*HARMAN TO A.C.*

[S.P. 18, xl. 120.]

Right Honourable,—On Saturday the 17th September in the afternoon I having got the three convoys together, I weighed from before the harbour of Harwich and stood off to sea with the wind southerly; on Wednesday night following I was so far as the headland called the Scaw, and that night one of our convoys which was Mr. Noble left us through his own neglect, and as yet I cannot hear no tidings of him, whether he be taken by any of the enemy's ships, or lost by foul weather, for we have had great deliverance from both, for twenty-four hours' time before we came into the harbour we had much foul weather, and had much-a-do to keep our ships from being ashore on the coast of Norway, and since my

THE LAST WINTER 85

arrival at Gothenburg with the other two ships, which was on Friday the 23rd of September I was informed by the merchants that there was riding under the Scaw a fleet of Hollander men of war containing forty-eight East India men which they convoyed.

They so much admire how we should 'scape them : the two convoys will be ready very suddenly, for here is great store of masts ready : so having no more at present to acquaint Your Honours with, I take leave and remain, &c.

WILLUGHBY HARMAN.

Aboard the Katherine
in the harbour of
Gottenburg, this
26th Sept. 1653.

1251. $\frac{Sept. 27}{Oct. 7}$th, 1653.—*BOURNE TO A.C.*

[S.P. 18, xl. 126.]

Right Honble.,—I even now received yours of yesterday's date for answer whereof you may please to receive this short account (viz.) That this day I have been aboard the several ships and frigates in this port whose names I gave you by mine sent by Yr. Honrs. the last night. The Newcastle and Centurion will put us to the utmost of our skill to supply them with main masts out of the stores we have, we must be forced to lengthen them with oak. As for the boltsprits and other masts and yards, we shall be able to fit these, but I wish those frigates yet abroad may come in better found as to masts, or else that we may be stronger in stores.

As for other stores, I expect a sufficiency to come down from London and Yarmouth to dispatch this squadron, but as to the victualling part, I am not able to resolve you in what capacity we are, for as yet I cannot meet with the victuallers' agent, yet I suppose we shall be able to complete them that are here, with all sort of provisions, but a little oil upon that wheel would not be amiss.

Most of these ships I find very much out of repair as to carpenters' work and they want caulking all over, within and without, the winter approaching requires it to be done which will take some time (here being very few carpenters in this place, considering the business to be despatched), so as I doubt I shall be constrained to take off the carpenters again from the new frigates building at Woodbridge and other places upon this coast, which I would not willingly if it may be avoided, for they are too backward and need no pullback.

I have cast about me the best course I can take to carry on the work and you may be pleased to believe I am sensible of the stress that lies upon the present affairs. As for the house you gave me command to treat about, I have had a pass or two at a distance with the owner, and I suppose his price may be about £340, possibly something may be abated but I judged it not advisable to move any further at present, neither indeed have I any desire as to my particular, yet in my judgment suppose it may be accomodable for your ends if this war hold.

The town at present is very nasty and sickly, and the truth is something like a prison to me, but the Lord can make it otherwise if he please to grant his presence (here being little else but what is of a vexing quality).

Give me leave a little to wonder that this garrison should at this season be dismantled whereas there was never so much use of it since it was appointed, and considering the present affairs occasion so great a number of men belonging to the fleet to be here (many of whom must be awed by authority) as also here being very many Dutch prisoners, concerning whom I have often desired to know the State's pleasure, as to the manner and place for securing them, but as yet have no answer.

Until Your Honours shall please to put the cash into other hands (which thing I earnestly desire) I pray please to settle some way wherein I may be supplied with money to carry on the service here; which is all at present from

Yr. Honrs.' very humble servant,

N. BOURNE.

Harwich,
27 Sept. 1653.

1252. $\frac{Sept. 29}{Oct. 9}th$, 1653.—*BOURNE TO N.C.*

[S.P. 18, xl. 144.]

Gentlemen,—Besides those ships sent in before, which were eight in number, there arrived here yesterday the Advice, Assurance and Half Moon, very much shattered, the Advice I doubt whether she can be repaired here, her defects are such, the Assurance hath lost all her masts save her mainmast, the other lost all her anchors save one, and by the badness of her main capstan (which was ill put off hand) the whole was very much endangered.

These frigates parted with the Worcester, Diamond, Reserve, Foresight, Portsmouth and some others which went up the Swin. I have no tiding of the Hamborough fleet—the Lord send good.

It's very evident that the principal cause of the loss of the masts in the Newcastle, Centurion,

Assurance and others was the badness of the chainplates, which generally broke like rotten sticks. It were not amiss to enquire after such miscarriages, and give more than ordinary charge concerning this for the future, there being the whole safety of all depending thereon many times. Upon survey I find all these ships very much out of repair in their hulls, as well as their masts; what shift I shall make for carpenters I know not unless I take off the hands from the new frigates again, which I am unwilling to do.

If it were practicable, I should desire some ten or twelve carpenters to be sent down in the hulk who might help her hither, and then help us upon the frigates who are hastened.

I pray hasten away the hulk and those stores demanded, without which we can do nothing.

I have herewith also sent a demand for some other provisions which I desire may be put on board the hulk in case she be not come away before: we are in want thereof very much.

Concerning the house. I have treated with the owner who is not very forward to part with it. He hath been offered lately £320 for it. Since then he hath bestowed cost. I suppose £340 will buy it. But did I know where to provide a conveniency otherwise for storehouse room I am slow to deal in it, not but that I judge it a very good pennyworth to any private man. I have signified so much to the Commissioners of the Admiralty.

I pray please to employ some persons who may carefully see these stores and provisions sent to us, for our wants admit of no delay, and order Mr. Scott to send blocks ready fitted to careen, and heave out masts by the hulk with what else he knows necessary for the business.

I pray cause some instrument belonging to the

Office of the Ordnance to be sent down speedily both to receive accounts of the remains as also deliver out stores that are laid up at Landguard Fort.

I find divers prizes spoiled here for want of present sale, the charge to maintain a company [of] knaves about them eats up all.

I pray make the Commissioners of the Admiralty sensible of it, so that they may speedily be sold here and at Yarmouth.

I have not else but remain
Yr. very assured friend,
N. BOURNE.

Harwich,
29 Sept. 1653.

I pray whether any other help come you let us have 3 or 4 carpenters acquainted to make masts here being work enough of that kind.

N. B.

1253. $\frac{Sept. 29}{Oct. 9}$, 1653.—*INSTRUCTIONS OF C.o.S.*

[S.P. Dom. Commonwealth, xl. 141.]

Instructions for Samuell Ward, Joseph Larke, Methuselah Turner and Samuel Cooper appointed Commissioners for considering and giving relief unto sick and wounded men in the service of the Commonwealth, and the widows, children and impotent parents of such as are or have been slain in the said service since the 1st of January, 1648, as also for ordering of prisoners in the war.

(1) That the said Commissioners do acquaint themselves with the constitution of the Chest at Chatham and the condition thereof and present their opinions touching the management thereof at present and for the future.

(2) That they take an account forthwith and as often as they see cause what sick and wounded men the hospitals of this nation can accommodate for cure according to the late resolves of Parliament, and that such sick and wounded men (immediately after their being set on shore) be ordered to such hospitals, and in such proportions as may be most suitable to the nature of them, and may best conduce to the real relief and cure of the diseased, who are to receive the allowance of the house during their continuance there, for and towards their maintenance, but when that allowance is found incompetent the said Commissioners are to make a convenient supply.

And if the hospital shall not be able to receive the numbers set on shore they shall take special care to see them provided for in other places at the most reasonable rates attainable, due respect being had to the condition and state of the diseased parties, and the great charge the State is exposed to in these exhausting times.

(3) That the Commissioners thus constituted give reasonable and timely direction to the mayors and chief officers of all seaport towns to make provision for all sick and wounded men as they shall be set on shore from any of the ships in the State's service, and to provide and send down what chirurgeons or other means are necessary for their relief.

(4) That the Commissioners aforesaid, or any two of them, do seriously consider the condition and damage of all such persons as are or shall be wounded in the service of the Commonwealth, and give them such allowance as they shall adjudge requisite, not exceeding £10 gratuity to any person, nor £6 13s. 4d. yearly pension to any. And in such cases wherein they or any two of them

do judge a greater allowance to be given they are to certify their opinions, with the grounds, to the Commissioners of the Admiralty and Navy and act further therein as order from them shall be given.

(5) That the said Commissioners are likewise to take care that all such monies as the Parliament have or shall please to order to the orphans of those that have been, or shall be, slain in the service at sea, shall be so settled and improved for the use and benefit of the orphans, according to the real intent of the Parliament as that it may be secured from all embezzlement whatsoever.

(6) That the said Commissioners or any two of them shall likewise only consider the conditions of the widows and children and impotent parents of such as have been or shall be slain in the service, and to give such gratuities to them (not exceeding £10) as in their judgment be most agreeable to the rules of charity, and may demonstrate the State's sense of their suffering conditions, and in any extraordinary cases to report as before. In the proportioning also of relief to be given due enquiry is to be made, and respect had, to desert of the party wounded or slain in the service, the voluntariness of his spirit thereunto, courage, faithfulness and continuance therein, the nature of his employment, whether as officer or common seaman, the condition of his family, the number of his children left, and poverty of relations to which relief is given, etc. And also a vigilant eye to be had to the certificates that are brought to evince the truth of the sufferings of any, that they come from known credible persons, and so thereby deceit in the business of the State's bounty may be prevented. In order to which the clerk of the cheque in every ship of the State's service shall of

course, and ordinarily at the coming in of the said ship, but more especially, and extraordinarily, after any fight or engagement with the enemy, send to the Commissioners a true list of all such seamen, soldiers and officers that were wounded, or slain in such service respectively, mentioning to those that are wounded in what manner, whether by loss of limb, or whatsoever else may render the parties more remarkable, and so his relief the less questionable by the said Commissioners : which list is to be signed by the captains of the ships on which such persons have been entered, or in case of his death, or wounds which shall disable him, then the master or lieutenant, or other superior officer that shall survive the said engagement, which list, so signed by the captain or other officer as aforesaid, as also by the clerk of the cheque, is to be transmitted to the Commissioners, to the end that they may be able to prevent or discover any who shall upon false pretences or certificates, claim the relief, which is only intended for such as have endured the brunt of a real service.

(7) The like rule to be observed when any sick men are sent on shore for their necessary refreshment and recovery.

(8) The said Commissioners are likewise to take care that so soon as any mariners or soldiers are recovered of their wounds or sicknesses that (unless disabled by loss of limb) they are returned to their respective ships with all possible speed.

(9) The said Commissioners shall with due care order the disposal of all such prisoners as shall be taken at sea, and provide for their maintenance not exceeding 4d. per day for each common man and inferior officer until an opportunity be presented to employ them in some useful service, whereby the public charge may be eased, which the

said Commissioners are to enquire after, and accordingly to prosecute, and 12d. per diem for commission officers only, such as are sick and wounded are to be disposed to hospitals and other convenient places, where means may be used for recovery of their health and cure of their wounds.

(10) That an exact and orderly account be kept of all allowances made to any, that the abuse of double or further relief (which some by indirect means have obtained) may be prevented, and that the Commissioners do follow such further orders and instruments as shall be from time to time given by the Parliament Council of State, or Commissioners for the Admiralty and Navy.

Signed in the name and by order of the Council of State.

A. HOWARD,
President.

Whitehall,
29 Sept. 1653.

1254. $\frac{Sept. 30}{Oct. 10}$, 1653.—*HUTCHINSON AND PETT TO A.C.*

[S.P. Dom. Commonwealth, xl. 150.]

R^t. Honble.,—We desire your Honours should know that yesterday afternoon came to anchor within Queenborough five frigates, the Landrell,[1] Worcester, Reserve, President and Foresight, some of which have been off from the ground more than three months, and all of them out of victuals, we humbly desire therefore you would be pleased to signify your pleasure what shall be done with them, that accordingly present care may be taken of them, they being all very useful frigates.

We also humbly desire to know which of these

[1] *Sic.* ? Laurel.

ships mentioned in the margin [1] now at their mooring are appointed for the winter guard, for that care shall be taken to hasten their dispatch.

There are some 40 or more of Dutch prisoners brought home in some of these ships that are very able, and seem to be willing to work. We desire to know whether your Hon^{rs}. will give leave to their working here where there is now much business to be done, or whether we shall send them to London with the rest.

There is also a prisoner lying in Upnor Castle at 5s. a week charge, committed for firing the Fairfax. If your Honours please to order it, he may now be tried by a Council of War.

We are now upon the [repairs] of the Resolution and shall go on to make a dispatch of them as soon as we can.

We rest

Y^r. Hon^{rs}. very honourable servants,

R. HUTCHINSON.
PETER PETT.

Chatham Hill,
30 Sept. 1653.

Margin.—Resolution, James, George, Triumph, Andrew, Victory, Rainbow, Vanguard, Paragon, Unicorn, Fairfax, Lyon, Entrance, Arms of Holland, Princess Marie, Duchess, Crow, Kentish.

[Prefixed by shorthand notes of the reply to be given.]

1255. $\frac{Sept. 30}{Oct. 10}$, 1653.—*COMMITTEE OF COUNCIL TO S.G.*

[**A.o.H.** Translated.]

High and Mighty Lords,—We have received your H.M.'s dispatch of the $\frac{20}{6}$th $\frac{September}{October}$, from

[1] Names given at the end.

which we see that your H.M. have been pleased to adopt and convert into a resolution part of the proposal made in our letter two days previously, in which your H.M. gives orders for us to prepare victuals and stores for the warships belonging to this port, to enable them to serve throughout the winter. But we do not see therein that any measures are taken with regard to that on which our ability to carry out the said order chiefly depends, namely the funds, without which, as far as we are concerned, nothing at all can be done, and we beg your H.M. to accept this as a formal notification of the fact, and therefore not to be surprised, however matters go, that we are taking no steps in the business, until such time as we shall be provided with the means.

But, in addition to this, it seems to us very doubtful whether it is entirely advisable to retain all the State's warships on active service throughout the coming winter, as seems from your H.M.'s said order to be contemplated; and whether, by so doing for that time, great sums of money will not be spent uselessly, the ships worn out, the store consumed and the crews wearied, so that, in the spring, when we shall stand in the greatest need of them, they will not be in a fit condition to be made ready for sea as quickly as necessity will probably require, so as to enable them to meet the enemy's fleet in due time; whereas their ships, either the whole or the greater part of them, will be laid up during that season, and we are already beginning to hear of their doing so; so that they will come out well prepared and refreshed after their rest; and in our opinion the same thing would be advantageous also on this side, with a view not only of saving such great and needless expense, but of avoiding the danger, indeed, of losing a number of our ships, if they pass the whole winter in the North Sea, without, probably, getting one opportunity during all the time of seriously engaging the enemy; although your H.M. may perhaps have special objects, for reasons unknown or incomprehensible to us, for keeping so many excellent ships in active service notwithstanding the alleged difficulties. For we cannot think it necessary or advisable, with a view only of protecting the wine-ships, and bringing them safely out and home, as was done this last year; for, when we have had experience how easily the enemy, without risk to themselves, or damage to their ships, can lie in their own harbours and watch for their return, when they happen to pass along their coasts, although on that occasion we were marvellously lucky, in that the fleet had not been scattered by bad weather, as often happens about that time of year, we can provide a much more certain defence for the said trade, with very little risk and at less cost to the country, by allowing the master of each ship to sail the long way round on his own responsibility, without forming themselves into a fleet and appointing officers, in which case it is not likely that the English would bring their fleet into action to look out for, or to come to meet, single vessels, which was well worth their while last season, with a view of meeting and capturing, or destroying, *en masse*, such a rich fleet that had been so long assembling. But, in this way, we should only have single cruisers to provide against, either State's ships or ships fitted out by individuals, and if these were encountered they might easily be held in check and driven off, or overcome, by some of our quickest sailing frigates to be kept in active service, for which purpose twenty or four and twenty would be amply sufficient, if twelve of them were sent to cruise off Ushant at the entrance of the Channel, and the remainder along the coast of these Provinces, beginning from the Wielings up to off Texel, and then outwards to the Doggerbank, in four squadrons of three ships each to protect the passage of the merchantmen against the English cruisers, with permission to withdraw if they find the enemy in too great force, and with orders to attack if they see their advantage, by which means news of the enemy's position and strength could also be sent both to the Bay of Biscay and home here ; whilst it is most unlikely for them to meet any ships in the winter season out there ; there is no channel in which specially commissioned ships or other cruisers could remain for any length of time on the watch for the ships sailing round the long way, being too much subject to storms, long nights, foggy weather and other enemies to navigation. In which case the remainder of the ships of war of these Provinces having been laid up in accordance with our views, could be cleaned, provided with all necessaries and sent to sea towards the end of February or beginning of March, either to oppose the designs of the enemy or to attack them. All the new ships and other first-raters expected from the Mediterranean will then come in very well, and will give us the means of launching a fleet so strong, that (under God's blessing) they will not have to give way before any English fleet. The only difficulty in the way is that the crews, who are now in good order and of the numbers required, if paid off, might be lost and by evil means become diverted to other services, of which we are somewhat apprehensive ; but, to prevent this, instead of absolutely paying them off, recruiting could be discontinued and the officers and sailors paid off for a period of three months, but we could keep in touch with them and retain them in the service under a mutual promise, by paying them one Rix dollar per week, giving them, moreover, permission to work or do anything they chose for their own advantage, until the drum shall sound again to summon them once more on board. And this should be done only in the case of experienced seamen, whose services are of importance to the country, there being no fear that people who engage as soldiers or unskilled hands would run away, or be lost or be inveigled away by foreign nations; these should be paid off at once, and left to support themselves till the spring on the money they receive and what they can earn by their handiwork; and in the coming spring they will present themselves of their own accord.

We have been anxious humbly to submit all these our views and opinions to your H.M. to be so used on behalf of the State in the wise counsels of your H.M., as your H.M. shall consider to be most advantageous to the country, &c., &c.

(Signed) D. E. van Schellinga.
Your H.M.'s very humble servants, the Committee of the Council for Admiralty, and by their command.
(Signed) Dav^r. De Wild.

Amsterdam, the $\frac{30th\ September}{10th\ October}$, 1653.

1256. Oct. $\frac{1}{11}$, 1653.—*HAYWARD TO C.o.S.*

[S.P. 18, xli. 2.]

R^t. Honble.,—Having formerly received an order from Rear-Admiral Lawson[1] to take into

[1] *Cf.* No. 1219.

custody and convoy such merchant ships as were bound for the port of Hamburg, the which having performed and being at anchor in the river Elbe, I received an express from the honourable General Monck by the Nonsuch ketch that as soon as the masts and powder that was there bought by the Resident were laden, to set sail with them directly for the river Thames and, endeavouring the performance thereof, we did on Thursday the 22nd of September, set sail out of the river Elbe, the wind being then at south-east, and with that wind that night we run 14 leagues west-nor-west to sea hoping to have met with Captain Hill with a squadron of frigates which we heard lay thereabouts to meet us, but we not finding them, and the wind coming about westerly, we stretched away to the norward, being informed by general expresses from Resident Bradshaw, and also by common report, that a party of twelve Hollands men-of-war were sent out of the Texel on purpose to intercept us, but notwithstanding this endeavour to surprise, contrary winds and much foul weather which for 7 or 8 days together we have had, we are by God's assistance safely arrived upon our own coast with those that came out of the Elbe mouth with two excepted, which is an Iceland bark laden with fish which was taken by the Dutch and retaken by Captain Oddy, captain of the Nonsuch ketch, and another small ketch as I suppose bound for London. They lost company with us on Monday night, the 26th of September, and not seen since by any of us: the fleet with us are four men of war, two ships laden with mast, a small ship laden with powder, and four or five and twenty ships and vessels laden with merchant goods, most bound for London.

The wind at present is contrary, but we shall not fail, God willing, to endeavour what possibly may be to take all opportunity of wind and weather to follow our former order. This at present is all I have to trouble your Hon^r. withat. Only beg leave to subscribe myself,

     Y^r. Hon^{rs}'. humble servant,
         JOHN HAYWARD.

From aboard the
 Gillyflower, 2 leagues
 off Scarborough.
 1st Oct. 1653.

1257. *Oct.* $\frac{9}{19}$, 1653.—*BOURNE TO A.C.*

[S.P. 18, xli. 4.]

Right Honble.,—By yours of the 29th September I received an order to the Governor of Landguard to maintain a guard here as occasion requires, as also the copy of an order signed by his Excellency the Lord General for a troop, and it is no more than is requisite to keep up the authority of the service. I would not be too bold, yet am apt to think the state of this place and the present affairs here were not fully known or foreseen, by whom the order was procured for the slighting and demolishing this garrison, but being upon the place, we are sensible of it already by the boldness of several who durst not adventure before the like kinds. I formerly hinted something hereabouts to your Honours, yet I understand they proceed to throw down not only the line but a fort, which was wont to be the mainguard and the only place I had to commit or secure any persons found contemning or disobeying your commands, and the truth is without some such place be continued, and a guard to maintain the honour of your service committed to my trust, I shall humbly desire to be removed rather than be forced to see such violence and insolence committed, and have not power to suppress the same.

Yesterday we had a taste of what we may look for frequently, wherein I was forced to be more mild than otherwise I should if I had been in another capacity, yet I was forced to make a shift to reduce them with more trouble than I will declare, and what I have suffered already as to this part, besides the care of all other matters, is not fit for me to relate. But I am sure it will be much for the honour and benefit of the service, and for the encouragement of honest instruments when the pride and insolence of men's spirits dare not shew itself. I have presumed to stop the throwing down the fort and mount until I know your Honours' sense hereof, which I humbly crave speedily, as also your resolution to the house and other particulars formerly propounded to you, without which I am in the dark.[1]

The Mary prize and the Gift sail this day, the captains having received their orders sent them from General Monck.

Your business goes on but slowly in comparison of what I desire, yet we lose no time, neither are idle, but the work is great about the mastheads and other carpenters' and caulkers' work, the ships being generally much shaken; we have little help, and the weather uncertain and rainy. I shall endeavour to improve that help we have to fit out some of the frigates. The old hulk we formerly had is sunk, and without the other come speedily I cannot do what I would.[2] If the stores will afford it, I desire a supply of 6 masts for mainmasts to be ordered down, which with what I have

---

[1] *In margin:* whether the house shall be taken and the mount continued.
[2] *In margin:* hulk to be speeded.

will put us into a reasonably good condition to recruit another squadron.[1] The Martin frigate came in hither this morning who came lately from Newcastle, but brings little news, but concerning the Bristol frigate, the Portland, Amity and another whom he saw in Aldborough Road, I suppose they have orders to direct their course.

If anything be expected from me in that kind I desire to know your Honours' pleasure that so I may be able to direct in case any other come hither upon that account.

If you will have the Advice or Malago Merchant be sent away, please to signify the same. Just now (since the writing of the former part) I received your letter of yesterday's date and understand your pleasure as to the payment of the frigates under which I am concluded as to my private opinion, and what your Honours command shall be obeyed by me as far as I may, but at present I believe the greatest part of the seamen and many officers are absent, and by that time they are returned and paid, some of the ships will be ready to sail, and then we may expect to have many gone when the ships shall sail, and could they be supplied with clothes at any honest rates aboard, I am humbly of opinion that one work at the last were best (but this with submission).

As for the purchase of the house your Honours may remember I was always slow in promoting it, and although I am clear from any temptation of desiring to make my habitation here, yet possibly I might be thought to do what is too common (viz. to drive on private designs under public pretences) and therefore could I have done less in faithfulness to your service I was resolved never to have moved it, but since it's not thought fit to con-

[1] *In margin:* masts of 26 and 27 yards long.

clude about it, I shall only acquaint your Honours that I have provided as far as I can, and promised to give my answer to-morrow, and in case it be otherwise disposed, and we want it hereafter, I hope I shall be blameless. But had I been to act for myself, I would have made short work.

    I confess the present place I am in doth little content me, were it not in pure obedience to commands which I am willing to observe, yet have shuffled through such inconveniences and lived at such expenses that I have no reason to desire a continuance as to myself. I hope you will excuse my plainness. I have not often intimated anything of this nature, and were I not too sensible of some discouragements which I have been accustomed unto, I should have been silent altogether, for I bless God I desire to trust Him as to outward things, and not be found seeking myself, yet not unfaithful to my family. This was far beyond my thoughts at the beginning, but I hope the candour will interpret my clear intention, and please to rest assured I am and shall be

    Yr Honrs'. very faithful and ready servant,
                                                N. BOURNE.

Harwich,
2 Oct. 1653.

    I have taken boldness to write two lines to my Lord General in order to the guarding this town, being doubtful whether a sufficient number can be spared from Landguard Fort. I desire your furtherance herein that some small company of foot may be sent hither, and that the fort which was the place of the mainguard may be kept up so long as the present state of affairs continue at this height.

1258. *Oct.* $\tfrac{4}{14}$, 1653.—*MYNGS TO A.C.*

[S.P. 18, xli. 17.]

Honourable,—In pursuance of your order of the 21st September, on Friday the 1st of October, I, at Dover, received on board the Vice-Chancellor of Poland and his retinue, and the 3rd landed him at Dieppe; the 4th about 2 o/c in the afternoon some ten leagues off of Dieppe espied twenty-three sail of ships, after which made sail, among which were three Hollands men of war, two of which stood out and fought us, but receiving some damage they bare away to leeward of the fleet, so we forthwith stood with the fleet, whom we brought by the lee and brought into the Downs.

One Captain Allinson, a private man of war came in after they struck, to us, and maimed two of them, coming along with us, securing the rest into the Downs.

We have received two very dangerous shots, on [in] our main mast, the other, through our foremast, which must be very well fished, if not unserviceable.

We lost only our master, none wounded. I have sent to Dover to see if can be fitted, if not, must be forced to come up in the Hope.

Y^r honours' humble servant,
CHRISTOP^R. MYNGS.

From on board the Elizabeth frigate
in Downs, this 4th Oct. 1653.

1259. *Oct.* $\tfrac{4}{14}$, 1653.—*COMMISSION FOR JUDGE ADVOCATE BY BLAKE AND MONCK*

[S.P. 18, xli. 18.]

(*Locus sigilli.*)

Robert Blake, George Monck, John Desborough and William Penn, Admirals and Generals appointed by Parliament to command the fleet, and for this expedition.

To Mr. John Fowler, appointed Judge Advocate of the Fleet.

Whereas among other things for the better regulating and governing the fleet or fleets of this Commonwealth at sea it is referred unto us, or any one of us, to call a Council or Councils of War of captains or other officers as to us or any of us shall seem expedient for the service of the Commonwealth in the government of their fleet or fleets, as aforesaid ; also to appoint a Judge Advocate to attend the said Councils of War, and to do and perform the said duties of that place in as full and ample manner as any Judge Advocate of a Fleet or Army might or ought to do by virtue of his said employment, and forasmuch as the said place is now vacant, and we are well satisfied of your fidelity and ability to manage the said trust, we do by virtue of the power given unto us, constitute and appoint you to be Judge Advocate of the Fleet for this ensuing expedition, and do hereby authorise and require you from time to time to attend all Court Martials that shall be called on board this ship, or any other in the fleet for trial of offenders trespassing against the laws of war and ordinances of the sea established by Parliament ; also to examine all such persons as are now in custody for offences committed against the said laws of war, or any other that shall be found trespassers in the like nature, during your continuance in the said employment ; also to examine all such persons upon oath as shall be produced as witnesses for or against them in order to the due proof of the matter of fact laid to the charge of them, or any of them, or to the clearing of them, and to observe such further instructions and directions as you shall from time to time receive from us for the service of the Commonwealth.

In consideration whereof you are to have and receive from the State after the rate of 8 shillings per diem, and this shall warrant your so doing.

Given under our hands and seals the 4th Octr. 1653.

(Signed) GEORGE MONCK.
WILLIAM PENN.

Copia Vera,
J. FOWLER.

1260. Oct. $\frac{5}{15}$, 1653.—ORDER OF A.C.
[Add. MS. 22546, fol. 141.]

By the Commissioners of the Admiralty and Navy. Forasmuch as it was thought fit in pursuance to a reference from the Council dated the 2nd of February, 1652,[1] that the fleet for this last summer should be divided into three squadrons, and that there should be one occasional Vice-Admiral, and one occasional Rear-Admiral allowed unto each of the said squadrons as the General should think fit and the service require. And whereas the persons mentioned in the annexed list [2] have been employed by the Generals of the fleet as occasional flag officers, in this last summer's service accordingly.

It is ordered that the Commissioners of the Navy do cause a bill to be made out unto the said flag officers in reward to them for wearing the flag during the time mentioned in the said list after the rate of seventeen shillings per diem unto a Vice-

---

[1] *I.e.* Feb. $\frac{2}{12}$, 1652/3. This is not among the documents in this collection.
[2] Not included.

Admiral, and fourteen shillings per diem to a Rear-Admiral, their wages as captains included.

JOHN DISBROWE.
WILLM. BURTON.
NATH. RICH.

1261. *Oct.* $\frac{5}{15}$, 1653.—*PETT TO A.C.*
[S.P. 18, xli. 21, 22.]

R^t. Honble.,—I did well hope we should have dispatched the service with quietness and have done it till this morning, but even now comes the Unicorn's company at least 200 of them, and with much peremptoriness in a mutinous way told me that they would not go aboard to do any duty till they had their money. I used all the arguments I could to please them in a fair way, and was assisted by Captain Lane and Captain Bourne, but nothing could prevail, therefore we must either submit to pay them which will not only in my opinion be very dishonourable to the service and beget an extreme ill precedent, and which I am confident will no way be pleasing to you, or else I shall humbly desire that a troop of horse may be forthwith sent down, which certainly will be of singular use : this being done, I doubt not but to give your Honours a good account of getting the Unicorn, Fairfax, Laurel and Kentish to the Hope timely next week. I humbly crave pardon for this troubling of you which I did well hope to have avoided, and rest at your service,

PETER PETT.

Chatham,
 5 Oct. 1653.

R^t. Honble.,—All the arguments that could possibly be used either by myself or those captains appointed to attend here will prevail nothing with the Unicorn, Laurel and Kentish's men to invite them to duty till their ships come into the Hope which might soon have been effected, could they have been persuaded. We promised them all their money as soon as they should arrive at the aforementioned place, leave to see their friends and dispatch their business 6 or 8 days, nay that they should have their money paid here, if they would but fit the ships for sailing, but this morning they cried one and all for London, and I think are gone, which I thought my duty to acquaint your Honours with, and humbly desire you should know that the service shall not be neglected, and do hope notwithstanding to get the four ships and frigates away next week; meantime humbly leave to your Honours' wisdoms when and where to pay these men. I desire to have a list of the winter guard, for that there is the Happy Entrance and some other Flemish prizes that are to be launched that we may accordingly hasten them.

The troop is come down this morning so shall make use of them only in pressing necessities, and do hope notwithstanding this late disturbance, to answer your Honours' expectation in fitting out the ships from home, of which we only desire timely notice.

I am
Y^r. Hon^{rs}'. very humble servant,
PETER PETT.

Chatham,
5 Oct. 1653.

In margin :

Matthew Macline } Unicorn's men headed the
Jno. Gregory } mutiny yesterday that I
Kendall } took notice of myself.

1262. *Oct.* $\tfrac{6}{16}$, 1653.—*DE WITH TO S.G.*
[A.o.H.]

Noble and Powerful Lords,—My Lords,—My last letter to your Lordships was written on the $\tfrac{19}{30}$th September from the rendezvous, and I trust it reached your Lordships safely. In this letter I gave a plain and faithful account, and had previously sent a statement of the deficiencies of victuals on our ships. After the five return-ships and various Baltic ships had been brought by the fourteen King's[1] ships and fireships to the rendezvous between Skagen and Kleine Helms, we sailed on the $\tfrac{22}{2}$nd $\tfrac{\text{September}}{\text{October}}$ with a Southerly wind from the said place with all the ships that had come in, except the above-mentioned King's ships, which we left lying at the rendezvous. We made every effort to reach Flekkefiord, in the hope of finding the ships from Bergen there; but owing to rough weather and contrary wind the ship Malacca, which was very leaky, was unable to keep the water down. On the $\tfrac{25}{5}$th $\tfrac{\text{September}}{\text{October}}$ we put into Maerdon with all our ships. I have lost no time in sending out expresses both overland and by sea, to carry information to the ships in Bergen and in all the harbours in the North Sea, telling the masters lying in those places to repair without loss of time to Flekkefiord, and to await our coming off the mouths of the shallows there, so as to enable us to continue our journey from that place in the same way, as soon as the ships have come from Bergen. On the $\tfrac{26}{6}$th, after inspecting the Malacca, it was decided that she should unload her cargo into other ships, as she was unfit to sail home; every effort was made to get the unloading done. On

[1] *I.e.* Danes.

the $\frac{28}{8}$th $\frac{Sept.}{Oct.}$, I received a letter dated from off Bergen the $\frac{9}{19}$th September, informing me that the three return-ships, and the Straits vessels and West Indiamen were still lying there, intending to join us with the first favourable wind, and that a contrary wind, storms and rough weather had obliged them to remain there, and to wait for a fair wind, which, as soon as they got, they would proceed on their way without loss of time. Since I sailed out, my Lords, I have not had the slightest news or succours from your Lordships. The short supply of provisions we have can be seen from the statement of the $\frac{9}{19}$th September. I have waited very patiently for a favourable wind and for the ships from Bergen. For the greater part of the time since we left home we have had southerly, south-west and south-east winds, which has protracted our voyage very much. I trust God Almighty will grant us soon a favourable wind and a safe voyage with all our ships and the vessels we were sent out to fetch. With regard to this place, there is neither credit, money nor provisions to be got on shore for such a number of people as we are here. All which I beg to submit for your Lordships' information. I am very anxious to have news as to the position of the enemy on our coasts, &c., &c.

(Signed)   WITTE CORN : DE WITH.

<small>Done on board the ship *'t huijs te Swieten*, lying in Maerdon, this $\frac{9}{19}$th September (*sic*) [*should be* October], 1653.</small>

Whereas the State's fleet under our command, on their sailing out the $\frac{1st}{11th}$ September, 1653, was victualled, in accordance with the instructions of the Boards to which they severally belong, for not longer than two months, and the provisions on board the said ships are now, therefore, beginning to be very sensibly reduced ; and a general survey of supplies was made a few days ago, and the ships best supplied made over some of their provisions to those who were worst supplied, so that every captain will have to make sure that his victuals will last out till the East Indiamen and other ships are convoyed home by us. They must, therefore, meanwhile be careful so to economise their provisions, as to have something still in store at the end of the time, and not suffer their crew to perish of hunger ; it being understood that those captains who give their crews less victuals than is customary, will have to satisfy them for the same either in victuals or money, and accounts are to be kept of the same. Every captain, moreover, is to be careful to fix these orders up on his quarterdeck, so that the same may be read by the officers, sailors and soldiers, and that they may rely on the same being carried out.

Memorandum how to make the victuals last out for the support of our men in this temporary scarcity : 3 to 4 lbs. of bread per week for every man, 3 [lbs.] of meat or bacon per week ; at ten or eleven o'clock every morning a basin of groats or peas and a basin of stockfish ; at four o'clock in the afternoon, the same. On meat-days a basin of groats, peas or beans, with a basin of meat ; in the evening a basin of groats, peas or beans again. Every one to manage his own butter and cheese, in such a way as he can make his supply suffice.

Done on board the ship *'t huijs te Swieten*,
lying in Maerdon, this $\frac{9}{16}$th October, 1653.

1263. *Oct.* $\frac{7}{17}$, 1653.—*BISDOMMER TO BEVERNING AND VAN DER PERRE*

[Thurloe S.P. i. 529.]

My Lords,—The Lords Commissioners of their High and Mighty Lordships, who have been at the Helder for the speedy equipping of the remainder of the damnified ships, are yesterday returned hither, and do advise, that upon Sunday last seventeen men-of-war set sail—directed their course to meet with Vice-Admiral de Witt, who is looked for back every hour with the East India ships, the rest of the fleet. We do hear, that the seventeen men-of-war also sent to meet with twenty-three English ships from Hamburg, laden with ammunition, arrived there after the English were gone from thence. That they missing of them presently set sail to join Vice-Admiral de Witt, if they could meet with him. The States of Holland have given a strict charge for inquiry to be made, who those merchants are, that from time to time send ammunition of war from Amsterdam to Hamburg. It is said here, that as soon as de Witt is come back, the lord of Opdam is to take possession of all the fleet, and therewith to convoy the wine fleet for France. The Lords Commissioners, who are come from the Helder, do inform me just now that they have lately received a letter from Grave William, wherein he writes, that a caper[1] had taken six of the twenty-three English ships, that came from Hamburg. We should be glad to have it confirmed.

The Hague, 17 Oct., M.S.

[1] *I.e.* privateer.

1264. *Oct.* 7/17, 1653.—*ADVERTISEMENTS FROM LONDON*

[Clar. MS. 46, fol. 327.]

London, 7th October, 1653.

We have near 200 men-of-war in the River, betwixt this place and Chatham, and about thirty more at sea, most to the westward. Our Fleet was much prejudiced by the late ill weather; but the safe arrival of our ships from Hamburg[1] doth make all good again, they were eighteen in all, richly laden, but we were chiefly solicitous for four in one whereof there was 50,000lb. worth of hemp and other naval provisions, in another 4000lb. worth of powder, and in the other two masts and woodwork; their convoy had left them, because they could not be ready by the appointed time, and we despaired of ever seeing them again; but they are come safely to Scarborough, having been many days at sea, without sight of an enemy, which we know not whether to admire, as the stupidity of the Dutch or our own good fortune; but this breaks the heart of the malignant party, and animates our own, with the other little successes which we daily have, among the rest one of our frigates[2] (having before lost her masts in a sharp fight with three Dutch men-of-war) brought in twenty small Dutch vessels from the French coast into Dover. Nor are we without our losses, a rich Barbado-man being taken the last week to the westward, either by the Dutch, or those pirates at Brest, at whom we are much offended, especially since the new Court of Admiralty they have there erected, and resolve to know from the French whether they will own the matter.

We have lately launched some new ships in this

[1] *Cf.* No. 1256.   [2] *Cf.* No. 1258.

River, and the General, with many of the officers, honoured one of them with their presence ; as I take it, it is called the Swiftsure of about seventy guns. Our Admiral Monke intends to go in her this winter with above sixty more. Blake is in the west, and it is believed will no more to sea, either for the indisposition of his mind, or body ; and though Monke be the General's creature, yet if a more saintlike person equal to that employment could be found out, it is possible it [sic] might be laid aside at present ; he is constantly with the Committee of the Admiralty, but talks of going to sea again within twelve or fourteen days, probably it will be three weeks first. Our seamen have been clamorous since their return, but we are paying them off as fast as we are able.

1265. *Oct.* $\frac{5}{15}$, 1653.—*BOURNE TO A.C.*
[S.P. 18, xli. 35.]

Right Honble.,—In my last I gave your Honours account of my taking this season to observe the state of your affairs upon the Coast and accordingly have been at Woodbridge, South[w]old, and Yarmouth.

At South[w]old I met with very great complaints from the bailiffs for want of money to discharge the quarters of the sick and wounded sent on shore, being about £500 in arrear ; the people, generally, very poor, and unable to forbear it, which causes great discontent, and may discourage them for the future if the like occasion may present, which I think my duty to present your Honours withal. At Yarmouth I understand there is about 200 sick and wounded yet remaining, part whereof is ordered to be sent up to London. I found some provisions there aboard a ship sent from the fleet, the greatest part being defective beer, which I ordered to be surveyed and disposed accordingly, that so the ship might no longer lie upon dead charge to the State.

I have given orders for the laying the standing rigging and cables for the two new frigates there, which I have also surveyed, and find they are not like to be ready this three months : some hemp I bought now, and more is wanting, which is taken order for, as I am informed.

The frigates at Woodbridge may be ready built, the one about three weeks, the other about ten weeks hence. In several particulars, as opportunity hath offered, I have endeavoured to serve the public.

As for the hulk and hoy with stores, I have no news of either which I thought necessary to signify : to the end your Honours may know we are not in a capacity to do what may be expected. I could gladly see some of the frigates in a better posture than they are, which will soon be, if I be supplied, else not. I shall proceed to repair the Advice frigate, and shall not grudge either at the number of ships, or quantity of work that shall lie before me, though never so course [? coarse] or troublesome, be it what it will, if I have matter to work upon.

I hope the next week will shorten our business upon some of the frigates, of which your Honours shall have a most particular account by my next.

The greatest part of the seamen are absent, and the work now will lie much upon their hand to dispatch. I wish some course may be taken to draw them down. I know none more like to take effect than the report of money to be sent down to pay them off.

Concerning the Dutch prisoners, I have observed a great number at Yarmouth, being fishermen, amongst which are very many boys, and aged infirm persons, who are neither able or willing to do any service against this nation, in their men-of-war, if at home, yet lie upon the same charge here as the rest. I thought it my duty to give this intimation, and leave it to your wisdom to consider thereof, as you shall see cause, but doubtless the charge is great, which may be prevented.

I shall not enlarge further to your trouble at present, but shall remain

Y^r. Hon^{rs}'. faithful and humble servant,
N. BOURNE.

Harwich,
9 Oct. 1653.

1266. *Oct. $\frac{12}{22}$, 1653.—ORDER OF A.C.*
[S.P. 18, lix. 105.]

By the Commissioners of the Admiralty and Navy.

It is ordered that the Commissioners for the Navy do cause the ships and frigate hereunder mentioned forthwith to be refitted for this winter's service, and that such seamen as the captains thereof shall present be entered on board the same.

WILLM. BURTON.
THO. KELSEY.
GEORGE MONCK.

12 Oct. 1653.

Mathias	Adventure
Tiger	Amity
Reserve	Worcester
Diamond	Gt. President
Foresight	Marmaduke
Portsmouth	Phœnix
[torn]	
Raven	
Pelican	

1267. Oct. $\frac{13}{23}$, 1653.—DECISIONS OF COUNCIL

[Archives of Hague.]

Whereas Vice-Admiral de With has communicated to us, the undersigned, the instructions he received for this expedition from My Lords Delegates of the States at the Helder, on the $\frac{19}{29}$th August, 1653, wherein amongst other things he is first charged to convoy home the East India return-ships and the merchantmen coming from the Sound, together with the ships from Bergen in Norway which were previously ordered to come to Flekkefiord; and whereas the said Vice-Admiral has further informed us as follows:

First, that most of the State's ships under his Honour's command were victualled when they sailed out, the $\frac{1st}{11th}$ September, for not more than two months, in accordance with instructions received by them from the respective Boards; and to make the scanty supplies last out, the Vice-Admiral, with a view of promoting the service of the country, on the $\frac{7}{17}$th October ordered the ration to be reduced by a third throughout the State's fleet.

Secondly, that the Vice-Admiral has dispatched expresses eight several times, both by land and sea, to Bergen, and has received only one answer on the $\frac{8}{18}$th October, written on the $\frac{28}{8}$th $\frac{Sept.}{Oct.}$ and $\frac{1st}{11th}$ Oct., by Commodore Jacob de Baer of the East India return-ships, in which he states that the said ships are lying there, and purpose to sail out and join us with the first favourable wind. The Vice-Admiral sent an answer to the said letter by express forthwith, earnestly desiring the said ships to come into Flekkefiord as quickly as possible. We learn this morning that the said ships have been still lying there over six days, so that we can hardly expect the said fleet except with long delay; whilst, in addition to this we have now about 400 merchantmen with us, four East-Indiamen, four flutes laden with spices taken out of the leaky ship Malacca, and the State's fleet consisting of seventy-four ships, which forms a mighty fleet, and ought, under present circumstances, to be convoyed with every possible protection, considering also the long nights, short days, storms and unfavourable weather that one must expect here every day, all which is a great anxiety to us. And having taken all the above into consideration we have decided—with a view of protecting and preserving the above-mentioned great and costly fleet—to sail in a body to off the Vlie or Texel, it being, of course, understood that we send notice hereof to their H.M. with all possible speed. And we, the undersigned, have thus decided and determined, believing it to be for the good of our beloved Fatherland and of the Chartered East India Company, trusting that Government will be pleased to approve of the same.

Done on board the ship *'t huijs te Swieten*, this 14/24th October, 1653.

(Signed)

WITTE CORN: DE WITH.	MIGHEL ADR.
GERRARD DEMMER.	D' RUIJTER.
JACOB JUNIUS.	PIETER FLORISZ:
ADRIAEN NICOLAESZ: KEMPEN.	FRANS CRYNSZ: MANGELAER.
PIETER VAN BRAKEL.	PIETER MARCUSZ.
JACOB ADRIAENSZ: PENSZ.	WILLEM VAN DER SOEN
	A. VAN DER HULST.
Cap^{n.} JAN G. VERBURGH.	T. VAN DER WERFF.
	E. MEESSEN.
JACOB CLEIJDIJCH.	JACOB CORN: SWART.
JAN WAGENAAR.	

Compared, &c.

THE LAST WINTER

1268. *Oct.* $\frac{10}{16}$, 1653.—*DE WITH TO S.G.*

[Archives of the Hague.]

Noble and Powerful Lords,—My Lords,—My last letter was written on the $\frac{6}{16}$th instant in Maerdon, informing your Lordships of our state and plans, and I hope the same will have come safely to hand. I have further to report to your Lordships that on the $\frac{7}{17}$th instant we held a general survey of the provisions on board all the State's ships; owing to scarcity the ration has been diminished by a good third, as may be seen from the enclosed paper. On the $\frac{11\text{th}}{21\text{st}}$ instant we left Maerdon with all the State's ships, the return-ships and the merchantmen in our company. On the $\frac{12\text{th}}{22\text{nd}}$ we were joined by about 170 merchant-ships from Flekkefiord, so that at that time we had about 370 to 380 merchant-ships with us altogether. On the $\frac{14}{24}$th, off Cape Naze, we fell in with Captain van der Soen and his squadron, consisting then of fifteen vessels. On the $\frac{15}{25}$th we were joined by Captain Egbert Meesen with his squadron of fifteen ships. From neither of these Commodores last dispatched by your Lordships have we been able to glean the slightest news of the enemy, which causes us the greatest surprise, for the enemy's fleet to be kept so secret. We have been informed, moreover, by the said Commodores and the captains with them, that they were not victualled for longer than till the middle of November. We are very much astonished to think that such a body of ships should be sent out with such small supplies of provisions at this season of the year, when storms and unfavourable weather may be looked for every day. I gave orders for a second and more searching survey, and the general result may be seen from the accompanying statement; this scantiness of provisions has much perplexed us. Further, my Lords, we have been speculating about the return-ships and others lying at Bergen in Norway, which, as far as we can judge, ought to have been at the rendezvous at Flekkefiord some considerable time ago, so that we are very much afraid that the said ships will only be able to get very slowly from that place at this season of the year. We have also taken into earnest consideration the fleet that we have with us at present, consisting of seventy-four ships of war, four return-ships, four flute-ships laden with spices out of the leaky ship Malacca, which was left behind in Maerdon owing to her unfit condition, and about 380 merchantmen, and together with these, the long nights, short days, the storms and unfavourable weather that we must look for every day, and the scarcity of our provisions; and the Council of War, having carefully considered all these unfavourable circumstances, has passed the resolution contained in the accompanying document, trusting therein to meet with your Lordships' approval. I have just received a dispatch from their H.M. of the $\frac{26}{6}$th $\frac{\text{September}}{\text{October}}$, and another of the $\frac{27}{7}$th of $\frac{\text{September}}{\text{October}}$. With regard to the resolution of the $\frac{26}{6}$th, I beg respectfully to submit, whether, when the fleet arrives off the shallows of the Texel and the Vlie, it will not be best for the State's ships to sail in as well as the others, because at the present season storms and unfavourable weather must be expected, and great accidents might be liable to occur if they lie off the shallows, the more especially as most of them will have exhausted their supplies of provisions, and I may say that at this time of the year they cannot be victualled outside; and if your Lordships have been pleased to determine that the said ships shall revictual as quickly as possible, it is fit from every point of view that they should sail in, it being understood, of course, that the crews remain on board, and that the provisions are made ready for the fleet as quickly as possible, together with a large supply of water, to be sent to us on our arrival; and our men will also need to fit themselves out again, and to be provided with more clothes, for, according to their report, they thought they should be only two months out. In reply to the dispatch of the $\frac{27}{7}$th $\frac{\text{Sept.}}{\text{Oct.}}$ I must say that we are in the highest degree astonished at receiving no news of the enemy; it would be of the greatest possible service to the country at this juncture, and we should very thankfully take advantage of it. I have further to inform your Lordships, that after we had made the enclosed decision, a small vessel was dispatched to Flekkefiord to keep a look-out for the ships that might come in there to the rendezvous from Bergen in Norway, with orders to the said ships so arriving to wait there for us or for further orders from your Lordships. I also think it my duty to state that none of the ships under our command have careened or been cleaned for a considerable time, as your Lordships are aware, and we have not therefore a single quick-sailing ship or yacht in the whole fleet. But attention should be paid to this point; and clean ships give one a great advantage in an engagement with the enemy; with their clean ships they always get the wind of us, and are much too swift in their manœuvres for us. It is, therefore, a matter of necessity that a portion of our ships should be careened or cleaned from time to time, if we are to get proper service from them. With regard to the two ships 't huijs te Swieten and 't huijs te Cruijningen, their portholes cannot be used on account of the inflow of water at their sills when under sail, so that it will be necessary to fit both of them as soon as possible with new bulges,[1] each 16 inches thick, weighted with iron; they will then draw a good foot less water, and their guns will be able to be used conveniently. If this is not done, the guns on the broadside in each ship are quite useless at sea, and I beg your Lordships to accept my opinion absolutely in this matter, &c., &c.

    (Signed) WITTE CORN: DE WITH.

Done on board the ship *'t huijs te Swieten*, this $\frac{18}{28}$th October, 1653.

1269. *Oct.* $\frac{17}{27}$, 1653.—*RUIJTER TO S.G.*

[Archives of Hague.]

 Noble and Powerful Lords,—My Lords—My last was dated the $\frac{15}{25}$th of September; since that time we have been lying under the Holmen, S.E. of Schagen, awaiting the coming of the East Indiamen and some other traders to the East; they came in to us on the $\frac{20}{30}$th of that month, with fourteen Danish ships under the command of Admiral Willekens, who had acted on behalf of this country. They anchored together to the east of Schagen, the wind being W.S.W., and very cold, so that we were unable to speak one another at that time and until the morning of the $\frac{21}{1}$st $\frac{\text{Sept.}}{\text{Oct.}}$, when Vice-Admiral de Witte and I, with Rear-Admiral Peter Florisz, went on board him, and received a kindly welcome. We lay there for the rest of that day, it being very cold, and

---

 [1] Buijak = belly, *i.e.* a bulge. Evidently the measure suggested is that of 'girdling' or 'furring.' *Cf.* Mainwaring, *Seaman's Dictionary*, or *Boteler's Dialogues*, N.R.S. lxv. p. 92.

the wind S.W. ; towards evening the wind shifted more towards the south ; early on the morning of the 22nd we got under sail, the wind being S.S.E. and blowing very cold, and did our best to make Flekkefiord in Norway, where our rendezvous was, in order to meet the rest of the ships from Bergen and other places, but were prevented on the 23rd by severe weather, the wind being W.S.W., so that we were driven too low, towards evening the ship Malacko began to hoist distress signals and was very leaky, so that she was obliged to seek some roadstead, and we ordered three ships of war to accompany her, which on the 24th came with her to Maerdon and we stood on and off till the 25th, when we were compelled by stormy weather to run in there with the whole of the fleet ; on the 26th it was decided to unload the ship Malacko into the empty merchantmen ; and we lay there, detained by contrary winds till the 11th/21st October, when we sailed out with an East wind, with 160 ships. On the 12th/22nd we arrived off Flekkefiord, whereupon 200 ships came out from there and from other arms of the sea, and we remained floating on and off, patiently waiting for the ships from Bergen till the 14th/24th inst. On that day we were joined by Commander Willem van der Soen with sixteen ships of war ; on the 15th/25th Commander Heckberdt Meeusen [1] came in, in the ship Brederode, also with sixteen ships of war, so that we now muster seventy-six ships of war and a good 400 merchantmen, and are all driving very much to the west, the weather being still and hazy. We have therefore taken the opinion of the Council of War, and decided to steer our course towards the Fatherland, as we have little or no provisions left to last us longer than 26 or 28 days

[1] *I.e.* Egbert Meesen. *Cf.* No. 1268.

at the outside, and are having only two meals a day throughout the fleet, and the greater number are drinking water. And as long, dark nights and severe storms by day must be expected so far North, we have determined it will be best to convoy the ships homewards, for it is impossible to procure provisions for such a fleet in Norway ; and if we were obliged to put into port there, great difficulties would be certain to arise in the fleet ; and the ships that came out last are just as badly off as we are ; in a word, we cannot assist one another, so that we are obliged to make for home ; thus done in latitude 56° 40′, 18 nautical miles from the coast of Norway.

To write to the Directors, that Master Jan Noose of Flushing, (*sic*) on the $\frac{15}{25}$th of October, coming from Hargyn ; and also to Heer Lamsen, &c., &c.

Your Noblenesses' Humble Servant,
(Signed)   MICHIEL ADR. RUIJTER.

Done on board the ship
t'huijs te Cruiningen,
the $\frac{17}{27}$th of October, 1653.
To the North of the Sand.

1270. *Oct.* $\frac{19}{29}$, 1653.—*DE WITH TO S.G.*

[Archives of Hague.]

Noble and Powerful Lords,—My Lords,—My last letter was dispatched to your Lordships by express galliot, Master Jan Corn : Turck, on the $\frac{16}{28}$th instant, and I trust the same will reach your Lordships in due course. In the said letter to your Lordships I enclosed the resolution we had passed, and a statement of the insufficient supplies of provisions on the State's fleet, and also submitted that the ships have not been in port or

THE LAST WINTER

cleaned for a considerable length of time, and that they are very foul and slow-sailing, and some of them very leaky, and it is very necessary to take measures in this matter. We truly have not a single quick-sailing ship or yacht in the fleet, and this arises from their foulness. With regard to the ships lying in Bergen in Norway, for which we have been waiting over six days, I have a foreboding that they will be able to make their way only very slowly from that place this winter; the more especially as the commodore of the return-ships, in a letter to me of the $\frac{28}{8}$th $\frac{\text{September}}{\text{October}}$, wrote that the pilots he had engaged at Bergen made great difficulties of being able to sail from that place to Flekkefiord this winter, if the contrary wind held till the end of this month. Nevertheless, as I wrote in my former letter, I have taken the precaution of sending an express to Flekkefiord to await their coming; and if your Lordships should be pleased to decide to send us as quickly as possible to Flekkefiord, to wait for the said ships there, we shall require provisions and water for the State's fleet without delay, and also orders for our fleet to sail home as quickly as possible, for it is impracticable at this season to victual the ships at sea; and therefore it is in the highest degree advisable that the said ships should sail in without delay, with a view of avoiding accidents by storm and rough weather. I beg that orders may be sent to me from your Lordships as quickly as possible, both off the Texel and the Vlie. I have further respectfully to submit, if the above plan is decided upon, whether it would not be best for a letter to be written forthwith to Resident Elseveijr, directing that all the Baltic ships, escorting ships and others, should repair to the rendezvous in Flekkefiord, and wait for convoy there. And with a view of keeping the crews on board the ships I think it would be necessary for their wives and friends to have an intimation from the several Boards, so as to be able to prepare clothing for them on the coming voyage. I beg further to submit to your Lordships' consideration that the Vlie is two-thirds better than the Texel as a port for the ships this voyage, for the reason that one anchor and one cable will hold better there than three in the Texel, and we can sail out better from there with a poor wind. And now, if we had flute-ships with provisions with us, as I have repeatedly begged and proposed, it would not be necessary for us to put in now, but we could continue our voyage forthwith to Flekkefiord, which is now prevented by scarcity of victuals. It therefore remains my opinion that it is in the highest degree necessary for ships with stores and provisions to sail with us, and the victualling ought to be done in shore ; it being understood, at the same time, that the principal officers and captains should have a suitable monthly allowance, so that they could live honestly, without being obliged to take their pickings out of the rations weighed out to the sailors and soldiers, which I have thought it my duty to write to your Lordships. I also think it right to report to your Lordships that the worthy preacher D. Robertij Junius (requested by their H.M. and your Lordships and besought to come on board the State's fleet for one voyage, to admonish every one on board, officers, soldiers and sailors, and to persuade them by his preaching to repent and to live good Christian lives, and to encourage them to bear themselves valiantly against the foe) has not only so influenced them by his preaching that they are better and more devout men, but has made them haters of sin, and continues to kindle their courage against the enemy, especially in all his sermons and in daily prayers, exhorting them to unity, peace and quiet among themselves, and to obedience to their respective superiors, so that I wish very much indeed he could have stayed for a longer time with our fleet. He has preached a number of times on different ships, both in my squadron and in others, both when we were in, and after we had left, the Dunes, to the number of seventy times in all, as appears from the extract from his Honour's diary. I wish, as he knows so well how to adapt his exhortations to the capacity of seafaring men, that when the fleet is in the shallows, he might have leave of absence and minister to the fleet in general. I think it would be an excellent thing for the fleets, and consequently for our Fatherland, if he could train the style of the preachers who have never been to sea, and shew them how to proceed on board ship. I think that if his Honour were asked by your Lordships he would not refuse to do this service to our country and to God's church. And I beg, moreover, that people may be found for these posts, of some years and experience, to go to sea with us as preachers; for I fear that young men, with little experience, would perhaps be causes of offence instead of edification, which would be both unbecoming and dangerous on board fleets like ours, &c., &c.

(Signed) WITTE CORN: DE WITH.

Done on board the ship *'t huijs te Swieten* a little to the south of the East Sands of the Doggerbank, this $\frac{19}{20}$th October, 1653.

1271. *Oct.* 21/31, 1653.—BOURNE TO A.C.

[S.P. 18, xli. 61.]

Right Honble.,—I received yours dated the 19th instant, and shall attend what is therein signified. But the postmaster at Ipswich hath several times before this abused you in keeping letters twice the time allotted, and this came to my hand but this afternoon, which I thought myself obliged to give an account of for sometimes your affairs may suffer much prejudice by him.

This coming very late, I received another signed by General Monck, with an order for Capt. Thomson, &c.

In my last from Yarmouth about 4 days since, I received advice that there were three or four small men of war, with many busses seen about 8 or 10 leagues N.E. from Yarmouth, upon receiving whereof I thought good to order Captain Thomson and the Cat to look abroad, and discover what they could of them, having respect to their own safety.

In my last I gave your Honour an intimation of some impatient expressions in the seamen tending to something worse, for the want of their money, and this morning something more appeared, for as I was going out of my quarters early I met with a great number in the streets, whom I passed by saying little, but observing what they would do or say, and presently they began to call for money and clothes. I demanding of them to what ships they belonged, they answered the Assurance and Mermaid.

I gave them fair persuasive language with promises of making speedy provision for them in case they would orderly go aboard and follow their business, which they seemed to accept and went away.

But suddenly after I understood that many more belonging to other ships were come ashore, with whom these mingled, and went up into the fields. This I judge my duty to acquaint your Honours withal, that you may please to give what other orders you see cause, and resolve what to do as to the payment of them, or otherwise, for I find this generally rooted in them, being, I doubt, too much encouraged by some others (although I cannot yet learn out the principal) yet doubtless the officers of those two where the first breaking out of it was, cannot well quit themselves from blame. I can do no more than I have endeavoured.

That troop which was ordered hither by the Lord General's command is drawn off again, and whether they returned or no is unknown to me, but it's but need, for I am informed yesterday many of them were rambling abroad in the country, and have put down all the gates and stiles near hand, and they were very unruly, as I am advised by those who come and make their complaint to one that cannot remedy them. As for the garrison, your Honours know it is upon the matter slighted by command, and we have only about 30 soldiers that can be spared from the Fort at Landguard.

I humbly offer the consideration of the matter to your Honours whether you shall see good, the men shall be speedily paid off quite, or not paid till they be in the Rolling [1] Grounds, or whether you will pay one moiety now, and the rest when they are out.

I know the latter will much distemper them, yet I cannot but think many of them will be gone when they should sail. I am not worthy to advise, neither am I satisfied which is best, but I am bold to say that if your Honours had seen cause to pay

[1] Rawling.

them off at their first coming in there would have been much money saved, and the frigates manned seasonably and with more satisfaction; excuse me herein.

As for the Advice, Constant Warwick, and Centurion (the two former especially will take up this 20 days or more to perform those works which are absolutely necessary to be done upon them, and so consequently it will be near a month before they can be ready to sail), what your Honours will please to resolve concerning these when you pay the five that are near ready, whether to pay them off quite, or leave 4 or 6 months' pay in hand till they be in the Rolling Grounds, or what else. I humbly submit to your determination, but to pay them quite off will be much more acceptable. Excuse me that I am so full of words about this particular.

I shall gladly follow your orders wherein I am able to make them practicable. Your Honours know the state of the business that I need add no more, but crave leave to be esteemed

Y^r. Honours' faithful servant,

N. BOURNE.

Ipswich,
21 Oct. 1653.

I was bold to crave your Honours' pleasure in two or three particulars in my last, but the weighty affairs admit not the consideration thereof.

1272. $\frac{Oct. 26}{Nov. 5}$, 1653.—*DE WITH TO S.G.*

[Archives of Hague.]

Noble and Powerful Lords,—My Lords,—My last letter to your Lordships was dated the $\frac{25}{4}$th $\frac{Oct.}{Nov.}$,[1] from off the Vlie. On the morning of the $\frac{26}{5}$th $\frac{Oct.}{Nov.}$,

[1] Not included in this collection.

the wind being W.N.W., the three return-ships sailed into the Vlie, so that the great and rich treasure we were sent out to fetch is now (God be praised) brought safely into port, excepting the Bergen ships, of whom no report can be made. As soon as the ships had sailed in, we made every effort to get off Texel. There is no doubt, my Lords, that great hunger is being endured on several of the ships in our fleet, and we are in sight of land without having any orders to put in, which creates great discontent among the sailors and soldiers of which I beg you kindly to be assured. I have just received a letter and resolution from their H.M., dated the $\frac{22\text{nd}}{1\text{st}}$ $\frac{\text{Oct.}}{\text{Nov.}}$, but cannot gather therefrom that the State's fleet is to put into port. I shall continue patiently to await orders to remove the discontent of the sailors and soldiers, which seems to be more than usually rife after this voyage ; and I beg faithfully to report the above to your Lordships, and do not hesitate to say that the sailors themselves are adopting measures such as we have many a time, to our regret, seen at home. I yesterday informed your Lordships, amongst other matters, that my wife is lying sick to death, that I have moreover a family of ten children living, and for eighteen months I have not slept soundly at home for more than four nights, and during the last seven months I have been on board eight different ships, going straight from one to another, to promote the service of the country ; and I therefore once more humbly make my request, on account of the sad news of my wife's illness, that permission may be sent me without delay to go home at once, &c., &c.

(Signed) WITTE CORN : DE WITT.

Done on board the ship *'t huijs le Swieten* this $\frac{29}{18}$th $\frac{\text{Oct.}}{\text{Nov.}}$, 1653.

1272A. $\frac{Oct. 26}{Nov. 6}$, 1653.—*MAYOR OF COLCHESTER TO LIEU^T OF TOWER (COLONEL JOHN BARKSTEAD)*

[S.P. 18, xli. 861.]

Right Honble.,—Yours of the 22nd I received, being very much obliged for the same. I shall observe the order, God willing. I am ashamed that I trouble your Honours so much, and that I have another request. The case is this: many seamen that travel from port towns beyond us up to London wanting means come to me, and many prisoners out of Holland of our men are of late set on shore in our coasts, who have not anything to help themselves, sometimes 20 or 30 in a day, and truly it pities me that our men should fare worse than Dutch prisoners, which I am confident they do many times, many of them being newly recovered of sickness fall sick again upon land. My request is that I may have an order from Y^r. Honours (and some others, if you think meet) that I may let such poor creatures have needful relief. I have relieved many, giving them sometimes 6d. and sometimes 12d. a man. I am out near £5 in 14 days' time, and truly I can't do otherwise seeing their necessity. I have hinted it to Commissary —— in a letter wherein I returned him thanks for dispatching the order. If your health permit, I desire you to speak with Justice Highland who will acquaint your Honour how the business for our poor town goes, in which I shall not mind you, knowing you are always extreme ready to engage yourself and friends for us. I would gladly have a word from your Honour to the bearer whether my other letter came to your hands last week, in which was a list of such men as are thought by us just and fit to proportion the taxes of our town.

I have sent a list this week to Justice Highland, but I am too tedious, for which I crave pardon. Desiring your Honour's health,

I remain,
>Your Honour's at command,
>>THO. PEEKE.

Colchester,
26 Oct. 1653.

Endorsed: Mr. Tho. Peeke from Colchester to Colonel Barkstead, Lieutenant of the Tower.

1273. $\frac{Oct.\ 28}{Nov.\ 7}$, 1653.—*ADDITIONAL ARTICLE OF WAR*

[B.M. Add. MS. 9300, fol. 285.]

An additional Article to the Laws of War and Ordinances of the Sea.

That all mariners and others employed, or which have been employed in the service of this Commonwealth in their fleets, or otherwise at sea, shall after the time of their respective discharges, demean themselves with all duty and respect to the public peace: And if any person who hath been, is, or shall be so employed, hath committed or abetted or shall commit or abet any mutinous or seditious act, whereby the peace of this Commonwealth may be, or hath been endangered; every such person shall be proceeded against, and suffer pains of death, or otherwise, in the same sort and manner, as by the laws of war and ordinances of the sea already established, he might have been proceeded against for any act of that nature, in case of being in actual service.

Provided, That every person comprised within

this Article, be proceeded against within three months after the offence committed, and not otherwise.

Friday the twenty-eighth of October, 1653. Ordered by the Parliament, that this additional Article to the Laws of War and Ordinances of the Sea, be forthwith printed and published.

HEN: SCOBELL,
Clerk of the Parliament.

London, Printed by John Field, Printer to the Parliament of England. 1653.

1274. $\frac{Oct.\ 28}{Nov.\ 7}$, 1653.—*A LETTER OF INTELLIGENCE FROM THE HAGUE*

[Thurloe S.P. i. 557.]

Upon Saturday the 1st of November news came to the Hague by a galliot sent to Scheveling that de Witt with the East India ships, which were in the Sound, and near 400 other merchants ships, were left the day before within 15 leagues of the Texel. Those of Norway, three East India ships and above 100 merchantmen were not then with them, but are since arrived. The next day after church and Monday were spent in consultation what to do with the fleet, and upon Monday night the general sense of the States was that the Lord Admiral Opdam, Witte Wittesen, John Evertson de Ruijter, and the whole fleet (as well those come from the Sound, as the others, which were ready here, in all 112 men of war) should immediately set sail for Margate Road, with design to take prizes (of which it was supposed this season, with such a surprise, would afford many rich ones), to block up the river, and to sink vessels at the two entrances into the Thames, that of the channel, and the other over the flats. Some objected that such an attempt would disturb the treaty, but more believed that it was the best way to advance it, and that those in England who really wished peace would be glad of it; and that such a strength from hence (to which it was propounded to send in a short time thirty-five ships more, as fast as they could be made ready) would countenance all their agreements for peace. Thus it was left upon Monday night, but the next day M. Opdam informed the States that the fleet was not victualled for such a design, most of the ships not having 20 days' victuals left, some not 8 days; and that they could not rely upon seasonable weather at this time of the year to give them liberty to victual at sea, as was proposed by some, the several admirals here being at present well stored with biscuit and flesh. Whereupon (with the foulness of many of the ships) he informed that there was a necessity the fleet should go into harbour to victual and clean.

These arguments (which were seconded by some of the sea-officers) prevailed with the States to lay the question aside, until the fleet should be visited: to which purpose M. Opdam was sent to the Texel on Wednesday, news being brought upon Tuesday night that all the men of war were, without orders, gone into the Texel: and upon his report on return the question is to be resumed. Amsterdam was most for the going to the Thames, but if that be not thought fit, they moved that a positive order be sent that no merchant ships should go to sea until March, and that the like advice be sent unto all foreign parts to continue there until that time: 'tis believed the one or the other will be speedily ordered, but I think it cockpit-lay[1] it

---

[1] This obscure phrase appears to mean something like a 'a hundred to one chance': 'lay' being a wager or bet. It was unknown to the *Oxford English Dictionary*.

will be the last : and do believe that the other was never intended really, but only pretended to countenance the present addresses to England.
7 Nov., N.S.

1275. $\frac{Oct. 31}{Nov. 11}$, 1653.—*ORDERS OF A.C.*

[S.P. 18, xli. 86.]

31 Oct. 1653.
By the Commissioners from the Admiralty and Navy.

Whereas the said Commissioners are informed that some seamen belonging to this Commonwealth that have been taken prisoners by the Dutch are of late set on shore at and near Colchester, and that Mr. Thomas Pecke, mayor there, hath disbursed some monies for their relief and enabling them to travel to London. It is ordered that the said moneys so disbursed, and what further the said Mr. Pecke shall see cause to lay out upon the like occasion, not exceeding in the whole £20, be reimbursed unto him by Bill from the Commissioners of the Navy, upon an exact account thereof presented unto them by the said Mr. Pecke. And this shall warrant their so doing.

GEORGE MONCK.
WILLM. BURTON.
THO. KELSEY.

Bill passed dated
9 Oct. 1654,
upon this order for £14 10s. 0d.

1276. $\frac{Aug. 31}{Sept. 10}$ to *Nov.* $\frac{1}{11}$, 1653.—*JOURNAL OF DE RUIJTER THE YOUNGER*

[Archives of Hague.]

$\frac{31st\ August}{10th\ September}$, *Wednesday.*—Item on the $\frac{31st\ August}{10th\ September}$ I came on board the ship 't huijs de Kruijnijngen of Amsterdam in the service of their H.M.

God Almighty grant us his blessing, and permit us to do good service for our Fatherland. Amen. Continued lying with a S.S.W. wind till the $\frac{1st}{11th}$ September.

$\frac{1st}{11th}$ *September, Thursday.*—Item early in the morning of the $\frac{1st}{11th}$ we got under sail with a S.S.W. wind, blowing a steady breeze, and sailed out of the Spaniard's Shallow with forty-two ships of war and a party of merchantmen. At noon we saw the whole fleet coming out of the Vlie, and we joined them in the evening. I should think there must be a good 300 ships bound for all parts. In the evening we had the spires of Brandaris[1] 3 miles E.S.E. of us. Wind, S.S.W., course N., made tolerable progress during the night until the morning of the $\frac{2nd}{12th}$ September.

$\frac{2nd}{12th}$ *September, Friday.*—Item early in the morning of the $\frac{2nd}{12th}$ we had showery and rainy weather; wind S. by E., course N.N.E., a tolerable breeze. At noon I calculated the Vlie was N. and N. by E. of us, 17 to 18 miles. Continued sailing N.N.E., made tolerable progress. In the afternoon about fifty ships parted from us and sailed off alone, both Brazil and West India traders, and ships bound for France and Spain. We got a wind due S.W., and in the evening calculated we were 23 to 24 miles N. by E. of the Vlie; continued sailing N.N.E. through the night, a light breeze, till the $\frac{3rd}{13th}$.

$\frac{3rd}{13th}$ *September, Saturday.*—Item in the morning of the $\frac{3rd}{13th}$ we were over against where the sand rises, on the east edge, in 24 fathoms; we saw the westward bound ships still to the west of us; fair weather, wind southerly. At noon we were on the north edge of the Sand; continued our course N. by E. until evening, a gentle breeze,

---
[1] S.E. of Terschelling.

about 5 miles N. by E. Wind S.W. with a tolerable breeze all through the night till the $\frac{14}{14}$th instant.

$\frac{14}{14}$th September, Sunday.—Item on the $\frac{14}{14}$th fine weather in the morning, a gentle breeze from the S.W.; during the night had sailed 10 miles[1] N. by E. Were close on the Jutish reef in 28 fathoms, and continued sailing till noon, when we cast a line in 24 fathoms on the reef, a coarse bottom. We calculated the Naze in Norway to be 11 miles[1] N. of us. Continued our course N.E. by E. all through the night till early in the morning of the $\frac{15}{15}$th instant.

$\frac{15}{15}$th September, Monday.—Item early in the morning of the $\frac{15}{15}$th the wind shot round through the South, to S.E. by E., we sailed due N.E. by E., until about noon, when we turned again S.S.W., with a stiff breeze and with our main-topsail. I calculated that from the evening of the $\frac{14}{14}$th till noon on the $\frac{15}{15}$th we had sailed 12 miles N.E. by E. I conjectured Vlecker to be N.N.W. of us across the sea. About 4 or 5 o'clock we saw the Holms 6 miles S.E. of us (?) in 22 fathoms, with a stiff breeze, wind E.S.E.; towards sunset we turned again, had our main-topsail still up; the weather became better during the night and we set our fore-topsail until the $\frac{16}{16}$th instant.

$\frac{16}{16}$th September, Tuesday.—Item about 7 o'clock on the $\frac{16}{16}$th instant we turned again S.S.E., the wind in the E., blowing a gentle breeze, with misty airs and drizzling rain. About 3 o'clock the wind shifted to the S.S.E., then we turned again Eastwards, with a light breeze. At sundown we found 26 fathoms on the north edge of the reef, about 7 miles off land. About ten o'clock at night, the wind shifted to the S.W. with thick rain, and we

[1] German miles.

sailed E.S.E. under shortened sail; at 2 o'clock at night we made sail again, the wind southerly, and remained so till the $\tfrac{17}{17}$th instant.

$\tfrac{17}{17}$th September, Wednesday.—Item early in the morning of the $\tfrac{17}{17}$th we saw four ships coming towards us, on the weather-side of us; five of our yachts made up to them. We were abeam of Skagen, wind S.E. by S. We lay over to the S.W. with a stiff breeze to get under the land, which we reached about midday in 18 fathoms of water, about half a mile from shore. A fishing boat came alongside, they said that on the $\tfrac{14}{14}$th instant six English ships had been in that part; we then anchored in 19 fathoms, wind S. by E. Directly afterwards there came two ships from Sweden, bound for Dunkirk with pitch, tar, hemp and staves, so they said, and we let them pass, and lay there through the night with showery weather, until the $\tfrac{18}{18}$th instant.

$\tfrac{18}{18}$th September, Thursday.—Item early on the $\tfrac{18}{18}$th the wind was S.S.W. and S.W. by S., we got under sail to run to our rendezvous S.E. of the Hook of Skagen (the Skaw); the weather misty, with rain; tacked about the whole day, but with little profit. The tide fell very strong to the north, and we came to an anchor at nightfall in 30 fathoms of water. We had the Northern Lights through the night, with a great deal of rain at times, wind southerly till the $\tfrac{19}{19}$th instant.

$\tfrac{19}{19}$th September, Friday.—Item early in the morning of the $\tfrac{19}{19}$th we got under sail to tack towards the Chief.[1] Wind S.S.E., with a great deal of rain, and we tacked for about six glasses; then the wind shifted to the S. by W. in heavy rain; and the tide fell very strong towards the north, so that we were obliged to anchor again

[1] t'Opper. Probably not a place-name.

about 10 o'clock, and lay to until after midday. Then the wind blew from S.W. by W. and W.S.W. Then we got under sail and sailed south, off and on, but could do little good, because the tide set so strongly towards the north. In the evening after sundown we anchored. We had advanced about 1½ miles to the south, and lay to during the night with a stiff breeze, till the

$\tfrac{10}{20}$*th September, Saturday.*—Item in the morning of the $\tfrac{10}{20}$th the wind began to rise more and more; towards noon we struck our yards and lowered our topmasts, and let the anchor down, and then swung round until the anchors caught. It blew a stiff gale from the S.S.E. About 9 o'clock in the evening the weather began to abate somewhat, and we continued lying there; during the night the wind shifted to S.W. by S. until the morning of the $\tfrac{11th}{21st}$ instant.

$\tfrac{11th}{21st}$ *September, Sunday.*—Item early in the morning of the $\tfrac{11th}{21st}$, we began to raise our topmasts and to cross yards; then we hove our anchors and got under sail to tack towards the Chief. In the afternoon it began to be boisterous again; at three o'clock it began to rain hard, and to blow from the S.S.E. Captain Claes Aldersen had the top of his mainmast carried away down as far as the shrouds; we also had a sharp tussle. We all anchored together in 8 fathoms, in quiet and rainy weather, and lay there during the night with tolerable weather; wind S.E.

$\tfrac{12th}{22nd}$ *September, Monday.*—Item early in the morning of the $\tfrac{12th}{22nd}$ we got under sail, and sailed to the South of Vice-Admiral de Wijtte, and anchored close up by him. He hoisted the white flag for all the captains to go on board, and ordered every one to make their ships clean and clear in every way as they should be. In the forenoon to-day we had the wind E.N.E., we then cleaned one side, which was very necessary. In the afternoon we cleaned the other side. We had very fine weather. About 2 o'clock the wind shifted to the N. with a light breeze, and we distributed the water amongst the ships as far as we could from our water ships. The weather continued good, during the night we got a westerly wind till the $\frac{13\text{th}}{23\text{rd}}$ instant.

$\frac{13\text{th}}{23\text{rd}}$ *September, Tuesday.*—Item early in the morning of the $\frac{13\text{th}}{23\text{rd}}$ we had a S.W. wind, fair weather. We got to work upon one side of our ship. In the afternoon a stiff breeze began to blow up, but towards evening we had a gale from the S.S.E., with heavy rain; lay there during the night till the

$\frac{14\text{th}}{24}$ *September, Wednesday.*—Item in the morning of the $\frac{14}{24}$th there was an improvement in the weather, but the sea was rather lumpy, so that we could not clean as before. In the evening two of our advice-yachts came out of the Sound, with our preacher and a Fiscal on board, and brought news that the East Indiamen with fourteen King's ships . . . (*sic*). Continued lying there with fair weather.

$\frac{15}{25}$th *September, Thursday.*—Item in the morning of the $\frac{15}{25}$th we worked on our other side and made it clean, and sent our lieutenant ashore for some refreshments for the crew. To-day Captain Wagenare brought in a Swedish ship [1] that had sailed from England, bound with cloths from London to Dantzig, and they said that a great number of English ships were at sea.

$\frac{16}{26}$th *September, Friday.*—Item before daybreak on the morning of the $\frac{16}{26}$th I sent our boat ashore to fetch off the lieutenant and the refreshments;

[1] *Kraaier.*

but it began to blow rather hard till towards evening, when the weather began to improve a little. Then our boat came on board, but brought only six barrels of meat with them. At sunset the wind shifted to the W.N.W., and we had fine, good weather, and continued lying there till the morning of the $\frac{17}{27}$th instant.

$\frac{17}{27}$th *September, Saturday.*—Item in the morning of the $\frac{17}{27}$th Vice-Admiral Wijtte Cor : de Wijtte hoisted his small flag to summon the principal officers on board, with regard to a Dantzig ship, sailing from London to Dantzig. It was decided by the Council of War to allow her to pursue her voyage free and unharmed. This morning we got under sail to anchor the ships in order. Then in the evening the wind blew from the E. with fair weather all through the night until the

$\frac{18}{28}$th *September, Sunday.*—Item in the morning of the $\frac{18}{28}$th fine weather ; wind S.S.E. This morning our preacher held a service. We had a good 400 men on board ; about half-past nine he went to hold a service on Vice-Admiral de Wijtte's ship, and at 11 o'clock on board Rear-Admiral Pijeter Floorsen's.[1] We continued on the look-out for the coming of the fleet from the Sound. Remained lying to during the night, with fair weather, wind S.S.E., till the $\frac{19}{29}$th instant.

$\frac{19}{29}$th *September, Monday.*—Item before daybreak on the morning of the $\frac{19}{29}$th we careened, and made both sides clean. This morning our advice-yacht came out of the Sound and reported that the East Indiamen and the merchantmen and the King of Denmark's ships were following in all haste ; to-day, towards evening, we saw several sail coming from the S.E. Then we weighed anchor and sailed to meet them, and stood off to the northwards

[1] Florissen. *Cf.* entry for $\frac{\text{Sept. 21}}{\text{Oct. 1}}$.

under our foresails only till the evening, when we anchored again with a stiff breeze, south wind, and lay thus the whole night till the

$\frac{20}{30}th$ *September, Tuesday.*—Item early in the morning of the $\frac{20}{30}$th, the wind W.S.W., a stiff breeze. We saw several ships round about. At eight o'clock we got under sail; then we caught sight of the Royal Admiral with other King's ships, with five East Indiamen and some more merchant-ships; we came up with them about 10 or 11 o'clock, and spoke the Admiral, but we could not understand one another very well on account of the strong wind. We sailed together to the S.E. side of Skagen, and so anchored together in good order, but were prevented from going on board by the strong wind from the S.W., and so we anchored close under Skagen, the wind W.N.W., a strong breeze continuing all through the night till the

$\frac{21}{1}st$ $\frac{Sept.}{Oct.}$, *Wednesday.*—Item in the morning of the $\frac{21}{1}$st, the wind W.N.W., and Vice-Admiral de Wijtte signalled for us to come aboard. I and Rear-Admiral Pijeter Florissen went together with him on board the Danish Admiral's ship, to greet him. The Admiral's name was Heer Wyllekens, who had served the prince a good eleven years; he was a very pleasant man. We remained with him till about 3 o'clock, when we separated, each returning to his own ship. Then we had a stiff breeze, wind W.N.W., lay to till the $\frac{22}{2}$nd $\frac{Sept.}{Oct.}$

$\frac{22}{2}nd$ $\frac{Sept.}{Oct.}$, *Thursday.*—Item early in the morning of the $\frac{22}{2}$nd, the wind S.S.W., a stiff breeze. I went on board Vice-Admiral de Wijtte's ship, and he ordered me to go on board the Danish Admiral and greet him in his behalf, and say that we were signalling our ships to get under sail, so as to sail towards Flekkefiord and collect all our ships that were to rendezvous there, but that the

Danish ships should continue lying there till further orders. With the sun in the S.S.E. we sailed round the Skagen reef, with a S.S.E. wind blowing a stiff breeze, clear weather until the evening. At sundown Robbeknuyt [1] was 2½ miles S.E. of us. We then furled our foresails close and drifted before the wind, which was S.E., with a stiff breeze, until 10 o'clock, at the end of the first watch. Then the wind shifted W.S.W., a stiff breeze, we then set the foresail; the breeze continued till the $\frac{23}{3}$rd $\frac{Sept.}{Oct.}$.

$\frac{23}{3}$rd $\frac{Sept.}{Oct.}$, *Friday.*—Item in the morning of the $\frac{23}{3}$rd our ships were much scattered; the two East Indiamen were a good mile and a half to the rear. We had the wind S.W. by W. and W.S.W., a stiff breeze; course N.W. At noon we sighted land about Maerdon, but could not get any information about it. Then the wind shifted to the S.W., stiff weather. Captain Mangelare's mainyard was shattered by the wind. At noon it began to blow very strong, so that we were all obliged to lower our topsails. About 4 o'clock in the afternoon we came close under the land between Maerdon and Flekkefiord; one of the East Indiamen, the ship Malacke (*sic*), was very leaky and laboured heavily, but there was no chance of helping her. This evening a number of merchantmen ran in, but we stood off to sea again, because it was too late, and sailed off S.E., with a stiff breeze until 2 o'clock at night, when we stood in again to land, or Westwards, until early in the morning of the $\frac{24}{4}$th $\frac{Sept.}{Oct.}$

$\frac{24}{4}$th $\frac{Sept.}{Oct.}$, *Saturday.*—Item early in the morning of the $\frac{24}{4}$th we hoisted our main topsail, but took it in again about 8 o'clock, on account of the stiff breeze, a south wind. At noon we stood off

---

[1] On the coast of Jutland between Hantsholm and the Skaw.

THE LAST WINTER 145

from land between Maerdon and Flekkefiord ; a south wind, stiff breeze. We saw a large ship on our lee, and conjectured it must be the East Indiaman Malacke ; the strong breeze continued, wind south, and we lay by during the night with boisterous weather, wind S.W., until the

$\frac{25}{5}th$ $\frac{Sept.}{Oct.}$, *Sunday*.—Item in the forenoon of the $\frac{25}{5}$th we came to land about three miles above Maerdon, fearing the boisterous weather; bore down towards Maerdon, and put in there at four o'clock in the afternoon with all the ships. Continued lying there through the night, till the $\frac{26}{6}$th $\frac{Sept.}{Oct.}$

$\frac{26}{6}th$ $\frac{Sept.}{Oct.}$, *Monday*.—Item early in the morning of the $\frac{26}{6}$th I went on board Vice-Admiral de Wijtte's ship, and he also summoned the Commodore of the East Indiamen on board, to decide what we should do with the ship Malacke, which was very leaky ; and it was resolved that all the cargo should be taken out of the ship. A fluteship came in to-day, which had sailed on the $\frac{22}{2}$nd $\frac{Sept.}{Oct.}$ from Texel, with seventeen ships of war ; this evening the wind began to blow very strong from the south, and continued so all night with much rain till the

$\frac{27}{7}th$ $\frac{Sept.}{Oct.}$, *Tuesday*.—Item in the morning of the $\frac{27}{7}$th, boisterous weather, wind S.S.E. Later in the day, very boisterous weather, wind due S.E. In the evening we fetched another anchor from the East Indiaman Malacke, on account of the strong wind. Nothing particular after that till the $\frac{28}{8}$th $\frac{Sept.}{Oct.}$

$\frac{28}{8}th$ $\frac{Sept.}{Oct.}$, *Wednesday*.—Item on the $\frac{28}{8}$th we ballasted our ship with about 56 last of stone, and fetched water to fill our casks. It was tolerable weather. Nothing in particular further. In the evening a galliot came in from Bergen in Norway, saying that twenty-seven ships were lying there, two warships, three East Indiamen, and the remainder Straits-traders, which would come to or near the rendezvous in Flekkefiord as soon as possible ; nothing further in particular until the

$\frac{29}{9}th\ ^{Sept.}_{Oct.}$, *Thursday.*—Item on the $\frac{29}{9}$th, good fine weather, an easterly wind and clear weather. We were busy unlading the ship Malacke ; nothing besides in particular. Wind northerly through the night till the

$\frac{30}{10}th\ ^{Sept.}_{Oct.}$, *Friday.*—Item on the $\frac{30}{10}$th, fair weather. To-day a party of loaded 'flensen' from Langesunt[1] and other places, with their cargoes, passed on their way to the rendezvous in Flekkefiord. Nothing further in particular, and we lay thus till the $\frac{1st}{11th}$ October.

$\frac{1st}{11th}$ *October, Saturday.*—Item early in the morning of the $\frac{1st}{11th}$ we hauled out from the shore, wind E.S.E. and drifted between the islands up to Vice-Admiral de Wijtte and moored there. Very showery weather all day. In the evening Vice-Admiral de Wijtte hoisted the white flag to summon all the captains on board each one to give in a return of his victuals ; and it was found that, taking one with another, there were not above five weeks altogether. Then the wind N.E. all night until the $\frac{2nd}{12th}$ October.

$\frac{2nd}{12th}$ *October, Sunday.*—Item in the morning of the $\frac{2nd}{12th}$ our preachers held services on several of the ships. In the afternoon five ships, laden with cargoes in Norway, came in. The wind continued N.E. ; fine weather all day till the $\frac{3rd}{13th}$ instant.

$\frac{3rd}{13th}$ *October, Monday.*—Item in the morning of the $\frac{3rd}{13th}$ very boisterous weather, wind E.N.E. We determined to leave this place to-morrow. The

[1] *I.e.* Langesund.

weather continued very bad, with rain and wind, till the evening, when it blew a strong gale from the east. At night the wind E.S.E. and towards morning diminishing, and shifting S.S.E.; then the weather improved.

$\tfrac{14}{14}th$ *October, Tuesday.*—Item in the morning of the $\tfrac{14}{14}$th, the wind S.S.E.; tolerable weather with fog and mist; no chance of putting out; lay here all day, with rainy weather. Nothing further in particular to-day until the

$\tfrac{15}{15}th$ *October, Wednesday.*—Item in the morning of the $\tfrac{15}{15}$th, fair weather with fog and mist; wind S.S.E. Services were held on several of the ships in our fleet; then good weather with mist. In the evening the wind steadily S.E. by E. with calms all the night, fair weather, until the $\tfrac{16}{16}$th instant.

$\tfrac{16}{16}th$ *October, Thursday.*—Item in the morning of the $\tfrac{16}{16}$th, foggy weather; wind S.S.E. with light breezes all day. Nothing further in particular. until the

$\tfrac{17}{17}th$ *October, Friday.*—Item in the morning of the $\tfrac{17}{17}$th it was appointed by Vice-Admiral de Wijtte and the principal officers that a survey should be taken of victuals, because there was a scarcity in the fleet; and orders were issued that meals should be served twice a day, and it was so appointed. Then fair weather, wind W.S.W. Nothing further in particular till the

$\tfrac{18}{18}th$ *October, Saturday.*—Item in the morning of the $\tfrac{18}{18}$th, fine weather, wind W.S.W., bright sunshine. To-day the Governor of Vlecken, whose name is Mägenys Arent Vet, visited our ships. In the afternoon it was very foggy; wind northerly till the

$\tfrac{19}{19}th$ *October, Sunday.*—Item early in the morning of the $\tfrac{19}{19}$th, the wind N.E., the breeze began to increase. To-day six services were held in our fleet. Then wind E.N.E., a good breeze all day, and during the night until the $\frac{10}{20}$th October a stiff breeze.

$\frac{10}{20}$*th October, Monday.*—Item in the morning of the $\frac{10}{20}$th, wind very variable, sometimes E.N.E., sometimes E., and sometimes E.S.E., so we sent a galliot to sea, to see what the wind was outside; they found it was E., blowing a stiff breeze; but the pilots did not think it advisable to sail out, and it was then decided to continue lying there till early in the morning of the $\frac{11\text{th}}{21\text{st}}$ instant.

$\frac{11\text{th}}{21\text{st}}$ *October, Tuesday.*—Item early in the morning of the $\frac{11\text{th}}{21\text{st}}$, as soon as it was day, we got under sail and sailed out of Maerdon, by the S.E. channel; wind E. by N., blowing a topsail breeze, with clear weather. On getting outside we saw ten or twelve ships coming from the E., who came up with us. It was well past noon before the East Indiamen got out of the shallows. We then lay by under our mainsails, so as not to be carried into Flekkefiord, because the current sets very strong to the W.; then in the evening the wind dropped after the first watch, wind E.S.E. Then it shifted to the N.E., a topsail breeze. We then stood in to the coast, N.W. by W., under our mainsails, till the $\frac{12\text{th}}{22\text{nd}}$ instant.

$\frac{12\text{th}}{22\text{nd}}$ *October, Wednesday.*—Item early in the morning of the $\frac{12\text{th}}{22\text{nd}}$ we were off Flekkefiord, and saw a number of ships coming out, but there was little wind, and we got much scattered one from another by the strong tide, which flowed very irregularly. We made every effort to get up with Vice-Admiral de Wijtte, but could not. We were a good 160 ships out of Maerdon and elsewhere, besides those from Flekkefiord, which came out at midday with their fleet. I should think a good 200

ships from Flekkefiord. At sundown we had the
Naze six miles N.W. of us. We then had calms
and clear weather, and drifted westwards, though
we had had our sails up; all through the night,
calms, and we got much scattered by the current,
until the morning of the $\frac{13th}{23rd}$ instant.

$\frac{13th}{23rd}$ *October, Thursday.*—Item early in the morning of the $\frac{13th}{23rd}$ the breeze was E.S.E. We had
drifted so far to the W. that we had the Naze
S. of us, four miles distant. The warships
from Westerryse were some of them with us, viz.
Commodore Wyllem van der Saen, with Jan
Amijrael and some others, but we missed a good
200 of the ships, and could not imagine how the
ships had been lost sight of, because there had been
no wind all through the night, so that we could
not see Vice-Admiral de Wijtte with the East
Indiamen. This morning we questioned Captain
Jan Amijrael, as we sailed up to him; he said
there were no ships lying in Westerryse, but that
all the ships had put to sea. We saw two more
ships of war to our lee, who fired shot after shot.
We sailed up to them, in hopes they were bringing
tidings of the ships from Bergen. They were
Captain Jacop Swart and Captain Kleijdijck of
Rotterdam; they said they saw twenty-four to
twenty-six ships in the N.W. I then immediately
hoisted the white flag, and the captains came on
board, and we decided to make towards them, and
when we had got down to them with the wind,
Captain Swart fired continually to signify to the
ships most to windward to come on, but no one
came on, so we were obliged to lie to, so as to remain
at our rendezvous. Off the Naze this afternoon
Captain Boogert joined us out of Flekkefiord. We
got a wind from the S., then lay over to the E.S.E.
In the evening we had the Naze four miles N.N.W.

of us; we then tacked to the W.S.W., with a south wind. We were 109 sail there, among which were seventeen warships. We sailed W. by S., making about six miles to the W.; we then turned again, till early in the morning of the $\frac{14}{24}$th instant.

$\frac{14}{24}$th October, Friday.—Item early in the morning of the $\frac{14}{24}$th there was a ship of war to the N.W. of us, which fired shot after shot, whereby we guessed they had discovered the fleet or that they were in sight; we then lay over to the west again. Shortly afterwards we saw the fleet, with Vice-Admiral de Wijtte, they were bearing down towards a body of ships on our lee. In the night we had had a great deal of rain and thick weather. When we came up with the ships to leeward, it proved to be Commodore Wijllem van der Saen with sixteen ships of war. In the evening we saw another body of ships to the N.E. of us again; we sent a galliot off to them at once, and in the evening lay over to the W. all through the night until the

$\frac{15}{25}$th October, Saturday.—Item early in the morning of the $\frac{15}{25}$th we saw nineteen ships to the N.E. of us, among which were sixteen ships of war under the command of Captain Heckert Meusen,[1] Admiral Tromp's ship,[2] and three merchantmen, which had sailed out of Texel on the $\frac{2nd}{12th}$ October. Vice-Admiral de Wijtte immediately summoned the captains on board to a council, and also the commanders of the East Indiamen, and we all decided the best thing we could do would be to sail for home, on account of the scarcity of provisions, because we could not remain at sea more than 26 or 28 days longer at the furthest; and we had also 400 merchantmen and five East Indiamen and

---

[1] *I.e.* Egbert Meesen.   [2] The Brederode.

THE LAST WINTER 151

seventy-six ships of war with us. Towards evening we got a wind from the S.S.E., and sailed towards the S.W. with a good topsail breeze ; at sundown we took in our topsail with the greater part of the fleet. Then the wind S.S.E., course S.W., and towards midnight the wind blew from the S.S.W., and we sailed W. till the morning of the $\frac{16}{26}$th instant.

$\frac{16}{26}$*th October, Sunday.*—Item early in the morning of the $\frac{16}{26}$th the wind dropped, and we drifted through the day on account of the calm ; towards evening a little breeze came from the N.E. We sounded bottom at 46 fathoms. I then calculated we were on the west edge of the reef. A gentle breeze all through the night till the

$\frac{17}{27}$*th October, Monday.*—Item early in the morning of the $\frac{17}{27}$th the wind blew from the south, a slight breeze ; towards evening we sounded 42 fathoms between the reef and the sand. The calm continued through the night until the

$\frac{18}{28}$*th October, Tuesday.*—Item before daybreak on the $\frac{18}{28}$th the wind came from the N.N.E., a gentle breeze, made little progress. Towards noon the breeze began to increase and we sailed S.S.E. In the evening we were on the north edge of the sand. Then the wind N.N.W., a good breeze. In the first watch the wind fell, shifted to the east and remained in that quarter till before daybreak, when it was due E.S.E., a good breeze, till the $\frac{19}{29}$th instant.

$\frac{19}{29}$*th October, Wednesday.*—Item early in the morning of the $\frac{19}{29}$th, we sounded 22 fathoms on the sand, Texel 30 miles S. of us. Then the wind E. by S. and E.S.E., a topsail breeze ; course S. by E. At noon we sounded 18 fathoms ; about 2 hours afterwards 26 fathoms on the south edge of the sand, Texel S. and S. by E. of us. At sundown I calculated we must be still 24 miles S. by E. (*sic*) of Texel. The wind continued E.S.E., a topsail breeze, with sky overcast ; course South ; in the first watch we took in our main-topsail ; the wind S.E. by E., a strong breeze till the

$\frac{20}{30}$*th October, Thursday.*—Item early in the morning of the $\frac{20}{30}$th the wind S.E. by E., a stiff breeze and [hoisted] the main top-sail again ; we sounded 26 fathoms. Calculated we had sailed 10 miles S.W. by S. during the night, from sundown to sunrise. At noon we saw four Zierikzee fishing-boats, which were sailing northwards on our lee ; one of our ships spoke one of the fishermen. The wind continued S.E. by E., a stiff breeze. In the evening we sounded 25 fathoms ; continued our course S. ; during the day we sailed altogether S.W. and S.W. by S. seven miles. In the evening we took the topsails in, and sailed continuously through the night S.W. by S., until the $\frac{21}{31}$st instant ; made nine miles S.W. and W., until early morning.

$\frac{21}{31}$*st October, Friday.*—Item early in the morning of the $\frac{21}{31}$st, we had 18 fathoms of water. Calculated Garremuyden to be 17 to 18 miles S.W. of us. At noon we were then in latitude 53° 4', in a depth of 18 fathoms; but we still saw no land. I then reckoned we were in the shallow water of the Breeveertyen.[1] In the evening we sounded 20 fathoms ; then we lay over to the E. by N., and had 20 fathoms all through the night ; this night on a continuous course E.N.E., made five miles until the $\frac{22\text{nd}}{1\text{st}}\frac{Oct.}{Nov.}$

$\frac{22\text{nd}}{1\text{st}}\frac{Oct.}{Nov.}$, *Saturday.*—Item in the morning of the $\frac{22\text{nd}}{1\text{st}}$, fair weather, wind S.S.E. We sounded 19 fathoms, and saw five strange ships to the W.N.W. of us ; it was Captain Bruijnsvelt with

---

[1] Possibly the "Broad Fourteens."

THE LAST WINTER 153

four merchantmen, that had followed us from Norway. Then south wind; in the evening we lay over to the E., but made little progress till the $\frac{23rd}{2nd}\frac{Oct.}{Nov.}$

$\frac{23rd}{2nd}\frac{Oct.}{Nov.}$, *Sunday.*—Item in the morning of the $\frac{23rd}{2nd}$, smooth water, westerly wind, then the wind dropped all day. In the evening we anchored, and lay to till before dawn on the $\frac{24th}{3rd}\frac{Oct.}{Nov.}$, in 18 fathoms of water, with fine weather.

$\frac{24th}{3rd}\frac{Oct.}{Nov.}$, *Monday.*—Item early in the morning of the $\frac{24th}{3rd}$, we weighed anchor, and sailed E.S.E. towards land, and about 8 o'clock saw the Huysduynen[1] to the E. of us. The fleet did their best to sail in to he Texel. Thanks and praise be to the Lord, who has kept us so safe. But the East Indiamen were forced to remain outside. In the evening we anchored with Patten S.E. of us. About 10 o'clock in the evening we got under sail, the wind shifted to the N.W. about midnight, and then we sailed out round the Hook with the East Indiamen towards the Vlie until the

$\frac{25}{4}th\frac{Oct.}{Nov.}$, *Tuesday.*—Item early in the morning of the $\frac{25}{4}$th we were 1½ miles from the West end of the Vlie. We saw Schout by Nacht[2] Pijeter Floirsen 2 miles to the N.E. of us with his squadron and the Hof van Seelant. It was calm, with a slight breeze N.N.W. To-day the Hof aforesaid got inside the Vlie. In the evening we came off the Vlie with the three other East Indiamen, and lay at anchor till the $\frac{26}{5}$th $\frac{Oct.}{Nov.}$

$\frac{26}{5}th\frac{Oct.}{Nov.}$, *Wednesday.*—Item early in the morning of the $\frac{26}{5}$th the three East Indiamen sailed into the Vlie. This morning four ships of war came

---

[1] On the N. point of the Helder and on the S. side of the Helder entrance to the Texel.
[2] *Cf.* Vol. I, p. 177.

out of the Meuse, Captain Jan de Liefde with
Captain Krijste Jan Eldersen, Wijllem Arensen's
ship and Captain Warremon's ship. Then we got
under sail and sailed towards Texel, wind W.N.W.,
a tolerable breeze. We had been informed that
quite seventy merchantmen had got in on the $\frac{23rd}{2nd}$
and $\frac{11th}{3rd}$. In the evening at sundown the south
end of the Texel was 2½ miles S.S.E. of us, and we
had the wind in the N.W. by W., a tolerable breeze,
and sailed S.W. by W., with seventy ships of war.
The weather continued good during the night; at
2 o'clock we anchored, with the light on the
Huysduynen 2½ miles E. by S. of us; wind S.W.,
fair weather till the $\frac{27}{6}$th $\frac{Oct.}{Nov.}$

$\frac{27}{6}th$ $\frac{Oct.}{Nov.}$, *Thursday.*—Item in the morning of
the $\frac{27}{6}$th, Vice-Admiral de Wijtte hoisted his small
flag from the quarter-deck, to summon myself and
Rear-Admiral Pijeter Floirsen on board. It blew
a stiff breeze from the S.W. We got under sail
to get a little more room, and it began to blow
harder and harder. About 3 o'clock we anchored
with the Kijch Dunes[1] about 3½ miles E. of us.
The gale continued, and we lay (?) anchored with
three cables with topmasts lowered fore and aft.
The ship Breederaede lost an anchor this evening.
We continued lying at anchor in 15 fathoms of
water, a stiff breeze, wind S.W. About 10 o'clock
in the evening the wind shifted to the W.N.W.,
with clear weather, and after midnight the wind
was due N.W., but a stiff breeze and boisterous sea
till the morning of the $\frac{28}{7}$th $\frac{Oct.}{Nov.}$

$\frac{28}{7}th$ $\frac{Oct.}{Nov.}$, *Friday.*—Item in the morning of the
$\frac{28}{7}$th the weather began to abate a little, with fine
clear sky; wind N.W. by W. In the afternoon

---

[1] About a mile S. of the Huysduynen—*i.e.* just south of the
entrance into the Texel.

THE LAST WINTER

the weather began to get rougher again, wind W.N.W., a cloudy sky. We remaining lying to with seventy ships of war, an ammunition-ship and a victualling-ship, altogether seventy-two ships. We lay to through the night with very boisterous sea, wind W.N.W., the ships laboured severely till the

$\frac{29}{8}th$ $\frac{Oct.}{Nov.}$, *Saturday*.—Item in the morning of the $\frac{29}{8}$th, rough weather as before, with several gusty showers of rain the whole day; during the night the weather moderated a little, but in the morning watch it began to get rougher again, with heavy rain.

$\frac{30}{9}th$ $\frac{Oct.}{Nov.}$, *Sunday*.—Item before daybreak on the morning of the $\frac{30}{9}$th the weather began to get very rough again; wind W.N.W., and sometimes N.W. During the day several ships slipped their anchors in the gale from the N.W., and sailed towards Texel. The Lord God bring them in in safety. Amen. At noon our anchor broke out from the bottom, we let fall our sheet anchor, which we dragged a little. Wind as before, very strong. In the evening several ships cut their mainmasts overboard. We had a heavy gale through the night from the N.W. and N.W. by N., until the $\frac{31st}{10th}$ $\frac{Oct.}{Nov.}$

$\frac{31st}{10th}\frac{Oct.}{Nov.}$, *Monday*.—Item early in the morning of the $\frac{31st}{10th}$, wind N.N.W., with heavy snow and hail. We saw Vice-Admiral de Wijtte lying without his mainmast, and ten other ships without their mainmasts, and one without any mast at all. It blew very hard all through the day from the N. and N. by W. In the evening Captain Boogert got adrift, and another ship cut her mainmast away. The wind continued N.N.W., rough weather. May the Lord God come to our assistance. He is our Salvation. Amen. All through the night we had very rough weather; wind from N. by W. to W.N.W. until the

$\frac{1st}{11th}$ *November, Tuesday.*—Item early in the morning of the $\frac{1st}{11th}$ the wind was north, very rough weather, with showers of hail and snow. Two more ships got adrift from their anchors. This morning we took counsel what was best to do to save the ships and our lives, and are very ready to choose the best plan; but we could not decide to cut away the sheet with the bower-anchors, each with two cables, since this would leave us with only one anchor and one to anchor which should hold[1] with three cables. About noon our bower-rope broke in half, the second rope, so that a rope and a half and an anchor were lost, and two cables quite spoilt. At noon we had a strong gale from the N.; after that the weather began to moderate, thank God. Towards evening the wind was due N.N.E. with tolerable weather. We counted still forty-seven ships, twenty-three of which were dismasted.

LIST OF CAPTAINS AND SHIPS, WITH THE NUMBERS OF THEIR GUNS AND CREWS, NOW IN THE FLEET OF THE COMMODORE.[2]

From Zealand.	Carrying.	
	Guns.	Men.
Captain Jan Pouwelsen, the ship Neptunus	28	134
Captain Joos Banckert, the ship de Liefde	26	86
Captain Jan Sichalsen, the ship 't Wapen van Sweeden	28	95
Captain Fr. Mangelaer, the ship de Liefde	30	110

[1] This is extremely obscure, but apparently the meaning is that there would be one cable left from each anchor cut away, which would leave three for the single anchor left.

[2] This would appear to be a list of Ruijter's squadron in this last voyage to Norway.

	Carrying.	
	Guns.	Men.
Captain Cornelis Evertsen the younger, the ship Vlissingen	26	110
Captain Claes Jansen Sanger's ship, commanded by Jan Jansen van de Eijcke, master; the ship 't galjas van Middelburch . . .	26	104
Captain Cuijper, the ship der Gaes . . .	27	109
Captain den Haen, the ship den Haesinvelt .	30	108
Captain Fortuijn, the ship den Endracht . .	24	98
Captain Loureijs Pensier, the ship St. Jan .	26	100
Captain Loncke, the ship de Fama . . .	30	110

From Friesland.

	Guns.	Men.
Captain Jooris Pietersen van den Broucke, vice commodore [Admiral]; the ship Westergo .	28	98
Captain Bouckhorst, the ship St. Nicolaes .	23	85
Captain van der Parre, the ship Albertijne .	24	70
Captain Aldert Pietersen Qua Coer (sic), the ship de Shaepherder	28	80
Captain Becks, the ship Sara	24	85
Captain Wagenaer, the ship Graef Hendrick .	30	100
Captain Degelcamp, the ship Gelderlant . .	24	80
Captain Gabriel Anteunissen, the ship Meedenblick	26	100
Captain Reijnier Sekema, the ship Hector van Troijen	24	75

From Amsterdam.

	Guns.	Men.
Captain van Velsen, the ship Gelderlant . .	26	90
Captain Jan Egbertsen Ooms, the ship Gouda .	28	86

From Rotterdam.

	Guns.	Men.
Captain Jan Arentsen Verhaeff, Rear-Admiral, the ship Rotterdam	30	120
Captain Jongenboer's ship, commanded by Lieut. Jan van Es:, the ship Gelderlant . .	26	100
Captain Jan Jansen van der Valch, the ship St. Pieter	28	122

The last comers from Texel.

Captain Jan Gidionsen Verburcht.
Captain Isaak Sweers.
Captain Lucas Albertsen.
Captain Douwe Anckes.
Captain Sijmen van der Hoeck.
Captain Claes Sael.
Captain Manuel Salijnex.
Captain Pieter Salomonsen.

1277. *Nov.* $\frac{2}{12}$, 1653.—*WASSENAER TO S.G.*

[Archives of Hague.]

Noble and Powerful Lords,—My Lords,—On the $\frac{27}{6}$th $\frac{Oct.}{Nov.}$, I got under sail in the evening, with Messrs. Herberts and Taemsz, Delegates of the Amsterdam Board of Admiralty, outside the harbour at Amsterdam, and made for Texel, the wind blowing a steady breeze from the S.S.W. On the $\frac{28}{7}$th $\frac{Oct.}{Nov.}$, the wind was contrary, N.W. and N.N.W., and we were obliged to tack against a strong breeze, making but little progress till towards evening, as we had both wind and tide against us. As night fell we anchored in the Balg between the island of Wieringen[1] and Texel; it blew a gale during the night. On the $\frac{29}{8}$th $\frac{Oct.}{Nov.}$, the wind was westerly, and blowing a gale; we remained lying at anchor; the gale continued, blowing hard in the same way all through the night. The $\frac{30}{9}$th $\frac{Oct.}{Nov.}$, wind as before, with a strong gale; we still remained lying at anchor. The master of my ship said he had seen some ship's timbers floating past, from which we conjectured some ships must have suffered damage; the gale continued; that evening at 7 o'clock our small anchor and rope were carried away, and during the night our pinnace. On the $\frac{31st}{10th}$ $\frac{Oct.}{Nov.}$, the wind was N.W., blowing a gale; but towards noon the weather grew somewhat calmer, and at two o'clock we weighed anchor; but the gale began to increase again and we were obliged to remain lying where we were. In getting under weigh the yacht of the Lords Delegates got aground in breaking out her anchor; she was under her foresail, and came to anchor again; at 7 o'clock

---

[1] An island inside the Texel on the way to Amsterdam.

in the evening she floated off, and got under sail and in order to avoid the shallows came closer in to Wieringen to anchor. It blew a stiff gale that night, mixed with rain, and we had thunder and lightning. At daybreak on the $\frac{1st}{11th}$ November, the wind was N. and N.N.W., blowing a gale as before with rain and sharp showers. The yacht of the Admiralty Delegates was lying close to us at anchor; and, seeing that the bad weather held out, and that it was impossible to make the Texel or the Helder, I made a signal for the pinnace of the said yacht of the Lords Deputies and went in her on board them, when we resolved, as we were in want of fresh water and other supplies, to run gently under our foresails only (the weather being so rough that we could not hoist our other sails) towards the west end of Wieringen, and we dropped anchor in that place towards evening. On the $\frac{2nd}{12th}$ November, the wind N. and N.N.W., we weighed anchor at daybreak, in company with the yacht of the Admiralty Delegates, and got under sail, tacking towards the New Deep. We saw some ships of war lying off the Schilt[1] and we spoke one of them, the ship den blaeuwen Arent;[2] they said they had come in on Sunday last, with nine feet of water in the hold. With her was lying the ship Purmerlant, belonging to the Amsterdam Directors, Captain Andries Sylbrantz:; they said the fleet was still lying outside, and that Commander de Ruijter was coming in. We also spoke the ship den Swarten Leeuw,[3] belonging to the Amsterdam Directors, commanded by Captain Hendrich de Raet, who had come in on the $\frac{25}{4}$th $\frac{Oct.}{Nov.}$, on account of leakiness. Captain Gerret Teemsz. of Enkhuijsen had also

[1] On the S.E. side of the Texel island.
[2] The Blue Eagle.   [3] The Black Lion.

come in ; and Captain Adriaen Brijnsvelt of Friesland, and Captain Pieter Salomonsz., belonging to the Amsterdam Admiralty, were both lying there also. When we came off the New Deep, we found Captain Cornelis Huijser's ship aground there. Commodore de Ruijter in person also came up with us, together with Captains Jan Egbertsz: Ooms and Jan van Campen ; they stated that the storm and tempest at sea had been so great that, to their knowledge, the following ships[1] had perished therein :—the ships commanded by Captain Cleyntie, Captain Marcus Hartman, Captain Ooms aforesaid, Captain Swart, the King's ship, Captain Rootjes, together with Commodore Schoonvelt with the ship den gouden Reael,[2] and Captain Wagenaer, belonging to the Friesland Admiralty, with numbers of their crews, not being able to specify how many. All the Zealanders, and some others as well, had made for the Meuse, Goedereede[3] and Zealand ; twenty-four or twenty-five of the ships were dismasted, and almost all of them had exhausted their supplies of provisions.

Commodore de Ruijter and the above-named captains were of opinion that, if the weather continued favourable, Vice-Admiral de With, from whom he had parted company this morning, would also endeavour to put in to-morrow with the ships he still had with him. We have also been visited by Messrs. Appeldoorn and de Zee, from the West-Friesland and the North Quarter Board, and by a gentleman, whose name I do not know, from the Friesland Board. We all purpose to-morrow, as soon as it is daylight, to ride up to Captain Ooms' ship, which is aground between the Huysduynen

[1] *Cf.* list in No. 1286.
[2] This ship does not seem to be in the list in No. 1286.
[3] Goree.

and Callant's Eye, on the shore, to save her guns and everything else aboard her that is sound, and also to make inquiries as to what may still be left of the other ships which are lost, whereon we shall report to your Lordships in our next. On reaching this place I received their H.M.'s dispatch of the $\frac{30}{9}$th $\frac{Oct.}{Nov.}$, and immediately afterwards their resolution of the $\frac{28}{7}$th $\frac{Oct.}{Nov.}$, together with its enclosures, and a letter to the Commodore to be appointed for the thirty ships of war proceeding to Ostend, the tenor of which I shall carry out to the utmost of my power, &c., &c.

(Signed)   J. VAN WASSENAER.

On board my yacht, lying
in the New Deep this
$\frac{2nd}{12th}$ November, 1653.

P.S. — Adriaen Jacobsz. van Huijsduinen, master of an advice-galliot in the employ of the Amsterdam Directors, reports that on the $\frac{29}{8}$th $\frac{Oct.}{Nov.}$, he set sail from Bergen in Norway two hours before dawn; that he left all the ships still there to the number of from fifty to sixty, lying in three separate divisions, some at Bock op der Zee in the Roads, some in Strudshavn, and some a short mile from that place; they have been unable to get away on account of the strong contrary winds, as your Lordships will see from the letter of Commodore den Baer, which I have sent to their H.M.

(Signed)   J. VAN WASSENAER.

1278. *Nov.* $\frac{3}{13}$, 1653.—*DE WITH TO S.G.*

[Archives of Hague.]

Noble and Powerful Lords,—My Lords,—We have thought it our duty to inform your Lordships that on the night of the $\frac{26}{5}$th $\frac{October}{November}$, we received a letter, enclosing a list, from Commissary Croon off the Texel shallows. In this letter he informed me that twenty of the ships are to victual here off the Texel shallows, and that supplies of provisions for them are lying ready in small craft and fishing-boats in the New Deep. I thereupon asked for instructions from their H.M., how close in shore I should anchor, saying I would not, on my own responsibility, bring the State's fleet so close in shore as is necessary to enable us to victual at sea. In the morning of the $\frac{27}{6}$th $\frac{Oct.}{Nov.}$, we made every effort to get a little nearer in shore, and several victualling-ships came out, but put back again on account of the rough weather; in the afternoon the weather was so rough we were obliged to anchor. At night it blew a strong gale from the W. On the $\frac{28}{7}$th, $\frac{29}{8}$th, $\frac{30}{9}$th and $\frac{31st}{10th}$ $\frac{October}{November}$, we had an extraordinarily severe gale; several of our ships dragged their anchors and cut their masts overboard; during the night we lost two anchors and several cables, and were obliged to cut our mast overboard also. On the morning of the $\frac{1st}{11th}$ November, we counted twenty-six ships lying there unshattered, twenty-three had cut their masts away, and one had lost all her masts. The rest, to the number of seventy, were missing; I am afraid they will have suffered terrible damage. On the $\frac{2nd}{12th}$ instant, we had a soft gale from the N.N.W. Commodores de Ruijter and Pieter Florisz: informed me that each of them had only one and a half cables on board, that their ships were very leaky and unfit to remain at sea. I therefore ordered them to sail into the Texel so as to avoid further mishaps, and also had a few other ships, which had lost their masts and rudders, towed in by other vessels. We are now making every effort to rig up a stump. Last night we

THE LAST WINTER

received their H.M. resolutions as follows:—two of the $\frac{26}{5}$th $\frac{Oct.}{Nov.}$, one of the $\frac{29}{8}$th and a letter of the $\frac{30}{9}$th $\frac{Oct.}{Nov.}$, and beg to submit the following remarks in this connection, first, with regard to the resolution of the $\frac{26}{5}$th $\frac{Oct.}{Nov.}$, I have thought it necessary for the service of the country not to divide the State's fleet, so as to prevent our being insulted if we fall in with the foe; and I have therefore brought the fleet to the nearest shallows and caused them to sail in, and was holding the State's fleet in accordance with the following resolutions of their H.M., vizt. of the $\frac{26}{6}$th $\frac{Sept.}{Oct.}$, and the $\frac{3rd}{13th}$, and $\frac{8}{18}$th October, 1653; and when the great calamity came upon us there was no possibility of sailing in. I trust that your Lordships will have duly received my letters sent off on dates as under, vizt. the $\frac{10}{20}$th and $\frac{19}{29}$th October, and the $\frac{24th}{3rd}$, $\frac{25}{4}$th and $\frac{26}{5}$th $\frac{October}{November}$, in which I faithfully stated my views to your Lordships. It has further come to my ears that the merchants in the Meuse have complained that I did not provide a proper convoy for the ships. I beg your Lordships to believe me when I say, that I had only one ship belonging to the Meuse under my convoy, and I sent Captain Ruth Jacobsz. to convoy her; and I beg that discrimination may be used in giving credence to such complaints. We now purpose, my Lords, as soon as God Almighty grants us wind and weather, to sail with all the ships that are now with us in to the Texel, because we cannot hold out at sea any longer, and there is not one of the ships but has suffered severe damage. At present we have the wind from the north quarter, which makes it impracticable for shattered ships to get into the Texel, &c.

Done on board the ship *'t huijs te Swieten* lying off Texel, this $\frac{3rd}{13tb}$ November, 1653.

I have to add, my Lords, that, after writing the above, we got wind and weather so far favourable that we were able to sail in to the Texel this afternoon with forty-two or forty-three of our ships, shattered and otherwise. Thanks be to Almighty God, who has been our guide and brought us to this haven. There are still several ships lying outside the shallows, with their masts and rudders gone, and I have given orders for them to be towed into the Texel. I beg to submit the above for your Lordships' information.

    (Signed)   Witte Corn: de With.

Dated as above.

1279. *Nov.* $\frac{4}{14}$, 1653.—*A LETTER OF INTELLIGENCE FROM THE HAGUE*

[Thurloe S.P. i. 571.]

Sir,—They are debating and busy at present upon the sea and maritime affairs, and the Vice-Admiral hath advertised, that in the winter season it is impossible to ride at an anchor upon the coast of Holland: notwithstanding they were minded, that he should stay out, and now this tempest happening, they are very much troubled, and do wish that their fleet had come in, but de Witt hath writ that he durst not stay upon the coast; and he being forbid to come in, he resolved to keep out in open sea, nevertheless those ships that want provisions must of necessity come in.

They are at a fine pass here now: the English having hindered us all this summer from acting, do rest in the winter: and we think to have gotten much by fighting with the sea, the winter and the tempest, *remotis Anglis*.

Letters of the 4th of November are come from the commissioners, giving to understand that the

English are making ready a very great fleet : pre-supposing that the Vice-Admiral de Witt is still in Norway, and that with eighty frigates and eight of their great ships from Chatham they will go to visit him. But in the winter men ought to be quiet, as here at present they do most certainly repent themselves for having been so rigorous and violent against Admiral de Witt, having commended him to stay out at sea, notwithstanding that those of Zealand, who are used to sail and trade more in the winter than in the summer, were properly the cause of it ; and now cometh advice upon advice that the fleet have suffered very much in this last storm. Some say that ten ships were cast away, others speak of fifteen, others of twenty, yea, some of thirty : certain it is, that it blew a fierce storm upon Sunday, Monday and Tuesday ; and that although it was neither full or new moon, yet there was such a high tide at Rotterdam, that the like was never seen. The Wednesday they had just celebrated an action of thanks for the happy arrival of their fleet, and the next day came news that so many of their fleet were cast away. They make account at present, to keep out but thirty ships at sea, unless that the preparations of the English do oblige them to set forth more.

Nov. 4/14th, M.S.

1280. *Nov.* $\frac{4}{14}$, *1653.—DE WITT TO BEVERNING*

[Thurloe S.P. i. 575.]

My Lord,—The fleet of this state having been now some days upon the coast, hath by a mighty storm, which God Almighty hath been pleased to send and to continue some days, according to the reports as we hear, suffered great damage, but we have not as yet any certainty what damage hath been done; and their High and Mighty Lordships, foreseeing the worst, have resolved to call in the fleet, to keep out at sea this winter season only some frigates. In the meantime their Lordships have proceeded to the election of two new Vice-Admirals and three Rear-Admirals.

In Portugal our businesses do not meet with that success as was expected. I am in haste.

Nov. 4/14th.

1281. *Nov.* 4/14, 1653.—*BEVERNING TO DE WITH*

[Thurloe S.P. i. 575.]

My Lord,—We thought it our duty concerning the equipping and constitution of the sea-forces here, to advise their High and Mighty Lordships, that we are informed that the fleet of eighty-nine or ninety ships, whereof is mention in our former from time to time, hath steered their course out of the river, and part of them for Portsmouth, and part for the Downs, the first about sixty ships, which are already at Portsmouth, or there daily expected, and the other of sixteen or eighteen frigates which stay for the Lord Whitelocke to convoy him past the English and Scots coasts, which may afterwards remain about the North parts.

Westminster, Nov. 4/14th.

1282. *Nov.* 5/15, 1653.—*WASSENAER TO S.G.*

[Archives of Hague.]

Noble and Powerful Lords,—My Lords,—[? I am enclosing] to your Lordships the resolutions passed by the Delegates of the several Boards and Committees of Directors here present, with regard

THE LAST WINTER 167

to the dismasted ships, and their order to the Naval Agents and Commissaries here to go the following day to inspect the ships that had their masts still standing, and to report to us upon their condition; from their verbal report and written statement, which I am sending to your Lordships, it appears that only four of the ships aforesaid can be made ready in these parts to put to sea again. It has therefore been determined to send all the rest each to their respective districts, so that they may be made ready there again with the least possible delay.

Besides the four aforesaid ships, the least damaged of which will require at least fourteen days before she can be made ready, there are two more ships now lying ready in the Vlie, belonging to the Board of West Friesland and the North Quarter, the one called den Herder,[1] the other 't Wapen van Hoorn, in addition to the ship Frisia, which, according to the report of Heer Heuvel at Nieuhuijs is lying ready in the Vlieter, waiting only to complete her supplies and crew; and these are all the ships in these parts from which their H.M. can receive any service for the next fourteen days or three weeks. We suppose that their H.M.'s former resolutions will be altered in part in consequence of the good news, vizt. that two of the East India return-ships, together with some of the State's ships coming from the Mediterranean, the Straits-traders, and others that have been lying in Bergen and thereabouts, are some of them off the coast and inside the shallows, and one of the return-ships has already arrived in the Texel. We have also heard a great deal of firing from about the Vlie, and suppose that some of them have put in there. We have also had news, by a flute

[1] *I.e.* Shepherd.

coming from France, that Commodore Tromp likewise is off the coast. The good God grant he may get in quite safely, &c., &c.

(Signed) J. VAN WASSENAER.

On board my yacht, lying
in the New Deep, this
$\tfrac{5}{15}$th November, 1653.

1283. *Nov.* $\tfrac{6}{16}$, *1653.—BOURNE TO A.C.*

[S.P. 18, xli. 116.]

Right Honble.,—Since my last to you we have paid all the ships appointed unless the Mermaid.

The Assurance was paid last, upon whose pay I laid a stop of 40s. a man until the frigate be in the Rolling Grounds, and they make their appearance there aboard, the reason of this distinction in pay was because this company was second to the Mermaid in deserting their duty and capitulating about their pay, and I thought it expedient to do this for the conviction of themselves and others.

The Mermaid I reserved to the last, which tomorrow I purpose to command out into the Rolling Grounds, when they shall be paid the rather because this company was not only the first that broke the hedge and invited others thereunto, but also as an aggravation of their former boldness and insolence they mingled themselves yesterday with the Assurance's crew (whom I had brought to a willingness to accept their pay with the fore-mentioned condition) and sought anew to stir up and provoke their spirits to distemper. But I suddenly quelled that spirit, and proceeded to pay off the said ship: and committed one of the most refractory and stubborn to be secured at Landguard fort with the rest of this company's, there being now 4 of the worst together, so that the business as to pay is now finished upon the matter, and we are quiet.

The Advantage came in yesterday from Yarmouth. I shall give order for her refitting and to-morrow they shall make way to enter upon her. Their men coming in at this season have an expectation of pay, and I purpose in case there be any considerable sum left to advance £300 or £400 by way of imprest to the captain.

Yesterday also came into the Rolling Grounds the Greyhound, who by the captain's relation hath met with extraordinary bad weather, and forced to Yarmouth Roads (that being the first place they could recover) which I am apt to believe, for we had about a week since the sorest storms at N.W. and N.N.W. for 3 or 4 days here that hath been known for many years. He waits for your Honours' orders, the wind at present being northerly.

Here is the Assurance, ready to sail, the Newcastle, Expedition, Convertine and Middleborough within a few days will be ready, they wanting some men at present.

I have taken all courses and means to lay a stop upon the men to prevent their going away, both by water and land, and have wrote as effectually as I may to the Mayor of Colchester and the constables of other towns that lie upon the pass of London : yet they find ways to run.

I desire your Honours' commands as to this part that when these ships are ready to sail and have so many men as will manage them, whether they shall sail for the Rolling Grounds or Hosely Bay, or Yarmouth Roads, where they will keep what they have in better order and government, and be in a way to increase their number.

Here are about a dozen pressed and sent from Yarmouth, but I desire your Honours would direct a word both to that, and to all other Corporations and towns who press men, that care may be taken in employing such faithful and able instruments as may not put the State upon charge of paying press and conduct money to such who signify nothing as to our present service and employment (most of them they press being boys and others very unfit for the work, and poorly clothed) which I shall send back so soon as others present. Most of the carpenters and caulkers being now put upon the Centurion, Andrew, Constant Warwick, Advantage and Recovery, I hope will hasten their dispatch, but some of them have taken up much help being greatly deficient when they came in.

I would gladly visit my family and habitation (having had a long spell upon this quarter) and now wait when your Honours please to grant my desire, and the rather because I find much alteration in my body, being much distempered. I shall give you no further trouble at present, but crave leave to assure you I am most humbly and no less heartily,

$\qquad$ Y^r. Honours' at command,
$\qquad\qquad$ N. BOURNE.

Harwich,
6 Nov. 1653.

1284. *Nov.* $\frac{4}{14}$, 1653.—*WASSENAER TO S.G.*

[Archives of Hague.]

Noble and Powerful Lords,—My Lords,—I have safely received your Lordships' dispatch of the $\frac{4}{14}$th instant, with extracts from your Lordships' resolutions of the $\frac{1st}{11th}$ and $\frac{3rd}{13th}$ instant; and in accordance with your Lordships' commands,

I have made their contents known to Vice-Admirals de Ruijter and Pieter Florisz. The former does not accept them entirely, but I hope to be able to persuade him to do so, especially if any assurance can be given him that he will not be obliged to transport his household to Amsterdam. I have already done all I possibly can to influence him, and shall persevere in my endeavours, and do not doubt I shall accomplish the matter. I am astonished, that no mention is made at all in your Lordships' letter of the disaster that has overtaken our fleet, of which I partially informed your Lordships in my letter of the $\frac{2nd}{12th}$ instant, with which a messenger was dispatched quite early the following day, and, as far as I can judge, ought to have reached the Hague before your Lordships' letter was sent off. But it seems that the messengers take their time, and I think orders should be issued on this point. Your Lordships will have seen from my letter of the $\frac{5}{15}$th Instant, that two return-ships and some other merchantmen, that have been lying in and about Bergen, have come in, partly here in the Texel, partly in the Vlie. Yesterday the ship der Goes, commanded by Jan Richwijn, came in here dismasted. He reports that he left Rochelle with twenty-five other ships, among which were seven warships coming from the Straits, vizt. the ships commanded by Commodore Tromp, Captain Michiel Fransz. van der Berck, the said Jan Richwijn, the younger Boer from Zealand and Captain Slord, with the ship Utrecht, and the English prize carrying forty-two guns.[1] He thinks

[1] It is difficult to identify this ship if the Leopard had already, as reported in No. 1227, reached Holland, as the other vessels taken in Appleton's action off Leghorn were armed merchantmen, quite small vessels (*cf.* Spalding's *Life and Times of Richard Badiley*, p. 204).

that the others must all have put in to the Wielings on account of the bad weather.

Herewith, &c., &c.
(Signed)   J. van Wassenaer.

On board my yacht lying
in the New Deep, this
⁷⁄₁₇th November, 1653.

P.S.—Immediately after writing the above the Delegates here from the Admiralty Board of Amsterdam received a letter from Commissary Jacob Agges, of which I enclose a copy and beg to refer your Lordships to its contents.

1285.   Nov. $\frac{10}{20}$, 1653.—BOURNE TO A.C.
[B.M. Add. 22546, fol. 146.]

Right Honourable,—The last night I received a letter from Mr. Blackborne wherein he signified your Honours' pleasure that I should, by my next, return an account of what ships are, and lately have been under my charge in this port, and also their present station. The substance whereof I humbly conceive I have formerly given your Honours.

The Convertine, Newcastle, Assurance, Expedition, Mermaid, Centurion, Middleborough, Constant Warwick, Advice, Recovery, and Malago Merchant, were appointed to this place by the Generals, who gave them orders to be speedily fitted, and I have several times given your Honours an account of our progress, as may appear by divers letters, wherein I have oft troubled you with complaints, and the truth is if provisions timely demanded had been seasonably sent down you had before this time been out of care for the fitting these ships, the contrary exercises my thoughts now for I would gladly see an end of this voyage.

The Mermaid's company being first in demanding pay, and deserting their duty, were the last paid, and before they had a penny I caused them to sail, and afterwards were glad to receive it with a rebate of 3ᵈ. per man deposited in their captain's hand till they sailed quite away, which to-morrow God willing they shall do, and those of them that appear not (unless discharged) shall forfeit that 3ᵈ. also which I have signified this day to them.

The Assurance's company being second to the former I paid last but she, with depositing 4ᵈ. in their captain's hands, and yesterday they sailed down below the ships, having everything on board, 4 of her company being chiefly active in raising up that evil spirit amongst them, I committed to Landguard Fort, where now they remain very seemingly sorrowful. I shall not release 3 of them without your Honours' orders, because they are not only guilty as to what I formerly intimated but also they have embezzled some provisions out of the ship they belong unto. I crave your directions what I shall do concerning them, whether the keeping of their pay, which is about a year's time, will satisfy for their thievery, and their imprisonment for their insolence, if it seem good to your Honours I shall proceed accordingly. The Convertine, Expedition, and Newcastle stay only for men.

The Middleborough and Malago Merchant are upon the matter ready also.

The Centurion, Advice, and Constant Warwick having had very much work done to them in their hulls and new masted, are yet imperfect, but the next week I hope will give a good blow to those works if the weather prove seasonable.

The Recovery deserves little cost to be bestowed on her, having robbed the stores long enough (if I may so say) she lies still at present till better ships are despatched.

The Advantage came in two days since and they are doing something upon her.

The Greyhound I advised your Honours in my last (dated the 6th instant) was arrived in the Rolling Grounds being forced to Yarmouth Roads by a violent storm, I then desired your orders concerning her.

And this is what account I am capable of giving both of the ships under my charge of late, as also their stations.

The ungrateful and disingenuous spirit in the seamen I lament, who are neither sensible of what is the public or their private interests but are below the beasts that perish. I hear that Ipswich and other parts are full of them, but here are few enough, they love not this air, since I have banished strong waters and sent some of them over the water.

I advised your Honours in my last of men prest and sent from Yarmouth, but they are not such as must do your work, which I signified to the bailiffs of that town and hope if they send any more they will be of another magnitude.

The Wildman, a fireship, in the beginning of the last summer, being leaky and having some provisions in her for the fleet, coming in hither by order, I have kept here till now, to receive in, and deliver out the remains of provisions taken from other ships under the State's pay (this being your own ship) and now have sent her up to Deptford with several remains of provisions (the greatest part whereof is not good) and have cleared all other vessels in which they were.

The Concord, according to the liberty given me is reduced to a naked hulk, and hath only two men upon charge to look to her, she being useful to take in guns and other provisions from the ships that come hither to be careened and tallowed.

THE LAST WINTER 175

I have not else to trouble your Honours about but crave pardon for this long discourse, and although my service be little worth, yet I shall always endeavour to manifest that I am, most really and readily to be commanded whilst I am

N. BOURNE

Harwich, 10th November, 1653.

1286. *Nov.* $\frac{10}{20}$, *1653.—A LIST OF THE DUTCH SHIPS that were cast away in the storm on the 29, 30 and 31 Oct., 1653. N.S.*

[Thurloe S.P. i, 582.]

1. The Liberty, all the men lost.
2. Prince William, Captain Boceman, all the men saved.
3. Gouda, John Egberts,[1] captain, half the men saved.
4. The Moerian, Captain Tol, half the men saved.
5. King David, Captain Vogelsang, all the men drowned.
6. Ship Amsterdam, Captain von Kempen,[2] all the men drowned except 14.
7. Captain Cuyper.[3]
8. A flute with provisions.
9. The Golden Lyon, Jacob Pens, captain.
10. Flushing, Captain Jacques.
11. The Crowned Love, Captain Hartman.
12. St. Vincent, Captain Kleyntje.
13. Ship, Wagenaer.[4]
14. Captain John Rootjes.
15. The ship Justice, Captain Swarts, all the men drowned.

Sent and received here 10 Nov. o.s.

[1] This is the Captain Ooms of No. 1277.
[2] or Campen. *Cf.* No. 1277.
[3] The ship der Gaes. *Cf.* No. 1276.
[4] *I.e.* the Graef Hendrick, commanded by Captain Wagenaer. *Cf.* No. 1276.

1287. *Nov.* 11/21, 1653.—*ADVICE sent by the Dutch Ambassadors to the States-General from Portsmouth.*

[Thurloe S.P. i, 583.]

There was brought hither on Saturday last 5/15th of this month £18,000 to pay off the ships that belong to this place. Here are come 10 men of war from London to be paid here, and when the men come on board to be paid, they are kept on board, and not suffered to go on shore again to fetch their cloaths, and to take their leave of their friends. These ships lye ready between Portsmouth and the Isle of Wight to go to sea: some of their names are Fairfax, Essex, Charity, Speaker, and Worcester. In the harbour of Portsmouth lye 7 ships more, all unfit, besides two that will be soon ready.

Here is a ship building of 60 guns, which will be ready against May.

Here is expected from Plymouth the ship Hannibal, with some merchantmen.

Here is yet great discontents among the seamen: I saw five of them put into prison for rising against their captain.

It will be three weeks first before their fleet will be ready to put out to sea. It is said, the general rendezvous is to be in the Downs. General Monck is to go in the ship Swiftsure, or Fairfax.

Portsmouth, Nov. 11th/21st.

1288. *Nov.* 12th/22nd, 1653.—*MONCK TO C.o.S.*

[S.P. 18, xli, 138.]

Right Hon[bl.],—This morning I called a Council of War of the respective commanders in the ships now riding here to know their state, an account whereof will appear by the enclosed list to the Commissioners of the Admiralty that a timely supply may be made according to their respective wants, also that the ships and frigates now fitting out at Deptford and Woolwich may be hastened down hither, where upon arrival I shall take care to quicken the commanders and other officers in their duty, in order whereunto your Lordship's commands to the Commissioners of the Navy will be of no small recommendation to their dispatch ; and upon their coming down hither you may expect an account thereof with their condition from time to time ; having nothing more at present but to assure you that I am, [etc.]

GEORGE MONCK.

Aboard the Swiftsure,
now in the Hope,
the 12th Nov., 1653.

1288A. *Nov. $\frac{12}{22}$, 1653.—A LIST OF SHIPS now in the Hope with their present state.*

[S.P. 18, xli, 138 (i).]

	Men on board.	
Swiftsure	230	Wants some of her dry provisions, but are expected down every day.
Fairfax	40	Hath most part of his beer on board, but no other provision. Hath but 8 guns.
Unicorn	20	Wants all his provisions and 4 of his guns.
Hannibal	60	Wants nothing but men.
Mathias	104	Wants only 10 tons of beer.
Laurell	100	Is every way fitted, and wants only men.
Kentish	100	Wants only men.
Paul	50	Hath only 17½ tons of beer on board and wants everything else.
Katherine	120	hath but 6 weeks' bread and beef, no butter nor cheese, jam, beer, but will carry 6 months of all provisions.

1289. *Nov.* 19/29, 1653.—*HATSELL TO N.C.*
[S.P. 18, cl.]

Gentlemen,—Since my coming home I have given dispatch to the several ships in the margin.¹ The Welcome and Cocke had much carpenters' work done to them to make them strong and staunch for a winter's tugging in the Channel, some of them have dipped a little deep in my store of cordage for their supply. And now is come in the Portland and Nonsuch who will want of that commodity also, which I shall give them, and when all mine is done I must crave Y^r Honours for a supply. I have urged all means, and got little or none since I came home.

I have given order to the frigates and ships that are to the westward that if they meet with any vessels with hemp or cordage (be they of any nation) to bring them in, and I shall do my best to get some from France, though I have cause to doubt that all endeavours that way will prove fruitless, yet I shall make an essay.

The Nonsuch came in on Saturday having met with a great Dutch man of war off the Lizard, with whom she had a pretty sharp scuffle, in which the boatswain and trumpeter of the Nonsuch were slain, her Lieutenant, Master and Chaplain wounded, her main and foretop masts with her foreyard, disabled, her rigging much shattered, and sails very much shot, for supplying of all which all hands concerned are at work. My store of sailcloth is all ended in supplying those ships already dispatched and the Portland wanteth near a whole suit, which I shall get her provided withal. I have

---

¹ Assistance, Sapphire, Elias, Welcome, Hampshire, Hector, Little President, Hopewell pink, Cocke ; Portland, Nonsuch, now in hand.

THE LAST WINTER 179

to desire you to issue an order to the subcommissioners of prize goods here to furnish me with ten or twenty balletts of royals, part of that linen cloth which was taken by the Sapphire, there being a good quantity of royalls in that parcel, as we judge by the outside of the balets which I conceive and offer you accordingly to be very useful for the Navy, and shall wait your pleasure therein.

The rosin that I wrote you of, that was supposed to be near 40 tons, I have had exactly weighed, and it wants somewhat of 18 tons, the one half thereof I shall send to Portsmouth the first wind, there being a vessel bound thither. I shall get what more I can of that commodity, and will advise you.

I understand of two or three Dutch men of war towards the mouth of the Channel, whither are sailed the Assistance, Hampshire, Richard and Martha, Sapphire, Elias and Hopewell pink, who if they met with them will, I hope, give a good account, etc.

I have had some trouble with sick men which came out of several ships, especially the Welcome, out of whom came near 60, which I was constrained to quarter in tippling houses, and some in the country, most of them are returned and put aboard again so that I judge there are not above 40 or 50 at most sick ashore of all the ships, which lodge in tippling houses to their great detriment.

I have written to M^r. Blackborne to desire him to take his time, and to move the Commissioners of the Admiralty to appoint the taking of a house to keep them altogether, and to have persons to have care of them, which would not only be far the better for the poor men, but of less charge to the State—pray second it.

These poor men are (many of them) out of clothes, and how to supply them I know not.

The Cocke was a very noisome sickly ship, but I have caused her to be cleansed and her ballence to be taken out, which was very loathsome, and clean to be put in. She had many men sick, and had one chirurgeon, he being turned over to another ship when they came from the Fleet. I have gotten an honest able man, and shipped him and paid his impress and gratuity.

The chirurgeon of the Welcome by reason of the great sickness amongst them had spent near all his medicaments, so I have paid him £5 on account.

I am earnestly solicited by the captains and clerks of the cheque to pay the money allowed for sick men which they crave every six months, I have not paid them any since I came down, judging it must come from the Prize Officers, but ours here have no order for it—pray give me your thoughts and help in it. I have been tardy in troubling you all this time. I shall earnestly attend your answer to each particular desired, which is all at present I have to offer you, do remain [etc.].

HENR. HATSELL.

1290. *Nov.* 1⁄2⁷, 1653.—*MONCK TO A.C.*

[S.P. 18, xli, 158.]

Gentlemen,—Yours of the 16th instant I received, and am glad to hear you have given effectual orders for a speedy supply of those ships with me in the Hope and that there are some ships ready to fall down unto us which is a great furtherance to the service, and do desire that the rest may be fitted out with all the expedition that may be.

I have appointed the Assistance, Nonsuch, Sapphire, Hampshire, Richard and Martha, Hopewell pink and two Dutch prizes to ply between the

THE LAST WINTER

Lizard and Scilly, and have ordered Captain Roger Martin, commander of the Bristol frigate, to command them, which I think will be a sufficient guard for the place, and have also ordered Captain Martin to appoint two ships of force to ply to and again before Brest, and beyond Scilly if the service requires it.

I am heartily sorry to hear the Council of State hath taken away the embargo, which will be a great hindrance towards the manning of the great ships unless they be speedily got down to the Hope.

The Captain of the Cocke, notwithstanding I have given him orders to make his immediate repairs to the ship under his command, as yet is not gone down. I do therefore desire that you will order him forthwith to repair on board or else I shall be forced to give that command unto another.

I am very glad to hear that Captain Goodson intends to go to sea with us, and shall expect him accordingly. Not more at present, but that I am [etc.]

GEORGE MONCK.

Swiftsure, in
the Hope,
the 17th November, 1653.

I have written unto Captain Lane to make his repair on board the Triumph but cannot as yet hear from him, and do therefore desire if you think it convenient to let Captain Jordan have the command of her in case he doth not speedily come. The Worcester and Adventure is come down here.

In case Captain Jordan commands the Triumph, then I do desire that Captain Goodson may command the George, and I shall find out some honest man to command the Unicorn.

1291. Nov. 18/28, 1653.—*A LETTER OF INTELLI-
GENCE FROM HOLLAND*

[Thurloe, S.P. i, 593.]

De Ruyter informed their Lordships upon the 22nd instant, that the third East India ship from Bergen was seen upon the coast and had set her course towards Zealand whereto she belonged; but appears since, that the said Ruyter was mistaken, for that the Resident de Vries writes from Denmark, that ship, with 60 merchantmen from several parts with two convoyers, lye still at Vleckeren,[1] and that at Gottenburgh were some English ships laden with masts and two convoyers. So that now the commissioners of the Admiralty and those of the States General are daily consulting together, what fleet is fit to set forth to sea this winter, and what ships are sufficient to fetch home the fleet at Vleckeren, and to way-lay the English at Gottenburg, and a list is to be brought into the assembly of all such ships as they intend for these exploits. In the meantime, upon the desire of Holland, the Admiralty of Amsterdam are commanded to send 15 or 16 men of war, to lye ready towards the Dogger Sand, there to look for and expect the fleet from the Eastland and the ships with the guns from Denmark, which are expected with the first, according to the advice from the Resident. And just now the Admiralty of Amsterdam have advised their Lordships, that the Eastland fleet of 80 sail and with them the ships with guns, having with them 360 guns, are arrived in the Vlie. So that now it is very probable they will keep out no great fleet this winter, save some ships to cruize to and again in these seas, and they have already discharged 30 men of war, which were hired vessels, and if they

[1] *i.e.* Vlecker.

could get seamen enough together after they were discharged, they would discharge near their whole fleet for this winter, but for that reason chiefly, they will keep abroad some part of their fleet.

In the meantime they equip very vigorously against the spring, being much encouraged by the arrival of their fleets this latter end of the year, and especially these last 80 with the guns. Thirty of their new frigats are built and will be equipped and fitted against February. They have ordered 30 other new ships to be built forthwith, and to be set on the stocks before the winter begins, and all utmost diligence is used to form this war against England in a better manner than heretofore, wherein their intention is to settle a constant fleet of 100 sail of ships of war as a standing body, which they hope to have in readiness in February or March next, besides two other squadrons to convoy their merchantmen, and they are contriving a constant maintenance for them. Only the States of Overyssel have advised their Lordships, that they shall not be able to raise their share towards the sea equipage so speedily as they hoped, and desire to be excused and that it may not be ill taken.

The Hague,
  Nov. $\frac{18}{28}$th.

1292. *Nov.* $\frac{18}{28}$, *1653.—MONCK TO A.C.*

[S.P. 18, xli, 162.]

Gent^n.—Yours of the 17th instant I received with the copy of a letter from Commander Willoughby then enclosed, and have appointed the Laurel, Mathias, and Martin to ply between Dungeness and to the westward of Boulogne, who set sail accordingly yesterday in the afternoon, and have also dispatched a letter to Commander Willoughby with a blank order for him to appoint any frigate as he shall think fit to ply in that station in lieu of the Mathias, who is then to sail to Ellen Road and follow Captain Howet's order, and as to yours of yesterday's date, I have also designed four frigates, now at Harwich, viz., Newcastle, Constant Warwick, Mermaid and Assurance to ply between the Dogger Bank and the Riff, supposing it to be the best place to answer the service expected from them.

According to your order I shall also issue commissions to Captain Goodson to command the George and Captain Jordan the Triumph withal, desiring that Captain Hill may be removed into the Unicorn, Captain Smith into the Worcester, and Captain Allen into the Advice, if you shall think fit, also the lieutenant of this ship to be commander of the Princess Mary (till the launching of the new frigates), whose honesty as well as ability will gain your consent for his remove into one of them of considerable force.

I was yesterday informed by John Poortmans that you have received order from the Council for payment of the prize money which is to be managed by him though he had business enough before, yet (in regard it is your desire) he is willing to undergo the trouble thereof, and saith also that you intend my own or partner's hand shall go for receipt of the money, wherein I desire to be excused, considering that if he should miscarry I must be accountable for the same unavoidably, though you intend it not, and therefore I judge that his single receipt will be sufficient if he have instructions to dispose of it, but according to the order of myself and partner. It will be necessary that the money be speedily sent down if you make proclamation thereof, as you

THE LAST WINTER 185

intend, and in order thereunto I shall send up John Poortmans to receive it, except it can be procured and sent down by content, which I had rather should be.

There is Captain Robert Plumby, commander of the Sampson, who is honest and valiant and confirmed by M‍ʳ. Willoughby's recommendation unto me, my desire therefore is that he may be in your eye for command of the frigate now building at Shoreham.

By a letter this day from the Officers of the Ordnance, I understand they have received your order to take security from all gunners to give in a faithful account of the stores committed to their trust which I do conceive will hardly be practicable, for the security will thereby be engaged to account for such gunners if they should be slain or die otherwise during their employment, and 'tis possible, if not probable, some imposition may be made after their death, which will not be reasonable for the security to answer for: also, if any gunner dies at sea the place must stand void to the prejudice of the service, except the party succeeding do put in security which (if it be had) will hardly be procured there, and therefore do humbly offer as my weak opinion that as special care be taken to place honest men as can be, and to make a particular declaration that any such persons as shall be found to offend by embezzlement, &c., shall undoubtedly suffer death according to the Laws of war, which I conceive will be more terrible than the other.

I am [etc.],

GEORGE MONCK.

Swiftsure, in
the Hope,
the 19ᵗʰ Nov., 1653.

1293. *Nov.* $\frac{1}{2}\frac{9}{0}$, 1653.—*WARRANT BY MONCK*

[S.P. 18, xli, 164.]

Whereas it hath pleased the Lords to destroy and make unserviceable a considerable part of the Dutch fleet which lay before the Texel, so that it's thought necessary to send three or four frigates to annoy the enemy thereabouts, you are, therefore, on sight hereof, wind and weather permitting, to set sail with the ship under your command in company with the Newcastle, Assurance, and Mermaid, and ply between the Dogger Bank and the Riff, or thereabouts to intercept all such Dutch merchant ships daily expected from the East country laden with masts, hemp pitch and tar, observing such instructions and directions as you shall receive from Captain Nathaniel Cobham, commander of the Newcastle frigate, till further order, and this shall be your warrant given under my hand and seal on board the Swiftsure, 19th November, 1653.

GEORGE MONCK.

To Captain Richard Potter,
commander of the Constant Warwick.
The like to Captain Philip Holland,
commander of the Assurance.
The like to Captain James Alleson,
commander of the Mermaid. These   a true copy.

1294. $\frac{Nov. 22}{Dec. 2}$, 1653.—*BOURNE TO A.C.*

[S.P. 18, xli, 171.]

Right Hon[ble].,—This morning I received a letter from General Monck with intelligence of the great and immediate appearance of the Lord against the Dutch in the late storm, which is much to be acknowledged of all who wait for him.

And thereupon he hath issued out orders to

the Newcastle, Assurance, Constant Warwick and Mermaid to ply over and by betwixt the Dogger and the Riff to intercept the Holland ships out of the Sound, etc. The two first are ready to sail, and shall, God willing, to-morrow, proceed accordingly, but the Mermaid sailed hence about a week since, but was 2 days ago in Yarmouth Road, and I have sent to stop her if it come time enough. As for the Constant Warwick she will not be ready this 8 days at soonest to sail, of which I have formerly advised the General, therefore presume he mistook her for the Expedition, which is ready, and thereupon I have given order to her in the room of the Constant Warwick.

The Middleborough is ready all the want is men so likewise others.

The Centurion is careened, and all carpenters' work finished. The Advice is likewise done as to that part except tallowing, which shall be done this week, if the Lord give us reasonable weather, as also the Constant Warwick.

I hope I may with Y^r. Honours' approbation, and without prejudice to the affairs, repair homewards next week, myself and family being not well. I shall at present trouble your Honours no further, being in expectation to receive your command in answer to my last, so crave leave to remain [etc.],
N. BOURNE.

Harwich,
2nd Nov., 1653.

1295. $\frac{Nov.\ 28}{Dec.\ 8}$, 1653.—*MONCK TO A.C.*

[S.P. 18, xli, 182.]

Gentlemen,—I understand that you are in some dispute amongst yourselves whether or no you shall fit out the great ships presently, or towards the spring. I shall make bold to offer my thoughts concerning it. In case you are not assured that we shall have a speedy peace with the Dutch I conceive the service will suffer very much unless they be expedited out for these reasons. First, because you will not get them manned; second, that then the Dutch will get their summer fleet ready before yours, which in case they should, instead of our blocking them up in their harbour we shall be by them blocked up in ours, so that one of the chiefest advantages against them will be for to get out our summer fleet before theirs, and all the objection that I know you have against it is only for cleaning of the ships against the spring; let not that hinder the furtherance of them, for we shall take care to keep them clean, and every way fit for service, if not, lay the blame on us, and do desire, if you are not assured of a peace, that you would settle officers in them, and speedy them forth as soon as you can.

I hope by the latter end of this week we shall, with twenty sail of men of war, sail to the westward, and therefore do desire that you would quicken the victuallers and their instruments for a speedy furnishing of those ships that are here and coming forth of the river, with all things they stand in need of.

Here enclosed is a list of such ships as are now in the Hope, which is all at present from [etc.]

GEORGE MONCK.

Swiftsure in the Hope,
 the 28th Nov., 1653.

(*No list attached.*)

THE LAST WINTER 189

1296. *Dec.* 2nd/12th, 1653.—*PROCEEDINGS OF C.o.S.*

[S.P. 25, lxxii, p. 151.]

Council of State, Friday, Dec. 2, 1653.

That General Blake and General Monck be appointed and commissionated Generals of the Fleet in pursuance of an order of Parliament of this day.

That the Parliament be humbly moved that Major-General Disbrowe and Vice-Admiral Penn may be appointed to be two of the Generals of the Fleet, and that they may be joined in a Commission with General Blake and General Monck, and M^r. Sadler is desired humbly to move the Parliament herein.

That Rear-Admiral Lawson be appointed Vice-Admiral of the Fleet instead of Vice-Admiral Penn.

That Colonel Rob. Blake, Colonel George Monck, Maj.-Genl. Disbrowe, Vice-Admiral William Penn and John Carew, Esq^{rs}. be humbly offered to the Parliament to be of the number of the persons who shall be appointed Commissioners for the Admiralty and Navy.

1297. *Dec.* 3rd/13th, 1653.—*MONCK TO A.C.*

[S.P. 18, xlii, 12.]

Gentlemen,—Having received order from the Council of State this morning that no opportunity might be lost to sail from hence with such ships as are ready, I did forthwith call a Council of War to know their present state, and do find about 20 sail will be ready the 6th instant, if some part of their provisions and stores which they want, be sent down in time, about which I have already writ to the respective officers concerned for their supply, but do desire it may be seconded by you, that so if wind and weather permit, I may set sail accordingly by the time aforementioned.

Since the embargo hath been taken off seamen are very hard to be got, although all care and diligence hath been used to answer that want, and I doubt we shall be forced to sail with 20, 30 and 40 men short to each ship except 4 or 5, which are full manned. I hope some care will be taken that the ships which follow may bring men enough for themselves and us, as well as for those ships at Portsmouth, which I understand there is great want of by a letter from M^r. Willoughby, and in order to that, give me leave to offer that I suppose it would be of some concernment if the masters of merchant ships were enjoined to allot more wages to seamen with them than the State doth, also that care might be taken for their impresting in every seaport town in England by the chief magistrate of such places, and upon notice given I shall take care to send some ships or vessels for their reception.

I am informed by John Poortmans that he hath no order for disposal of the prize money in his hands, which I desire you will send down very speedily by reason of our sudden sailing from this place, and the seamen's expectations thereof being very high. Not more at present but that I am [etc.],

GEORGE MONCK.

Swiftsure, in the Hope,
3 Dec., 1653.

1298. Dec. $\frac{3}{13}$, 1653.—*RUIJTER TO S.G.*

[A.o.H. Translated.]

Noble and Powerful Lords,—I safely received, on the $\frac{1st}{11th}$ Instant, your Lordships' letter of the $\frac{29}{9}$th $\frac{\text{November}}{\text{December}}$, being in effect an answer to mine of the $\frac{22}{2}$nd $\frac{\text{Nov.}}{\text{Dec.}}$, and stating that your Lordships had been pleased to confer upon me the Vice-Admiraltyship of the Province under the direction of your Lordships' Admiralty Board at Amsterdam, and that I, in my letter above referred to, had endeavoured to excuse myself from the acceptance of this office; on which account your Lordships are expecting me in Amsterdam. In reply to which I beg to assure your Lordships that I am most deeply grateful to your Lordships for conferring upon me the said office of Vice-Admiral, the more especially as I am not one who seeks high office, but serve more for love and for the good of our beloved Fatherland, than in any way to seek important positions. Wherefore I beg your Lordships will be pleased to discharge me from the aforesaid office, and permit me to finish my service in the Province of Zealand, where my fixed home is. But, in order to comply with your Lordships' gracious purposes and plans, as soon as I learn your Lordships are to meet again on matters of business, I shall at once repair to Amsterdam without loss of time, and shall endeavour by word of mouth to satisfy your Lordships more at large, and to convince you on this matter.

Herewith, etc., etc.,
(Signed) MICHIEL ADR. RUIJTER.
Middelburg,
the $\frac{5}{15}$th December, 1653.

1299. *Dec. $\frac{16}{26}$th, 1653.*—*INSTRUCTIONS BY GENERALS*

[Sloane MS. 3232, fol. 79.]

Instructions for all commanders in chief of squadrons, for all flag commanders in their divisions, and for all captains of ships at sea, in the service of the Commonwealth.

By Robert Blake, George Moncke, John Disbrowe, and William Penn, Admirals and Generals, of the fleet set forth by authority of the Commonwealth of England, and for defence of the same.

Whereas there are, and may be from time to time, sundry exorbitances and miscarriages amongst sundry persons in the fleet, for restraining whereof General Councils of War cannot be so frequently called as were requisite; for preventing therefore of the same, and for regulating and governing the fleet, in better order for the future, according to the laws of war, and ordinances of the sea, ordained, and established by Parliament of England, we have thought expedient, and do hereby order as followeth.

That the first article of the said laws and ordinances be duly observed by each commander, of and in the fleet, according to the true intent and tenure thereof.

That the chief flag, (or commander of each squadron,) with the assistance of the Council of War of the squadron under his command do fully determine, sentence and punish all offences committed against any and every of the articles of the laws of war, and ordinances of the sea, by any person belonging to any of the ships in his respective squadron, provided that no execution or sentence of loss of life or limb do proceed (if the fact do so deserve) until that we, the Generals, be made acquainted with the crime, (the criminal being still secured) as also with the dispositions against and defences made by the offender, with all circumstances thereon depending, and the same delivered to the judge advocate of the fleet, to be enregistered, and kept upon record. Provided also that no sentence for the cashiering of a captain of any vessel of war of the State's, or in their service, do pass until that we Generals have had information of the whole, and that the proceedings be delivered as abovesaid to be recorded.

That each commander bearing flag, subordinate to the chief commander of any squadron, calling to council with him the commanders of the ships of his division that shall be present, to the number of three at the least, have hereby power to determine, sentence, and punish all offences against any and every of the said laws and ordinances of the sea, that are or shall be committed, within the ship (or any ships of the division) under his command. Provided that no sentence of loss of life or limb, do pass upon any person, or of cashiering of any captain, until we, the Generals, be made acquainted with all circumstances of the proceedings, and likewise provided that no sentence of cashiering any lieutenant, or master of any ship of war of the State's, or in their service shall pass until the chief flag or commander of that whole squadron be informed as aforesaid, and that the information and dispositions be remitted to record, as in the former section is expressed.

And it is hereby likewise ordered, that whensoever any vessels consisting of three ships of war, or more, shall be sent as commanded, towards any guard or station, the commander of that party, shall have, and hereby hath the same power to punish, any manner of crime, or person that is hereby given unto the flag commanders of a division, during the time of their stay abroad.

It is farther ordered that the captain of each particular ship of war, of the State's or in their service, calling to his assistance the lieutenant of the said ship (if any be thereupon allowed) with the master, his mate, clerk of the cheque, gunner, boatswain, and carpenter thereof have hereby power to examine, bring to trial and punishment, any person belonging to the ship whereof he is commander, for any and every offence committed against any of the said laws and ordinances of the sea, or against such orders as have been formerly or shall be made by us for retaining of mariners within board of their respective ships, for the containing of them in their duties whilst aboard, and for the punishing of any who shall attempt to carry them thence without leave first obtained, and this order is farther to extend to the punishing in like manner, of any offence committed on shore, in any place or harbour into which any of the ships that are or shall be in the service of the State, shall be sent, (or may have occasion to put in) by any person of or belonging to any such ship or vessel, as also of any offence committed against any orders already made or hereafter to be made by us, for the prevention of fire, or any other accidental mischance by miscarriage of light, taking tobacco, selling strong water or strong drink within board, or the breach of future orders for the avoiding of mischiefs or inconveniences in the fleet. Provided that no sentence of loss of life or limb do pass, nor the cashiering of any officer having a commission or warrant for his place, but that all such officers be remitted unto the commander of the party (if remote from the fleet) or to the flag commander of that division, or to the next superior commander in that squadron (or if he also be absent) to the chief flag or commander thereof according to the power by us devolved unto every of them in the preceding sections, and that each person within their cognizance respectively may receive sentence, and undergo execution thereof condign to his demerits, reserving the case of loss of life or limb, or cashiering of captains, to our own immediate knowledge.

And it is lastly ordered that according to a former order of 16th May 1653, all commanders of ships of war in the service of the State, do without delay repair on board the flag of the division under which they are ranked, or the chief flag of the squadron, at all such times as a pendant or other signal for a council of war shall be put forth by any of the said flags, upon penalty of forfeiture of one day's pay for the first neglect, and the like for the second, unless cause allowable be shown to the contrary (in which case they are to send the officer nearest them in place or command [sic] to execute their absence) and upon refusal of payment to be taken into custody by the Marshall General of the fleet, until the same be made, and the same person offending a third time, to be presented and proceeded against at the next General Council of war, as a contemner of order and discipline, given under our hands and seals of anchor on board the Swiftsure this 16th day of December 1653.

GEORGE MONCKE,
WM. PENN.

1300. Dec. $\frac{16}{26}$th, 1653.—*MONCK TO C.o.S.*

[Thurloe, S.P. i. 636.]

Rt. Honourable,—Since my departure from the Hope, in obedience to your commands, with such ships as were then ready for service, on the 12th instant it was resolved at a council of war,

that the fleet should ply between the Isle of Wight
and Beachy, and over upon the coast of France,
so near as with safety we might, in hopes to have
met with those Dutch merchants' ships with their
convoy of 30 men-of-war, whom we expected till
now, supposing they would have come through
the Channel this last eastwardly wind; but
hearing nothing of their motion, and the wind
being now westwardly, it was yesterday thought
fit, with advize of the respective commanders in
the fleet, that we should sail for Ellen Road, and
there to ride in a ready posture upon any intelligence we shall receive of the enemy's motion:
and in order thereunto have appointed several
scouts for discovery of any fleet, as interception
of any vessels they may meet withal in enmity
with this Commonwealth. The enclosed [1] is a list
of what ships are now in a body, which I humbly
present you with, and remain,

  Your Lordship's most humble servant,
        Geo. Monck.

Swiftsure, at an anchor off the Culver Cliffs. 16 Dec. 1653.

1301. *Dec.* $\frac{16}{26}$*th*, 1653.—*POORTMANS TO BLACKBORNE*

[S.P. 18, lxii. 102.]

Sir,—After the letters coming herewith were
sealed I received this further in command from
the General that Colonel Whyte might be sent
down to be advised with about a more orderly
way of gunning the fleet for the future.

I desire you will please to send me some
instructions for stewards and cheques, about 100

---

[1] Not given in the Thurloe papers, but *cf.* No. 1303.

of each, for I want them very much, there being many persons entrusted with these employments which have no instructions at all.

Y^r. most affectionate friend and servant,
JOHN POORTMANS.

Swiftsure,
  16 Dec. 1653,
    at the back of the Culverts.

1302. *Dec. $\frac{17}{27}$th*, 1653.—*ORDER BY THE GENERALS*

[S.P. 18, xlii. 80.]

On board the Swiftsure, 17 December 1653.

By the R^t. Hon^{bles}. Robert Blake, George Monck, John Disbrow, and Wm. Penn, Admirals and Generals of the Fleet of the Commonwealth of England.

For the future prevention of abuses, and those sad and lamentable events which have formerly and likewise lately happened by unresistable accidents of implacable fire to several vessels of the Navy and others, so far as may stand with the providence and mercy of Almighty God towards the fleet entrusted to our charge and conduct set forth by authority of Parliament of the Commonwealth of England for the defence thereof. It is hereby strictly ordered as followeth :

That no person of or in the fleet presume (after the watch is set) to have or keep any candles lighted between the decks or in any other part of this or any other vessel in service of the Commonwealth except such as are necessarily to be employed about the ship's use, and those to be carried in lanthorns only ; and that none but such be used in hold of this or any other vessel under pain of severe punishment, and hereof the lieutenant, the master, his mates, the quartermasters, boatswain and mates, with the yeomen of each vessel are to take especial care, and the Marshall General, with his deputies (in their several stations) are to take the offenders into immediate custody until censure do pass.

That no tobacco be taken between the decks of this or any other vessel of war, or in hold, or in the cabins of the same, under pain as aforesaid, and that all those mentioned in the former articles have a vigilant eye thereunto, and do endeavour to bring all delinquents to condign censure.

That no strong water or other strong drink be sold within board of this or any other vessel in the service, whereby mariners may be intoxicated, and rendered uncapable of, and refractory to, duty, besides manifold mischances and mischiefs ensuing thereupon; and the breach hereof to be under most severe censure and punishment.

That copies hereof be by the Judge Advocate delivered and dispersed through the several ships present, the same to be fastened in some convenient place, with the captain's name subscribed, whereby due notice may be taken of the premises.

Signed by their Honours' order,
JNO. FOWLER,
Judge Advocate.

Endorsed:
For preventing of fire in ships of the fleet.

1303. Dec. 17/27th, 1653.—*A LIST OF THE WINTER GUARD;* [1] *with the Commanders' Names, Number of Men and Guns and in what Staćon.* The 17th of December 1653

Ships now in Ellence Road

Ships' Names	Men	Guns	Commanders
Swiftsure	400	64	—
Fairefax	300	56	John Lawson
Unicorn	300	56	William Goodson
Marston Moor	—	—	John Bourne
Hanniball	180	44	William Haddock
Katherine	[130]	[36]	[Willoughby Harman]
Paule	120	30	Anth. Spatchurst
Halfemoon	150	36	Barthol. Ketcher
Reserve	180	44	Robert Clarke
Industry	100	32	Shadrack Blake
Worcester	220	56	William Hill
Pellican	180	42	William Whitchorn
Midleburgh	120	32	William Godfrey
Speaker	300	54	Samuell Howett
Ruby	180	44	Edmond Courtis
Pellican prize	[120]	[34]	John Simonds
Faulcon	[80]	[28]	Barthol. Yates
Heartease	150	36	Thomas Wright
Rosebush	120	34	Vallnit Tatnell

Ships at Portsmouth

	Men	Guns	Commanders
Dolphin	120	34	—
Guinia	[150]	34	—
Discovery	[180]	[40]	Thomas Marriot
Hound	120	36	Jonathan Hide
Sattisfaction	100	30	Michell Hutton
Great Charrity	180	44	James Terry
Saphire	140	38	Nicho. Heaton

[1] It will be noted that the men and guns do not always tally with those given in No. 1229. Figures and names in square brackets have been supplied from that list.

THE LAST WINTER

Ships plying between the Lizard and Scilly

Ships' Names	Men	Guns	Commanders
Bristoll	200	50	Roger Martin
Assistance	180	40	Willi. Crispin
Hampsheer	180	40	Robert Blake
Elias	140	36	John Best
Hopewell pink	—	—	—
Nonesuch	170	40	Thomas Penrose

Ships now in the River

Ships' Names	Men	Guns	Commanders
Taunton	—	—	Rich[d]. Lyons
Tyger	170	40	Gabr[ll]. Saunders
Marmaduke	160	42	John Grove
Raven	140	38	John Taylor
Black Raven	150	38	Samu[ll]. Dickerson
Convert	120	32	Isaiah Blowfeild
Mary Rose	—	—	Jeffery Dare
Litle Presidn[t].	[80]	[12]	Thomas Sparling
Bryar	90	24	Robert Samsom

Ships at Chatham

Ships' Names	Men	Guns	Commanders
Tryumph	350	60	—
George	350	64	—
Andrew	360	60	—
Lyon	220	50	John Lambert
Thomas and Lucy	125	34	Andrew Rand
Sophia	160	38	Robert Kerby
Cock	140	36	Garrett
Welcom	200	40	Thomas Bennett
Rich[d]. and Martha	180	46	Eustace Smith
Westergate	140	34	Samuell Hankes
Hector	100	28	John Smith
Litle Charrity	150	38	John Gifferyes
Mathias	220	52	Thomas White
Lawrell	200	50	Rich[d]. Newbery
Kentish	180	50	Edw. Witheridge
Expedition	140	32	Thomas Vollis

Ships plying between Isle of Wight and Cape Barffler

Ships' Names	Men	Guns	Commanders
Essex	250	56	Robert Saunders
Foresight	180	42	Rich[d]. Staynor
Dyamond	180	42	John Hermon
Portsmouth	170	42	Joseph Cubitt

THE LAST WINTER

Ships in the Hope

Ships' Names	Men	Guns	Commanders
Parrogan	300	56	George Dakins
Dragon	160	38	John Seaman
Tulip	120	32	Clarke

Ships now at Harwich

Convertine	220	44	John Hayward
Recovery	80	24	Roberthay (sic) Tubb
Maligoe Mch^t.	140	36	Henry Collins

Ships on the Scotch Coast

Vanity	—	—	—
Advantage	100	26	Edward Thomson
Primrose	90	26	John Sherwin
Dutchess	90	24	Edm. Smith
Sunn	40	16	--
Greyhound	90	20	--

Ships gone for Gottenbergh

Phenix	180	44	Nicholas Foster
Elizabeth	180	42	Christoph^r. Ming
Mary Prize	120	37	Henry Maddison
Guift	130	34	Edward Barret

Ships on the Coast of Holland

Centurian	200	42	Robert Nixon
Newcastle	160	40	Nathan Cobham
Mermayd	100	26	James Ableson
Advice	180	42	Francis Allen
Constn. Warwick	120	30	Rich^d. Potter
Assurance	160	36	Phillip Holland

Ships on the Coast of Ireland

Fortune	100	32	—
Mayflower	130	34	—
Parradox	60	14	--
Cignett	80	22	--
Nightingall	100	16	John Humpheryes
Fox	90	22	Robert Vessey
Cardiffe	130	36	Robt. Story

Ships for guard of the Collier trade

Ships' Names	Men	Guns	Commanders
Sparrow	60	12	John Whitwang
Swann	80	22	Thomas Wilks
Xth Whelpe	—	—	—
Society	140	44	Nicholas Lucas
Adventure frigg^t.	160	40	Peter Foot
Adventure Mechn^t.	160	38	Joseph Taylor
Armes of Holland	150	36	Robert Coleman
Falmouth	120	30	Robert Mill
Red Hart Pink	30	6	Southerne
Gr^t. President	100	44	Francis Parks

Ships in the Downes

Martin	90	14	William Vessey
Nonesuch	40	8	James Ody
Douke	90	12	Robert Clarke
Plover	100	26	—

Ships at Plymouth

Portland	170	38	Edward Blagg
Sampson	120	28	Robert Plumly

1304.   *Dec. 26th 1653*
        Jan. 5th, 1654.—REPORT OF FLEET
        COMMITTEE

[S.P. 18, xlii. 64.]

Memorandum

In order to the timely providing of a considerable fleet for this next summer's expedition in case the war with the Dutch continue, it is humbly offered :

(1) That there be for a main body 130 sail, thirty whereof it is supposed will be continually absent as employed for convoy of prizes, washing, tallowing, and refitting, with other contingencies incident to so great a body.

THE LAST WINTER

(2) To be designed for the Channel and Land's End 12.
(3) For Ireland, 6.
(4) For Scotland, 6.
(5) For the back of Scotland to intercept trade, 12.
(6) For the guard of the collier trade, 4.
(7) That the main body with the rest be ready by the latter end of March, but those appointed for the back of Scotland should be in their station by that time.
(8) That a large magazine of victuals, masts and all other stores be timely provided at Harwich.
(9) That so large a provision of all sorts of ammunition, with masts and cordage be provided, as after an engagement we be not too long without recruits, for want whereof the service may be much prejudiced.
(10) That what merchant ships shall be taken into the service may be of the bigger sort and best gunned, and that we may have the favour to present captains for them, which we suppose may conduce to the good of the service.
(11) That there be nine fireships, one for each flag.

Endorsed:
Memo^d. for the Fleet brought by Col. Clerk and Lt.-Col. Kelsey.

1305. $\frac{Dec. 29th, 1653}{Jan. 8th, 1654}$.—*MONK AND PENN TO GENERALS.*

[S.P. 18, xlii. 73.]

Gentlemen,—By a letter from General Disbrowe of the 26th instant, we have intelligence that there are a considerable number of Dutch merchant ships homewards bound from several ports in St. Martin's Island, which concurs with what is come to our knowledge, and do suppose this last eastwardly wind hath brought them into the westwardly winds' way, and do hope they will not escape the party of frigates under the command of Captain Bourne, now plying between the Isle of Wight and Cape Barfleur, and several other frigates appointed to ply almost at every headland, and over upon the coast of France, as opportunity gives leave, so that all our nimble frigates are now abroad, and we apprehend will better answer the service than by a main body in the Channel this winter, as you are sensible of, yet we have ordered Captain Bourne to endeavour an embodying with us upon the first coming up of an eastwardly wind, it being our intentions then to sail from hence with the main body and ply in that station, or where else may most conduce to the better intercepting of any ships that wind may bring from the coast of Holland.

There are five prizes lately taken by our frigates which came from Nantes, four whereof are in this road, the other is sent into Dover by the Kentish; the master of one of them informs us that he came from Nantes about 12 days since, where were no more in the river than those five which are now taken,

We are,
Y^r. very affectionate friends and servants,

GEORGE MONCK,
WM. PENN.

Swiftsure in
  Stokes Bay, the 29th
    Decr. 1653.

The Vice Admiral informing us that you are satisfied concerning Captain Matham, and that you are willing he should be employed in the service, we do desire you will signify so much in writing by your next, and we shall take care of him the first vacancy.

Endorsed :
For the Rt. Honᵇˡᵉ. the Generals of the Fleet at Whitehall.

1306. *Dec. 30th, 1653 / Jan. 9th, 1654*.—*N.C. TO A.C.*
[S.P. 18, xlii, 74.]

Right Honourable,—Whereas the sad news of the two ships' loss, which brought 54 masts from New England not to be paralleled, is come to our knowledge, we think fit to signify our earnest desire that your Honours would write effectually to the Generals to cause the captains concerned to be strictly examined and dealt withal, according as the crime shall be found, for the terror of others ; the rather for that we have credible information they were taken but 14 leagues from the Lands End, and were brought quite through the Channel to Flushing, were 6 days in their passage, saw no frigates of ours, and the ships that took them lying one day feasting off of Dungeness.[1]

We are according to your direction hastening what we may the ships bound for New England upon that account, wherein we are very sensible of how much concernment to the public service their speedy despatch both here and there is, especially as the state of affairs are now in our view. You were formerly acquainted by some of us of a necessity of sending a supply of goods thither for the lading of these ships, and of letters of credit to be given to the agents employed in the service there for drawing bills of exchange upon the Treasurer in case of need, and we had your verbal assent to what was propounded, upon which we shall and do continue to act that the service may not suffer by delays, yet we desire an order under your hands (as is usual in such cases) empowering us to act herein both in sending goods, and otherwise as the necessity of the service may require, wherein we shall use our best endeavours in husbanding what is committed to us to the most advantage.

We remain at y^r. Honour's commands,

E. HOPKINS,
ROB. THOMSON.

Navy Office,
30 Dec. 1653.

1307 (undated).—T. TAYLOR TO A.C.

[S.P. 18, xlii. 114.]

To the Right Honble. the Commissioners for managing the affairs of the Admiralty and Navy.

The humble petition and remonstrance of Thomas Taylor, Gunner of the Sovereign,

Humbly Sheweth—

That your petitioner having (within these few days by your Honours' favour and justice) had a copy of a paper given into y^r. Honours by Captain Read, formerly commander of the said ship, containing several examinations taken before him in nature of a charge against the petitioner, wherein he humbly conceived these two particulars are materially suggested:

(1) The want of powder during part of the engagement.

(2) That the Sovereign's guns reached not so far as the Dutch ordnance did.

To the first, the petitioner affirms he was as well provided of all materials incident to his charge and office as any ship in the fleet, having in a readiness between 2 and 3000 cartridges filled and fitted to the sundry natures of the guns, though the captain is pleased to name a far lesser number, and to mistake in other particulars in that paper. And he professeth in the providence of God he used his best and utmost endeavour with all faithfulness to serve the State in his place, was ignorant of, and much grieved for the neglect of his yeoman, and believes the reason why he made demur to deliver out the powder was in regard the boys came down without the cases, for want whereof y^r. Honours may conjecture how great danger there was to carry to and again in canvas or paper, cartridges among so many lighted matches, and in so great a hurry; so that the petitioner hopes and humbly prays y^r. Honours will not lay the blame of his yeoman's miscarriage upon him, when it was not at that part in his power to prevent it, being himself busied in making shot out of a cannon of 7 inches, whereby the mainmast of the Dutch Rear Admiral was shot by the board, and by that means was taken by our fleet.

As to the 2nd particular, it is conferred that some guns from the Dutch fleet shot farther than the Sovereign's, which y^r. petitioner humbly conceives to be for these 3 reasons :

(1) In that the Dutch allow a greater quantity of powder.

(2) For that they usually carry in their quarter

(whereas we perceived they slung their shot further) one or more of their best long guns, whereas ours are our chase pieces.

(3) But the most evident cause at that time was that by reason that the Sovereign then was at least a mile and a half to leeward, and therefore had not the advantage to carry a shot by a quarter part of the way with that to windward.

The premisses considered, your petitioner most humbly prays that if y^r. Honours shall not be satisfied with what is herein offered, y^r. Hon^{rs}. would be favourably pleased to appoint him a time of hearing, for which he hath waited there 6 months that so by y^r. Honour's favour and justice he may be restored to his employment, wherein he shall endeavour to do the Commonwealth faithful service.

And y^r. petitioner as ever bound shall pray, &c.

THOMAS TAYLOR.

1308. *Jan.* $\frac{2nd}{12th}$, 1654.—*MYNGS TO A.C.*

[S.P. 18, lxv. 1.]

Honble.,—In pursuance of your orders for the attendance of my Lord Ambassador Whitlocke the 15th November, we arrived at Gottenburg. Some foul weather. Parted company the day before, but through mercy are well arrived. My Lord and his retinue are well.

The 23rd my Lord set forward from Gottenburg to the Court. Contrary winds detained us until the 22nd December, we attempt[ed] once or twice to sail, but were forced in again : our ship's company hath been very sickly, above ninety men sick at a time, five died. At present, generally in a recovering condition. My Lord sent his packet by the Phœnix, who got out of port a day before us, the wind taking us short, as we were going out [of] harbour. Under the Scaw we met with three Hollands men of war, and some eight or nine merchant men with them. We fired some guns upon them, but our sickly condition, our enemy's odds, and a lee shore, were the reasons upon which we left them. A day or two after came up with the Phœnix who had been in fight with a Hollands man of war [1]—he had four men killed, eleven wounded and lost his bowsprit—the further particulars y^r. Hon^{our}. may expect from the next whom some two days since we left at an anchor thwart of these sands; we keeping under sail fetched in with Winterton where anchored under the stress of a southerly storm way over which forced him from his anchor to sea again. I shall use all advantages on our way to Portsmouth, our provision drawing towards an end.

      Y^r. Honour's humble servant,
           Ch. Myngs.

Yarmouth Roads,
 this 2nd January 1653.

1309. *Jan.* $\frac{3}{13}$, *1654.—MONCK AND PENN TO A.C.*

[S.P. 18, lxv. 3.]

Gentlemen,—We are now upon sailing, though this wind be but little to the eastward of the north, intending to ply in the station we formerly acquainted you with.

Several times we have desired that provision might be made for such sick and wounded men

[1] *Cf.* No. 1310.

as should be sent to Portsmouth, Gosport or the Isle of Wight, and you have informed us that order was already given thereon, which doth not yet appear, for Mr. Willoughby tells us that he knows not which way the quarters of those sick men already sent ashore will be paid. We pray that some speedy course may be taken for payment of what money shall grow due upon that account, or else the service will be slighted, and poor men suffer very much, of which we have had some experience already.

Hearing nothing of our commissions as yet, we cannot but remind you of them, that one of your number being of the Council will move effectually therein.

We are,
   Y^r. very affec^{ate}. friends and servants,
      GEORGE MONCK,
      WILL$^M.$ PENN.

Swiftsure,
near the Horse,
the 3rd Jany. 1653.

Since the writing hereof we have fallen down to Ellens Point, where we met with the Great President, Tiger, Tulip, Princess Mary, Recovery merchant, and Taunton.

1310. *Jan.* $\frac{3}{13}$, 1654.—*FOSTER TO A.C.*

[S.P. 18, lxv. 6.]

Honourable Gentlemen,—In order to a compliance with orders received from the Generals of the Fleet, enjoyning me to acquaint your Honours with my proceedings whilst apart from them, I humbly spread before you the dispensations of Providence towards us this present voyage, which hath been as followeth, viz.:

THE LAST WINTER

Having received on board the Lord Whitelock (Ambassador Extraordinary for Sweden) with his retinue and such goods as his Lordship was pleased to send on board, we set sail from the Hope the 6th November 1653, in company with the Elizabeth frigate, and such other ships and vessels as were appointed to attend the said Lord.

The seventh (being Monday about 8 at night the smack appointed to attend the said Lord Ambassador stood in for our own shore, and left us.

The 15th following, we landed his Lordship in the City of Gottenburg, where he was honourably received by the Governor and magistrates of that place.

The 30th, following, his Lordship began his voyage towards Stockholm, with rainy, blustering weather. The 3rd of December the wind came to the north and east. The Phœnix and Elizabeth frigates weighed anchor, and went to sea, the rest with the mast laden ships being then not ready to sail. The 4th ensuing, the wind came to the west-nor-west (a storm) which forced us room for Gottenburg again.

The 20th, following, the wind came to the S.E. (large enough to lead it out of that port); our men falling sick, provisions spending, and the time of great frosts approaching, there appeared a very great necessity to hasten to sea, for being there we could get home with winds that would keep us in that place; betimes in the morning we hastened to sail, the Elizabeth and the rest seeming to do the like. Being got to the sea, the wind came to the S.S.E. and blew very hard with much snow, which caused thick weather. We made what sail we could to fetch over upon the Jutish coast, which we did, and at 4 o clock anchored in ten fathom water. Betwixt 6 and 7 at night the wind came to the south-south-west with clear weather, at which time we see the land, and betwixt us and that a fleet of ships.

The 21st in the morning betimes we weighed anchor, and getting the weather gauge of them, endeavoured to discover what men of war were amongst them, and see only one ship of countenance, and a private man of war of eight guns, the fleet being Hollanders come from the Sound and seventy and two sail in number, some having six, some four, and others two guns apiece. Upon the discovery of our firing some guns amongst them, cut their cables and run towards the Sound. Before they got clear we boarded and manned three of them, clearly perceiving that if we took none before engaging their men of war, they would all escape whilst we were engaged, not doubting in the least (in the strength of the Lord) to be able enough to deal with them, I commanded the prizes to keep to windward of us, and about eight o'clock engaged them. After the passing of two broadsides the private man of war run after their fleet. We continued the dispute till 4 in the afternoon (all which time we passed broad sides, close board and board as fast as we could tack our ships). The enemy then run towards his fleet, we pursued him, and passing longst, gave him a broadside, and running out ahead of him, tacked upon him again, and gave him another broadside, each close board and board, we tacked again intending to board him, but ere we got up with him night came on and having our bowsprit shot by the board, our main and foremast dangerously shot through and through and scarce a shroud whole upon them, our hull being much shot, our best and small bower anchors shot in pieces, four of our men slain and eleven wounded. Being in an enemy's country and none to assist us, not knowing what men of war we might (possibly) meet withal, nor what weather might ensue—we pursued him into 6 fathom water (off the shore) his ship being all along upon the careen, he continued firing off some guns as he fled towards his fleet. By which (as also by his most exceedingly shattered sides) we judged him in a sinking condition, and by firing of guns called to his fleet for boats to save his men, who were about 4 leagues off at an anchor under an island. During this day's engagement there hath stood upon the shore about four hundred horse and foot who have had the perfect view of us all the day. The best gun we have in the Phœnix carries but 18 pound iron, we received shot from the enemy of thirty and six pound weight. The dispute (and with it the day) being ended, we stood with our prizes and being in this condition durst not expose ourselves to sea till we had strengthened our masts, and spliced our rigging which was our work all this night.

At four in the morning we weighed anchor the wind being then at east, we endeavoured to double it about the Scaw, which then bore north north east from us, the wind forthwith veered to the north north east. We continued plying to windward all the day, but our prizes did little good of it. About 3 in the afternoon three Hollands men of war (two of them very great ships) being come from Holland to convoy their fleet, came right before the wind upon us. We, seeing that, bore to our prizes, and seeing no hopes left to preserve them, took out all our men. I commanded to fire them, but our men being in such a strait, and having so little time, the enemy hastening upon us, they omitted it, by the time all our men are on board the enemy is all close up with us. They fired at us and we at them (unanimously resolving to sink or burn rather than to yield or call for quarter).

The two first shot they made (that raked us) the one shot the chain of our foreyard in pieces, and the other two-thirds of our maintopmasthead above the bearing.

They seeing us so disabled pressed exceedingly to get on board us—we bore what sail we could upon our maimed masts, and fighting through them, in one hour's time got without shot of them. They seeing we outstripped them so far after one hour's pursuit, bore to the prizes, who by this time were upon or near the shore, our men having cut away all their anchors, leaving them in the bottom of the Bay.

The 22nd, about 2 in the morning a Hollands man of war stood across our fore-foot, close to windward of us, standing over from the coast of Norway. At 8 in the morning the wind came fair for England, we bore away to sea. The 25th we came up with our own ships, come from Gottenburg (the morning after we had fought the enemy), having seen them two days before. But not knowing them to be our ships, stood not with them till our ship was refitted in the best manner we could. Captain Mings, in the Elizabeth, sent his boat on board and his Lieutenant, to know our wants, we both conclude to stay by our mast-laden ships till upon our own coast. But the 27th about 8 in the night a very violent storm running to the north northeast (as much wind as we could spoon [1] before it) we lost sight of them, but doubt not of their speedy safe arrival, there being no fear of their falling with any of the enemy.

[1] Spound.

In regard (by reason of southerly winds) we were put to the westward; had the Lord been pleased to have ordered the Elizabeth to have come out with us (which it seems was prevented by the so sudden shifting of the wind) we had undoubtedly destroyed that whole fleet.

I am sorry the Commonwealth is not bettered by those prizes, which was impossible for me to preserve, but am glad the enemy hath sustained so much damage by one small frigate.

The Swedes at Gottenburg report the King of Denmark is much troubled that he affronted our nation by their ships being stayed, and blames evil counsel for it. De Witt (when last in the Sound) endeavoured to comfort him with a cordial of their great victory obtained against us at sea, giving him a list of 22 sail of our ships sunk, and eight taken, boasting much of their still putting us to flight, but the King's own subjects is able to inform him that the Hollanders, and not we, are still the flying party, and that one day our small frigate fought and routed their fleet and men of war, and the next day made her way (the Lord helping us) through three of their ships coming to avenge the quarrel, the least of which (as to countenance) exceeded the Phœnix.

I desire and hope the Lord will help me to lay to heart this his so eminent appearings on the behalf of our nation, and by such weak means to make England a terror to other nations, by a mere act of his especial providence in remote corners of the world in such a manner as I want words to express.

The Lord Ambassador Whitlock is said to arrive in Upsall, four Swedes' miles from Stockholm, the 24th of December, when he is to have his audiences. Being (by reason of southerly winds) prevented from complying with the General's order (at present) being in Ousely Bay, I have sent to Major Bourne the condition of the frigate, and dimensions of our maimed masts, considering if I go for Portsmouth (according to orders received at my going to sea) and there not being masts to refit us, some time might be lost. According to his orders or advice, I shall, God willing, proceed.

In the interim, humbly craving your Honours' excuse for my prolixity.

I remain [&c.],
NICHOLAS FOSTER.

Phœnix frigate
this 3rd Jany. 1653.

Postscript,—The skippers of the ships (once in our possession) is now with their people on board the Phœnix.

Endorsed:
Captain Foster, from the Phœnix in Ousley Bay.

1311. *Jan.* $\frac{5}{15}$, 1654.—LETTER OF INTELLIGENCE FROM THE HAGUE

[Thurloe S.P., ii. 7.]

A great storm lately happened in the port of Texel, wherein about 16 ships perished, one of which of the East Indies, with above 200 men in her, three other ships of war and all the rest merchant-men.

Before the said port there was seen lately a squadron of 16 English ships of war, but in this season it is not possible for them to subsist upon that coast.

Jan. 5/15, 1654.

1312. *Jan.* $\frac{5}{15}$, *1654.—DISBROWE AND BLAKE TO THE PROTECTOR*

[Thurloe S.P., ii. 9.]

May it please your Highness,—Two of the Lords Deputies, Newport and Beverning, have this day been at the Lady Ashley, near Maidstone and returned about 6 o'clock in the evening, since which time Colonel Doleman hath been with us, and acquaints us that all is agreed unto by the Deputies, and that so much hath been signified by them in a letter to your Highness, that they doubt not but a confirmation will be sent from their masters by the same frigott that wafts them over. We replied we could not order her to stay any time upon that coast, without your Highness' directions and therefore asked him, whether any such desire had been represented from them in their letter, or any answer returned thereunto? He told us, there was not: so that we forbear any giving such orders, unless we receive your Highness' pleasure therein. We understand by Doleman, that they intend to go on board to-morrow. The Amity being in the Hope, we have appointed her to receive them in and transport them for Holland, which they seem rather to accept of than the Paragon, she drawing less water. We intend to tarry here most parts of to-morrow and shall be ready to receive any commands from your Highness, which shall be observed by,

Your Highness' most humble, faithful servants,
JOHN DISBROWE,
ROBERT BLAKE.

Gravesend, Jan. 5/15. 1654.

1313. *Jan.* 16/26, 1654.—*MONCK AND PENN TO GENERALS*

[S.P. 18, lxxviii. 26.]

Gentlemen,—There being little hopes of any agreement with the Dutch, we do desire that what we acquainted you with in relation to a general embargo may not be laid aside, for the great ships with the new frigates and merchant ships intended for strengthening the next summer's fleet will take up 16,000 men besides those ships already here, which are but poorly manned, a list of which merchant ships we send you herewith enclosed, conceiving them to be the most serviceable and fittest to be entertained; they exceed the number intended by four, but I suppose that some of them are not at home, which will take away the overplus.

We have appointed Mr. Pointer, now Cheque of this ship to be Cheque of the Sovereign, and Mr. Hedges, now Master of the Marston Moor to be Gunner of her, also Mr. Bodham to be Cheque of the great frigate at Woolwich, which we thought necessary to acquaint you with that there might be no interfering. Soon after the departure of Lieutenant Rockwell from hence we did appoint another to be Lieutenant of the Kentish in his room, supposing he could not well return under a month's time, so far as we could judge of the ground of his being sent for up, and the ship being appointed to sea, it was thought the more necessary but not with any intention that he should be a loser by it, wherefore we desire he may be appointed Lieutenant to one of the 3ᵈ ranked frigates now a-building, or else to one of the great ships which you shall think fit.

Had not the wind and weather been uncertain

since our last, we had been at sea; however, it is intended the first eastwardly wind to prosecute our former resolutions, not having more at present but to assure you that we are

Yours, &c.,
GEORGE MONCK,
WM. PENN.

Swiftsure in
Ellen Road,
the 6 Jany. 1653.

For the R*t*. Hon*ble*. the Generals of the Fleet at Whitehall.

1314. *Jan.* $\frac{8}{9}$, 1654.—*PENN TO A.C.*

[S.P. 18, lxxviii. 37.]

Gentlemen,—I hope that General Monck is with you ere this, from whom you will receive a full account of the state of affairs here to the day he went away, since which there hath little occurred worth your knowledge, only that the Centurion came into the fleet yesterday, whom I have ordered to ply between the Isle of Wight and Cape Barfleur, in company with the Worcester and 6 frigates more, already in that station, and hope in two or three days' time to make them up twelve. Here is also the Mary Rose and Nightingale; the latter, being very defective, I have ordered into Portsmouth harbour, likewise the Elizabeth and Nonsuch frigates which must be refitted, but the tides abating, I have ordered them to take in a month's victuals to keep them out till the next spring, in regard it will be lost time to send them into harbour till that time.

Not more at present but that I am, &c.,
WM. PENN.

Swiftsure in
Ellen Road,
the 9th Jany. 1653.

1315. *Jan.* 18/28, 1654.—*POORTMANS TO BLACKBORNE*

[S.P. 18, lxxviii. 103.]

Dear Sir,—After long riding here and in Stokes Bay the wind is come about to the N.N.E., where 'tis supposed it will settle for some time, so that it is thought necessary the fleet should sail, which we are now about to do, and intend to ply in the same station which you have been already acquainted with, or where else may most conduce to answer the service.

I pray forget not to send down some printed instructions for clerks and stewards with laws marshal and encouragements for the seamen by the Ports[mouth] waggon this week, also a copy of the Order to the Commissioners of the Navy expressing what each officer of a ship shall receive during their continuance in Petty Warrant; Captain Bourne also, after his service presented, desires he may not be forgotten as to his extra allowance while he was the General's Captain. My humble service to the Generals, and in particular to General Monck, also to Captain Kelsey, and my kind respects to my brother Creed, which is all at present, but commending you to the good hand of the Lord,

I remain, &c.,
JOHN POORTMANS.

Swiftsure in
Ellen Road,
the 16 of the 11 month 1653.

Pray be not unmindful of the chirurgeons I formerly writ of, here is great want of them.

1316. *Jan.* 30/30, 1654.—*PENN TO THE
GENERALS*

[S.P. 18, lxxviii. 138.]

Gentlemen,—Since my last, which gave you an account of our sailing from Ellen Road, we have plied in our appointed station between the Isle of Wight and Cape Barfleur, the wind having been for the most part to the northward of the east, and moderate weather. Little observable hath occurred, save only this that the Diamond frigate hath forced on shore on the French side a vessel which came from Newhaven,[1] where it is supposed she is bilged.

The Expedition also hath brought in a small vessel called the Hope of Camphire in Zealand bound for Bordeaux ; she is light, having only a few deal boards, besides ballast, in her.

I have appointed her to ride at the Spithead till further order. We have also met with several Hamburgers and Lubeckers come from Dunkirk, being light, they were most of them bound for Rochelle and Nantes. The Ruby, one of the squadron under the command of Captain Hill of the Worcester, did accidentally run on board a Virginiaman and sunk her, but 'tis supposed none were drowned except one.

If the wind continue eastwardly, as now it is, and the weather moderate, whereby the service may be answered to keep sea with such a body as this is, I shall continue in this station for aught I know to the contrary at present, and come within sight of the French shore once a day, as we have done hitherto for the most part, but have

[1] *I.e.* Havre.

a party of frigates lying so close under the shore as with safety they may.

Not more at present but that I am, &c.,

WM. PENN.

Swiftsure,
Cape de Hogue
bearing S.S.W. of us
about 6 leagues off,
the 20th January 1653.

This letter should have been sent last night according to its date, but being deprived of the opportunity, and the wind coming about to the S.S.E. hath occasioned the stay of it till our arrival here, whither it was apprehended most safe for the fleet to come, being bad weather, but the Essex, Kentish, Portland, Bristol, Taunton, Nonsuch, Great President, with the Marston Moor to command, are left in the station from whence we come. This day also the Portsmouth frigate came into the fleet, who being clean is a very good sailor, I have ordered to ply off the Land's End in the same station with the Sapphire, where I hope the Captain[1] of her will do good service, being a very active man.

WM. PENN.

Dated in Ellen Road
the 20th January 1653.

1317. *Jan.* $\frac{10\cdot20}{20\cdot30}$, 1654.—*FRAGMENTS OF JOURNAL*

[S.P. 18, lxxviii. 139.]

A Journal of our voyage from the 16th of the eleventh month to the 20th of the same.

16th. This morning, the wind being come about to the north-north-east, our foretopsail was loosed, to give notice to the fleet of the

---

[1] Joseph Cubitt (*cf.* No. 1303), the writer of one of the fullest accounts of the battle off the Texel (Vol. V, No. 1181).

General's intention to sail: the same morning a Council of War was called of the flag officers only, to advise about going to sea if the wind continue eastwardly, and how to order the fleet for the best advantage of the service and securities thereof, and after some debate thereon it was agreed that the fleet be in two bodies, thus disposed, the main body to keep it up to windward, with all the sail they could make, yet so as they may not be separate, and the station to be between the Isle of Wight and Cape Barfleur: the lesser body to be only frigates which are to ply as near the shore as with safety they may, and to endeavour to keep sight of the main body in order to a conjunction upon discovery of any fleet. Soon after this result a gun was fired and the foretopsail sheets hauled home to give notice to the fleet of the General's intention to weigh forthwith, which was accordingly done, and about three in the afternoon got to sail, and stood off all night with an easy sail, the wind as before, and a moderate gale.

17th. This morning we had the wind more eastwardly, a fresh gale. About nine of the clock a Council of War was called to let the respective captains know the General's intentions for the better ordering of the fleet during its continuance in this station between the Isle of Wight and Cape Barfleur, in order to which directions verbally given unto the commanders of the Marston Moor, Essex, Laurel, Kentish, Portland, and Nonsuch frigates to ply about 3 or 4 leagues off of Cape Barfleur and to give notice by the usual signs upon the discovery of any fleet, to which end they are appointed to keep sight of the main body and what frigates more should come into the fleet are to be sent unto them for strengthening that body; Captain Bourne appointed to command them, and to select two frigates out of his squadron to ply close under the French shore that no ships may pass by unseen.

At the same time the General orders the Elizabeth and Expedition to ply to the northward, and to keep as far to windward of the main body as they may well be discerned, and by signs, as in the instructions for sailing to give notice to the main body upon discovery of any fleet of ships.

After this every commander repairs to his charge, and the fleet prosecutes the aforementioned resolves—the remainder of the day we had the wind more eastwardly—a fresh gale.

18th. This day was fair weather and little wind yet that which was eastwardly, the fleet continuing in their station, making the English shore in the morning, and French shore in the evening. This afternoon came into the fleet the Convertine and Gillyflower and Lubeckers come from Dunkirk, then were also 8 Hamburgers brought in by the Paragon but were cleared—presently a hoy was also ordered for Ellen Road to give notice to all the State's ships of the fleet's station, with orders for them to hasten to the fleet.

19th. This day the wind as before though very little, being close weather—at night the Expedition brought in a prize come from Zealand, and bound for Bordeaux. She had little in her except a few deal boards.

The captain of the Diamond also gives an account of a vessel he forced on shore on the French side.

20th. This day the wind all northward, fair weather and a moderate gale. We endeavour to gain the English shore. In the afternoon the wind more eastwardly.

1318. Jan. 24th/Feb. 3rd, 1654.—*PACK TO A.C.*
[S.P. 18, lxv. 39.]

Right Honble.,—These are in humble wise to signify unto y^r. Honours that according to the orders and instructions to me given by the R^t. Honble. General Blake and General Desbrow the 5th inst. at Gravesend, having transported the Lords Deputies from the States General of the United Provinces in the Netherlands into Holland, and landed them at Helvoetsluys, their desire was that I should stay there for the space of eight days while they communicated the proposals with which they were sent to the States General, which I accordingly did, and upon the last day of the said limited time I received a letter by an express from the Lord Beverning and the Lo. Nieuport signifying that it was the States' desire that I should stay yet two or three days more, assuring me that it would be much conducing to the benefit of both nations through the hopes for peace between them, of which there was so great probabilities, the which was also certified me by my Lady Strickland, whose desire and endeavour it was to come over with me, but could not, in regard my Lord Beverning's despatch was so sudden, who came on board within 3 days after which was the 21st of this month, whom we landed at Harwich this present day, where I shall abide till I have your Honour's order for my future employment.

In the interim humbly taking leave,
I remain, &c.,
[*No Signature.*[1]]

On board the Amity frigate,
at Harwich 24 Jan. 1653.

[1] No. 1229 gives H. Pack as commanding the Amity. A. Porter, who writes from that ship in No. 1328, was apparently her " Clerk of the Cheque."

1319. *Jan. 25th / Feb. 4th*, 1654.—*BLAKE AND PENN TO A.C.*

[S.P. 18, lxxviii. 169.]

Gentlemen,—We are now going to sea, the wind being all eastwardly, where we suppose it is settled for some time. Our intentions are to ply in the same station you were formerly acquainted with, or where else may most conduce to the good of the service. Here is nothing more at present, having received no intelligence from our scouts at sea since we parted from them.

We are, &c.,
Rob. Blake,
Wm. Penn.

Swiftsure at the Spithead under sail 25th Jany. 1653.

1320. *Jan. 30th / Feb. 9th*, 1654.—*BLAKE AND PENN TO A.C.*

[S.P. 18, lxxviii. 200.]

Gentlemen,—Since our departure from this place with which our last acquainted you, we have kept sea, though little hath presented worth your knowledge, and yesterday the wind coming about all westward, it was thought necessary to gain this place in time lest we should be driven to leeward, but have left a considerable party of frigates to keep sea, which we apprehend will answer the service during the wind's continuance as now it is; a list whereof is herewith sent.

Upon intelligence received of several Dutch merchant ships now at Newhaven waiting only the opportunity of a fair wind to carry them home, we have appointed the Dragon, Tiger and Adventure frigates to ply to the eastward of that place, the better to intercept them, and less they should miss of them, have given notice hereof to the party of frigates now plying in the Narrow.¹ We have also appointed the Constant Warwick to ply off the Land's End as an additional strength to those ships already there, which will now be 6 in number, good sailing frigates, and have given the Commander-in-Chief, Captain Cubit, in the Portsmouth, strict order to keep sea as much as possibly he can, who being an active man, we hope will give a good account of that affair, which is all at present but that we are, &c.,

ROB. BLAKE,
WM. PENN.

Swiftsure in
Stokes Bay
the 30th Jany. 1653.
For the Right Honble. the Generals of the Fleet at Whitehall.

1321. $\frac{Jan.}{Feb.}$ $\frac{31}{10}$, 1654.—*HEATON TO BLACKBORNE*

[S.P. 18, lxxviii. 214.]

Sir,—The Generals at sea appointed me in company of 3 more to ply in the Soundings— few are to be met save pretended friends, indeed 15 days ago I met Beach and 3 frigates more which did mouth me a saker shot at 2 in the afternoon. When I had his wake I tacked and kept him company till night, it was so much wind and sea that we could not with safety open a topsail, since I have not heard of nor seen him. On the 26th instant, S.W. from Scilly, in 90 fathoms water, I met 5 sail, viz. 2 Ostenders, 2 Dunkirkers, and one Hamburger, with some from Malaga. Upon supposition of their going for Holland I thought it my duty to bring them to Plymouth, there to clear themselves.

¹ Between Cape Barfleur and the Isle of Wight.

On the 28th I see a fleet of our merchant ships homeward bound.

On the 29th, I endeavoured to get the wind of the same that I might the better secure them from pirates.

On the 30th as I plied in sight of the Lizard on the weather gauge of the fleet which was 28 in number I had sight of a Dutch man of war. By 2 in the afternoon I got up with him, and after some scuffling, through God's mercy I became master of her without hurt to any of my men.

The captain's name is Daniel Willebore, the ship is called the Walcheren of Middleburg of 20 [guns] and 70 men, 6 whereof was slain. He hath been 7 months from home—sold his prizes always in France. This ship lay commonly upon the west coast, with whom the Nightingale fought about 24 days ago near the Start. I hope God in short time will deliver Beach and the rest into our hands, or we shall make the sea too hot for them.

Not else at present, but desire to approve myself.

Yours and the Commonwealth's to be commanded which I am,

N. HEATON.

Sapphire,
Plymouth Sound,
31 Jany. 1653.

1322. *Feb.* $\frac{3}{13}$, 1654.—*BEVERNING TO S.G.*

[Thurloe S.P., ii. 67.]

High and Mighty Lords,—They are sending two more regiments from hence to Scotland and General Monck is designed to go commander in chief thither, but the time of his departure is not

yet resolved on. Certain it is, that they are sending 25 frigates to the north, to hinder all assistance from being sent to the Scots and the fleet is to be reinforced with 30 good ships more, that were prest this week in the river, to be ready in 18 days' time. Whether that be the reason, or any other concealed, which I am ignorant of, I cannot positively advise, but this is certain, that besides the 70 or 80 ships, that lie about Portsmouth, these 30 merchantmen more this week were contracted for, and are providing with men in all haste, to go and join with the fleet. Some think that they have advice here of the great equipage of your High and Mighty Lordships and of a precise order to have your fleet ready against the 1st of March; and that therefore the lords of the government here are resolved to have first a great and powerful fleet at sea; but I hope, that God will soon dispel all jealousies with a gracious blessing upon our treaty. I remain,
    High and Mighty Lords,
      H. BEVERNING.

Westminster, Feb. $\frac{3rd}{13th}$, 1654.

1323. *Feb.* $\frac{4}{14}$, *1654.—WETTEWANG TO A.C.*

[S.P. 18, lxxix. 22.]

Right Honourable,—Sir, after my service presented to your Honours, these are to certify you of my proceedings according to your Honours' order. I conveyed in company with the Red Hart pinck seven sail of Hullmen into Humber, where we left the Red Hart pinck having almost lost her rudder, which done, I went to Newcastle, and there was 30 sail of colliers which we went to the southward withal, so far as Flamborough Head, where we met with a Hollands man of war of 16 guns, which we gave chase to, but could not get him. The fleet would not stay, but plied to windward, the wind being southerly, so that we were put to leeward of them. The next morning we were following the fleet with all sail we could, it being the 25th January—near under the Head, we met with another man of war, which we chased, and took in 6 hours' time with 6 guns and 52 men, we killed him one and wounded 7 more, the wind blowing hard southerly, that we were forced for Newcastle, where I delivered the prize to the prize masters. We have washed and tallowed our ship, for she was very foul, and now we are a coming to the southward with 40 sail of colliers, but I had rather for my own part do you any other service, though never so much hazard, for the colliers will not keep together so that it is impossible to secure them. So having nothing else to acquaint your Honours, but that we hear of 3 or 4 men of war upon the coast, I take leave and rest, &c.,

JOHN WETTEWANG.

From aboard the Sparrow,
at Tynemouth Bar,
Feb. 4, 1653.

1324. *Feb. $\frac{4}{14}$, 1654.—BLAKE AND PENN TO A.C.*

[S.P. 18, lxvi. 9.]

Gentlemen,—Yours of the 30th of the last month, with another of the 2nd inst. were received, and have advised with several commanders and pilots in the fleet which are best acquainted with the harbour of Brest whether any of our frigates may safely ride before the mouth thereof, and do upon enquiry find that it will be very dangerous with a westerly wind which most commonly blows there, and if it do please God to afford them safety with that wind yet they dare not let slip or cut to follow any that shall be bound in with those winds, so that all things considered we do conceive the service may as well be answered if these ships already appointed to ply thereabouts be active in their duty in lying constantly near Ushant and the Seams as wind and weather will permit, and upon set eastwardly and northwardly winds to close into the harbour as with safety they may, and do also apprehend their present number, being 6, to be sufficient; if you should think fit to add any more we shall comply with you therein; and what orders you apprehend fit to give them we desire may be sent by land to such port as may with most expedition answer that service, which cannot be done by sea so long as the wind continues westwardly. For what you write about muster books to be sent to the Commissioners for Sick and Wounded, order shall be given thereon at the next Council of War.

We are sorry to hear that the treaty between the Dutch and this Commonwealth is come to no certain resolution, their delay portends no great hopes of agreement, the consideration whereof doth quicken our former endeavours that such of the fleet now here may be ready for service upon all commands, and so hope the like with you.

For fit commanders for those ships you mention we can give little account at present, only refer you to a former letter of General Monck wherein commanders for some of them were propounded.

For the Hare pink we suppose she is plying

in the Narrow but we shall send that she may repair hither for her orders, and desire you will do the like by land which we conceive will be the surest and speediest way.

Care shall be taken to send 6 frigates to the eastward to look after the four Hollands men of war you mention, and to do any other service which Providence shall present.

Understanding that the Master Attendant at Portsmouth hath no accommodation for his residence at the dock the better to carry on the service as other officers have, we do offer as a thing necessary that some suitable provision be made for him there, apprehending it will much conduce to the advantage of the service according to the present state of affairs.

This day came into the fleet the George, Convert and Recovery.

We are, &c.,

ROB. BLAKE.
WM. PENN.

Swiftsure,
at the Spithead,
4 Feb. 1653.

1325. *Feb.* $\frac{6}{16}$, 1654.—*PETITIONS TO THE PROTECTOR*

[S.P. 18, lxvi. 12.]

To His Highness Oliver, Lord Protector of England, Scotland and Ireland and his Council.

The Humble Petition of Judith Todd, widow, sheweth,

That her husband Thomas Todd did with much good affection and faithfulness serve this Commonwealth divers years in several of their ships since the year 1642 and for two years past discharged the place of Master in their service, but in this last expedition chose voluntarily to serve under the commands of Major Bourne, Rear Admiral in the Ship Andrew, with the fidelity and courage of your petitioner's said husband in that whole time of service and more especially at the engagement nigh the Kentish Knock was sufficiently manifested where her said dear husband to her very great sorrow received his mortal wound, and whereof he shortly died, having two months before that time a command conferred upon him by the General as the merit of his faithful and active service before, but seeing the said ship was not at present fitted for sea, chose rather to spend that time in your service.

Your petitioner by this sad stroke being deprived of so faithful a husband and left with one child, and for that your petitioner's said husband did spend his youth and time without any improvement of his outward estate for the well-being of your petitioner and her infant, being carried forth in his spirit for the public interest of this nation, your petitioner therefore humbly beseecheth Your Highness to take into consideration her very great loss and to vouchsafe some comfortable means towards her subsistence with her child, or otherwise to refer the same to the Honourable Committee of the Admiralty and Navy.

And she (as in duty bound) shall ever pray.

Monday, Feby. 6th, 1653.

His Highness is pleased to recommend this petition to the Commissioners for the Admiralty and Navy to order an allowance to the petitioner as to others in like cases.

J. S. M. KER.

My Lords,—Upon consideration of the great loss sustained by the death of Mr. Thomas Todd, especially to the family to which he was related, we are bold to certify that most of us upon our own knowledge and observation are fully satisfied that the said Todd was a very godly man, and one that feared God and faithfully served this Commonwealth, in the just defence of whose honour and right he several times engaged, and we have good cause to rest assured that at the fight with the Dutch fleet nigh to the Kentish Knock (under the command of the Rear Admiral in the Andrew) he behaved himself very gallantly, and there received his mortal wound of which he shortly died.

We humbly recommend the condition of the widow and her child to Your Lordships' consideration, and remain,

Right Honourables,
Y^r. very faithful and humble Servants,
WM. PENN,
JOHN TAYLOR,
WM. HADDOCK,
SAM. HONETT,
THOS. EVANS,
JOHN BOURNE,
ANTHY. EARNING.

3rd April 1653.

Right Honourable,—I may not omit to trouble you with a word concerning the husband of this petitioner. I have known him for many years, and all that time to be a most faithful and active man for the carrying on the great interest of this Commonwealth, so far as his capacity reaches, and that he personally served the State since the relief of Lyme, where he was actually employed amongst others that went on shore for that purpose, and for above two years past he served in the place of a Master in your service, where he had good approbation, but in the beginning of March last he being very zealously affected to the present cause chose rather to go as a volunteer under my command in the Andrew than embrace better offers as to his outward advantage. In which time and employment, he behaved himself not only as a godly precious man but with very much zeal and courage upon all occasion, and more especially at the engagement with the Hollanders' fleet nigh the Kentish Knock where he had his arm shot off close to his body, and some days after died. I cannot speak more in his honour than he justly deserves. I humbly offer the premises to your Honours' consideration, and commend the widow and her child to your favour, whose loss cannot be made up, but her life may be made more comfortable by your compassion.

I beg your honour's pardon that I have been so large, my heart being constrained thereunto, and so remain, &c.,

N. BOURNE.

We, who have hereunto subscribed our names, do certify the truth of this above written.

JOHN OKEY,
JOHN WATERTON,
HENRY BARTON,
WILLM. GREENHILL.

1326. *Feb.* $\frac{11}{21}$, 1654.—*BLAKE AND PENN TO A.C.*

[S.P. 18, lxxix. 87.]

Gentlemen,—Yours of the 11th instant we received and as to what intelligence you have that Beach with 2 ships more of Brest are gone northward, we do apprehend that he is now westward by what we hear, and that he hath not been northward very lately, neither can we learn anything of those 4 Dutch men of war which were reported to chase an English ship into Ryde Bay, as by the enclosed will appear; however, our endeavours are and shall be that the enemy have as little liberty as may be to range in the Channel.

Since our last we have kept sea with the main body of the fleet until now that the wind is come about all northwardly, which hath occasioned our arrival here, but have left a considerable party of frigates at sea to answer all emergencies. Little hath occurred considerable only the taking of 3 small vessels, according to the enclosed note. We have this day sent into Portsmouth harbour 7 or 8 frigates to wash and tallow, and so from time to time take the advantage to refit our ships, that upon all occasions we may be in a continual posture for service but do conceive more expedition might be used if a timely supply of victuals could be had, the want thereof causeth their stay in harbour three times so long as otherwise they might, which to prevent for the future it were advisable that some effectual course might be taken, there being none of the victuallers here now as we are informed.

Here is one Captain John Jefferies, commander of the Little Charity, who is an active man, and well reported for an honest man, and therefore have thought to propose him unto you for commander of the 4th frigate now building at Bristol, which is all at present, but that we are, &c.,

Rob. Blake,
Wm. Penn.

Swiftsure in
Ellen Road,
the 14 Feb. 1653.

Prizes taken between the 9 and 14 Feb. 1653.

Jacob Yeankes, Master of the pinke St. David of Horne 90 tons, his lading 2000 Dutch cheeses, 8000 pantiles, 21 firkins of butter, 2000 pipestaves, and some hoops, bound for Lisbon, taken by Captain Fran. Allin,[1] comm^r. of the Advice frigate.

Jose Johnson, Master of the Beane of Tragoose, twenty last laden with wheat, rye, beans, pease, and six pots of mather; came from Zealand, and bound for Bordeaux, taken by Captain John Umpheres,[2] commander of the Nightingale frigate.

Cornelius Petersen of Riga in Zeiftland, Master of the Arms of Riga, 120 tons nothing but ballast, bound for Nantes, taken by Captain Robert Sansum,[3] commander of the Adventure frigate.

Ships appointed to keep sea in the absence of the fleet (*i.e.*):

Marston Moor	Taunton
Portland	Foresight
Advice	Centurion
Ruby	Tiger
Assistance	Dragon
Nightingale	Adventure
Reserve	Great President
Rich^d. and Martha	Convert
Kentish	Industry
Princess Mary	Society
Essex	

[1] *I.e.* Allen. [2] *I.e.* Humphreys.
[3] In No. 1303 R. Samson appears as commanding the Bryar, the Adventure being commanded by P. Foot.

1327. Feb. 15, 1654.—F. WILLOUGHBY
TO A.C.

[S.P. 18, lxxix. 93.]

Right Honourable,—You may please to take notice that the Speaker, Bristol, Elizabeth, Diamond, Thomas and Lucy, Ruby and Westergate are all tallowed, the 2 last are gone to sea, the three first staying for a wind, the other 2 for victual.

Yesterday the Laurel, Worcester, Pelican, Nonsuch, Expedition, Mathias, Welcome and Elias came into the harbour, which with the Heartsease before in, we hope to have ashore next spring, no care being wanting to forward the State service.

Yesterday we carreened one side, this day have perfected the other side of the Sovereign, so that we hope on Monday or Tuesday next to have her in a capacity to receive her provision, if any may then be ready for her, which I much fear.

According to information from the victuallers we have not above three thousand five hundred men's victuals left in this port for 6 months. The greatest part of the fleet will suddenly be in want of a recruit. I should desire Y^r. Honours would please to take it into consideration, that some effectual course may be taken for a timely supply.

I am, &c.,
FR. WILLOUGHBY.

Portsmouth,
15 Feb. 1653.

1328. *Feb.* $\frac{18}{28}$, 1654.—*PORTER TO N.C.*

[S.P. 18, lxxix. 104.]

Right Wor^ps.,—Your Worships may please to be informed that in pursuance of an order to Captain Nicholas Foster and other captains, appointing them to ply between the Dogger Bank and the Riff for the space of a month after our arrival at the river of Humber (where we were to take into our company the Newcastle, Assurance, and Mermaid frigates according to the readiness they were in, and after the service performed by some of them for which they were designed) on the 11th inst. we arrived in Grimsby Roads, where understood that the Newcastle was not ready and the other two attending some merchant ships which they were to convoy for the river Elbe, so the next day set sail towards our station, and on the 13th about 7 leagues off from Flambrough Head (an hour and a half before day), we espied divers vessels, each having a light out, whom we chased, and by the time we had a competent light of the day, made two of them to be ships.[1] Captain Foster gave chase to her that was leewardmost, and we to the other, whom by 8 of the clock (or before) we came up with, he putting out a Holland's ensign, and a bloody Jack, who seeing that he could not go from us, tacked, seeking to gain the wind of us, but could not. As soon as 'twas fit, we fired a gun at him, who answered us for the same with two. We fought with him till 7 hours or more were expired before he would yield, notwithstanding we shot his foretopmast by the board the second (or third) broadside that we gave him,

[1] *I.e.* warships.

in all which long and hot dispute the Lord was so pleased to favour us that we lost but one man in the fight, one mortally, and 2 more slightly wounded, whereas we slew 8 of his men and wounded about 18 more. Captain Foster chased so far to leewards after the other ship (that pretends to be a Swede) that he could not fetch us till after we had taken this, whom we found to be a Zealander of 20 guns called the Sandenbergh of Siriacksea, appointed to waft those vessels which bore the lights (being about 40 sail of fishermen) whom we could not meddle with by reason of manning of him and repairing (in some measure) the rigging, which was extremely cut and broken. We received three shot through the diameter of our mainmast, by reason whereof (I suppose) it's altogether unfit for further service. Our main topmast cap was shot asunder, our sails generally torn, but (thanks be to God) we received little damage in the hull; our foreyards and foremast shot in divers places. We received one shot also in our mainyard, and as touching our prize (which we were ordered by Captain Foster to carry into Humber), she was so disabled that we were forced to tow her thither, and brought her to an anchor near Grimsby the next day, being the 14th instant, and as soon as we can have an opportunity of wind, we shall ply for Yarmouth or Harwich to refit our frigate.

This I thought my duty to give your worship an account of, as I am, &c.

ANTHO: PORTER.

From on board
the Amity frigate
in Grimsby Road,
the 16th Feb. 1653.

To the Rt. Worshipful the Commissioners of the Commonwealth's Navy at their office at Tower Hill, London.

1329. *Feb. $\frac{17}{27}$, 1654.—BLAKE AND PENN
TO A.C.*

[S.P. 18, lxxix. 116.]

Gentlemen,—According to your desire in a former letter, we have caused a survey to be taken of all the brass ordnance in the State's ships here, and in Portsmouth Harbour, and the persons entrusted, upon their return, do not find any amongst them to be defective. We also writ to M^r. Newbery, Officer for the Ordnance at Portsmouth, to take a survey of what guns were under his charge, from whom we have received no account as yet, and are informed he is now at London, where we hope he hath given you account of this, but by what we can perceive, there is small hopes of providing the Sovereign with a lower tier of ordnance this way, and do hope that some more effectual course is taken to supply that want before now, which we thought necessary to acquaint you with, in regard we understand she will be ready to take in provisions on Monday next.

We find that notwithstanding all our care to provide men for the fleet we do not only come short of our expectations, but many of those we have do also desert the service, although all due care hath been taken for prevention thereof, which it is conceived is chiefly occasioned by that general liberty given to merchants' men going to sea, not so safe, according to the present state of affairs, for we are informed that there is gone out of the western ports of this nation at least 3000 able seamen, this last eastwardly wind which we fear will be very much wanted to man this next summer's guard.

We are, &c.,
ROB. BLAKE,
WM. PENN.

Swiftsure in
Stokes Bay,
17 Feb. 1653.

1330. Feb. 22 / Mch. 2, 1654.—*E. ALKIN TO BLACKBORNE*

[S.P. 18, lxvi. 54.]

Hon^{d.} Sir,—I make bold to trouble you with a line or two to beseech you to afford me your good word to the Honble. Commissioners for the Navy for a little money, for truly Sir I am a very weak woman, having many infirmities upon me which have been procured in my endeavours to serve this Commonwealth.

As for the ten pounds that was ordered me that Major Bourne paid, I paid six pounds of it at Harwich[1] and at Ipswich, disbursed money for the relief of the poor Dutch prisoners, seeing their want and misery to be very great, could not but have some pity towards them (though our enemies), and as for the money I had besides at Harwich, the Mayor had the account of it to a penny, so that indeed I brought up but poor three shillings to town, therefore, good Sir, make my case known that I may have something ordered now for my relief being now in a course of physick, and I shall as ever I have been if God spare my life and health to the utmost of my poor endeavours be serviceable to this Commonwealth. So with my prayers for you and yours.

I rest [&c.]
ELIZABETH ALKIN.

22nd Feb., 1653.

[1] Harridge.

1331. Feb. 25, 1654.—*BLAKE AND PENN TO A.C.*
Mch. 7.

[S.P. 18, lxvi. 71.]

Gentlemen,—Yours of the 16th and 18th with another of the 21st present we received, whereby we understand that care is taken for furnishing the Sovereign with a lower tier of ordnance which she will be ready to receive so soon as they can be sent down, and therefore desire the more expedition may be used.

Your orders to the commanders of those ships to the northwards for repairing to the fleet in order to a conjunction are very reasonable, having respect to your intelligence about the enemy's intention to be at sea with 120 sail of ships by the first of the next month ; but for calling off those ships whose stations are to the westward, especially those at the Land's End, where they do considerable service, we have suspended at present, having credible intelligence that Beach is yet thereabouts. But if your next speak the treaty at the same uncertainty we then desire your further opinion as to calling them off, which we shall advise and do therein as may most conduce to the good of the service. In the meantime (you being best acquainted with the state of affairs in relation to the enemy) we hope some effectual as well as timely care will be taken to [supply] the fleet with men, the want whereof is very considerable, and do very well approve of, and join with you in the report presented to the Lord Protector and Council about an embargo, it being as we conceive the only way to answer the service in that particular, and would have been more effectual if it had been sooner put into operation provided that the war with the Dutch go on.

We are still here with the main body, the wind

having been westwardly and northwardly, with blowing weather so that we have had little intercourse with the shore. Our squadron is still at sea, from whom we heard the other day, but nothing worth your knowledge, save that through the goodness of the Lord they were in their appointed station, and in a good condition, notwithstanding the foul weather we have lately had.

We are [&c.]
Rob. Blake.
Wm. Penn.

Swiftsure in Stoakes
  Bay, the 25th Feb. 1653.

1332. $\frac{Feb.\ 27}{Mich.\ 9}$, 1654.—E. ALKIN TO BLACKBORNE

[S.P. 18, lxvi. 74.]

Hon^{d.} Sir,—I beseech you to stand my friend to the Honble. Commissioners for the Navy (not knowing who else to make my case known unto), being in great strait through the weakness of my condition am inforced to make use of two nurses for my help, and have not sufficient to defray what my necessities require, desiring you to take into consideration that my sickness and many infirmities being procured by my continual watchings night and day to do service for this Commonwealth, and having implored others to do the like, have been inforced to sell my bed and other goods to make them satisfaction and to prevent their clamour. I therefore humbly request I may [have] a little money ordered me or my pension mended, or else be put into some hospital, my days being but short, and to prevent a miserable end of them, my charge being very great for physic and necessary attendance for my preservation, and I shall think myself

THE LAST WINTER 245

ever bound to you for all your favours, hoping I shall be no more troublesome to you, but shall while I live pray for you and yours and rest.

Your poor servant in distress,

ELIZABETH ALKIN.

Feb. 27, 1653.

1333. *Mch.* $\frac{3}{13}$, 1654.—*A LETTER OF INTELLIGENCE*

[Thurloe S.P. ii. 130.]

Sir,—Many of their men of war are already fallen down towards Texell and the Commissioners of the Admiralty on Monday last gave orders that the workmen should labour all night as well as day upon those ships yet preparing, which may be ready the next week : so soon as they are ready, they are dispatched away with all speed, though not one ship manned. Most have not above 12 or 20 men aboard. This week the drum shall beat for men, that their fleet be manned with all speed, which I cannot believe be done in less than . . . months' time. They would be put to it for men but that many entertain service in hopes of a peace. As I conjecture the reason of this sudden preparation was upon a flying report that your fleet was designing for the Sound. They will send a convoy with their East India ships outward bound, a fleet for the Straits, to keep the French and the Turks in, and will have a fleet in readiness about home. All this must be done out of the number I sent you the list of. Their East Country fleet of 150 sail are arrived here. It is now the season to send out merchantmen for all ports, many are ready but attend on the conclusion with you.

March 13th, 1653/4. N.S.

1334. Mch. $\frac{4}{14}$, 1654.—*BLAKE AND PENN TO A.C.*
[S.P. 18, lxvii. 25.]

Gentlemen,—Yours of the 2nd instant we received with some intelligence that the Dutch intend to be at sea with a considerable fleet very speedily, with this advice to have the fleet in such a posture as may answer the service, which we have not been slack in so far as lies in us, and shall endeavour to continue the same, but do somewhat wonder that the ships in the river make no more expedition to us. The enclosed[1] is a list of the ships here and in Portsmouth harbour, by which you will perceive not only our present condition, but also that the ships appointed to ply between this and the Land's End are now in the fleet, except the old Warwick, which is inconsiderable.

We have writ to our partners that the Martin, Merlin, Drake and Nonsuch ketch may be ordered hither, and we shall send the Pelican frigate to keep company with the Pearl in the Narrow, which we apprehend will as well answer that service there, and those small vessels more useful to us here, and therefore desire your concurrence.

The wind is now at north-east, which hath occasioned our falling down to Ellen Road, where we shall be ready for any opportunity of service that may present, and if the wind continue here put forthwith to sea.

We are [&c.]

ROB. BLAKE.
W$^{M.}$ PENN.

Swiftsure in Ellen Road
the 4th March, 1653.

[1] Not in S.P. 18.

1335. *Mch.* 10/20, 1654.—*AN INTERCEPTED LETTER TO SIR WALTER VANE*

[Thurloe S.P. ii. 153.]

The joy here is very great, being assured of the peace with England. Such a number of people and ships lie idle here and have nothing to do, that it is incredible, who would be glad to be at work again, if it so pleased My Lord Protector. The great preparations in the meantime, that are made in England, do still put the people in some kind of fear, that all is not right as it should be. The men of war are equipping, but slowly. . . . Everybody doth desire peace but few believe that England will make it to hold any long time. . . .

Your devils of English capers have taken at the mouth of the Vlie seven ships that came from Hamburg laden with fruit from Spain. The devil take them all.

Amsterdam. March 20th, 1654. NS.

1336. *Mch.* 14/24, 1654.—*BLAKE AND PENN TO A.C.*

[S.P. 18, lxvii. 81.]

Gentlemen,—One from General Monck of the 9th instant with another from yourselves of the 11th we received, and shall consider of one or more fitting vessels to secure the trade about Lundy, though we conceive it is one part of the station whereon the Irish squadron ought to ply.

Before yours came to hand we had received on board several ships of the fleet about 400 of the soldiers lately sent down, but shall suspend the remainder till we hear further from you, only desire that a proposition of beds may be hastened to us for them, which is the greatest want at present.

Yesterday we got the Sovereign into Stokes Bay, where all endeavours shall be used to enable her for service, as well as the rest of the fleet, which we are not slack in, and do hope that those ships in the river will receive the like dispatch, and, as they are ready, be hastened hither in order to a conjunction—which is all at present, but that we are [&c.]

Rob. Blake.
Wm. Penn.

Swiftsure in Ellen Road
the 14th March, 1653.

We desire you will not forget to hasten away orders to the Martin, Merlin, Drake, and Nonsuch ketch, now in the Narrow, to repair to the fleet for the reasons mentioned in our former letter.

1337. *Mch.* $\frac{18}{28}$, 1654.—*COMMISSIONERS FOR SICK AND WOUNDED TO A.C.*

[S.P. 18, lxvii. 94.]

To the R^{t.} Honble. the Commissioners for the Admiralty and Navy.

By the Commissioners for sick and wounded.

In pursuance of the General Order of the 27th January last, we have perused an account of disbursements for sick men brought to us by Mr. Edward Hayward, of Chatham, and Mr. Tho. Whitton, of Rochester, for taking care of whom they were warranted from the Commissioners of the Navy, Mr. Hayward's bearing date the 13th January 1652, and ending the 10th November following; Mr. Britton's the 10th June last and ending the 14th November following, and find Mr. Hayward charge himself with £550 (which agrees with a certificate from the Treasurer of the Navy), of which hath been disbursed £539 6s.—£43 6s. 1d. whereof is expended for diet for the sick, wherein they exceed not 1s. a day for a man and £103 5s. 0d. for other emergencies, viz. : £81 16s. 0d. to doctors and apothecaries for physic, £20 for nurses, candles and fire, &c., in extraordinary occasions, 20s. for shirts for 5 sick men, and £9 for bringing sick on shore.

The consideration of whose pains and faithfulness in their husbanding the State's treasure doth induce us at their request humbly to commend them to your Honours for the allowance following, i.e. To Mr. Hayward for 302 days at 2s. a day and £5 towards travelling charges divers times to London, £35 4s. 0d., which we consider to be below his desert, but he be in the State's service, and under salary for another affair. To Mr. Whitton for 158 days at 3s. a day in regard it was his whole employment, and £5 for his travelling charges, £28 14s. 0d., so that the whole amounts to £603 4s. 0d. which we humbly desire may be regarded by your Honours and the Commissioners of the Navy for payment, the imprest being abated, and remain [&c.]

SAMUEL COOPER.
JOSE LARK.
SAMUEL WARD.

Little Britain,
Mar. $\frac{16th}{26th}$, 1653.

1338. *Mch.* $\frac{18}{28}$, 1654.—*BLAKE AND PENN TO A.C.*
[S.P. 18, lxviii. 2.]

Gentlemen,—Yours of the 16th instant we received, and the same day did arrive here the Martin, Merlin, Drake and Nonsuch ketch, out of whom we took as many men as they could [?] towards manning the Sovereign and have remanded them to their former stations, the Martin only excepted, whom we intend shall ply about Lundy for securing of trade between the Welsh and Irish coast, which by General Monck we understand is infested with Brest pirates.

We are glad to hear that the treaty with the Dutch is likely to produce its expected and desired end, however our endeavour shall not be slacked so to equip that part of the fleet here as may answer all emergencies, so far as lies in us.

Since that Beach is taken by the Constant Warwick and brought into Plymouth, we suppose there are now no considerable ships to deal withal, and do therefore offer it unto you that the Portsmouth frigate may be commanded to the fleet with the ship Royal James wherein Beach was taken, conceiving they will be more useful here to attend that motion of the main body.

We desire to recommend unto you for officers in the great new frigate at Woolwich the persons following, viz. :

For
- Carpenter, John Pack, now carpenter of the Fairfax.
- Boatswain : Tho. Clemens now Boats^n of this ship.
- Gunner : Tho. Swan, now Gunner of this ship,

of whose ability and honesty we have very good testimony, also one Thos. May, midshipman here, for Boatswain of the 4th rate frigate at Bristol, which is all at present, but that we are [&c.]

Rob. Blake.
W^m· Penn.

Swiftsure in Ellen Road
the 18th March, 1653.

1339. *April* 18/28, 1654.—*MILL TO A.C.*

[**S.P. 18, lxix. 44.**]

R^t Hon^{bles},—These are to advise your Honours that on the eleventh instant, the Portsmouth, Middleborough and myself were together between the Isle of Bas and Ushant, and in the morning very early, we did espy 45 sail of Frenchmen, with whom we did forthwith engage, which came from Saint Malos, the most part of them bound for the Newfoundland—some of these ships had 20, 18, 16, 14 guns apiece, some more, some less. I sunk two and brought in one here with me, which is 150 tons, and hath 9 guns. The Middleborough, she is here likewise with two prizes, but whether the Portsmouth hath taken any I know not. When we did engage with them it was very foul weather, so that we could not carry out our lower tier of guns, none of us, but what we did was with our upper tier of guns. We did disperse the fleet, some foremasts and some mainmasts shot by the board, some are gone one way, some another, so that we could not board them by reason of the foulness of the weather, but if it had pleased God to have given us fair weather we had taken and spoiled the most part of them. In this engagement I had my main topmast shot by the board, and my mainmast shot in one place, and cracked in another place, and foremast shot through in the middle, and main-yard shot and foreyard shot and bowsprit broken, and all our sails and rigging torn to pieces. As soon as the engagement was over I shaped my course for Plymouth, it being very thick, misty and violent stormy weather. We fell in within two miles of the shore before we saw land, and the land we first made was the Island of Lew, and the wind was at south-south-east, so that we could not by any means weather the Ramhead nor the Dodman. I did endeavour what possible could be to get into sea, but could not, ever expecting when the mast would go by the board, so that I was enforced, for the securing of the ship, to put into this harbour, and with the first opportunity shall for Plymouth to have the ship repaired again. The Middleborough and prizes are forced in here by storm of weather, as we were. I have not heard of the Portsmouth since the engagement. We have sunk five, and have three in this harbour.

What the Portsmouth hath done since we parted from her, I know not.

Having not else at present to acquaint your Honours with, but remain [&c.]

ROB. MILL.

Fowey, the 13th April, 1654.

1340. *April* 21/24, 1654.—*SACHEVERELL TO A.C.*

[S.P. 18, lxix. 59.]

R^{t.} Hon^{bles.},—Since my last to your Honours about three weeks since, here hath nothing happened, either of action or intelligence of any consequence in these parts; if there had, I should soon have given your Honours an account, only according to your Honours' order we keep still plying in the narrow between Dover and Calais, together with the Merlin, Drake and Nonsuch ketch, where we are all ready to attend whatever shall be your Honours' farther pleasure. Here hath no ships of the enemy, either outwards or homewards bound, passed through the Channel of late, but only Hamburgers and Lubeckers, and such like, some whereof we have stayed on suspicion in Dover pier, but are now cleared again.

I was the last week at Dunkirk, from where I conveyed a very rich convoy of merchant vessels bound for London, who sent unto me often times for convoy before I went over, and being some four or five days wind-bound there, I could not return for Dover so soon as I expected to attend my Lord Protector's order to sail for Dieppe in order to the transporting the Earl of Bolingbroke and the Lord Mandeville for England, so that the Drake being present was sent upon that service. However, I hope the service I was then upon was not contrary to your Honours' desire.

This day here came by six of our merchant ships in the service who came from the fleet at Portsmouth, and were bound up the river, and also the Rear Admiral Badiley in the Vanguard came into the Downs yesterday, being the 13th instant. In my last I gave your Honours an account of some miscarriage of our private men of war who still infest these parts, and do much disservice to the Commonwealth in enticing our seamen and raising mutinies and violence on our men, when at any time we send our officers to press men for the State. However, I hope their time will not be long to continue amongst us. The 10th of this instant one Captain Welch, in a private man of war met with a ship belonging to Lubeck, who came from St. Martin's, and being then in Dover I saw him standing into the Road to speak with me. And this Welch, standing off to sea, met with him in sight of me, and made him sail to leeward for Rye road, where he very grossly abused him and his men, and made him by force sign a bill to a merchant in Dover to pay him a sum of money for his freedom, although he had the General's pass from the fleet, and other sufficient testimony besides, of his being bound for, and belonging only unto, Lubeck.

The next day I put accidentally under the Ness myself when this Captain Welch and the Lubecker were, and upon complaint by the skipper to me of his sad abuse, I called the business to a farther account before the Sub-Commissioners for Prize goods at Dover, who could do no less than acquit the man from any further trouble. This being one particular abuse, I could do no less (though something tedious) than give your Honours account, there being many other such miscarriages amongst them, so that whatever vessel they meet with, whether free or unfree, they will be sure, if they can, to make a spoil of them. So having not else at present to trouble your Honours, humbly committing you and your great affairs to the wise disposal and direction of our good God, I humbly take leave, and subscribe myself [&c.]

BEN. SACHEVERELL.

From aboard the Pearl
frigate, riding in the
Downs, this 14th April, 1654.

1341. *April $\frac{1}{7}$, 1654.—BURTON TO A.C.*

[S.P. 18, lxix. 63.]

R$^{t.}$ Hon$^{bles.}$,—The Brier frigate came into the roads last night, and this day I had all the officers before me. What one did say, all did affirm to be truth, as per enclosed appeareth. And for my opinion of this business, I cannot see any fault in the petitioner, Tho. Ridley, for when he that carry the light lay by the lee or short at any time, all the fleet must do the same, but he that carried the light was to blame, for when he laid short or by the lee, he should have put abroad two lights, and then all the rest of the fleet should have put abroad one light apiece, so every ship should have seen one another, but before he that carry the light put abroad 2 lights the rest ought not to put abroad any, for if they do, then they cannot know him that carry the light. I cannot find any great fault in the Brier's company neither, for they say the night was dark, and rainy weather, and the vessel they sunk was a low small vessel, and they could not see her till they were so near her as they could not shun her. In case one merchant ship had run aboard another in the same kind, the law of the sea is to pay half the loss at the least. The Brier is gone to Harwich to victual. She cannot carry above 5 or 6 weeks' victuals at most, therefore she is not so fit to lay at North Seas as the Sparrow pink or the Weymouth pink, which are both at Newcastle. In case they come, if you please, I shall send one of them with the North Sea men—here is 30 or 40 sail ready to sail, and stay a purpose for convoy. Likewise the Iceland convoy is thought long, for the owners are with me to hear every post.

The Southwold, Aldborough, and Wells men are most of them yet to sail. I hope the next spring tide I shall get the frigates out into roads, and then I shall come and wait on you.

Not else, but the tender of my service,
I rest [&c.]
WILL^{M.} BURTON.

Yarmouth,
April 17, 1654.

P.S.—Came to me Capt. Smith in the Tarrenton which have taken an East Indiaman of the Dutch of 900 tons richly laden with 4 chests of silver, which he and the Captain of the Plymouth have aboard, two in each ship, being they took him together.

The Tarrenton have broke his bowsprit and his best bower anchor, and I having no supply for him here, of masts nor anchor, have sent him into the Rolling Grounds of Harwich where Major Bourne may supply him.

He lost his prize in a thickett[1] but believe she is gone up to London.

The enclosed will give you a further account. Not else. I rest.

1342. *April* $\frac{17}{27}$, 1654.—*SMYTH TO A.C.*

[S.P. 18, lxviii. 64.]

R[t.] Hon[bles.],—In pursuance of your order of the 25th of March, Captain Stainer and myself have been on the Dogger Bank, and plying near to the Riff the 13th inst. at half an hour past eight at night, being thick foggy weather, we espied a ship and bore up with her, being to windward. In an hour's time I clapped her on board, fearing lest by reason of the darkness of the weather she might escape. I having intelligence of six of their men of war that were to come convoy for the Sound, and thought that this might be one of them, and to give him enough that the next day we two might be the better able to deal with the other five, but it proved an East India ship, called the Rose of Amsterdam; she was outward bound, and had been in Norway and bound for Holland. The men in her forced the master back for the Texel—we killed him 16 men, and wounded him many. She is a new ship of about 800 tons which never had been at sea, she hath but 26 guns, a very rich ship, as the men reported. She had in her four chests of silver, two of them Captain Stainer hath on board, and two I have on board.

Captain Stainer's lieutenant is in her and one Mr. Harrigate, which is master's mate with me,

---

[1] *I.e.* fog.

who is a very able man. We have either of us 20 men on board her.

It continued thick foggy weather from the 13th until the 16th, and on the 15th at ten in the morning we lost sight of her, we being the length of the head 20 leagues off at sea, the wind at E.N.E. I do not question but she is come safe into the river of Thames. I having given him an order to bring her to London in case we should part company, of which I thought good to give your Honours notice that further care may be therein taken. For the laying of her on board we have broke our bowsprit close by the stem, and she hath shot our best bower anchor in pieces, near to the nut, and the catheads away.

I do entreat your Hon[rs]. that you would be pleased to give order that I may have a bowsprit and best bower anchor of 2700 sent to me, either in Yarmouth Roads or into the Rolling Grounds, for if I should go for Harwich, or come for the river of Thames, I should not be able to keep my men, but they would run away, being but lately pressed, and having little pay due to them. I have not seen Captain Holland nor Captain Parke since we set sail from Bridlington Bay. The 9th we left the company of the Phœnix, and hath not seen her since. And the last night, being on the back of Yarmouth, Captain Stainer chased one ship to the eastward, and I gave chase to another to the southward, and came up to her, being a ship belonging to Sturteene,[1] under the Queen of Sweden, which had her pass, and since we have not seen one another, but hope to meet in Yarmouth Roads this night or to-morrow. Your [&c.]

JER. SMYTH.

Yarmouth Roads
  the 17th April at
  4 in the afternoon.

[1] Possibly Stettin.

1343. *April* $\frac{17}{27}$, 1654.—*STAYNER TO A.C.*

[S.P. 18, lxix. 65.]

R$^{t.}$ Hon$^{bles.}$,—These are to acquaint you that according to your order of the 25th March, as soon as it came to my hand the 4th April, I did make what haste I could to execute that order, but the ships that were expected to be with me I never saw since the 5th, which was the next day, only the Tarington, which hath been with us ever since. I wrote to you the 12th instant from our station, by a ketch which was appointed to be with the Tarington and us, but I understand by Major Burton that letters are not come to hand, therefore I shall give you an account of all that hath been worth since the 7th instant. We meet with a fisherman of Ameland that gave us notice that the second of this month there came home an East Indian man of 12 guns and that there rideth two or three hundred sail of ships at the Texel, bound to the Sound, with a convoy of 10 sail, those ships are to bring back a fleet of ships that comes from France.

We hath meet several Hamburgers and Danes that came from London, but hath not seen one fisherman in the sea that proves enemies. The 13th instant the Tarington and us being together, we met a Hollander bound for the East Indies. After a short dispute he yielded, it being in the night, we lying by her sent our boat on board, the Tarington coming thought she had not been yielded, clapt her on board, by which means she hath lost her bowsprit, and since she being moored between us, we taking out the prisoners, before that I could give orders to my lieutenant who commands on board of her. We lost company of her, it being exceeding thick and foggy. I hope the prize is in safety by this time; before she departed from us we understood that she had money that lay in the main hatch way, we thought that the seamen would have embezzled it. We took it out. Captain Smith had two chests and I had the other two. The men says that there is much money in the hold.

She is a very great ship, and well laden, as is credibly informed by the officers that were taken in her. The master was slain, and six or eight and twenty men. We hath lost one man and one wounded. The Tarington had none slain nor wounded, but had two drowned in entering on board. In consideration that we were no more in company but us two, and the Tarington disabled by the loss of his mast, I thought good, our time being expired within two or three days, to come for Yarmouth, where I might receive further orders, but in consideration that there are none, Major Burton and I think it fit I should go to sea towards the Holland's coast for three or four days until you shall send me instructions, for then I shall be into the roads again to wait your pleasure, so I rest [&c.]

RICH. STAYNER.

From Yarmouth,
the 17th April, 1654.

To the Rt. Honble. the Commissioners for the Admiralty, Navy at Whitehall.

Hast post hast.

1344. $\frac{Apl. 21}{May 1}$, 1654.—*PROCEEDINGS OF C.o.S.*

[S.P. 25, 75.]

The Articles of Peace Union and Confederation betwixt His Highness the Lord Protector and the States General of the United Provinces of the Low

Countries, together with the ratification thereof by His Highness were this day read (the same being signed by His Highness and passed under the great seal of England), and consented to by the Council, and it was ordered that it be offered to His Highness as the advice of the Council that the same be delivered as His Highness' ratification of the said articles to the Lords Ambassadors of the said States General.

1345. $\frac{Apl.\,25}{May\,5}$, 1654.—*PROCEEDINGS OF C.o.S.*

[S.P. 74, p. 57.]

That it be referred to Mr. Secretary Thurloe to send forthwith for the Heralds, and to give them such orders that the proclaiming of the peace concluded betwixt His Highness and the States General of the United Provinces of the Netherlands to-morrow may be put into an effectual way according to the Council's Declaration lately published.

INDEX

AABARTS

AABARTS, Albart, i, 413
Abel, Father (Rear-Admiral), v, 130
Aberdeen, v, 35, 140
Ableson, James (Captain), capt. of the Mermaid, vi, 201
Abramsz., Reijmont (Gunner), iv, 186
Abuses. *See* Complaints.
Acken (*or* Ackeren), Jan van (skipper), iii, 226, 234 ; orders to, ii, 72
Ackersloot, Adrian Corn. van (Captain), his instructions, v, 321
Acklam, — (Captain), v, 63
Actions: Fleets and Squadrons:
 Off Dover, i, 8, 172, 192–195, 220, 221, 227, 237, 238, 250 *sqq.*, 276 *sqq.*, 295 *sqq.*, 423
 capture of Dutch Northern Fishing Guard, i, 17, 385 *sq.*, 399, 408
 Off Plymouth, ii, 105 *sq.*, 116, 121, 142, 158, 195, 222, 300
 Kentish Knock, ii, 268–280, 282 *sqq.*, 286, 288 *sqq.*, 294 *sq.*, 301, 304, 306, 357; vi, 16, 233 *sqq.*
 Dungeness, iii, 89 *sqq.*, 100 *sq.*, 106 *sq.*, 116, 143, 151, 205, 230, 252; vi, 15 *sq.*
 Portland, i, 14, 15 *n.*; iv, 68, 72, 78 *sqq.*, 88 *sqq.*, 93 *sqq.*, 100 *sqq.*, 108 *sqq.*, 118 *sqq.*, 163 *sqq.*, 180 *sqq.*, 188 *sqq.*, 194 *sq.*, 227 *sqq.*; vi, 17

ADMIRAL

 Gabbard, v, 16–24, 69 *sq.*, 71 *sqq.*, 81 *sqq.*, 89 *sqq.*, 96 *sqq.*, 109 *sq.*, 116 *sqq.*, 120 *sqq.*, 124 *sqq.*, 137 *sq.*, 144 *sq.*
 Texel, v, 162 *sqq.*, 341, 348 *sqq.*, 354 *sqq.*, 364 *sqq.*, 371 *sqq.*, 382 *sqq.*, 396 *sq.*, 419 *sq.*, 427 ; vi, 1
Actions, Single ships :
 Amity, v, 239 *sq.*
 Constant Warwick, vi, 7
 Diamond, iii, 100
 Dragon, ii, 134
 Elizabeth, vi, 104, 113
 Fairfax, iii, 237
 Helena, iii, 188
 Lily, vi, 55
 Merlin, v, 347
 Nonsuch, vi, 178
 Phœnix, vi, 209, 212 *sq.*
 Portsmouth, iii, 133, 350
 Smyrna Merchant, v, 278
 Tiger, ii, 373.
 See also Gibson, Richard
Adams (Captain), iii, 12 ; lieutenant to General Blake, i, 11 ; captain of the Mary Rose, i, 11 ; recommended for captaincy of 4th rate, v, 381
Adelaar, Jeroen (Captain), i, 389; capt. of the Middelburgh, iv, 310
Admiral (*or* Amijrael), John (Captain), capt. of the Brack, v, 185 ; trial for desertion, v, 220, 240 *sq.*, 243 *sq.* ; battle of the Texel, v, 363

ADMIRALTIES

Admiralties, Dutch :
  Zeeland, at Middelburg, i,
    55 ; ii, 31, 45, 47, 53, 55,
    86 ; iii, 51 ; iv, 117, 358 ;
    v, 136 ; ships to be ready
    for sea, ii, 119 ; delegates
    from, v, 202, 219, 223 ;
    ships chartered by, v, 219,
    286, 404, 422. *See also*
    Navy ; Finance
  North Holland, at Amsterdam, i, 55, 120, 271, 377,
    382 ; ii, 22, 41, 45, 46, 78 ;
    iii, 16, 57 ; iv, 358 ; v, 74,
    134, 220 ; vi, 135, 182 ;
    ask to be exempted from
    joining other boards for
    hiring 100 ships, i, 122 ;
    ask for letters of marque
    &c. to be made out, i, 362 ;
    for convoy for Baltic trade,
    i, 376 ; ii, 14 ; for convoy
    for ships from Spain, ii, 14 ;
    demand share of shipbuilding grant, iii, 82 *sq.* ; to
    States General concerning
    contraband, iii, 387 *sq.* ; to
    States General concerning
    preparations for campaign,
    iii, 390 *sq.* ; delegates to
    inspect ships, v, 191, 202,
    223, 337 ; vi, 68, 158 ;
    wages of ships' crew, v,
    219, 223 ; survey of condition, v, 358, 393 ; De
    Ruyter made Vice-Admiral
    of the Province, vi, 191.
    See also Discipline ;
    Finance
  North Quarter or W. Friesland, i, 55, 154, 275, 382 ;
    iv, 359 ; v, 43, 55, 74, 133,
    218 ; vi, 160, 167
  South Holland or the Maas at
    Rotterdam, i, 55, 74, 382 ;
    iii, 152 ; iv, 389 ; v, 113
    sq., 189, 220, 386, 422 ;
    naval expenditure, iii, 195

ALDERNE

sq. ; delegates from, v,
    202
  Friesland, at Harlingen, i,
    55 ; v, 186, 219 *sq.*, 287 ; vi,
    160 ; ill-equipped ships, ii,
    94
Admiralty Court, to try case of
  murder, ii, 262
Adriaen, Jan (Captain), found
  innocent of charge of cowardice, vi, 46
Adriaansse, Jan (Gunner), Gunner of Brederode, i, 278
Adriaensen, Hendrick (Captain), i, 389 ; capt. of the
  Sampson, iv, 310 *and n.*
Adriaensen, Jacob (Captain),
  iii, 226 ; v, 23
Adriaenszoon, Allert, capt. of
  the St. Jacob, fireship, i, 265
Adriaenszoon, Pieter (Captain),
  ii, 363
Aecks (*or* Aech), Simon van der
  (Captain), i, 388 ; ii, 49, 353 ;
  capt. of the Amsterdam, iv,
  310 *and n.*
Afield, —, v, 92
Agges (*or* Aggens, *or* Aggelsz.),
  Jacob (Commissary), ii, 334,
  374 ; iii, 47 ; v, 60, 318 ; vi,
  172 ; letter from, ii, 383
Albemarle, Duke of, four days'
  battle, i, 47 *and n.*
Alberts, Cornelis (Captain), iii,
  239
Albertsz., Lucas (Captain), i,
  388 ; ii, 49, 147, 181, 185,
  353 *sq.* ; iii, 225, 233 ; vi,
  157 ; capt. of the Drie
  Coningen, iv, 309
Aldeburgh, iv, 340, 370, 395 ;
  v, 64, 257, 268, 293, 300, 400,
  408, 416, 428 ; vi, 1, 58, 60,
  102 ; sick and hurt at, v, 410
Aldern, Captain, iii, 430 ; iv,
  176
Alderne, Thomas (Captain),
  (Victualler of the Navy), ii,

INDEX

ALDERNEY

76; iii, 430; letters from, v, 279; vi, 29
Alderney, Isle of, iv, 90, 164
Aldersen, Claes (Captain), vi, 140
Aldertszoon (*or* Allertsz.), Peter (Captain), i, 196, 198, 234, 251, 264, 382, 393; iii, 224; ordered to ply into Downs, i, 219; convoy to St. Martin's, iii, 220; battle of Portland, reported dead, iv, 182, 189
Aldgate, Abraham (Captain), capt. of the Martin, i, 25; took Ostender, i, 25, 26
Aldworth, Rt. (Commissioner of the Navy), i, 70; iii, 307, 317, 324
Aleppo, vi, 24
Alford, Richard, letters of reprisal on behalf of, i, 72
Alfordness. *See* Orfordness.
Algiers, fund for relief of captives at, ii, 258; iii, 304 *and n.*, 329
Alkin, Elizabeth, v, 159, 248; vi, 9; letters from, v, 247; vi, 242, 244; her petition, iv, 102, 104, 140; vi, 242, 244
Alkmaer, v, 234
Allart, Cornelis (Captain), v, 45
Allein, Fr. (Commissioner for Ireland and Scotland), iii, 431, 432
Allen, Francis (Captain), vi, 201, 237; letter from, iv, 256 capt. of the Recovery, vi, 52; capt. of the Advice, vi, 184
Allen, Samuel, iv, 342
Allertss., Claes (Captain), capt. of the Nieucasteel, iv, 314
Alleson, James (Captain), capt. of the Mermaid, vi, 186
Alleyn (*or* Allen), — (Alderman), iii, 97, 332, 343; iv, 176
Allinson, Captain, capt. of privateer, vi, 104
VI.

APPELDOORN

Alteren, Pieter van (Fiscal Advocate), iii, 190; iv, 248, 258
Ameland, v, 195; vi, 258
Amerongen, van (Delegate), v, 237
Ames, Joseph (Captain), capt. of the Samuel Talbot, v, 20
Amsterdam, iv, 98, 137, 186, 247; v, 23, 43, 55, 58, 113, 119, 187, 238, 264, 286, 326, 421; vi, 39, 112, 136, 158, 171, 191, 247
Commanders of Admiralty ships from, i, 261; ii, 336, 342
Commanders of Director's ships from, i, 262; ii, 337, 342; vi, 159
Commanders of Vice-Admiral De With's squadron from, i, 265
list of ships, iv, 310; vi, 157
meeting of Delegates at, v, 237
See also Admiralties, Dutch.
Anchorages and Rendezvous. *See especially* the Downs, Dungeness, Margate, Isle of Rhé, St. Helens, Schoonevelt, the Swin, Texel, the Wielings.
Anckes, Douwe (Captain), vi, 157
Anderson, Joseph (mate), v, 78
Andrewes, Nathaniel (Victualler of the Navy), letters from, v, 279; vi, 69
Anthonissen (*or* Axtennisz., *or* Antamissen), Evert (Commodore), i, 388; iii, 155, 224; iv, 373, 382; v, 28 *sq.*, 238, 318, 323; capt. of the Hollandia, iv, 309; v, 185; battle of the Texel, v, 355
Anthoniszoon, Gabriel (Captain), ii, 80, 147, 190; vi, 157; capt. of Medemblik, ii, 147
Appeldoorn, —, vi, 160

R

APPLETON

Appleton, Henry (Captain), i, 68, 70; vi, 46, 171; capt. of Leopard, in command convoy squadron Mediterranean, i, 68
Archer, Anthony (Captain), capt. of the Paradox, i, 66; capt. of the Fortune, vi, 51
Aren, Jacob (Captain), battle of the Gabbard, v, 74 *n.*
Arensen, Jan Willem (Captain), v, 127; vi, 154
Arentsen, Al (Captain), ii, 181
Arianssen (*or* Arentszoon), Pieter, i, 393, 397; ii, 337
Ariaen, — (of Schevelingen), iv, 186
Arkinstal, Thomas (Captain), i, 13; master of the George, i, 13; petition to the Admiralty committee, iii, 352
Armorer, Nicholas (Royalist agent), ii, 225 *and n.*
Army, Committee of the, i, 355
Arnold (*or* Arnot), John (Bailiff of Yarmouth), iii, 345, 444; iv, 343; v, 62; letter from, iv, 342
Arthur, — (Vice-Admiral of Dorset), iii, 188
Arthur, John (Sub-Commissioner for Weymouth), iv, 139
Articles of War: committee appointed to prepare, iii, 163, 272; printed by order of Parliament, iii, 293–301; additional article of war, vi, 133
Artificers, Dutch: carpenters, etc., to be paid off, vi, 64; shipwrights sent to the Texel, vi, 26
Artificers, English: shipwrights, of Portsmouth, refusal to work, ii, 372; lack of, iv, 219; dockyard artificers, in want of pay, iii, 326; from Norway, iii, 371; from

BACON

Sweden, iii, 371; shortage of carpenters, vi, 86, 88 *sq.*
Arundel, iv, 387
Arundel Castle, spare powder from, to be sent to Plymouth, i, 222
Aryons, Willem (Captain), battle of Portland, iv, 69
Aukes, Douwe (Captain), ii, 147, 149; capt. of the Struisvogel, ii, 147
Aulberghen, Baron of, iii, 85
Ayscue, Sir George (Admiral), i, 67, 68, 70, 179, 181, 268, 281, 286, 287, 292, 325, 327, 339 *n.*, 344, 346, 357 (2); ii, 13, 39, 53, 66, 70, 97, 111; iv, 334 *and n.*; letters from, i, 341; ii, 56; capt. of the Rainbow and in command of Barbados squadron, i, 67; to hasten into Downs, i, 315; to convoy ships, i, 337; took seven Dutch ships in Straits, i, 342; his squadron in the Downs, i, 363; Dutch attempt to attack, i, 363, 369, 372, 401; ordered into Channel, ii, 17, 33, 34; to arrange Channel convoys, ii, 60; action off Plymouth, ii, 105–108, 195; council of war, ii, 121; off Isle of Wight, ii, 189; resignation, ii, 265 *and n.*; report of fresh service, v, 340. See *also* Instructions

BACKEN, Jan (Captain), appointed Vice-Admiral, v, 318
Backer, Cornelis, (Dep. of Board of Admiralty), ii, 38, 72
Backstays, how fitted, i, 22 *and n.*
Bacon, Francis (Bailiff of Ipswich), i, 317; letter from, i, 369
Bacon, Nathaniel, i, 317

INDEX

BADILEY

Badiley, — (Captain), battle of Kentish Knock, ii, 282, 289 sq.
Badiley, Richard (Rear-Admiral), i, 2, 20, 68, 69, 70; iv, 203, 325; v, 33, 71, 79, 150; vi, 49, 253; letters to, iv, 230; captain of the Paragon, i, 18; action off Isle of Elba, i, 18, 19; command of convoy squadron in Mediterranean, i, 68; iv, 217, 300, 352; his return, v, 59, 65 and n., 187
Baer, Jacob de (Commodore), vi, 117, 161
Baermans, Jan Jansz., i, 265
Bagben, Nicholas (merchant), letter from, iii, 322
Baily, Simon (Captain), v, 18; capt. of the Lisbon Merchant, iv, 279
Baker, —, iii, 124
Baker,— (Captain), capt. of the Prosperous, i, 191
Baker, Cornelius (seaman), iii, 173
Balck, Augustyn (or Auke) (Vice-Admiral), i, 265, 351, 388; ii, 249, 251; iii, 31, 46, 156, 207, 220, 224, 240, 242, 243, 245, 250; iv, 122, 324, 335; letters from, ii, 331; iii, 30; to convoy Muscovy Fleet, ii, 249; convoy duty, iii, 257, 259; iv, 23; battle of Portland, iv, 69, 188, 190; his reported death, iv, 182, 189; capt. of the Vrijheijt, iv, 310
Balg, v, 359 sq., 362 sq., 394; vi, 24, 158
Ball, Andrew (Captain), i, 7, 67; ii, 124, 129, 131, 167, 175, 376, 386; iii, 168; letter to, iii, 420; capt. of the Antelope, i, 64; loss of, ii, 365, 374; capt. of the Adventure, i, 2;

BARFLEUR

took French ship, i, 3; capt. of Triumph, i, 4; iv, 20; killed Portland fight, i, 4; iv, 80, 83, 101, 172; instructions to, ii, 155; in charge of convoy to Sound, ii, 365, 374, 388; iii, 12
Balla Castle, iii, 371
Ballangowne Wood, iv, 107
Ballard, Michael (purser), purser of the Briar, his examination, iv, 129
Baltic. See Contraband; Stores, Naval; Commerce
Baltimore, Lord, i, 142
Bamford, James (Commander), letter from, v, 379; battle of the Texel, v, 379 sq.
Bancker (or van Banckers), Adriaen (Captain), i, 263, 393; ii, 337, 342, 346; iii, 241; iv, 192; capt. of Hollandia, iii, 222 sq.
Banckert (or Bancken, or Bancker), Joost (the Younger) (Captain), i, 425; ii, 64 n., 146, 187, 305, 354; iii, 208, 214, 218, 223 sq., 233; vi, 156; capt. of De Liefde, ii, 146; battle of Portland, reported dead, iv, 182, 189, 192
Bane, — (Captain), ii, 99
Banister, Sir Edward, iv, 256
Barbados, i, 67; iv, 235; v, 292; Ayscue's expedition, i, 75; took 27 ships for breach of Act of 1650, i, 76
Barbary States, i, 38, 42; relations with, i, 63
Bardesius, Hector (Captain), i, 262, 393, 417; iii, 224
Bardoel, Bastiaen (Captain), i, 262; iii, 190 sq.
Barentsz., Pouwels (skipper), skipper of Brederode, i, 278
Barfleur, Cape, vi, 223; Dutch rendezvous at, ii, 163; and Isle of Wight, ships plying

BARFOTE

between, vi, 200, 204, 219, 221
Barfote, William (merchant), iii, 330
Barker, John (Captain), iv, 96, 124; letter from, ii, 364; capt. of the Prosperous, i, 191; iv, 20; battle of Portland, iv, 80 *sq.*, 84, 101, 165, 188 *and n.*, 195
Barkstead, John (Colonel), iv, 326; v, 236; letter to, vi, 132
Barnard, Edward, letter from, v, 85
Barnes, Michael (Surgeon); petition of widow, ii, 95
Barnes, Miles, iii, 451
Barnes, Robert (Master); master of Friendship, i, 286
Barning, Anthony; capt. of the Reformation, iv, 22
Barnstaple, iii, 386, 416; iv, 103; v, 36, 334
Barrett, Edmund, capt. of the Lily, i, 66
Barrett, Edward; capt. of the Swift, vi, 51; capt. of the Gift, vi, 201
Bartelszoon, Jacob (skipper), ii, 349; master of Parrot-tree, iii, 192
Bartelszoon, Lambert (Captain), i, 263, 392-3; iii, 222 *sq.*, 228, 239, 240, 249; iv, 192; v, 135; Tromp's orders to cruise near Shetlands, i, 394; to reconnoitre Downs, i, 425; took merchantman off Dover, v, 58
Bartery, — (Captain), iii, 47
Bartlett, — (Captain), letter to, iii, 172
Barton, Henry, vi, 235
Barton, — (Major), v, 342
Barton, Mr., iv, 256
Bas, Isle of, vi, 251; Dutch fleet sighted near, iv, 48

BECKE

Basch, van der (Captain), capt. of the Angel Gabriel, v, 185
Baskett, — (Captain), (Govr. of Cowes Castle), i, 16
Bates, Dr., iv, 241
Bathurst, Dr., v, 412
Batten, Robert (Captain); capt. of the Garland, ii, 239; battle of Dungeness, iii, 117, 230
Batz, Isle of; De Ruyter's squadron near, ii, 122 *and n.*
Baxter, Colonel, iv, 390
Bayley, Thomas (Captain), capt. of the Lisbon Merchant, iv, 22
Bayl, Geurt (Master) master of the Black Eagle, iii, 192
Bayners, — (Captain), found innocent of charge of cowardice, vi, 46
Baynes, Robert (Captain), i, 66
Bayonne, v, 40, 43, 132
Beach, Sir Richard (Royalist Captain), i, 23; capt. of The Sorlings, i, 25; taken by the Constant Warwick, i, 25. *See also* Privateers: Royalist.
Beachy Head, iv, 95, 169, 172, 392, 396; v, 251 *sq.*; vi, 196; Blake's fleet off, iv, 60, 164
Beale, William (Victualler of the Navy), letters from, vi, 29, 69
Beane, Edward (Light keeper, South Foreland); warrant to, iii, 303
Beare, Amos, Boatswain's boy of Tiger, i, 6; Master Attendant at Woolwich, i, 6
Beck, William (Captain), i, 66, 327; iii, 52
Becke (*or* Beckx), Hans Carelsen (Captain), ii, 147, 246, 255, 354; iii, 240; vi, 157; captain of the Sara, ii, 147; log of, ii, 211-216

BECKE

Becke, Robert, capt. of the Fair Sisters, v, 17
Becker, Jan (Captain). *See* Barker, John
Becker, Steven, iv, 286
Beecke (*or* Beke, *or* Beerk), Cornelis (Captain), ii, 64, 256, 354; iii, 223, 226
Beerman, Hendrick (Master), master of the Promised Land, iii, 193
Belevelt, — (Captain), ii, 343
Bellebruijn, Johan (Captain), iii, 217
Bence, Alexander, ii, 310
Bennett, Colonel, v, 406
Bennett, Thomas (Captain), vi, 200; capt. of the Welcome, vi, 51
Benson, —, letter from, vi, 39
Berch, (*or* Berck), Michiel Franz van den (Captain), iii, 197, 198; vi, 171
Berckman, Otto (Captain), iii, 223, 226 *sq.*; capt. of Leifde (fireship), i, 265
Bergen, v, 29, 40, 42, 44, 131 *sq.*, 265; vi, 26, 37 *sq.*, 61 *sq.*, 145, 171; Dutch merchants awaiting convoy, vi, 34 *sq.*, 54, 109 *sq.*, 117, 120, 123, 125, 131, 149, 161, 167, 182
Berkeley, Sir William (Vice-Admiral); loss of Swiftsure, i, 46
Berkstead, — (Colonel), iii, 140
Berlington. *See* Bridlington
Berry, —, ii, 239
Berry, Toby (Deputy Clerk of the Check), iii, 441
Best, John (Captain); capt. of the Elias, vi, 200
Bevan, Isaac; battle of the Gabbard, v, 97
Bevan, Rowland; letter from, v, 97
Beveren, — van, ii, 83

BLACKBORNE

Beverling, — (Ambassador), v, 118, 213 *n.*; vi, 217, 225; letters to, v, 403; vi, 29, 112; letters from, v, 389, 408; vi, 31, 70, 166, 228
Beverweerd, —, ii, 226 *and n.*, 229; asked to take command on Tromp's death, vi, 26
Bevesiers, iv, 190 *and n.*
Beyerlyncke. *See* Beverning
Bideford, iii, 416; iv, 103; v, 36
Bije, Jacob de (Advocate Fiscal), iv, 384; v, 58 *sq.*, 220 *sq.*; vi, 75
Bijl, Jan (*or* Jacop), (Mate), v, 61, 137
Bilboa, iv, 254
Birchell, —, iii, 396
Bird, Major (Sheriff of Ross), iv, 106
Biscay, Bay of, Dutch convoy to, iii, 66; v, 27; ports in: merchants' petition for delay of convoy from, iv, 23; Tromp's instructions to, iv, 26; his reply to petition, iv, 28; merchant ships from, iv, 358; intelligence to be sent to, vi, 97
Bisdommer, —, letters from, v, 412; vi, 112
Bishop, George (Intelligence), letter to, ii, 276
Bitter, — (Captain), capt. of the Marcuerjus, iv, 323; his instructions, v, 321
Blackborne, Robert (Sec. Navy Commissnrs.), iii, 307, 317, 324, 334, 404; iv, 40, 42, 45, 67, 140, 227; v, 263, 310, 398; vi, 172, 179; letters to, iii, 366; iv, 40, 42, 63, 67, 103, 131, 153, 156, 332; v, 25, 30, 50, 54, 89, 98, 106, 195, 247, 303, 367; vi, 196, 220, 227, 242, 244; letters from, ii, 388; iv, 227; v, 258

BLACKBURNE

Blackburne, James (Deputy Clerk of the Check), iii, 441
Blackenburrow. *See* Blankenburg
Blackness, iv, 151, 167, 169, 172, 228
Blackrock, iv, 300
Blackwall, ii, 170; iv, 387
Blackwall, Richard (Treasurer and Collector of Prize Goods), i, 111; v, 344
Bladon, iv, 291
Blagg, Edward (Captain), iv, 148; v, 16, 250; vi, 202; commissioned, iii, 376; capt. of the Marmaduke, iv, 293; capt. of the Portland, vi, 50
Blake, Benjamin (Captain), i, 7, 67; iii, 168; iv, 51; captain of Assurance, i, 6; took Portuguese ship of war, i, 6; capt. of the Triumph, ii, 239; discharged, iii, 418
Blake, Humphrey (Treasurer and Collector of Prize Goods), i, 111 *n.*
Blake, Robert (Captain), capt. of the Hampshire, vi, 200
Blake, Robert (Admiral and General at Sea), i, 4, 12, 14, 15 *n.*, 29, 54, 64, 84, 88, 107 *sq.*, 140, 153, 160 *sq.*, 189, 201 *sqq.*, 215, 233, 240, 257, 259, 267 *sq.*, 318, 350, 356, 362, 376, 409, 419; ii, 66, 69, 78, 82, 113, 168, 287, 326, 375, 386; iii, 31, 43, 58, 67, 168, 332, 353, 366, 397, 421, 436; iv, 33, 38, 48, 56, 170, 172, 193, 258, 260, 262, 273, 275 *sq.*, 334, 355, 385; v, 20, 42, 118, 148, 258, 381; vi, 16 *sq.*, 104, 225
Letters to, i, 110, 129, 132, 137, 216, 292 *sq.*, 307, 311 *sqq.*, 316, 320, 322, 324 *sq.*,

BLAKE

332, 340, 361, 363, 371; ii, 100, 110; v, 278
Letters from, i, 154, 161, 194, 249, 257, 290, 331, 336, 374, 406; ii, 95, 134 *sq.*, 139, 183, 272, 281, 311, 335; iii, 74 *sq.*, 91, 105, 114, 353, 397; iv, 47, 163; v, 68, 81, 94, 103, 111, 186, 208, 214, 228, 248, 256; vi, 79, 217, 226, 230, 235, 241, 243, 246 *sq.*, 249
Commanded against Rupert, i, 2, 5, 13; took French ship of war, i, 7; burnt Tunis ships of war, i, 24 *and n.*; took Plate fleet, i, 25; ordered to hasten forth fleet, i, 110; consulted as to his instructions, i, 130; orders to Penn, i, 154, 323, 406; orders to join the fleet, i, 185
Action off Dover, i, 8, 11, 172, 193, 423; Tromp asks for restoration of captured ship, i, 216 *and n.*, 256; Blake's reply, i, 257; ordered to stay Dutch ships, i, 246; petition from ship's comp. of the Worcester, i, 249, 250; to appoint convoy for Baltic trade, i, 312
Fleet off Shetland, i, 385; off Fair Isle, i, 403; council of war, i, 406; iii, 76; to repair to Channel, ii, 100, 110; to reinforce Ayscue's squadron, ii; 120, took Dutch merchantmen, ii, 134; took French men of war, ii, 166, 234, 344, 346; in the Channel, ii, 184, 222
Battle of Kentish Knock, ii, 268–280; iii, 53; reported off Maas, ii, 338; in Downs, iii, 68, 84, 125, 209; receives report of Tromp's

INDEX

BLAKE

fleet, iii, 75 (2); his commission renewed, iii, 77
Battle of Dungeness, iii, 91, 95, 107, 116 sq., 143, 230; complaint of his captains, iii, 92, 105; asks to be discharged, iii, 92
Battle of Portland, iv, 79 sq., 83, 88, 95, 100 sq., 118, 120 sq., 124, 163 sqq., 188; his health, iv, 204, 229, 232, 235, 241, 251, 325, 353; v, 68, 156, 256, 259, 263, 291, 310, 340; vi, 6, 114; in command of reinforcements, v, 67, 71 and n., 83, 85, 109, 116
Battle of the Gabbard, v, 23, 88 n., 93, 100, 117, 124, 145, 198; his death reported, v, 208; General of the Fleet and Admiralty Commissioner, vi, 189 See also Instructions; Operations and Movements.
Blake, Shadrach (Captain), capt. of the Samaritan, v, 19; capt. of the Industry, vi, 199
Bland, John (merchant), ii, 247
Blankenburg, v, 86, 93 n., 144
Blasques, iv, 300 and n.
Block, Joris (Captain), capt. of the Hollantsche Thuijn, iv, 324; battle of the Texel, v, 355, 364
Blogg, Richard (fisherman); reports Dutch fleet off Hartlepool, i, 383
Blocker, (or Bloeker), Pieter Adriensz. van, i, 262; iii, 225; iv, 25
Blount, Lieut.-Colonel, iv, 106
Blowfield, Isaias (Captain), iv, 294; vi, 51, 200; capt. of the Lily, iii, 146
Boceman. See Boermans
Bock op der Zes, vi, 161

BOOKS

Bodham, Mr., vi, 218
Boer, Jaep van (Captain), i, 239; capt. of the Eendracht, iv, 315
Boer (the Younger), v, 128; vi, 171
Boermans, Jan (Captain), i, 388; vi, 175; capt. of the Prins Willem, iv, 309 and n.; battle of Texel, v, 358
Boet, (or Boodt), Jacob Claesz. (Captain), i, 263, 393; iii, 225
Bogaert, Dirk (Captain), ii, 265; capt. of the Catherina, iv, 310
Bogaert, Fredrick (Captain), i, 262; iv, 338
Boger, Richard (Captain), ii, 162
Bolingbroke, Earl of, vi, 253
Bonch, Herman, ii, 223
Bond, Denis (of the Admiralty Committee), i, 130, 138, 190, 191, 209, 211, 216, 241, 294; ii, 22, 36, 75; iii, 425, 446; iv, 317
Bondt (or Bont), Davidt Janss. (Captain), i, 388; capt. of the Maen, iv, 308
Bonker, John. See Barker, John
Bonkier, John (Captain), capt. of the Shepperd, v, 185
Bonnell, Benjamin (agent for Sweden), iii, 371
Bonner, — (Captain), letter from, iii, 18; capt. of the Marmaduke, ii, 128, 170; took Dutch merchantmen, iii, 18
Bonner, Mr., iv, 318
Bonteboer, Pieter Tueniss (Captain), capt. of the Swarten Arent, iv, 308
Boogert, — (Captain), vi, 149, 155
Books mentioned, William Lilly's *Almanachs*, i, 20; *Zealander's Choice*, Joseph Hill, i, 24 and n.; Corbett's

BOOSSE

Fighting Instructions, iv, 262 n.; *Life of C. Tromp*, v, 147 n.

Boosse, Gerrit Jacobz., capt. of the Vercken (fireship), i, 265

Booth, Sir William, capt. of the Adventure, i, 29; took Algerine ships of war, i, 29, 30

Bootsmasz, E. van (Lord Commissioner), ii, 362

Bordeaux, iv, 26, 90; v, 40, 43, 115, 132 sq.; vi, 221, 224, 237; report from, iv, 24

Bordessen, Hector (Captain), ii, 351

Boreel, — (Dutch Ambassador to France), iii, 61

Bos, van den (Captain), battle of the Texel, v, 360

Boshuijsen, Jacob van (Captain), iii, 196

Bostock, Richard, i, 209 n.

Boston, i, 316; iv, 357

Boswell, Sir William (Ambassador at the Hague), i, 75

Bouckhorst, — (Captain), ii, 62, 79, 80, 86, 188 sq.; capt. of the St. Nicolaes, vi, 157

Boudesteijn, —, (Fiscal), v, 220

Boulogne, iv, 89, 97, 118, 153, 193; vi, 183

Bourgonien, (*or* Bourgoigne), Jan (Lieutenant Commodore), ii, 363; iii, 225

Bourne, John (Rear-Admiral), ii, 239; iv, 56, 78, 115, 245, 254, 296, 301, 319; v, 105; vi, 107, 204, 220, 234
Fight off Portland, i, 16; iv, 74, 125 n., 166; capt. of the Assistance, i, 16, 65; iv, 20 n.; Rear-Admiral of the Blue, i, 16; iv, 20 n., 189 and n.; his squadron to the Sound, ii, 249, 251, 315; capt. of the Resolution, vi, 49; capt. of the

BRADSHAW

Marston Moor, vi, 199; to command squadron between Isle of Wight and Cape Barfleur, vi, 224

Bourne, Nehemiah (Rear-Admiral) (Major), i, 185, 196, 198, 217; iii, 344, 397, 405, 426, 436, 452; iv, 45, 55, 58, 75 sq., 127, 145, 217 and n., 294, 297, 305, 369, 386, 390; v, 31, 66, 186, 188, 192, 207, 217, 248 sq., 258, 260, 272, 301, 314, 423; vi, 1, 107, 216, 233, 242, 256
Letters to, iv, 78; v, 104; letters from, iii, 367, 383, 393; iv, 55, 58, 76, 112, 131, 132, 144, 145, 149, 242, 243, 321, 322, 332, 343, 345, 348; v, 26, 75, 79, 292, 342; vi, 56, 82, 85, 87, 100, 114, 128, 168, 172, 186
Capt. of the Speaker, i, 64; action off Dover, i, 8, 10 sq., 172, 194, 250 and n., 251 and n., 252 and n.; Rear-Admiral, i, 185; battle of Kentish Knock, ii, 282; appointed Navy Commissioner, iii, 278

Boutgee, Willem Willemszoon, capt. of the Coning David (fireship), i, 265

Bowden, Robert (Captain), capt. of the Constant, i, 73

Bowes, Robert, iv, 290

Boynton, — (Colonel), iv, 45

Brackel, John (Captain), battle of the Gabbard, v, 74 n.

Brackman, Daniel Cornelisz., i, 263, 393

Bradshaw, John, Lord, on committee to prepare articles of war, iii, 272; President of C.O.S., iv, 53, 56, 61, 76

Bradshaw, Richard (British Resident at Hamburg), ii,

INDEX

BRADSTOW

387; iii, 34, 126, 426; iv, 157; vi, 99; letters from, i, 326; vi, 41, 78; instructions to, iii, 40
Bradstow. *See* Broadstairs
Brahel (*or* Brakel *or* Braeckel), Pieter van (Captain), i, 388; ii, 384; iv, 323; vi, 118; capt. of the Bommel, iv, 309 *and n.*; capt. of the Groningen, v, 185; trial for desertion, v, 220, 240 *sq.*, 243 *sq.*; battle of the Texel, v, 360
Brake Head, i, 370, 373
Brandaris, vi, 137 *and n.*
Branders, — (Captain), iii, 222
Brandley, William (Captain), i, 385; iii, 65; capt. of the Portsmouth, i, 65; action off Dover, account of, i, 209, 210; recommended capt. of the Outward, ii, 328; capt. of the Essex, vi, 49
Brandling, John, i, 317
Bras, Arien (Captain), capt. of the De Drye Coningen (merchant), i, 234
Brasset, — (French Resident), ii, 303
Braxton, Mr., iv, 256
Brazils, The, soldiers for, v, 282
Brederode, Wolphert van (Captain), i, 388; orders to, ii, 375, 383; capt. of the Hoop, iv, 310
Breen, Pieter van, capt. of the Ste. Pieter, iv, 308
Breesound, v, 140 *sq.*
Breeveertyen, vi, 152 *and n.*
Bressa Bay. *See* Breesound
Brest, iii, 330; v, 210, 296; vi, 181, 231, 235; Ruyter's squadron in, ii, 159, 165. *See also* Pirates
'Brest pirates.' *See* Privateers: French

BROWNE

Brewer, Erasmus (Captain), i, 25, 26
Brewster, —, R. (Commissr. of the Navy), iii, 307, 317
Bridgewater, v, 36, 39
Bridlington, iv, 351 *n.*; vi, 257
Brighton, De Ruyter's squadron off, ii, 99
Briel (*or* Brill), iv, 248, 378, 384; v, 104, 145, 312, 420; vi, 25
Brinckers, Poppe (Captain), capt. of the Bracke, v, 362; battle of the Texel, v, 362
Brion, Barne (Captain), ii, 131
Bristol, iii, 441; iv, 99, 131, 138, 364; v, 35, 38 *sq.*; vi, 236; ships for Straits and Bilboa exempted from embargo, i, 305
Broadridge, — (Master), master of the Triumph, battle of Portland, iv, 80, 83
Broadstairs, iv, 393 *n.*
Broeche (*or* Broeck), W. P. van de, ii, 25, 38, 72; iv, 360
Broeckhuysen, Witt. van (Delegate), letter from, v, 386
Brom, Jan (Master), master of flyboat Gideon, iii, 191
Brome, Gilles Jansen (Captain), iii, 241
Brookes, —, ii, 101
Broucke, (*or* Brouch *or* Broeck), Joris Pietersen van den (Rear-Admiral), ii, 57, 146, 188 *sq.*, 353, 355, 382; vi, 157; capt. of the Westergo, ii, 146; death of, ii, 111, 143
Brouwer, Cornelis Jansz. (Captain), i, 218, 262, 417; iii, 190 *sq.*; iv, 338
Brown, John, ii, 67
Browne, —, i, 108
Browne, — (Captain), iii, 49; capt. of the Hercules, i, 191; to be tried for misconduct, iii, 338

BROWNE

Browne, Arthur, capt. of the London, v, 17
Browne, Major, v, 71 *and n.*
Browne, Mr., i, 115
Brun, — de (Spanish Ambassador at The Hague), iii, 139; iv, 351
Bruyne, John De, letter to, vi, 72
Bruynseret, — (Captain), capt. of the Brede, v, 186
Bruynsvelt, (*or* Brijnsvelt), Adriaen (Captain), ii, 343; iii, 224, 240; vi, 152, 160
Bucker, Andries (Master), ii, 265
Buckingham, Duke of, v, 207
Bugia, Action at, i, 29
Bullock, Christopher (Surgeon), v, 206; letter from, v, 388
Bulter, Joost (Captain), battle of the Gabbard, v, 120 *sq.*; capt. of the Town and Country: his death, v, 22, 69 *and n.*
Bunn, Thomas, capt. of the Greyhound, vi, 50
Burgh, van der (Captain), i, 388
Burdick, John, Master's mate of the Worcester, i, 250
Burgis, Thomas, iii, 365
Burton, Thomas (Surgeon), v, 206; letter from, v, 388
Burton, William (Admiralty Commissioner), letters from, vi, 72, 254
Burton, William (Major) (Bailiff of Yarmouth), v, 62, 401; vi, 107, 116, 136, 258 *sq.*; letters from, iii, 442
Bushel, — (Master), his ship taken, iv, 176
Bushell, Edward (merchant), iii, 56
Bushell, John (merchant), iii, 56
Business, Distribution of, among the several Committees. See 'Orders of the Council of State,' *passim*

CAMPEN

Buskill, Nathan, capt. of the Hector, i, 65
Butterboxes, v, 70
Button, Edmund (Captain), iv, 9; lieut. of the Worcester, i, 250; capt. of the Sampson, iv, 21; killed, battle of Portland, iv, 21 *n.*, 79, 166
Buys (*or* Bays), Ruth Jacobsz. (Captain), i, 261, 393; ii, 336, 342, 345 *sq.*; iii, 224
By, — de (Advocate), iii, 55
Byllevelt, Willen, supercargo of the Lastdrager, i, 397

CADE, — (Captain), capt. of the James, iii, 332
Cadiz, i, 319; iv, 150, 222; v, 252 *n.*; supply base, i, 2, 7, 13; arrival of silver fleet, ii, 14; departure of five ships, ii, 349; Dutch men-of-war off, v, 301
Cadman, James (Captain), v, 19; vi, 50; capt. of the Eagle, i, 66; capt. of the Pearl, iv, 21.
Caerelsen, Hans (Captain), iii, 239
Calais, i, 197, 212; iv, 97, 108, 112, 121, 132, 142, 151, 162, 191, 196, 261, 354, 367, 372, 374 *sqq.*, 379; v, 49, 58 *sq.*, 84, 135, 190, 252; Dutch rendezvous off, ii, 58; v, 52, 71
Callant's Eye, vi, 161
Camp, Hendrick Jansen (Vice-Admiral), iii, 225; action with Fairfax, iii, 237
Campen, Abraham van, i, 218, 262, 417; ii, 337, 342, 351 *sq.*; iii, 224; battle of Kentish Knock, ii, 358; battle of Portland: killed, iv, 189

CAMPEN

Campen, Gillis Mathijsz. (Captain), i, 265, 393; ii, 342, 379; iv, 310; capt. of the Golden Lion, ii, 379; capt. of the Bromel, v, 185; capt. of the Groningen, v, 359; battle of the Texel, v, 357

Campen, Jan van (Captain), i, 389; ii, 336, 342; iii, 225, 233; iv, 122, 323; v, 130, 185; vi, 46, 160; capt. of the Overijssel, iv, 310 and n.; battle of the Texel, v, 362

Camperdown, v, 139, 350, 373, 425

Campes, Gillis Thyssen (Captain), i, 388

Canaries, v, 214

Canterbury, iv, 157

Capelman, Jan Warnaertssen, capt. of the Alckmaer, iv, 315 and n.

Carbrancy, John, battle of Portland, iv, 89

Carew, John (Admiralty Committee), i, 294; ii, 89, 101; iii, 318, 340, 407, 415, 427, 440, 447; iv, 67, 136, 160; v, 33, 81; letter to, iv, 368; letter from, iv, 289; v, 400; vi, 73; appointed Navy Commissioner, vi, 189

Carleton, Dudley, i, 74

Carlington, v, 140

Carlisle, iv, 290 *sqq.*

Carlisle, Robert (Master), master of the Hopewell, iii, 34

Carpenter, Walter, i, 281

Cartensz., Dirck, iv, 186

Carter, John (Bailiff of Yarmouth), i, 378, 384

Carter, Paul (Master), master of the Ann of Newcastle, iv, 291

Carteret, — (Lieutenant), i, 46

CHATHAM

Carteret, Sir George, to be Vice-Admiral of French fleet, ii, 54, 366

Cary, Mr., v, 107

Caskets, iv, 164; vi, 56

Cats, Dingman (*or* Singeman), (Commodore), i, 263, 388; iii, 222 *sq.*, 228; iv, 192; v, 127; battle of the Gabbard, v, 74 n.; his instructions, v, 320

Cats, Jacob (Dutch Ambassador), letters from, i, 239, 245, 271; arrival of, i, 48

Cats, Jan Pauwelsen (skipper), iii, 236

Cats, Johan van. *See* Galen

Catwyck, v, 118, 224, 341, 382

Causes of the War, i, 48

Centsen, Bastrain (Captain), his instructions, v, 321

Cerstyaensen, Cerstijaen, i, 393

Challoner, Thomas, ii, 73; iii, 96, 121, 122, 148

Chant, William, capt. of the Tiger, i, 186; to repair to Yarmouth, i, 186

Chapman (*or* Chaplin), — (Captain), iv, 127; capt. of the Entrance, iii, 49; to be tried, iii, 164, 173; capt. of the Golden Cock, battle of Texel, his death, v, 390 n.

Chapman, Edmund, capt. of the Recovery, i, 65, 180

Chatham Chest, iii, 274 *and n.*, 358; iv, 223, 288; vi, 89

Charost (*or* Chadost), Comte de (Governor of Calais), i, 235; ii, 303

Chatham, i, 110, 130, 139, 288; ii, 248; iii, 433; iv, 31, 99, 112, 134, 144, 153, 282, 284; v, 31, 76 *sq.*, 98, 106, 187, 215, 249, 270, 272, 300 *sq.*, 344 *sq.*, 392; vi, 29, 53, 73, 107, 113, 165, 248;

CHELSEA

complaints against officers, i, 70; building of fort at, i, 107; list of ships at, vi, 200
Chelsea, vi, 71 sq.
Chessons (Captain) iv, 96
Chester, — (Colonel), capt. of the Swallow, under Rupert, ii, 135
Cheneys, Thomas, letter from, iv, 53
Chilworth Mills, iv, 364
Cholmley, Sir Hugh, iv, 45
Christchurch, iii, 372
Christiaensen, Christiaen (Captain), iii, 242
Christienson, Peter (Master), ii, 265
Claes, — (Captain), ii, 63; iv, 324. *See* Sanger, Claes Jansz.
Claese, Dirk (Captain), ii, 265
Claesz, Jan (of Monickendam), iv, 186
Claeszoon, Salomon, i, 362
Claeszoon, Tymen (Lieutenant-Commodore), ii, 382; iii, 187, 239; capt. of the Westergo, ii, 382; battle of the Gabbard, v, 23, 74, 240, 242
Clark, Robert, capt. of the Martin, i, 66
Clarke, — (Captain), capt. of the Tulip, vi, 201
Clarke, Robert (Captain), v, 209, 228; vi, 50, 199; letters from, i, 358; v, 31, 49; capt. of the Reserve, i, 65; capt. of the Drake: action with privateer, v, 49
Clay, Robert (Captain), carpenter of the Tiger, i, 6; capt. of the Sapphire, i, 6
Clemens, Thomas (Boatswain), vi, 250
Clerck, Marinns de (Captain), ii, 339; iii, 224
Clerk, Colonel, vi, 203

COAST

Clerk of the Cheque, propositions concerning, iii, 373; iv, 225
Cleydick (*or* Cleydyck), Jacob (Captain), iii, 224, 246; battle of Portland, iv, 123; his death, iv, 188
Cleydyck (Kleydyck *or* Kleidijck), Jacob (Captain), v, 130, 134, 239; vi, 118, 149
Cleydyck, Jan, i, 261
Cleyntge (Cleyntien *or* Cleyntie), Ariaen Geritsz. (Captain), i, 264; iii, 224 sq., 240; orders to, iii, 39; battle of the Gabbard, v, 74 n.; his ship lost off the Texel, vi, 160
Coach, Peter, Gunner's mate of the Worcester, i, 250
Coal Trade, i, 412; ii, 175, 373; iii, 28, 35, 428, 450; iv, 50, 160, 290 sq., 303, 325, 352, 381; v, 408; vi, 7, 229
Crews of colliers impressed, iii, 166; iv, 201, 205; v, 292; age limit for men in, iii, 393; lack of men for, iv, 53; reported blockade of Hull and Tynemouth, iii, 333; of Newcastle, iv, 205, 235, 259; collier fleet intercepted by Dutch, iv, 318 sq., 328 sqq., 331, 335 sqq., 346, 350 sqq., 356, 358, 361, 385, 394; list of ships for guard of, vi, 202
Coast Defence, Dutch: land preparations, i, 98
Coast Defence, English: i, 368, 373; ii, 12, 90; iii, 340; v, 405; vi, 83
Isle of Wight, i, 107; iii, 111, 127, 130, 140, 157; Reinforcements ordered for Orkney and Shetland, i, 223; for Deal, i, 356; power to impress men in

COBHAM

Kent, i, 357; Yorkshire ii, 19; Newcastle and Tynemouth, garrisons of, ii, 228; Downs, iii, 103; soldiers for Kent, Suffolk, Essex, iii, 110, 112, 130, 141, 145; Dutch landings in Kent and Sussex repulsed, iii, 106, 108, 135, 144 Guns for defence of Portsmouth, iii, 141; fear of invason, iii, 346; ships for, v, 95, 405; vi, 180, 183 sq., 219; coasts of Ireland and Scotland, v, 414. See also Lights; Summer Guard; Squadrons; West and North Guard; Soldiers

Cobham, Nathaniel, vi, 186, 201; capt. of the Newcastle, vi, 50

Cock, Nathaniel (Captain), capt. of the Blossom, v, 20

Codde, Isaac (Captain), iii, 225, 233; v, 220, 281, 287; orders to, iii, 39; capt. of the Postpaert, iv, 323

Coebergen, — (Delegate), v, 239

Coenders, — (Captain), v, 219, 287; battle of the Gabbard, v, 23

Coendraet, Hans, iv, 186

Cogshall, Thomas, coxswain of the James, i, 11

Cokyard, —, ii, 131

Colaert, — (Admiral), i, 20; French Commission, i, 20; action with Capt. Heaton, i, 21, 22

Colchester, v, 259; vi, 71, 132, 136. See also Peeke, Thomas

Cole (Captain), iv, 127, 144, 151; capt. of the John, iv, 58, 113; battle of the Texel: his death, v, 353

Coleman, Robert (Captain), capt. of the Globe, v, 18;

COMMERCE

capt. of the Arms of Holland, vi, 202

Colery, Joris (Captain), i, 261, 388

Collins, Captain, iv, 256

Collins, Henry (Captain), iv, 280; v, 16; vi, 201; capt. of the Malaga, i, 67

Colman, William (seaman), v, 397

Colster, Willem van (Captain), iii, 197

Colt, — (Captain), capt. of the John, i, 191

Commerce, Dutch:
Brazil, i, 121, 273; vi, 137
Baltic, exempted from embargo, i, 85 and n.; to pay only half shipping dues, i, 103; Blake to interrupt trade, i, 302; merchant fleet for, ii, 385; iv, 311; v, 46, 59, 119, 201, 208, 245; vi, 109, 182; ships captured, v, 237; vi, 212
Caribbean, i, 77, 390
White Sea, ii, 248–51
Dutch East India Co.: orders to Blake to intercept fleet, i, 301, 331; company's ships to join Dutch fleet, i, 377; convoy of fleet for, ii, 366; iii, 108; iv, 361; impress of E. I. C. ships, v, 108, 183 sq., 297, 305 sq., 335; advice boats sent to fleet, v, 193, 265; news of return ships, vi, 26, 29, 34 sq., 37 sq., 55, 61 sq., 142, 161, 167, 171
West Indies, company to be formed at, i, 412; iii, 179, 181; ships from, taken, v, 216, 235; return ships, vi, 110
Spain, silver fleet, i, 412; ii, 14, 15, 260, 349 sq.; iii, 43, 61 and n.

276 INDEX

COMMERCE

Guinea, ii, 366; v, 108, 183
Mediterranean, ii, 16, 366; v, 108, 183, 193; vi, 26, 61, 110, 167, 171
Norway, iv, 311, 359; v, 46, 59; vi, 146, 167, 171
trade with England forbidden, iii, 150, 170, 182
rise of price in corn, v, 119
homeward fleet expected north about, iv, 358, 361, 371, 373, 375, 381; v, 29, 40, 42 *sqq.*, 108, 130 *and n.*, 131, 139 *sq.*, 141, 197, 207 *sq.*, 210, 232, 246, 253 *sq.*, 283 *sq.*, 301, 305, 336, 340
seven Hamburg ships taken, vi, 247
English fleet hinders Dutch trade, v, 102 *sq.*, 106, 140, 148 *sq.*, 153, 194, 217, 229, 233, 263 *sqq.*; vi, 7, 186 *sq.*
stagnation of trade, ii, 224; v, 119 *sq.*, 312; vi, 10
trade with Hamburg, interruption of, ii, 260; v, 265; illicit, vi, 112
prohibition of export, iii, 60
channel closed for Dutch trade, vi, 5, 14
overseas trade compared with that of 1914, vi, 13
See also Convoys; Excise; Fisheries; Netherlands: foreign relations

Commerce, English:
i, 329; ii, 371, 377; iii, 50, 133, 280; v, 296, 346
Baltic, convoy to be appointed, i, 312
Barbados, i, 377, 412; v, 292; ships taken by Dutch, vi, 113
Brittany, iii, 133, 321
E. I. Co., i, 377; v, 90, 278
Hamburg, naval stores from,

COMMERCE

iii, 446; vi, 41 *sq.*, 81; their arrival, vi, 7, 113
Levant, i, 377
Mediterranean, ii, 76
New England, iii, 50, 64; vi, 81, 205 *sq.*
Sound, Dutch attacks on, in the, ii, 66; iv, 143
Venice, v, 251 *sq.*
Virginia, ii, 77; vi, 221
higher rates to be paid for naval stores, as encouragement, vi, 80
See also Coal Trade: Convoys; Fisheries; Stores
Commerce, Neutral
Denmark, iii, 413
Hanseatic, Dutch interference with, iii, 388 *sq.*
naval stores from Hamburg, iii, 446
Spanish, silver for Ostend, iii, 166
French, vi, 6, 26, 112, 178; Newfoundland fleet, vi, 251
See also Stores: Naval
Commerce, Protection of:
Dutch, Cruising ships and squadrons for, i, 322; ii, 22–26; 41–45, 250, 312, 366; iii, 23, 187, 390, 399; influence of, on Dutch strategy, i, 376, 377; ii, 14, 15, 38; v, 46, 63, 283; vi, 2, 13 *sqq.*, 26, 63, 65, 96 *sq.*; protection of the E. I. Co., iv, 359; v, 108, 120; proposed to discontinue organising the trade in fleets, vi, 96. *See also* Operations and Movements
Commerce, Protection of:
English, ii, 29; iii, 164; v, 229, 278; vi, 7, 13 *sqq.*; cruisers and squadrons for, ii, 11, 20, 135; iv, 283, 369; v, 95, 121; vi, 7, 81, 250; ships warned of

INDEX

COMMISSIONERS
position of Dutch fleet, iii, 291, 301; guard for colliers, vi, 202. *See also* Convoys; Dungeness; Squadrons
Commissioners, of the Admiralty, *passim*; of the Navy, *passim*; special, appointed after Dungeness, iii, 96, 98, 105, 121, 132, 167, 178; their instructions, iii, 98, 123, 127, 146; a report from, iii, 121, 147; petition for resident commissioners at several ports, iii, 346 *sq.* proposals of committee for Irish and Scotch Affairs, iv, 236, 253
Commissions and Warrants, Penn, as capt. of the Triumph i, 161; as Vice-Admiral of the fleet, i, 189; as capt. of the James, i, 318, 323; as commander of a particular squadron, iv, 33; Ruyter, as Vice-Commodore, ii, 27; as Vice-Commander, iv, 285; Monck as General, iii, 110, 178, 317; Richard Suffeild as capt. of the Duchess, iii, 353; John Fowler as Judge Advocate of the Fleet, vi, 105; warrant to intercept Dutch merchantmen, vi, 186
Complaints, Dutch:
Ruyter, of his captains, ii, 152, 174
of his ships, ii, 144, 182, 186; vi, 25
De With, of his seamen, ii, 220 *sqq*; iv, 258
of his ships, vi, 121, 124 *sq.*
of his fireships, ii, 237
of lack of ships and equipment, iv, 281, 354 *sq.*, 380; vi, 77
of slowness in equipment, vi, 40, 77
of his captains, ii, 313 *sq.*,

COMPLAINTS
359; iii, 53 *sq.*; iv, 258, 384; v, 351, 355 *sqq.*, 384 *sq.*
of being superseded, iii, 15 and n.
of Amsterdam Admiralty, ii, 369, 377
Tromp, of his ships, iii, 20; iv, 207, 377; v, 151
of his fireships, v, 47
of lack of ships and equipment, v, 289
of delay in equipment, v, 189
of lack of stores and ammunition, v, 48
Evertsen, of unfounded charge against him, vi, 25
Evertsen and Ruyter, of bad treatment by De With, vi, 25
Admiralty Boards, of ships and men, ii, 324
of ships, undermanned, ii, 322; iv, 257
of lack of respect to delegates, v, 394
of lack of promised financial assistance, vi, 64
of consequent delay in fitting out, vi, 66
officers and seamen, of lack of leave, v, 387
soldiers, of lack of leave, v, 387
merchants, of their convoy, vi, 163
Complaints, English:
Blake, of his captains, iii, 92, 105, 147
Bourne, of unserviceable men, iv, 346
Monck, of slowness in refitting, v, 301
Ambassadors, of treatment of Dutch prisoners, vi, 71
bailiffs, of sick and hurt allowance not supplied, v, 268

COMPTON

seamen, of wages withheld, v, 276
at impress, v, 276
complaint against Chatham officers, i, 70
complaint against victualling, i, 242; iii, 176; v, 78, 231, 256 sq., 267, 270, 274, 276, 295, 328, 343, 375, 391; vi, 114
of unfit men pressed, i, 269; iii, 400
against capt. of the Francis, i, 358
against Navy Commissioners, ii, 125, 128
against capt. of the Marmaduke, ii, 128, 170
against Capt. Wyard, iii, 16
against privateers, iii, 40, 92; iv, 39
Compton, —, ii, 262
Condé, Prince of, v, 115
Conders, Jan (Captain), trial for desertion, v, 240, 242
Conduct Money, i, 139, 226; iii, 104, 159, 163, 312 sq., 366, 415; iv, 139, 163; v, 37; vi, 170; for volunteers, iii, 275; v, 37; for sick and wounded, iii, 273, 339
Coninck (or Coninch), Fredrick de, i, 262; v, 254, 281
Conington, iv, 256
Constable, Sir William (President, C.O.S.), iii, 14, 140; iv, 236; v, 393
Contraband, i, 165; iii, 150, 388 sq., 429; iv, 351, 388; v, 253; Dutch declare ammunition and victuals contraband, iii, 150, 152, 170, 184; trade in contraband from the Baltic, iii, 190 sq.; iv, 143, 379, 387, 390, 396; v, 27; export of, from Holland, iv, 349
Contyn, Adrien (Captain),

CONVOYS

battle of the Gabbard, v, 74 n.
Contsen (or Comtsen), Bastiaen (Captain), iii, 224, 228; iv, 192; took English ship, iii, 231, 252, 254
Convoys, Dutch:
ii, 176, 345, 370; iii, 80, 241, 253, 257, 258, 390, 399, 436; iv, 179, 187, 316, 359; v, 44 sqq., 59, 61, 119, 139, 187, 217, 265; vi, 26, 63, 85, 137, 161, 182
Baltic, i, 376; v, 245; vi, 182, 245
Brazil, iii, 242
Caribbean, i, 77 sq.; iii, 213, 266
Channel, i, 179, 260; ii, 62, 79
charge for convoys, ii, 22, 24; iii, 195
E. I. C., France and Spain, iii, 10, 23, 33, 35 sq., 39, 66, 138, 160, 186, 210, 213 sq., 225, 233, 242, 259; iv, 222; v, 27, 252, 336, 395; vi, 258
E. Indiamen to Sound, ii, 375; v, 246, 335, 404; vi, 256
E. Indiamen outward bound, vi, 245
convoy for wine fleet to France, vi, 112, 196
Mediterranean, ii, 16, 41, 44, 128, 311; iii, 242, 259
Straits, i, 220, 235; v, 336
St. Martin's, Tromp at, iv, 23 sq., 30, 32; petition from Biscay ports for delay, iv, 23; Tromp's instructions to, iv, 26; his reply to petition, iv, 28; in straits of Dover, iv, 65; their safe arrival, iv, 142
Silver fleet, ii, 14 sq., 18, 38, 41 sqq., 72, 77, 260, 350
Sound, for return ships, vi,

INDEX

CONVOYS

2 *sqq.*, 26, 35, 76, 79, 109, 117, 136 *sqq.*; outward bound, vi, 5, 49, 53, 61; arrival at Texel, vi, 153 *sqq.*; merchant ships sail from, without convoy, vi, 38 *sq.*, 46, 48; reported 26 taken by English, vi, 46, 48; De With's instructions to convoy, vi, 59; merchantmen from Sound join De With, vi, 143; Muscovy fleet from, ii, 250, 332, 334 Texel, i, 235; ii, 16 convoy for fleet expected north about, v, 284, 336
See also Denmark: Foreign Relations
Convoys: English:
ii, 11, 168; iii, 87; iv, 157, 260, 283, 293, 307, 372; v, 34, 49, 211, 225, 265, 278, 329, 346; vi, 42, 166, 229
to and from Baltic and the Sound, i, 312, 326; ii, 365, 374, 386, 388; Gothenburg, vi, 182, 208, 214
to and from Channel Islands, i, 287; ii, 370; iii, 439
Coastwise, i, 153, 203, 224, 305, 316; ii, 104, 124; iii, 429; iv, 59, 173, 174
Fisheries, v, 411; vi, 255
France, ii, 19, 97; vi, 253
Hamburg, vi, 33, 78, 84, 87, 99, 239
Iceland, vi, 255
Ireland, i, 267; iv, 320
Ostend, i, 337
Scotland, i, 202; iv, 174 *n.*
Sound, *see* Baltic
Spain, iv, 254
Texel, i, 128, 133
for the coal fleet, ii, 373; iv, 290, 292, 303, 318 *sq.*, 328 *sq.*, 335 *sqq.*, 346, 350, 356 *sq.*, 373, 394; vi, 7, 229 *sq.*
VI.

CORN

E. I. C. ships, v, 121
prizes, iv, 253, 260, 282; v, 145, 187
for victuallers, ii, 98, 137, 167; iii, 25, 34; iv, 141, 253, 347; v, 196, 343
demands for, ii, 154, 174, 375; iii, 49, 59, 131, 174, 387
ships for, i, 62, 68, 136, 153, 186, 224
Conway, Lord, letters to, v, 197, 213
Coode, Isaac (Captain), battle of the Gabbard, v, 74
Cook rooms, position of, i, 12
Coolbrant, — (Master), i, 390
Cooper, Samuel (Commissioner for Sick and Hurt), instructions to, vi, 89
Copenhagen, ii, 66; v, 109 *n.*; vi, 54; Dutch merchant ships awaiting convoy, vi, 35, 55, 62
Coppe, Jacob Janssen (Captain), capt. of the Catrina, iv, 323
Coppe, John Jacob, v, 74 *n.*
Coppin, James, i, 414; capt. of the Hart, i, 66
Coppin, John (Captain), ii, 239; iii, 88, 111; capt. of the Entrance, i, 64; capt. of the Speaker; his petition, iii, 373
Coradall, Henry, action off Dover, account of, i, 227, 228
Corbet, — (Captain), iv, 137; capt. of the Mary ketch, iv, 22
Corbett, —, i, 246; ii, 73
Corbin, Angel (Captain), capt. of the Mary ketch, v, 62
Corff, Jan Claessen (Captain), ii, 198, 256, 354; capt. of the St. Maria, ii, 65
Corn, Ary (Captain), capt. of the Vergulde Buys, ii, 343

S

CORN

Corn, Jersen (Master), ii, 343
Cornelissen, Adrian (Master), master of the Princess of Rotterdam, iv, 137
Cornelissen, Pieter (skipper), iii, 226, 234
Cornelissen, Geroen (skipper), ii, 185, 191; orders from De Ruyter, ii, 140 (2)
Cornelissen, Simon, master of the Star of Hoorn, iv, 98
Cornelissen, Ysbrant, iii, 226 *sq.*, 237
Cornelisz., Reijer (Master), v, 322
Corneliszoon, Jacob (Captain), capt. of the Wassende Maen, i, 379
Corneliszoon, Matheus, i, 262
Corneliszoon, Meyndert (Captain), capt. of the Liefde, i, 124
Corneliszoon, Reynst, i, 264, 407
Corneliszoon, Symon, i, 261
Cornelius, —, (Captain), vi, 52; capt. of the Fox, v, 16
Cornelys, Adrian (Captain), found innocent of charge of cowardice, vi, 46
Cornwall, iv, 163
Corstiaensen, Corstiaen (Rear-Admiral), i, 261; ii, 336, 342; iii, 156, 220, 224; battle of Portland: reported dead, iv, 189
Cort, Jacob, Paulussen (Captain), i, 261, 351, 368, 388, 393; iii, 224, 240; capt. of the Star, iv, 309
Cortenaer, Egbert. *See* Meeussen
Cortuere, Pieter Elych, v, 44 *n.*, 133
Cottenburg. *See* Gothenburg
Cottington, Lord, iv, 105
Couckebacker, N—, iii, 198
Courteis, Edmund. *See* Curtis

CRISP

Courts Martial. *See* Discipline: Trials
Cowes, iv, 137; ship lying at, to be sent to Downs, i, 215
Cox, Owen (Captain), i, 68; v, 298; vi, 50; letters from, v, 251, 364; capt. of the Constant Warwick, i, 18; action off Isle of Elba, i, 18; retakes Phœnix, i, 19, 20; v, 150; battle of the Texel, v, 365 *sq.*; capt. of the Phœnix, v, 366; his death, v, 373, 390 *n.*
Coxe, —, capt. of the Falcon, vi, 52
Coytmor, Robert (Navy Commissioner), i, 225, 344; ii, 34, 73, 293, 373, 387; iii, 34, 113, 399; letters to, i, 249; ii, 373; iii, 113, 399; letter from, iv, 149; Secretary Admiralty Committee, i, 53; to report on State's ships, i, 185, 319; ii, 118; to hasten out ships, iv, 326
Crallo, Martin, petition of, ii, 171
Cramer, Barent (Captain), i, 265, 351, 388; ii, 331; capt. of the Edan, iv, 309; capt. of the Swarte Bull, v, 361; battle of the Texel, v, 361
Cramp, — (Captain), capt. of the George Bonaventure, iii, 312
Crapnell, George (Captain), vi, 50; capt. of the Merlin, v, 18
Creed, Mr., iii, 430; iv, 175; v, 107; vi, 220
Creswell, Thomas, letter from, i, 364; reports sighting Dutch fleet, i, 364
Crisp, — (Captain), capt. of the Prosperous, v, 390 *n.*; battle of the Texel: his death, v, 390 *n.*

INDEX 281

CRISPIN

Crispin, William (Captain), v, 18; vi, 50, 200; capt. of the Assistance, iv, 293

Croeger, Hendrick (Captain), i, 389; battle of the Texel, v, 363; capt. of the Marcus Curtius, iv, 310

Croeg, Hendrick, iv, 25

Crofwik, Roger (Navy Commissioner), iii, 324

Croisic, iv, 136 *and n.*

Cromarty, iv, 107

Cromer, iv, 372

Cromwell, Henry, letter from, i, 138

Cromwell, Oliver (Lord General), i, 190, 209, 211, 239; iii, 112; v, 91; vi, 232; letters to, v, 81, 364; vi, 217; letter from, v, 266

Croon, Commissary, vi, 162

Crossing, Phillipe (merchant), letter from, iii, 322

Crossnesse, Ericke. *See* Johnson

Cruijck (*or* Cruyck, *or* Kruijck), Astriaen (Captain), capt. of the Vogelstruis, battle of Portland, iv, 123, 189 *and n.*, 195

Cruisers. *See* Commerce; Intelligence; Squadrons Employed

Cruys, Wessel Janszoon (Master), master of Wassende Maen, i, 379

Cruijs, Pieter (skipper), ii, 349; v, 127

Crynsen, Cryn (skipper), ii, 208, 349

Cubitt, Joseph (Captain), v, 20; vi, 51, 227; letter from, v, 367; capt. of the Tulip, iii, 408; iv, 21; battle of the Texel, v, 367 *sqq.*, 390 *n.*; capt. of the Portsmouth, vi, 200; capt. of the Sapphire, vi, 222 *and n.*

DARTMOUTH

Cullen, v, 185

Cullen, William (Mayor of Dover), iii, 173, 319; letter from, v, 66, 211

Culmer, John, ii, 335

Curtis, Edmund (Captain), iv, 21; v, 17; vi, 50; letter from, iii, 399; capt. of the Guinea, i, 67; capt. of the Ruby, vi, 199

Cuttance, Roger (Captain), i, 330; iv, 293; v, 17; vi, 49; capt. of the Pearl, i, 65; took Dutch ship, iii, 132; capt. of the Sussex, iv, 20

Cutting, John (Captain), iii, 366

Cuyper, Cornelis (Captain), ii, 64 *n.*, 199; iii, 224, 228, 233; iv, 194; capt. of the Gaes, vi, 175 *and n.*

D., F., offers a gunnery invention to the Dutch, iii, 84

Dakinge (*or* Deakins, *or* Dakins *or* Deacons), George (Captain), ii, 243; iii, 77, 177; iv, 293; v, 16; capt. of the Advice, i, 65; capt. of the Worcester, iv, 20; battle of Portland, iv, 81, 84; capt. of the Andrew, vi, 49; capt. of the Paragon, vi, 201

Daniel (*or* Daniells), John (Captain), ii, 101; capt. of the Maidenhead, iv, 294

Dantzic, i, 329; v, 266; vi, 76, 141 *sq.*

Darby, — (Lieutenant), i, 46; lieut. of the Sandwich, i, 46

Dare, Jeffery (Captain), petition of, iii, 400 *sq.*; capt. of the Exchange, v, 18; capt. of the Mary Rose, vi, 200

Dartmouth, iii, 386; iv, 67 (2), 103, 137, 148, 305; v, 298;

DAVIS

petition of inhabitants for convoy for fishing fleet, iii, 387
Davis (*or* Davy), Robert (Captain), vi, 51; capt. of the Dolphin, v, 20
Dawkins, Rowland, letter to, i, 130
Dawson, George (Customs Officer), ii, 247; iii, 419; v, 50
Dawson, Henry (Mayor of Newcastle), iii, 451
Day, — (Captain), capt. of the Advice, i, 16; killed Portland fight, i, 16
Day (*or* Dey), John (Captain), ii, 240; iv, 293; capt. of the Old Warwick, i, 65; capt. of the Advice, iv, 20; battle of Portland, iv, 73, 80, 83; court martial, v, 429
Day, Thomas, letter from, v, 211
Daym, Jan (Captain), iii, 248
Deal, iii, 441; iv, 50, 77, 96, 130, 135, 147, 176, 332; v, 66, 299; 500 barrels of powder to be sent to, i, 242, 269; reinforcements for, i, 356; Deal Castle, i, 369, 373; v, 77; Dutch fleet sighted off, iv, 32; proposal for hospital in, iii, 273
Deane, Edward, ii, 162
Deane, Humphrey (skipper), iii, 239
Deane, Richard (Admiral and General at Sea), i, 4, 14, 15 *n*., 54, 319, 385; iii, 110, 283, 369, 400, 407, 415, 435; iv, 33, 38, 48, 139, 156, 172, 232, 260, 262, 273, 275 *sq*., 284, 353, 392; v, 67, 112, 125, 129 *n*., 266
Letter to, iv, 149; letters from, iv, 47, 152, 163, 245, 252, 295, 299, 305, 319,

DENMARK

347, 361, 368, 385, 386, 389; v, 31, 35, 53, 64
Ordered to send troops to Orkney and Shetland, i, 223; his commission as General, iii, 110, 178; battle of Portland, iv, 79 *sq*., 83, 101, 124, 163 *sqq*.; list of ships under his command, v, 16 *sqq*.; battle of the Gabbard, v, 21, 72; his death, v, 72, 84, 92 *sq*., 100, 106, 114, 144, 190
Deans, Captain (Treasurer and Collector of Prize Goods), v, 344
Dearloo, v, 417
Declaration of Paris, i, 52
Degelcamp, — van (Captain), ii, 80 *and n*., 191, 343 *sq*.; capt. of the Gelderlant, vi, 157
Delft, v, 282, 288, 402, 412
Demmer, Gerrard, vi, 118
Denaru, Jan Pieterszoon (Captain), ii, 352
Denich, Frans, ii, 356
Denmark, Foreign Relations: with England, ii, 66, 103, 205, 312, 313, 316, 364, 376, 385, 388; iii, 12, 13, 40, 126, 413, 426, 448; vi, 215
Negotiations for a treaty, ii, 335; report of treaty with Netherlands, ii, 368; v, 118, 194; report of closer alliance, ii, 384; the King and his Navy, iii, 448; vi, 35; reported to be arming their fleet, iv, 251
English fear Danish squadron may join Dutch, v, 51; reported English success against, v, 71; breach with Sweden, v, 211; suggested exchange of ships with Netherlands, v, 244 *sqq*., 254, 281, 283, 290, 313, 386; warships to

INDEX

DENNIS

convoy Dutch merchantmen, vi, 62, 79, 109, 122, 141 *sqq.*
Dennis, Robert (Captain), i, 67, 69, 70; ii, 180; capt. of the John and in command of Virginia squadron, i, 67
Deptford, i, 110, 185, ii, 133; iii, 65, 405, 427; iv, 44 *n.*, 87, 99, 231; v, 76, 215, 276, 292, 301, 345; vi, 53, 83, 174, 177; two frigates to be built at, i, 140; state Ships not to be brought to, i, 184
Desborough. *See* Disbrowe
Desbrough, G. (Major), iv, 177
Dessoen, — (Captain), ii, 345
Deurloo, iv, 193 *and n.*
Deyckers, Jan (Captain), i, 262
Dickinson, Samuel (Captain), vi, 200; capt. of the Black Raven, vi, 52
Dieppe, iv, 388; vi, 104, 253
Dimlington iv, 394; rendezvous at, iv, 341 *and n.*
Dingle Bay, iv, 300 *n.*
Dircxszoon (*or* Diricksen, *or* Dercksen), Arent (Captain), i, 264, 351, 393; ii, 337, 343; iii, 225, 245; v, 239; capt. of the Monnich, iv, 314
Dirckszoon, Dirck (Captain), capt. of the Amsterdam, ii, 343
Dirick, — (Captain), capt. of the Shepherdess, v, 185
Disbrowe, John (Major-General), i, 187; iii, 131, 132, 360; vi, 107, 203, 225; letter from, vi, 72, 217; appointed Navy Commissioner, vi, 189; General at Sea, vi, 6, 104, 189. *See also* Instructions
Discipline, Dutch: Fiscal appointed, ii, 328; iii, 70; captains, iii, 70, 236; iv,

DODMAN

26, 182; v, 153 *sq.*; misconduct of, in action, v, 73, 88, 100, 102, 117, 178, 198, 200, 205, 220, 319, 351, 355 *sqq.*, 384 *sq.*, 402, 413; trial of, ii, 311, 315, 367; iii, 26, 53–56; iv, 384; v, 191, 205, 220 *sq.*, 239 *sq.*, 243, 264, 287; vi, 41, 75
Seamen, mutiny of, ii, 235; iii, 60, 62 *sq.*, 73; iv, 207, 247 *sq.*, 257 *sq.*; v, 223, 281, 317; desertion of, v, 201; measures to prevent, vi, 24; indiscipline in capture of prizes, v, 48; at the battle of Texel, v, 170, 172; vi, 25 *sq.*
Discipline, English: iii, 128, 164, 169, 381, 409; iv, 147 *sq.*, 391; v, 177; vi, 100 *sq.*
Captains, trial of, iii, 163 *sq.*, 338, 364, 406, 412, 445; v, 429; vi, 205; officers cashiered, v, 141
Seamen, mutiny of, iii, 45, 73, 86, 311, 422, 438, 449; v, 65 *sq.*, 295, 429; vi, 8, 107 *sq.*, 128, 168, 173; instructions for punishment, vi, 192 *sqq. See also* Articles of War
Dispensier (*or* Pensier), Lourens (Captain), ii, 80, 87, 147; vi, 157; took English merchantmen, ii, 192; capt. of the St. Jan, ii, 147
Dixwell, — (Colonel), i, 356, 357; ii, 287
Dobbins, — (Commissary), iii, 431
Does, Jan Corneliszoon (Master), master of the Fortuyn, i, 124
Dockyard artificers. *See* Artificers
Dodman, vi, 252

DOGGER

Dogger Bank, iv, 359; v, 41, 44, 50 *and n.*, 217; vi, 97, 182, 184, 186 *sq.*, 239, 256
Doleman, — (Colonel), iv, 233, 353; vi, 217
Dorislaus, Isaac, iii, 364; instructions to, iii, 361 *and n.*
Dornford (*or* Durnford), Robert (Captain), iv, 153, 157; v, 18; letters from, iii, 133, 350; capt. of the Portsmouth: action with two Dutch men-of-war, iii, 133 *sq.*, 350 *sq.*
Dorset, iii, 127
Dorvelt (*or* Dorrevelt), Barent Pietersz., i, 123, 261, 351
Doumes, Andries (Captain), iii, 225; iv, 25
Douwes, Andries (Captain), ii, 364; court-martialled, v, 192
Douwes, Douwer (Captain), ii, 353
Douwes, Elcke (Master), master of the St. Mary, i, 221
Douweszoon, Andries (Captain), i, 264
Dove, David (Captain), vi, 50; capt. of the Tenth Whelp, iv, 21
Dove, John, iii, 317, 324, 439
Dover, i, 196, 198, 242, 311, 327, 339, 352; iii, 173, 441; iv, 50, 52, 77 *sq.*, 95, 104 *sq.*, 108, 126 *sq.*, 130, 134, 157 *sq.*, 236, 260, 282, 299, 303, 332 *sq.*, 355, 373, 376, 385, 392; v, 21, 26, 49, 71, 77, 104, 121, 139, 190, 208, 224, 299, 345, 408; vi, 104, 113, 204, 252 *sqq.*
Volunteers from, i, 9; rewarded, i, 241; Dover Castle, i, 190, 294; iv, 96, 303; gunners and ammunition wanted for, v, 52; packet from, i, 235; pier, repair of, i, 242; money

DRIVER

for the fleet to be carried to, i, 305, 310; ships refitted at, i, 343
Victualling station, ii, 75, 164, 169, 183; Dutch fleet off, iii, 107, 159, 332; v, 49, 58, 66; English fleet at, iv, 48; Dutch attack shipping at, v, 58, 70, 135. *See also* Actions: Fleet and Squadrons
Dover, Straits of, iv, 369 *n.*, 388; v, 250, 252, 285; Texel squadron to join De Ruyter at, ii, 91; Dutch fleet and convoy sighted, iv, 65; Dutch fleet after battle of Portland, iv, 183
Dovrevelt, Barent (Captain), capt. of the Amsterdam, iv, 310
Downing, Hon. George (Scout Master General), letter to, vi, 37
Downs, i, 107, 129, 196, 198, 202, 215, 217, 239, 302, 365, 417; iv, 78, 96, 102, 134, 144, 172, 234, 260, 299, 304 *sq.*, 324, 335, 350 *sq.*, 358, 364, 371 *sqq.*, 382, 384 *sq.*, 390, 393, 396; v, 21, 28, 31 *sq.*, 56 *sq.*, 81, 114, 121, 129, 134 *sq.*, 139, 190, 203, 221, 251, 298; iv, 57, 104, 166, 253
Rendezvous, i, 107, 154, 187; iv, 31; vi, 176; ships in, to be victualled for 5 months, i, 242; list of, i, 289; 10 Newfoundland fishery ships to remain in Downs, i, 224; Dutch fleet in Downs, i, 363; iii, 84; v, 49; list of ships in, vi, 202
Drew, —, ii, 67
Driver, John (Lieutenant), lieut. of the Hamburg Merchant, iv, 345

Drury Lane, iv, 256
Duijm (or Duym), Jacob Klaesz. (Captain), i, 262; capt. of the Sun, iv, 323; v, 23; battle of the Gabbard, v, 23
Duijm, Jan (Captain), battle of Portland, iv, 195 sq.; battle of the Gabbard, v, 74
Duijrekop, Leijn (Mate), iv, 354
Dun, — (of Berwick), iii, 371
Dunes, iv, 127
Dungeness, ii, 58; iv, 144, 391; v, 139 n., 250 n.; vi, 183, 205
Dutch rendezvous off, ii, 59; battle of, iii, 89 sqq., 100 sq., 106 sq., 116, 143, 151, 205, 230, 252; vi, 15 sq.; losses, iii, 108, 144, 230; Dutch anchored off, iii, 92; English ships warned to avoid, iii, 97, 113, 123, 127, 174. See also Actions: Fleets and Squadrons
Dunkirk, i, 218, 235; iv, 132, 142, 170, 196, 260, 274, 280, 283, 370, 372, 376; v, 22, 43, 49, 84, 86, 100, 200, 251, 253; vi, 221, 224, 253; relief of, ii, 166, 234; Tromp's fleet off, i, 211; v, 109, 124, 138; surrender to Spanish, ii, 344
Dunkirk, privateers of, i, 20, 135 n.; ii, 299
Dunottar Castle, i, 223; v, 35
Dunwich, iv, 53; v, 64, 257, 260, 268, 300; sick to be accommodated, v, 399
Durnford, Robert (Captain), vi, 50; capt. of the Portsmouth, iv, 278
Duyts, Jan (Captain), capt. of Ostend privateer, iii, 231
Dyck, Thomas Jansen (Captain), capt. of the Hoope, ii, 65

EADEN, Henry (Captain), capt. of the Phœnix, v, 17
Earning (or Erning), Anthony, (Captain), iv, 280; v, 19, 105; vi, 234; capt. of the Reformation, i, 191; to repair to Downs, i, 202 n.
East Mundham, v, 410
Eastland, v, 119, 201
Eckersen, Jan (Captain), v, 135
Eckersloodt, Adrijaen Cornelijssen (Captain), v, 418
Eclipse of the Sun, 1652, i, 7
Edam, i, 263; iv, 324; v, 23, 40, 74
Edwin, John (Captain), ii, 28; iv, 279; v, 19; capt. of the Oak, i, 16; iii, 103; iv, 22; battle of Portland, i, 16; iv, 73; capt. of the Cock, vi, 52
Eenarm, Cornelis Reiners (Lieutenant), tried for desertion, v, 240, 242 sq.
Eerckhove, Pauwels van der (Captain), iii, 233
Egbertsen, Jan (Captain), ii, 63, 147, 188 sq., 353; vi, 175 and n.; capt. of the Gouda, ii, 147. See also Ooms, Jan Egbertsen
Eichels, Jacob (Captain), ii, 187
Eijcke, Jan Jansen van de (Master), vi, 157
Elba, Isle of, action off, i, 18
Elbe, The, iv, 388; v, 265, 395; vi, 33 n., 99, 239
Elberszoon, Corstiaen, i, 261
Eldersen, Christiaen (Captain), iii, 225; vi, 154
Eldersen, Elveston (Captain), iii, 233
Eldertszoon, Corstyaer (Captain), i, 382; iii, 208, 210 sq.
Eldred, —, v, 33
Eles, Thomas (merchant), letter from, iii, 322

Elinch, —, v, 43
Ellis, — (Captain), ii, 73
Ellis, Nathaniel (boatswain), boatswain of the Sussex, iii, 382
Elseveijr, — (Resident), vi, 125
Elsinore, place of rendezvous, i, 311-12, 326
Ely, William (Light keeper, North Foreland), iii, 303 n.
Embargo: Danish, vi, 215
Embargo: Dutch, Baltic trade exempted from, i, 85 and n.; embargo on English shipping, i, 136; reported raised, i, 136
Embargo: English, 21 days' embargo on all merchant ships, i, 246, 248, 258; ships for Straits and Bilboa exempted, i, 305; 14 days' embargo on all ships except provision ships, iii, 322, 323; on merchantmen lifted, vi, 8, 181, 190, 241; general, vi, 218, 243
Embezzlement, i, 323; iii, 126; vi, 173; security for prevention of, iii, 25, 314; vi, 185; of prize stores, iv, 145 sq.
Emden (or Embden), iv, 98, 361
Ems, The, iv, 309 n.; v, 199, 235, 286
Enemy Ship, Enemy Goods: English claim, i, 324; iv, 32; vi, 31. See also 'Free Ships, Free Goods'
Engelen, Cornelis, i, 351
England: foreign relations, Anglo-Danish, ii, 66, 103, 205, 312, 313, 316, 364, 376, 385, 388; iii, 12, 13; Danish ships to be stayed, iii, 31, 45, 58, 126; France: Blake captures Vendome's squadron, ii, 166, 234, 344, 346. See also Privateers
England, its advantage of strategical position, i, 31, 33
Enkhuisen, iv, 185; v, 23, 185, 187, 194, 369, 421; vi, 159; commanders of Directors' ships from, i, 262; v, 74; ships from, v, 422
Erith, iv, 44 n.; v, 76
Erle, Sir Walter (Lieutenant of Ordnance), iii, 327
Es, Van (Captain), i, 430
Est, Jan van (Lieutenant), vi, 157
Eselen, Joost, iv, 186
Etaples, iv, 117, 191
Ethes, Richard (Deputy Mayor of Deal), iii, 356
Evans, Thomas, vi, 234
Evelyn, — (Major), letter to, i, 119; Governor of Wallingford Castle, i, 119
Evertsen, Cornelis (Captain), (the Younger), i, 234, 264; ii, 86, 146, 187, 305, 327, 354; iii, 156, 224 sq., 237, 238, 241 (2), 255; iv, 192; v, 135, 239; vi, 157; battle of Kentish Knock, ii, 294 sq., 301; capt. of the Vlissingen, ii, 146
Evertsen, Cornelis (Commodore), i, 263, 351, 393, 404, 407; ii, 342; iii, 222 sq., 232, 247; iv, 192, 384; v, 130; vi, 46
Orders from Ruyter, ii, 80; to cruise in Straits, iii, 239, 240, 257; convoy duty, iv, 179, 187 sq.; battle of Portland, iv, 188, 191; battle of Texel: taken prisoner, v, 390 n., 393
Evertsen, Jan (Captain), iii, 246
Evertsen, Jan (Vice-Admiral of Zeeland), i, 59, 235, 236, 263, 284, 321, 351, 353, 391,

INDEX

EWELL
393, 395, 426, 428 ; ii, 93 ; iii, 10 *sq.*, 33, 48, 66, 69, 78, 140, 156 ; iii, 223 *sq.*, 248, 259, 264 ; iv, 179, 192, 196, 251, 377, 384 ; v, 45 *sqq.*, 56, 130, 133 *sq.*, 200, 219, 223, 239, 286, 312 *sq.*, 403 *sq.*, 421 ; vi, 25, 27, 46, 134
Letters from, i, 86, 133, 379, 395 ; ii, 88
Commanding squadron at entrance of Channel, i, 76 ; temporary C.-in-C., ii, 88 ; battle of Dungeness, iii, 117, 151, 252 ; his journal, iii, 222 *sqq.* ; iv, 187 *sqq.* ; his squadron separated by storm, iii, 242 ; off the Start, iii, 244
Battle of Portland, iv, 89, 118, 120 *sq.* ; reported slain, iv, 171 ; battle of the Texel, v, 171, 350, 355 *sq.*, 383 *sq.*, 419 ; vi, 47 ; claims chief command on Tromp's death, v, 377, 385 ; refusal to serve under De With, vi, 25
Ewell, Zacheus, master's mate of the Worcester, i, 250
Ewont, — (Captain), i, 388
Ewyck (*or* Ewijck), G. van, iii, 392 ; iv, 223 ; v, 220 ; letter from, v, 393
Ewyck, S. van, iv, 360
Examinations, Committee of, i, 234, 337
Excise : Dutch, farmers of, v, 313
Eyk, Jan Janszoon van der, ii, 305
Ezekiel, — (Captain), v, 282

F. D., letter from, iii, 84
Faber, Teunis (Fiscal Advocate to the Fleet), v, 239 ; vi, 75

FINANCE
Fair Isle, rendezvous for Dutch fleet, i, 389, 392, 403 ; English fleet reported off, v, 45, 140
Fairlight, i, 197, 419 ; iv, 72, 95, 114, 153
Fairy Isle. *See* Fair Isle
Falkener, Joseph (Ordnance Officer), iii, 314, 316
Falmouth, iii, 441 ; iv, 187 ; v, 278, 301 ; Dutch ship stayed, i, 246
Fappenlain, Anthony (Lieut. Commander), his instructions, v, 320
Fareham, iv, 232, 296
Farn Islands, i, 380
Farnham, iv, 218
Faroe Islands, v, 40
Felstead, Humphrey (Captain), capt. of the Marigold, vi, 52
Femsen, Gerrit, i, 264, 393
Fenn, Henry (Captain), capt. of the Roebuck, v, 20
Fenwick, George (Colonel), ii, 167
Feverton, v, 410
Field, William, iv, 43, 44 ; v, 107
Fielder, Jo (Commissioner for Ireland and Scotland), iii, 431, 432, 446
Filey, iv, 329
Finance : Dutch :
Taxation for providing 150 ships, i, 85, 94, 103 ; iv, 312, 316 ; money for fitting out of 100 ships, how to be obtained, i, 121 *and n.* ; security required, i, 122 ; Admiralties asked to send quotas of expenses, i, 271 ; Amsterdam debt to Denmark, i, 273 ; expense of cruising squadrons, ii, 22–26 ; Amsterdam Admiralty asks S.G. for money, ii, 316 *sq.* ; vi, 64 *sqq.* ; for part share of

288 INDEX

FINANCE

shipbuilding grant, iii, 82 *sq.*; demand for a 'constant war fund,' iii, 392; levy of two hundredth penny, iv, 143

Admiralty Boards ask for funds, v, 388; vi, 64 *sqq.*, 95; military funds diverted for use of fleet, vi, 49; all orders for payments suspended, vi, 64. *See also* Pay: Dutch

Finance: English, iii, 109; iv, 138 *sq.*; vi, 176

Charge of the fleet and convoys, i, 141; payment for 40 extra ships, i, 224, 233; reimburse press money for same, i, 227; money for repair of Dover pier, i, 242; diverted for use of fleet, ii, 167, 168; iii, 98

Money required for building and victualling 30 frigates, iii, 64; money required for victualling and seamen's pay, iii, 175, 308; iv, 320

Assignments of money for the Navy, iii, 304 *sq.*; Navy estimates, iv, 57, 296; vi, 43; money required for reparations, v, 52, 294; for naval stores, v, 235 *sq.*; vi, 42; for sick and hurt, v, 247 *sq.*, 268, 293, 300, 344, 401; vi, 248 *sq.*; for shipbuilding, vi, 43

Lack of money, vi, 43; allowance for victualling, to be paid monthly, vi, 68 *sq.*, 73; money for building of dry dock, vi, 70. *See also* Pay

Finsse, — (Captain), iv, 193

Fireships: Dutch, i, 265, 351, 365; ii, 32, 47; iii, 33, 160, 185, 233; v, 23, 43, 186, 190, 312

FISHERIES

Ruyter's orders to captains of, ii, 64, 148; in De With's fleet, ii, 343, 354; Tromp's demands for, iv, 362, 378; v, 27 *sq.*, 47, 57; at the Gabbard battle, v, 23, 74 *n.*, 138; at the Texel battle, v, 169 *sq.*, 350, 356. *See also* Complaints

Fireships: English, i, 143, 164, 240, 280, 371; iii, 336; vi, 174

To be dispatched to Downs, i, 129, 307; to be 'hastened out,' i, 249, 347; instructions for, iv, 265; battle of the Texel, v, 350; list of ships, vi, 52

Fisheries: Dutch:

Herring busses, i, 17, 103; vi, 29, 60; fishing vessels taken, i, 401, 405; v, 129 *n.*, 139 *sq.*, 286; their men released, v, 139; small fishery exempted from embargo, i, 85

Greenland fishery, i, 125, 392, 412; iv, 349; Tromp to protect North Sea fisheries, i, 219; at Orkney and Shetland, i, 223; England to interrupt herring fishery, i, 302, 336; northern fishing guard taken, i, 385 *sq.*, 399, 408; release of fishing guard, v, 112

Fisheries: English:

Mackerel fishery, guard appointed, i, 137, 153; ships bound for Newfoundland fishery to remain in Downs, i, 224, 268; dismissed, i, 316, 319, 324; fisheries' ships exempted from embargo, i, 258

North Sea boats taken by Tromp's fleet, i, 379, 401, 412; ii, 92; distressed state

INDEX

FISHERIES

of Yarmouth, iii, 344 sq.; Greenland, i, 413; Iceland, i, 413; ii, 175; vi, 255; vessels taken by Dutch to be released, v, 112; Yarmouth herring fleet, v, 411. See also Newfoundland

Fisheries: French, i, 304, 358

Fitch (Colonel), v, 398

Flag, the honouring of the, i, 135, 170, 212, 251; Young's summons resisted, i, 179, 182; Tromp before Dover, i, 193, 420, 422

Flags, ensigns of prizes, how displayed, i, 12; colours of red, white and blue, i, 14; Dutch vanes in English ships, i, 16; flags, captured: dressing ship with, i, 23; colours of Ostenders, i, 27; the Prince's flag, i, 167 and n.; squadronal pennants, English, i, 185; squadronal pennants, Dutch, i, 236; Royalist colours, iii, 189; of command (English), red, blue and white, iii, 375, 376; colours demanded, iv, 321 sq.; v, 26; Dutch offer prize for capture, v, 319; a bloody Jack, vi, 239. See also Signals

Flag Officers: Dutch, Lieut-Admiral, i, 177; Vice-Admiral, i, 59; vi, 166; of Amsterdam, vi, 191; Rear-Admiral, vi, 166; Commandeur (or Commodore), i, 177, 261; ii, 2; Vice- or Lieut.-Commandeur, i, 177; ii, 2, 336; Schout-bij-Nacht, i, 177; vi, 153; appointments by Ruyter, ii, 57, 111

Flag Officers: English, Vice- and Rear-Admirals of Summer Guard, i, 127; iii, 374 sq., 424; vi, 106; Vice- Admiral of the Fleet, i, 177, 189;

FLUSHING

iii, 406. See also Generals at Sea; Rewards; Pay

Flamborough Head, i, 340; iv, 159, 318, 328 sq., 331, 335, 356 n.; v, 249; vi, 230, 239

Fleet. See Navy

Fleet Committee, report of, vi, 202 sq.

Fleetwood, Je. (Lieutenant-General), i, 305, 344; letter from, iv, 363; added to Admiralty Committee, i, 234; to appoint officers to prevent disorders, i, 353

Flekkefiord, iv, 360; v, 245; vi, 28, 37 n., 38, 54, 62, 78, 109, 119, 121, 125, 144 sq., 149; rendezvous, vi, 109, 117, 120, 123, 125, 143, 146, 148

Flekken, vi, 37 n., 38, 138, 147, 182 n.

Fleming, Sir Oliver, i, 223; ii, 158

Floriszoon, Pieter (Rear-Admiral), i, 264, 321, 351, 353, 391, 393, 429; ii, 363; iii, 11, 31, 138, 225, 233, 236, 248, 266; iv, 23, 28, 251, 315, 377; v, 45, 48, 56, 113, 130, 133 sq., 200, 239; vi, 29, 118, 122, 142 sq., 153 sq., 162, 171

Letters from, i, 379, 395; capt. of the Monickendam, iii, 199 sq.; iv, 178 n.; battle of Portland, iv, 118, 178 sqq., 186; battle of the Texel, v, 351, 356, 383 sq.

Flushing, iv, 98, 194, 197, 258, 370, 384; v, 34, 43, 58 sq., 114, 117, 126, 132, 136, 189 sq., 200 sq., 203, 210, 219, 223, 227, 243, 282, 288, 335, 365; vi, 124, 205

Commissioners of Director's ships from, i, 264; ships cleaned at, i, 382; return

INDEX

FLYPS

of Tromp's fleet from northern voyage, i, 410; Dutch wounded landed, v, 117. *See also* Privateers: Dutch
Flyps (*or* Flyp), — (Captain), ii, 190; iii, 254, 256. *See also* Philipsen
Fockes, Gerrit (Captain), iv, 334
Fockes, Sipke (Captain), i, 199, 235, 262, 285; ii, 351; iii, 224; capt. of the St. Mary, i, 207 *n.*; prisoner of war, examination of, i, 213; battle of Portland: reported dead, iv, 189
Foli, Jan, iv, 186
Folio, —, Mr., i, 115 *and n.*
Folkerts (*or* Folkertie), Willem (Captain), capt. of the Swarte Bull, iv, 324; battle of the Gabbard, v, 74 *n.*
Folkestone, iv, 134, 172
Fomeen, Andrew, battle of Texel: taken prisoner, v, 390 *n.*
Foot, Peter (Captain), capt. of the Adventure frigate, vi, 202, 237 *n.*
Fopsen, Jan (chief boatswain), iv, 186
Foreign Affairs, Committee of, i, 222, 247, 318; iv, 51
Forests, Abernethy, iii, 369 *sq.*; Glenmorieston, iii, 369; Waltham, iii, 290
Forster, Nic. (Captain), capt. of the Golden Fleece, iv, 16
Fort d'Outaô, i, 344 *and n.*
Fortuyn, Andries (Captain), ii, 80, 144, 147, 149, 187, 195 *sq.*, 256, 305, 354; iii, 224, 241, 247; v, 45; vi, 157; capt. of the Eendraght, ii, 147
Foster, Nicholas (Captain), i, 31; vi, 7, 201, 239 *sq.*; letter from, vi, 210; capt. of the Phœnix, i, 31

FREESTON

Foulsbury, iv, 141
Fowey, vi, 67, 138; v, 296
Fowler, John, vi, 198; appointed Judge Advocate, vi, 105
France: English Letters of Marque against, i, 59, 60, 72, 80, 81, 123, 162, 163, 247, 304, 330; Dutch ships taken under, i, 123, 162, 163; capture of Dutch merchantmen off coast, vi, 104, 113; action with French Newfoundland fleet, vi, 251. *See also* Letters of Marque: English
France, Foreign Relations: England, capture of Vendôme's squadron, ii, 166, 234, 344, 346; Netherlands, iii, 61. *See also* Privateers
Francis, Philip (Mayor of Plymouth), ii, 292
Franklin, —, proctor of Admiralty Court, i, 82
Fransz., Pieter, iv, 186
Fransz., Sijmon, iv, 186
Fransen, Essel (Lieutenant), iii, 240, 247
Frazerburgh, Dutch fleet off, i, 400
Fredericsen, Jan (Captain), iii, 245
Fredericxsz., Jan, iv, 186
Fredericsxz., Pieter, iv, 186
'Free Ship, Free Goods,' a Dutch claim: protests against captures, i, 123, 162, 163; capture of Hamburghers, iii, 19, 33, 59, 72; iv, 32, 250; capture of Lübecker, iii, 32; Tromp and the regulations, iii, 139, 170; ambiguity of S. G.'s orders, iii, 388 *sq.*
Freeman, John (merchant), iii, 413
Freeston, v, 410

INDEX

FRIESLAND

Friesland, or North Quarter, iv, 194; v, 195, 233, 265, 357; vi, 160; commissioners of Directors' ships from, i, 264; ii, 337; commissioners of Admiralty ships from, ii, 337, 343; list of ships from, vi, 157. *See also* Admiralties: Dutch

Frost, —, ii, 288

Fugge, — (Master), master of the Robert and Richard, i, 286

Fuller, — (Captain), iii, 282

GABBARD SHOAL, iv, 203; v, 72 *n*.; battle of, v, 16–24, 69 *sq.*, 71 *sqq.*, 81 *sqq.*, 89 *sqq.*, 96 *sqq.*, 109 *sq.*, 116 *sqq.*, 120 *sqq.*, 123 *sqq.*, 137 *sq.*, 144 *sq.*, 198; losses: Dutch, v, 84, 86 *sq.*, 91 *sq.*, 97, 99, 101, 110, 118, 125, 144, 173, 200; losses: English, v, 85, 93, 96 *sq.*, 110, 173

Gaeuw, Jacob (Captain), ii, 342

Galbraith, David, ii, 265

Galen (Cats) Johan van (Commodore), iii, 160; iv, 222, 308; his fleet before Porto Longone, iii, 61, 79; capt. of the Jaersvelt, iv, 310; his squadron in the Mediterranean, v, 150; killed, vi, 37

Galway, iv, 138

Garremuyden, vi, 152

Garrett, — (Captain), capt. of the Cock, vi, 200

Garrett, — (Lieutenant), ii, 292

Gatonbe, Nicolas, master of the Worcester, i, 250

Gauden, D. (Victualler of the Navy), letters from, vi, 29, 69

Gawdon, Mr., v, 328

Gelder, — van, ii, 208

Generals at Sea, a vacancy to be filled, i, 88; Blake re-

GILBERT

appointed, i, 88, 99; vi, 189; Deane appointed, iii, 110, 178; Monck appointed, iii, 178, 317; vi, 189; Penn appointed, v, 73 *and n.*; vi, 189; Desborough appointed, vi, 6, 104, 189. *See also* Instructions

Genoa, iv, 380; v, 191, 222, 237, 286, 297, 308, 322, 402

Gentlemen-Commanders, i, 32, 33, 40, 44

George, i, 13, 14

Gerritsen, Andries (Master), master of the Veere, ii, 79

Gerrit, — (of Hamburg), iv, 388

Gerritsz., Albert (Captain), v, 207, 231

Gesjasz (*or* Josjan), Lourens (Captain), ii, 348, 355

Gething (*or* Githings), Philip (Captain), capt. of the Tenth Whelp, i, 66; capt. of the Convert, v, 20; capt. of the Mathias, vi, 52

Gethinge, Richard (Captain), iv, 278; capt. of the Convert, iv, 21

Gibbes, John (Captain), capt. of the Garland, i, 64; to be examined before Council of State, i, 240, 257, 274

Gibson, Richard, i, 15 *n.*, 31; his reminiscences, i, 1; biographical note, i, 1; joins the Assurance, i, 7; fight off Portland, i, 17; purser of the Sapphire, i, 22

Gidionse, Jan (Captain), battle of the Gabbard, v, 74

Gifferyes, John (Captain), capt. of the Little Charity, vi, 200

Gifford, Benjamin (Governor of Landguard Fort), ii, 325

Gijsen, Jan (boatman), v, 136

Gilbert, Thomas (seaman), iii, 173

GILBERT

Gilbert, Thomas (Captain), iv, 294; capt. of the Cullen, iv, 22
Gilson, John (Captain), iii, 50; action off Dover, account of, i, 227; 228; capt. of the Speaker, battle of Dungeness, iii, 90
Glarges, C. de (or Glarsyes) (Dutch agent at Calais), i, 235; ii, 140, 189, 236, 346; iii, 68, 161, 209, 237; iv, 334, 354, 372, 380; v, 221, 227; letters to, ii, 61; letters from, iii, 165; iv, 381; v, 207, 231; reports of English Fleet, iii, 125; iv, 373; v, 58 sq., 190, 243
Goa, blockaded by Dutch, vi, 24
Godfrey, Michael (merchant), iii, 330
Godfrey, William (Captain), iv, 280; vi, 50; capt. of the Warwick, iv, 21; capt. of the Middleburgh, vi, 199
Goedereede. *See* Goree
Goffe, — (Colonel), ii, 158, 292; iv, 176; v, 186, 192, 393, 423
Golding, — (Captain), capt. of the Hound, took Dutch ship, ii, 242
Gomes, E., vi, 76
Goodman, Richard, iii, 445
Goodsonn, William (Rear-Admiral), i, 13; iv, 293; v, 20; vi, 181, 199; capt. of the Entrance, iii, 408; iv, 21; capt. of the Rainbow, iv, 245; capt. of the Unicorn, vi, 49; capt. of the George, vi, 184
Goodwins, i, 219, 351, 370, 373, 417; iv, 304, 389, 396; v, 28, 56, 135; Dutch merchantmen from Straits, i, 234; Dutch fleet off, ii, 263; v, 52
Goodwyne, Edward, iii, 282
Goossen, Felip (Captain), ii, 342

GRAVES

Gorcum, Pieter (Captain), i, 265, 393; ii, 185, 187, 209, 342; iii, 225, 233; orders to, iii, 39
Gordon, — (the Younger, of Straloch), iii, 371
Gore, The, i, 328; iv, 260 *and n.*; v, 52
Goree, iv, 184, 354, 367, 371, 375 sq., 377, 380, 383; v, 28, 41, 45, 47, 54 sq., 58, 94, 110, 133, 142, 172, 198, 200 sqq., 205, 219, 226, 244, 282 sq., 287 sq., 351, 355, 368, 383, 385, 420 sqq.; vi, 28, 160 n.; Victualling station, i, 381; ships refitted at, i, 382; De Witt's fleet, arrival after Kentish Knock, ii, 326
Gosnell, George, letter to, i, 119
Gosport, iv, 114, 220; vi, 210
Gothenburg, v, 42; vi, 7, 35, 81, 85, 182, 208, 211, 214 sq.; list of ships gone to, vi, 201
Gough, Bob, v, 94
Govertss., Hendrich, capt. of the Star, iv, 308
Govertsz, Jan, iv, 186
Graeff, Albert de, i, 265, 388, 393; ii, 336, 342; iii, 225, 233; capt. of the Hollandia, iv, 309
Graeff, Maerten de (Captain), i, 262
Grant, Laird of, iii, 370
Gravelines, i, 343; iv, 132, 183, 191; v, 120, 136; Texel squadron join De Ruyter, ii, 94
Graves, William (at v, 19 called Thomas) (Rear-Admiral), iv, 392; v, 425; capt. of the President, i, 257; ii, 239; iv, 20; battle of Portland, iv, 95, 114 sq.; capt. of the Andrew, iv, 278; Rear-Admiral, v, 19; battle of the

GRAVES

Texel, his death, v, 353, 373, 390 n., 428
Graves, Robert (Captain), v, 20 ; capt. of the Johnathan, iv, 280
Gravesant, v, 367, 369
Gravesend, i, 185, 258, 305 ; iv, 44 n., 55, 76, 86, 175, 243 sq., 332, 343 sqq., 352, 371 ; vi, 217, 225
Gravenzande, v, 127, 419
Graydon, John (Captain), capt. of the Hampton Court, i, 46
Great Blasket Island. See Blasques
Green, John (skipper), skipper of the John and Sara, iii, 239
Green(e), Thomas, ii, 157 ; letter from, iii, 280 ; v. 90
Greene, — (Captain), iv, 127, 144, 151; capt. of the John and Elizabeth, iv, 113 and n.
Greene, Edward, capt. of the Adventure, v, 19
Greene, Henrie (Captain), capt. of the Hector, privateer, ii, 39
Greene, John (Mayor of Lynn), letter from, iii, 312
Greenhill, William, vi, 235
Greenland, i, 392 ; iv, 310 n., 349 ; vi, 35. See also Fisheries
Gregory, John (seaman), vi, 108
Gregory, William (Captain), i, 66
Grenn, Philip Charel de, iii, 199
Grey, Lord, iii, 422
Grieck, Adrian (Captain), iii, 223, 226
Grimsby, vi, 239 sq.
Grisnez, ii, 62 ; iv, 118, 121, 183 ; v, 135 ; vi, 17
Groeningen, v, 69 ; list of ships from, v, 186
Groot, Cornelis de (Captain), iv, 337, 338

HAERKENS

Groot, Joachim (Master), master of the St. John, iii, 193
Grove, John (Captain), vi, 200 ; capt. of the Marmaduke, vi, 51
Gueldcrland, v, 233
Guernsey, i, 336 ; iii, 340 ; iv, 366 ; money shipped for garrison, i, 287 ; seamen impressed, iii, 162 ; iv, 324 ; De Ruyter's squadron off, iii, 261
Guildford, iv, 218
Gunfleet, v, 68
Gunnery, size of gunports, v, 122
Guns, Dutch. See Ordnance
Guns, English. See Ordnance
Gunston, Benjamin (Captain), iv, 279 ; capt. of the Chase, iv, 22
Gurdon, —, iii, 409
Gyselin, J., ii, 25

HAAN (or Haen), Leendert den (Captain), ii, 62, 79 sq., 86, 146, 189 sq. ; vi, 157 ; capt. of Haas in 't Veld, ii, 146
Hackworth, Thomas, iii, 73
Haddock, William (Vice-Admiral), ii, 239; iv, 22, 280; v, 17 ; vi, 199, 234 ; capt. of the Hannibal, i, 269 ; capt. of the Vanguard, ii, 17 ; V.-A. to Ayscue, ii, 17
Haeck, Symon van der (Captain), iii, 224
Haecxboot, Jan Fredericsen (Captain), iii, 225
Haecxwant, Leendert Ariensz (Captain), i, 261 ; iii, 186, 211, 225, 232 ; iv, 338 ; v, 287 ; orders to, iii, 38, 138
Haeffhoeck, — (skipper), iii, 39
Haepwant, — (Captain), v, 239
Haerkens, — (Captain), battle of the Gabbard, v, 74 n.

HAES

Haes, Jan de (Captain), iii, 224, 233; battle of the Texel, v, 355 sq.; taken prisoner, v, 390 n.
Hague, iv, 286, 312; v, 118, 193, 221, 243, 264, 377; vi, 68, 134, 171; return of Dutch fleet from northern voyage, i, 404
Haldersen, Claes (Captain), v, 420
Halewijn, Alewijn van (Delegate), iv, 311; vi, 75 sq.
Hall, — (Captain), ii, 124, 135
Hall, Edward (Captain), ii, 17; capt. of the Andrew, i, 64
Hall, Morgan (Master), master of the Anne, of Maidstone, iv, 50
Hallowes, Nathaniel (Navy Commissioner), iii, 324
Ham, Willem (Captain), i, 264; convoy to Channel vessels, i, 235; capt. of the Tobyas, iv, 313; capt. of the Sampson, iv, 316
Hamburg, i, 326; ii, 260; iv, 137, 158, 170, 250, 370, 388; v, 128, 265 sq., 329, 395, 425; vi, 42, 81, 112, 247; English men-of-war for, v, 411. See 'Free Ships, Free Goods;' Contraband
Hammocks (or Hamacoes), to be provided, i, 358 and n.; iv, 161; v, 187; want of, iv, 343, 363, 387; v, 26, 64, 67, 80, 95, 209, 211, 217, 229
Hancock, — (Captain), late capt. of the Maidenhead, ii, 101
Hancraft, — (Boatswain), v, 303
Hankes, Samuel (Captain), vi, 200; capt. of the Westergate, vi, 52
Hanley, Saite (Captain), capt. of the Princess Maria, v, 19

HARRIS

Hans, J. (Admiralty Committee), iii, 318
Hard, The, of Zealand, iv, 375 and n.
Hardenbrouck, P. H. v., iv, 313, 360
Hardinge, — (Major), iv, 62
Harditch, Francis (Captain), vi, 51; capt. of the Princess Maria, iv, 21; capt. of the Arms of Holland, iv, 279
Hare, Thomas (Captain), iv, 136, 221, 280; v, 18; capt. of the Ann Piercy, iv, 22
Harensen, Abram (Captain), ii, 199
Hargyn, vi, 124
Harlingen, v, 23
Harman, John (Captain), i, 29; v, 19; vi, 200; capt. of the Welcome, iv, 21; capt. of the Diamond, vi, 50
Harman, Roger (Captain), capt. of the Stork, vi, 51
Harman, Thomas (Captain), capt. of the Tiger, i, 29; took Dutch ship of war, i, 29
Harman, Willoughby (Captain), vi, 199; letter from, vi, 84; capt. of the Katherine, vi, 52
Harmer(s), Robert (Bailiff of Yarmouth), iii, 444; iv, 343; v, 62; letter from, iv, 342
Harpers, — (Delegate), v, 285, 307
Harrigate, — (master's mate), vi, 256
Harrington, —, i, 328
Harrington, Sir James (Colonel), i, 200, 286
Harris, — (Captain), iii, 88; capt. of the Middleborough, discharged, iii, 442
Harris, Isaac (surgeon), letter from, v, 388
Harris, Richard (Alderman of Barnstaple), iii, 435

HARRIS

Harris, Thomas (surgeon), letter from, v, 388
Harrison, — (Captain), i, 328, 363; ii, 67; capt. of the Vanguard, i, 269; superseded, ii, 17; orders to, i, 352
Harrison, Thomas (Major-General), Lieut. of Ordnance Office, i, 151; compensation for loss of office, i, 152, 153
Hart, — (Captain), capt. of the Golden Dove, i, 191
Hartlepool, Dutch fleet off, i, 383
Hartman, Marcus (Captain), ii, 145, 199; v. 130, 321; vi, 175; capt. of the Gecroende Lyfde, v, 126: his ship lost off the Texel, vi, 160
Harris, Mr. (surgeon), v, 206
Harvey, Francis (Secretary to Blake), iii, 418; letter from, iii, 366
Harwich, iii, 359, 429; iv, 290, 303, 319; v, 32, 34, 81, 146, 187, 188, 198, 206 sq., 217, 228 sq., 247 sqq., 253, 257 sq., 260, 262, 268, 270 sqq., 275, 280, 343, 380, 405, 408 sq., 411, 414, 416; vi, 1, 31, 57, 73, 83 sq., 116, 170, 184, 187, 225, 240, 242, 255 sqq.
complaint of victuals at, i, 242; victualling station, ii, 75, 98, 164, 183; v, 104; orders to commanders of ships at, iii, 112; warned to avoid Dutch fleet, iii, 123 (2)
English fleet off, v, 67; vi, 72; sick at, v, 314, 343, 396 sq., 399, 409 sqq.; vi, 57; refitting station, v, 293, 301; prizes sent to, v, 300; list of ships from, v, 315; vi, 201; garrison to be dismantled, vi, 86, VI.

HAYWARD

100; proposal to buy house for the Navy at, vi, 86, 88, 102
Hasilrig, Sir A., iv, 176
Haslcloch, Mr. (surgeon), v, 259
Haslewood, v, 410
Hasselaer, Geraert, v, 287
Hasselgants, — (Lieutenant), v, 186
Hastings, officers of Dutch frigate to be stayed at, i, 259
Hastings, — (Captain), capt. of the Dove privateer, i, 74
Hastings, Anthony (Captain), i, 46; capt. of the Sandwich, i, 46
Hatsell, Henry (agent for Admiralty Commissioners), i, 23, 26; iii, 131 n.; iv, 45, 67, 391; v, 186, 192, 376, 423; letter to, iv, 217; letters from, iii, 131, 354, 376, 435 iv, 40, 103, 147; vi, 178
Haulsholm, vi, 144 n.
Havre, iv, 65, 309, 388; v, 128; vi, 221 n.; Dutch rendezvous at, ii, 234; Dutch merchantmen at, vi, 226
Haward, Mr. (storekeeper), iv, 76
Hawley, — (Captain), iii, 313
Hay, — (Admiralty Commissioner), i, 287
Hay, Henrick (Lieutenant), sentence of Court Martial on, vi, 75 sq.
Hay, William, ii, 18, 180
Haye, — de, iii, 69
Hayle, Richard (Bailiff of Ipswich), letter from, i, 369
Hayward, Edward, vi, 248 sq.
Hayward, John, iv, 293, 299, 305; v, 18; vi, 51; letter from, vi, 98; capt. of the Gilliflower, i, 65; iv, 21; to convoy ships to Hamburg, vi, 33; capt. of the Convertine, vi, 201

T

HEANE

Heane, Colonel (Governor of Jersey), i, 330 and n.
Heath, — (Doctor), i, 29
Heath, Thomas, iv, 22, 279; v, 19; capt. of the Brazil, i, 67
Heathen, Richard (Captain), capt. of the Sapphire, iv, 279
Heaton, Nicholas (Captain), i, 23; v, 16; vi, 50, 199; letter from, vi, 227; trumpeter's mate of the Triumph, i, 23; capt. of the Sapphire, i, 21; action with privateers, i, 21; capt. of the Swallow, i, 23
Heck, Jan (Captain), iii, 225; iv, 184: capt. of the Eenhoorn, iv, 313
Heck, Jan (Captain), capt. of the Adam en Eva, iv, 314 and n.; acquitted of charge of cowardice, vi, 46
Heckas, John (Captain), capt. of the Unicorn, v, 185
Hedge, William (seaman), iii, 382 n.
Hedges, — (Master), appointed gunner of Marston Moor, vi, 218
Heelft, Bruyn van, i, 262
Heertjens (or Heertges), Dirck (or Jan) Pieterszoon (Captain), i, 389; ii, 331 sq.; v, 185; capt. of the Winthont, iv, 309 and n.; tried for desertion of flag, v, 220, 240 sqq., 244
Heidje, Teunis Willemsz., van der (Commander), v, 204, 223, 225; capt. of advice boat, v, 74
Hein, Piet, v, 403
Helder, River, v, 28, 39, 48, 58, 285, 297, 305, 307, 316, 322, 338, 341, 367, 388, 413; vi, 49, 62, 75, 112, 117, 153, 159
Heligoland, v, 395; vi, 44, 78

HILL

Hellingwerff, — (Lieut.-Commander), capt. of the Sevenwoolden, v, 186
Helmont, Commissary, iv, 282; v, 285, 307
Helston, v, 405
Helvoetsluys, v, 287 sq., 384; vi, 225; Dutch fleet off, ii, 298, 309
Hendrick, Abraham, i, 393
Hendricksen, Hendrick, iv, 338
Hendricxz, Pieter, iv, 186
Hendrickszoon, Jan (skipper), ii, 349; iv, 186
Herbert, Arthur, Earl of Torrington, i, 41
Herberts, — (Delegate), vi, 158
Herman, R. (Mayor of Exeter), iii, 336
Herman, Thomas (Captain), v, 250; capt. of the Welcome, iv, 279
Herne, Thomas (Victualler of the Navy), letter from, vi, 69
Hesilrige (or Heselrige), Sir Arthur, i, 295, 330; ii, 230; ordered to send powder from Newcastle, i, 203; to send guns to Tower of London, i, 267
Heussen, Coenraet van (Amsterdam Director), v, 191
Heuvel, Heer, vi, 167
Hewett, —, appointment as master of the Sovereign, cancelled, ii, 46, 91 n.
Hewitt, Thomas, letter from, v, 35
Heyden, vi, 47
Hide, Jonathan (Captain), iv, 137; v, 17; vi, 51, 199; capt. of the Hound, iv, 279
Highland, Justice, vi, 132 sq.
Hill, Richard (Commissioner of Prizes), ii, 108; iv, 364
Hill, Thomas (Captain), capt. of the Fleece, iv, 280
Hill, William (Captain), iii, 168; iv, 153, 173; v, 16, 104; vi,

78, 99, 199, 221 ; letter from, iv, 172 ; capt. of the Sapphire, iv, 20 ; battle of Portland, iv, 81 ; capt. of the Diamond, iv, 278 ; capt. of the Worcester, vi, 49 ; capt. of the Unicorn, vi, 184. *See also* Instructions
Hitland. *See* Shetland
Hobbes, James (boatswain), bosun of the Entrance, iii, 49
Hodges, Mr. (gunner), v, 302
Hodges, Luke (Commissioner of the Navy), iii, 307, 325
Hoeck, Sijmen van der (Captain), vi, 157
Hoeckboot, Jan Fredericksz. (Captain), tried for disobedience, v, 192
Hoen, Albert Corneliss. t' (Captain), capt. of the Princesse Royaele, iv, 314
Hola, — (Captain), i, 388 ; ii, 336
Holcomb, Humphrey, i, 291
Holden, John (Captain), capt. of the Convertine, i, 65
Holder, Thomas (Royalist agent), ii, 225 *and n.* ; letter to, ii, 225
Holderness, iv, 341
Holland, John (Navy Commissioner), i, 54 ; ii, 310 ; iii, 74 ; letter from, i, 268
Holland, Joseph, v, 92
Holland, Philip (Captain), iv, 21 ; v, 19 ; vi, 50, 186, 201, 257 ; capt. of the Cygnet, i, 65 ; to repair to Downs, i, 187 ; capt. of the Assurance, iv, 279 ; battle of the Texel, v, 390 *n.*
Hollesley Bay, v, 407 ; vi, 216. *See also* Hoseley Bay
Holley, Seth (Captain), vi, 51 ; capt. of the Arms of Holland, iv, 21 ; capt. of the Princess Mary, iv, 279

Holland, John (Navy Commissioner), ii, 170 ; iii, 277 ; complaint against, iii, 109, 169 ; his resignation, iii, 169
Holman, Benjamin (seaman), iii, 173
Holman, Richard (seaman), iii, 173
Holmen, vi, 122
Holmes, Sir Robert, failure to take Dutch Smyrna fleet, i, 46
Holms, vi, 138
Honett, Samuel, vi, 234
Hooft, Cor. Pietersen (Master), ii, 200
Hoog, Adrain van, letter to, v, 408
Hoola (*or* Holla), Cornelius (Captain), i, 134, 393, ii, 342, 345 *sq*; battle of Kentish Knock, ii, 358 ; capt. of the Leijden, iv, 309 *and n*. *See also* Hola
Hoolch, G. (Lord Commissioner), ii, 362
Hoorn, iv, 186, 313 ; v. 307 ; commanders of Directors' ships from, i, 262 ; wounded sent to, iv, 185
Hoorn, Count van, v, 287
Hope, The. *See* Tilbury Hope
Hopgood, Edmund, ii, 162
Hopkins, Edward (Navy Commissioner), iii, 344, 397, 450 ; iv, 40, 99, 131, 136, 217 *and n.*, 297 ; v, 236, 333 ; appointed Commissioner of the Navy, iii, 278
Hopkins, Robert (seaman), iii, 173
Hopwood, —, iv, 363
Hormer, Robert (Bailiff of Yarmouth), iii, 345
Horn, Count van, v, 204
Hosely Bay, vi, 169
Hosier, John (Captain), i, 269 ; iv, 150, 290, 292, 318 ; capt.

HOTHAM

of the Magdalen, iii, 34 ; his instructions for convoy, iv, 173
Hotham, Sir Jo., iv, 46
Houcbout, Jan Friedricksz. (Captain), i, 263
Houck (or Houch), Jacob Pietersz. (Captain), i, 262 ; iii, 225
Houlding, Anthony (Rear-Admiral), iv, 135 ; letter from, iii, 349 ; Rear-Admiral of the Red, i, 14 ; fight off Portland, i, 14 ; capt. of the Ruby, ii, 239 ; iv, 20 ; action with Dutch man-of-war, iii, 349, 351
Houten, Cornelis van, i, 262, 393 ; ii, 337, 342 ; battle of Kentish Knock, ii, 358
Houttuijn, Adriaen (Captain), capt. of the Casteel van Medemblick, iv, 314
Howard, —, ii, 225
Howard, A. (President C.O.S.), vi, 93
Howard, Captain, vi, 78
Howett, Samuel, i, 186 ; ii, 239 ; iii, 168 ; iv, 215, 278 ; vi, 49, 184, 199 ; capt. of the Foresight, i, 7, 67 ; to repair to Downs, i, 186 ; Rear-Admiral of the Red and capt. of the Laurel, iv, 20 *and n.* ; battle of Portland, iv, 124 ; capt. of the Speaker, v, 17
Hoxton, Walter (Captain), capt. of the Bonaventure, iii, 95 ; battle of Dungeness, iii, 91, 117, 230 ; slain, iii, 95
Hoxton, Rachel, petition for relief, iii, 409
Hubin, John; iv, 128
Hudson, Reinold (fisherman), master of the Marigold, reports capture by Dutch fleet, i, 378

HUYGHENS

Huijsduinen, Adriaen Jacobsz. (Master), vi, 161
Huijser, Cornelis (Captain), vi, 160
Huist, Abraham van der (Captain), capt. of the Groeningen, iv, 309
Hull, i, 316 ; ii, 12 ; iv, 245 ; v, 32, 54, 215, 272 ; vi, 35 ; Dutch man-of-war stayed, i, 246 ; victualling station, ii, 75, 98, 164, 169, 183 ; v, 104, 230 ; English ships off, warned to avoid Dutch fleet, iii, 113 ; sick and hurt to be accommodated, v, 268, 300
Hulst, Abraham van der (Captain), i, 261, 382, 388, 393 ; ii, 336, 342 ; iii, 225 ; v, 239, 358 *sq.* ; vi, 118
Hulten, Nicolas van, ii, 16
Humber, iv, 356, 395 ; v, 53 ; vi, 229, 239 *sq.*
Humphrey, John (Captain), vi, 50, 201, 237 ; capt. of the Nightingale, iv, 21
Humphreys, — (Captain), capt. of the Friendship, i, 191
Hunkin, — (Colonel), ii, 89
Hunsdown, v, 234
Hunt, J. (Admiralty Committee), iii, 340, 440, 447 ; iv, 67, 136, 160
Hunter, William (President C.O.S.), ii, 116, 127, 137, 138, 139
Hurley, William (Captain), capt. of the Constant, i, 73
Hurst, Thomas, ii, 162
Hutchinson, Richard (Treasurer of the Navy), i, 54 ; ii, 130, 156, 170 ; iv, 297 ; letter from, iii, 367 ; vi, 93
Hutton, Michell (Captain), capt. of the Satisfaction, vi, 199
Huybert, Corn. de, iv, 360
Huyghens, — (Deputy), iii, 399

HUYRLUYT

Huyrluyt (*or* Huijrluijt) Commodore), i, 179 *n.*, 388 ; convoy to merchantmen from Straits, i, 197, 219, 418 ; capt. of the Zeelandia, iv, 310 *and n.*
Huysduynen, vi, 48, 153 *and n.*, 154 *n.*, 160
Huyskens, Hendrick (Captain), i, 389 ; iii, 190, 193 *sq.* ; iv, 323 ; orders to, ii, 375, 383 ; capt. of the Westvrieslandt, iv, 309 *and n.* ; battle of the Texel, v, 357, 362
Hyde, Sir Edward, ii, 226, 231
Hythe, i, 195

ICEFZYL, v, 233
Ilfracombe, iii, 416 ; v, 296
Impress : of horses, iv, 51
Impress : of men, Dutch, v, 119, 289, 307 ; soldiers to be pressed, v, 119 ; protections, v, 201
Impress : of men, English, i, 294 ; ii, 66 ; iii, 111, 158, 209, 238, 302, 306, 312, 324, 325, 336, 341, 343, 356, 360, 393, 403, 416, 435, 442 *sq.*, 450 ; iv, 38, 42, 53 *sq.*, 58, 76, 87, 99, 103, 129 *sq.*, 134, 139, 163, 187, 201 *sq.*, 218, 233, 255, 324, 353, 357, 374 ; v, 32 *sq.*, 50, 63, 67, 187, 270, 310, 314, 339, 343, 376, 390 ; vi, 170, 174, 190, 253 ;
Authority to press : i, 226 ; iii, 103 *sq.*, 168 ; iv, 103, 217 ; v, 36, 38 ; difficulties of, v, 36 *sq.*, 50, 65, 79, 333 *sq.* ;
Men pressed : Scots, i, 405, 408 ; iv, 234 ; Welsh, iv, 234 ; bargemen, iii, 148 ; v, 406 ; crews of colliers, iii, 166 ; iv, 201, 290, 348, 381, 385 ; v, 292, 343 ;

INNISBOFFIN

from Channel Islands, iii, 162 ; Irish, iv, 234 ; watermen, iii, 129, 145, 410, 440 ; iv, 39, 99, 352 ; v, 115, 291, 309 ; vi, 72 ; from East India Co., iv, 234 ; in the West, v, 36-39, 158, 333 *sq.*, 405 *sq.* ; of unfit men, i, 269 ; iii, 400 ; for coast defence, i, 357 ; v, 412 ; transport of, iv, 44, 352 ;
Prest money : i, 139, 188, 226 *and n.* ; iii, 104, 312 *sq.*, 415 ; v, 37, 98, 406 ; vi, 169 ; imprest tickets, i, 139 ; iv, 163 ; v, 236 ; impress warrants: from outward and inward bound ships, i, 186 *sq.*, 191, 215 ; granted to privateers, iii, 96 ; iv, 231 ;
Privateers : pressed men desert to, iv, 39, 65 ; men to be pressed out of, iv, 231 ; protections : i, 138, 141, 184, 295, 352 ; ii, 109, 247 ; iii, 56, 103, 290, 445 ; iv, 50 *sq.*, 141, 218, 291 ; v, 36 ; resistance to impress : v, 37, 158 ;
Waterman's Company : petition from, v, 309.
See also Complaints ; Conduct Money ; Seamen
Impress : of ships and vessels, Dutch, v, 120, 282
Impress : of ships and vessels, English, i, 307 ; iii, 124 ; iv, 51, 204, 218, 234 ; v, 408 ; vi, 229 ; list of, iv, 366
Inch Keith, defence of, i, 403
Ingoldsby, — (Colonel), i, 344 ; ii, 101, 120 ; iii, 426, 431 (2) ; iv, 175, 236 *sq.*, 300, 302, 304 ; v, 393
Innisboffin (*or* Einsbuffin, *or* Ennisbussen), iv, 138, 283 *and n.*, 372 *n.*

INDEX

INTELLIGENCE

Intelligence, Dutch, v, 41 sq., 193, 199, 323 sq.; vi, 78, 110, 121;
Cruisers sent to seek, iii, 60, 68, 80, 137, 138, 139, 233; iv, 180, 187, 193; v, 29, 190, 199, 204; vi, 39, 63, 97; agents for, iv, 376;
Intelligence received and 'Letters of Intelligence,' iv, 334, 355, 371 sqq., 380 sqq.; v, 28, 43, 45, 58, 60 sq., 74, 129, 133, 136, 190, 207 sq., 223 sqq., 231 sq., 254, 285 sq., 297, 318, 325, 408 sq.; vi, 24, 77, 139, 141, 145 sq., 165
Intelligence, English, iii, 369; iv, 50, 259, 303, 344; v, 51, 76 sq., 141, 207 sq., 251; vi, 78, 243, 256;
Cruisers, i, 342, 344; iii, 360, 437; iv, 132 sq., 260, 283, 329; v, 33, 65, 92 sq., 142, 352; vi, 57, 60; of the Dutch Fleet, iv, 60 sqq., 67, 71, 164, 318, 322, 328 sq., 341; v, 25 sq., 54, 64; vi, 60, 243, 246; of Dutch merchant fleet, v, 210; vi, 34, 37 sqq., 203 sq.; postmasters to be hastened, v, 53; vi, 128
International Law, Declaration of War, Dutch, i, 412; reprisals, i, 58 sqq., 72, 79, 81, 99, 116, 160, 162; Paulet reprisals, i, 71, 74, 75, 116, 352. *See also* Contraband; Enemy Ship, Enemy Goods; 'Free Ship, Free Goods'; Reprisals, acts of; Visit and Search
Invasion of Netherlands, threat of, v, 155, 194, 197, 208; preparations against, v, 233 sq.

IVAN

Inventions: fire machines, Dutch, ii, 319; rumoured secret machines, English, ii, 320; a combustible projectile, iii, 84; Dutch infernal machines, v, 55; blunderbusses, Dutch, v, 412
Inverness, 3 Dutch prizes sent to, i, 385; convoy to, iv, 174 n.
Ipswich, i, 317, 384; iv, 290; v, 206 sq., 248 sq., 259, 268, 270 sq., 294, 342, 344 sq., 389, 409; vi, 128, 130, 174, 242; ships not to be restrained, i, 119; letter from bailiffs of, i, 368; victualling station, ii, 75, 183; sick and hurt to be accommodated, v, 249, 257, 260, 314, 396, 399, 410 sq.; vi, 57
Ireland, provision ships for, iv, 307; to be exempted from embargo, i, 248; iii, 323; convoy provided for, i, 267; iv, 320; ships and squadrons on coast of, iv, 216, 300; report of Dutch plan of attack on, v, 87; list of ships off the coast, vi, 201; Commissioners in Ireland, i, 336
Ireland (off Texel), v, 146, 423
Ireton, Thomas (Quartermaster General), i, 109; v, 114
Isaaxszoon, Abram (Quartermaster), quartermaster of Brederode, i, 278
Isaacszoon, Stephen (skipper), i, 348, 427
Issbrantssen, J., letters from, v, 317, 325, 337
Islands, their position one of the elements of sea-power 1, 33–47
Italy, v, 233
Ivan, P., letter from, v, 337

INDEX

JACKSON

Jackson, Anthony, action off Dover, account of, i, 227, 228
Jackson, Henry (surgeon), v, 206; letter from, v, 388
Jacobsen, Jan (skipper), battle of Portland, iv, 190
Jacobson, —, (Captain), ii, 73, 285
Jacobson, Jaspar (Master), master of the Peter of Hamburg (II), iv, 138
Jacobsse, Maarten (carpenter), carpenter of Brederode, i, 278
Jacobsz., Ruth (Captain), vi, 163
Jacobszoon, Jan (Captain), capt. of the Vos, ii, 343
Jacobszoon, Joris (skipper), ii, 349
Jacobszoon, Pieter (chief boatswain), iv, 338; chief bo'sun of the Brederode, i, 278
Jacques, — (Captain), capt. of the Flushing, vi, 175
Jacques, Joseph (Master), master of the Peter of Hamburg (I), iv, 137
Jaep, Broer (Captain), battle of Kentish Knock, ii, 296
Jaersvelt, Claes. Bastiensz. (Captain), i, 262; iv, 338; v, 130
Jager, Leendert Arentsen de (Captain), capt. of the Oranienboom, ii, 65
Jager, Uldinich de (Lieut.-Commander), court-martialled, v, 191
Jans, Huyge (skipper), ii, 62, 80, 86, 189 sq.
Jansen (or Janszoon), Allert (or Albert) (Captain), i, 235, 264, 393; ii, 343, 351, 363; iii, 225, 233, 240 (2); iv, 192
Jansen, Emme (skipper), iii, 238
Jansen, Gerrit (Captain), ii, 265

JENINGS

Jansen, Gillis (Captain), iv, 193; v, 239; vi, 76; his instructions, v, 321
Jansen, Heene, iii, 226
Janss., Cornelis (Captain), capt. of the Jupitar, iv, 308
Janssen, Fijs, iv, 186
Janssen, Michiel (skipper), ii, 84
Jansz., Lourens, iv, 186
Janszoon, Adrian (Captain), capt. of the Gloeyenden Oven, i, 339
Janszoon, Claes, i, 362; iii, 248; iv, 192
Janszoon, Dirck (Quartermaster), quartermaster of the Brederode, i, 278
Janszoon, Hendrich (Captain), capt. of the Graaf Sonderlandt, ii, 343
Janszoon, Huybert (Quartermaster), quartermaster of the Brederode, i, 278
Janszoon, Jacob (Captain), ii, 343
Janszoon (or Janssen), Gillis (Captain), i, 263, 393; ii, 342; iii, 156, 224, 228; v, 418
Janszoon, Peter (Lieutenant), prisoner of war, examination of, i, 214
Janszoon, Robber (Master), master of the Brederode, i, 278
Jariaensen, Stoffel (Captain). See Juriaenszoon
Jefferson, John (Captain), iii, 452; iv, 280; v, 17; capt. of the Thomas and William, i, 191; iv, 22
Jeffery (or Jeffryes), John (Captain), v, 17; vi, 52, 236; capt. of the Falmouth, iv, 293
Jenings, Richard (Bailiff of Ipswich), letter from, i, 369

JENNINGS

Jennings, Adam (merchant), iii, 413
Jensen, — (Master), master of the Concord (Dutch merchant), ii, 16
Jernants, —, ii, 338
Jeroensz. (*or* Jervensen), Ewont (Captain), ii, 342 *sq.*; iii, 225; capt. of the Zutphen, iv, 309 *and n.*
Jeroensz. (*or* Jervenssen), Hillebrand (Captain), i, 388; ii, 342, 379; iii, 186, 225, 233 *sq.*, 239 *sq.*, 256; iv, 309 *and n.*, 323, 372; orders to, iii, 39; battle of the Texel, v, 355, 357
Jersey, i, 336; iii, 439; iv, 45; seamen impressed, iii, 162; iv, 324; masts from, iii, 387
Jervoise, Henry, petition of, ii, 170
Jessell, William (Captain), capt. of the Hamburgh Merchant, v, 17
Jesson, Nathaniel (Captain), iv, 293; v, 20; capt. of the William and John, iv, 22
Jessy, Mr., v, 411
Johnson, — (Captain), iii, 25; capt. of the Convert, i, 191
Johnson, Alexander (seaman), iii, 449
Johnson, Edward, v, 93
Johnson (*or* Crossnesse), Ericke (Master), master of the St. John of Fredrickstadt, iii, 413
Johnson, George (Admiralty Committee), iii, 415; iv, 160
Johnson, Henry (shipbuilder), ii, 156; iii, 418; letter to, i, 139
Johnson, John, i, 136
Johnson, Jose (Master), master of the Beane of Tragoose, vi, 237

JORDAN

Johnson, Michael, ii, 39
Johnson, Mrs., v, 93
Johnson, Peter (Master), master of the Nantes of Rotterdam, iv, 98
Johnson, Richard (Captain), i, 135
Johnson, Sanders (seaman), iii, 382 *n.*
Jolas, David (Master), master of the Trinity, iii, 194
Jones, George, ii, 126, 130
Jones, Hugh (Master), master of the Anne, pink, i, 153
Jones, Roger, vi, 51
Jongeboer, Aert Jansz. de (Captain), ii, 62, 79, 80, 86, 189 *sq.*; iii, 39, 186, 240; vi, 157
Jongen, Jan (Master), master of the Fortune, iii, 191
Jongh, Jan Ysbrantoe de (Master), i, 397
Jongh, de, Isaac (Captain), i, 216 *n.*, 235, 261, 397
Jongstal, — (Ambassador), v, 118
Joons, Richard (coasting-pilot), iv, 337
Joosten, Ary (master carpenter), ii, 363
Joosten (*or* Joossen), Philip, i, 351, 393; ii, 255
Jordan, Sir Joseph (Admiral), i, 7, 67, 343; ii, 121; iii, 368; iv, 255, 278, 284; v, 20; vi, 49, 181; Capt. of the Pelican, i, 7; to repair to Downs, i, 202 *n.*; rear-admiral to Ayscue, ii, 123; battle of Kentish Knock, ii, 272; capt. of the Vanguard, iv, 245, 392; his journal, iv, 392 *sqq.*; v, 139–146, 422–429; capt. of the Triumph, vi, 184. *See also* Instructions

JORGASSEN

Jorgassen, Laurens (Captain), iii, 223, 226
Josias, Laurents, capt. of the Eenhorn (fireship), i, 265
Joyne, Anthony (Captain), iv, 279; v, 20; vi, 51; capt. of the Convertine, iv, 20
Jumper, William (Captain), capt. of the Sandados, i, 30; took French ship of war, i, 30; capt. of the Sandados prize, i, 30
Junius, D. Robertij (preacher), vi, 126
Junius, Jacob, vi, 118
Juriaenszoon (or Juridenz, or Juryaens), Stoffel, i, 262, 390, 391, 393, 397; ii, 337, 342; battle of Portland, iv, 190
Jutland, iv, 360; vi, 28; shoal, vi, 54 sq., 61
Juynbol (or Janbal), Dirck (Captain), i, 261; iii, 224; battle of Dungeness, drowned, iii, 118, 230, 252

KATTEWATER, vi, 61
Keijser, ——, iii, 388
Kelsey, Thomas (Lieutenant-Colonel), ii, 162; iv, 151; vi, 116, 136, 203, 220; letters to, v, 52, 66, 90, 92; letters from, iii, 158; iv, 65, 71, 302; v, 400; vi, 72; despatched to Dover Castle, i, 190
Kelshall, v, 310
Kempen (or Kemp), Adriaen Niclaesz (Captain), i, 263, 351, 392, 393, 396; ii, 255, 343; iii, 215, 225, 233; iv, 193; v, 130, 239; vi, 118; capt. of the Amsterdam, vi, 175
Kempinck, Cornelis (skipper), iii, 245

KILIOTS

Kendall, — (seaman), vi, 108
Kendall, George, letter from, v, 275
Kendall, William (Captain), i, 234; ii, 13; iii, 386; iv, 62, 278; v, 19, 273; vi, 51; letter from, v, 376; capt. of the Mary, i, 65; to hasten into Downs, ii, 18; capt. of the Success, iv, 21
Kennemerlant, v, 289
Kent, report of Dutch fleet off coast, i, 356; impress for coast defence, i, 357; Dutch landing repulsed, iii, 106; ships on coast of, prohibited sailing, iii, 177
Kentish Knock, battle of, ii, 268–280, 282–284, 286, 288–291, 294 sq., 301, 304, 306, 357; vi, 16, 233 sqq.; losses, Dutch, ii, 291; losses, English, ii, 291
Ker, J. S. M., vi, 233
Kerchoven, — (Captain), v, 127
Kerck, Cornelis Claesz (Master), iii, 209
Kerckhoff, Pauwels van der (Captain), iii, 225; battle of Portland: reported dead, iv, 189; capt. of the Dolphin, v, 219
Kerckhoff, Quieryn van den (Captain), i, 261; ii, 334
Ketcher, Bartholomew, vi, 199; capt. of the Half Moon, vi, 52
Key, W. (Master), master of the Providence, iv, 50
Keyser, Nanningh (Dutch Ambassador at Copenhagen), ii, 333, 375, 380; iii, 190; v, 290, 313; vi, 54, 61 sq.
Kien, Marten, v, 43, 132
Kijckduijn, iv, 185; vi, 154 and n.
Kiliots, iv, 24 and n.

King, John (Captain), i, 415;
  v, 16; vi, 50; capt. of the
  Nonsuch ketch, i, 66, 191;
  capt. of the Mermaid, iv, 278
Kinsale, victualling station, ii,
  164, 183
Kint, Cornelius 't, captured
  Dove, i, 74
Kirby, Francis (Captain), vi,
  51; battle of Portland, iv, 81,
  84; capt. of the Bear, v, 17
Kirby, Robert (Captain), vi, 52,
  200; capt. of the Sophia, v,
  17
Kirk, Anthony (Captain), capt.
  of the Speaker's prize, iii, 408
Kleine, Helms vi, 55, 62
Kleyntje (or Clentie), Adrjaen
  (Captain), ii, 364; iv, 323;
  v, 186; vi, 175
Knowlinge, Stephen, letter
  from, vi, 55
Knox, Robert (Captain), iv,
  294; capt. of the Charles, i,
  191
Koebrugge, Hendrick, skipper
  of the St. Mary, i, 221
Koeteringh, Jan (Captain),
  capt. of the Uijtrecht, iv, 308
Koningsbergen (or Konigsburg),
  iv, 136; vi, 39, 81 and n.
Koolbrant, — (skipper), i, 266
Korff, Jan Claessen (Captain),
  iii, 223, 233
Kraeger, Andries (Captain), iii,
  224
Krijnsen, Jan (boatman), v, 136
Kroeger, Erasmus (Master),
  master of the St. Matthew,
  iii, 194
Krauger (or Crouger), Hendrick
  (Captain), iv, 338; his instructions, v, 320
Kuiper (or Cuijper), Kornelis
  (Captain), ii, 146; vi, 157;
  capt. of the Der Goes, ii, 146
Kuiphuijsen, R. W. (Lord
  Commissioner), ii, 362

Lamb, David, iv, 141
Lamb, Mathew, protection
  granted, iv, 141
Lambe, Thomas (merchant), iii,
  327
Lambert, — (Major-General),
  regiment ordered for coast
  defence, ii, 12
Lambert, John (Captain), iv,
  278; v, 18; vi, 49, 200;
  capt. of the Ruby, i, 65;
  capt. of the Lion, iv, 20
Lamberts, Reijnier, iv, 186
Lambertsen, Peter (Master),
  master of the Berck Howter
  Church, iv, 136
Lamsen, Burgomaster, v, 286;
  vi, 124
Land Committee, i, 200
Landguard Fort, vi, 8, 18, 83,
  89, 100, 103, 129, 168, 173;
  letter from, i, 378
Land's End, i, 322; ii, 11; iv,
  178; v, 296, 405; vi, 55, 57,
  205, 226, 243, 246
Lane, Lionel (Vice-Admiral), iii,
  126, 147, 168; iv, 215, 293;
  v, 18; vi, 107, 181; capt. of
  the Victory, i, 64; V.-A. of
  the Blue, iv, 9, 20 n.; battle
  of Portland, iv, 125; capt. of
  the Triumph, vi, 49
Langdale, Sir Marmaduke, ii,
  225 and n., 229; letter from,
  ii, 225
Lange, Adriaan de (Master),
  master of the Fortuyn, i, 123
Langesund, vi, 62, 146
Langford, Richard (Captain), iv,
  294; capt. of the Elizabeth
  and Ann, iv, 22
Langham, — (Colonel), ii, 247
Langley, John (Admiralty Committee), iii, 334, 340, 403,
  407, 417, 427, 440, 447; iv,
  108, 136, 160; v, 33, 81
Lantdiep, v, 317, 322, 325, 337,
  339

INDEX

LAPPER

Lapper, Jan Jans. van (Captain) i, 388 ; ii, 333 ; iii, 190, 194 ; iv, 338 ; v, 130, 239 ; orders to, ii, 375, 383 ; capt. of the Phesant, iv, 309 *and n.* ; battle of the Texel, v, 364

Lardner, Richard, ii, 162

Larke, Joseph (Commissioner for Sick and Hurt), instructions for, vi, 89

La Roche, — (Captain), ii, 172

Laston, v, 410

Latley, Phillip, bo'sun of the Worcester, i, 250

Launt, William (Captain), capt. of the Tiger frigate, i, 202 *n.*

Lawson (Sir) John, (Admiral), i, 15, 67; iii, 168; iv, 112, 128, 134, 217, 244, 259 *n.*, 274, 303, 321, 394 ; v, 143, 180, 407, 413 *sq.*, 429; vi, 1, 42, 49, 60, 98, 199 ;
 Letters from, iv, 45, 242 ; vi, 32 ; capt. of the Centurion, i, 7 ; Vice-Admiral of the Red and capt. of the Fairfax, i, 14 ; iv, 20 ; fight off Portland, i, 14, 15 *and n.* ; iv, 94, 96, 111, 124 ; action off Dover, i, 195 ;
 Petition for his family in event of his death, iv, 45; wounded at battle of Lowestoft, 1665, i, 46 *and n.* ; flag in the George, v, 19 ; battle of the Gabbard, v, 83, 85 *n.*, 110 *and n.*, 144 ; in command of the blockade, vi, 1, 31 ; V.-A. of the Fleet, vi, 6, 189

Lawson, — (Master), iv, 129

Lebeck, Jan (Captain), iii, 209

Lechmere, B. (Admiralty Committee), iii, 317

Le Daugnon, Count of, iv, 27

LICHTEN

Ledgant (*or* Ledgart), William (Captain), iv, 279 ; v, 20 ; vi, 51 ; capt. of the Nicodemus, iv, 22

Lee Road, iv, 244, 290, 327, 343 *sqq.* ; v, 26, 64, 67, 78, 143 ; v, 214, 217, 249, 345

Leeuw, Cornelis de, iv, 186

Leeuwswelt, C. T. (*or* C. J.), ii, 38, 72

Leghorn, v, 210 ; vi, 171 *n.*

Leith, v, 32 *sq.* ; letter from, i, 399, 400

Lemnien, Gerrit van, i, 351

Lendersen, Adrian (Master), ii, 265

Lentsen, Bastiaen (Captain), battle of Dungeness : took Hercules, iii, 118

Leostoff. *See* Lowestoft

Letters of Marque : Dutch, grants of, i, 362 ; ii, 86 ; with French commissions, ii, 312

Letters of Marque : English, i, 358 ; ii, 94, 97, 104, 114, 124, 154, 167, 169, 264 ; regulations for the issue of, i, 359, 360 ; ii, 41 ; iii, 40 ; grants of, ii, 38, 39 ; petition for, iii, 445 ; for Scotland, ii, 73, 252 ; iii, 283 ; iv, 176 ; for Scilly, ii, 252 ; not to be granted, iv, 231, 233

Levenhuijsen, Reijnst Cornllisj (Captain), v, 289

Leverington, Thomas, gunner of the Worcester, i, 250

Leutnor, —, i, 234

Lew, Island of, vi, 251

Lewis, Thomas (Victualling Agent), v, 268 ; letter from, ii, 285

Leyden, siege of, i, 34

Leyer, v, 186

Licenses, English, to Danish ships, iii, 413

Lichten, Willem van, iii, 200

INDEX

LIEFFDE

Lieffde, Jan Evertsen de (Rear-Admiral), i, 261, 351; iii, 156, 228, 241

Lieffde, Jan de (Younger), iii, 264; vi, 154

Lier, van (Amsterdam Delegate), v, 191

Lieutenants, only one, even in flagship, i, 11, 189; number in each ship increased, i, 45; lieutenant-captain in a flagship, ii, 274; in 4th rates, iii, 372

Lievensz., Cornelis (skipper), iii, 80, 162, 226; iv, 380; v, 28, 39

Lights, Coast: English, iii, 177; warrants to light keepers, iii, 303

Lijere, W. van, iv, 360

Lilburne, Henry (Governor of Tynemouth Castle), ii, 229 and n.

Lilburne, Robert (Colonel), v, 32 *sq.*; letter to, iii, 369; letter from, iv, 105

Limbery (*or* Limmerie), John (Victualler of the Navy), ii, 76, 292; iii, 96, 109, 303; orders to, iii, 177

Limbery (*or* Limbey), John (Captain), i, 356; iv, 280, 321; v, 16, 258, 260, 262, 280; letter to, iii, 177; capt. of the Loyalty, granted letter of marque, ii, 38

Limerick, iii, 377

Lindesnaes, ships of Tromp's fleet take refuge at, i, 410

Lisbon, iv, 89; v, 148, 195, 210; vi, 237

Lisle, John (Captain), wounded in action off Plymouth, ii, 106, 117; petition of, ii, 371

Lisle, — P. (President of C.O.S.), ii, 154, 288; letter from, i, 117

LONDON

Littlejohn, John (Captain), vi, 51; capt. of the Peter, iv, 93

Littleton, John (Captain), capt. of the Peter, v, 18

Livorne, v, 119

Lizard, iv, 178, 187; v, 278; vi, 178, 181, 228; Dutch fleet sighted, iv, 40

Lizard and Scilly, ships plying between, vi, 200

Lizatie, John (Master), master of the Golden Cock, iv, 98

Loane, Richard (gunner), gunner of the Eliza, v, 78

Lochorst, Adam van, iv, 223, 360

Locke, James (Captain), capt. of the Constant Anne ketch, ii, 30

Locksmith, Robert, iii, 73

Lodington, Mr., v, 260, 262

Locnon, Andrew von (Captain), capt. of the Real of Gold v, 185

Loenen, Adriaen van (Captain), i, 389; capt. of the Patientia, iv, 310; battle of the Texel, v, 361

Logan, Andrew (Lieutenant), lieut. of the Sapphire, i, 45; sentenced to death by Court Martial, i, 45 *n.*

Logging, George (skipper), ii, 67; iii, 44

Loire, iv, 349; merchant ships awaiting convoy, iv, 23

Lomsen, Burgomaster, v, 219

London, victualling station, ii, 75, 164, 169, 183; Dutch project to block channel to, iii, 332, 390, 399; iv, 192; proposed that some hospitals be reserved for wounded seamen, iii, 273; iv, 232

London, Committee of the Militia of, i, 131

Long Sands Head, iv, 298, 395;
    v, 64, 68; Dutch fleet off, v,
    64, 67
Longland, Charles (Agent at
    Leghorn), letter to, ii, 388;
    iv, 227
Lonique (*or* Loneque), Cornelis
    (Captain), iii, 224, 241, 245;
    iv, 354, 355 *n.*; battle of
    Portland, iv, 123, 189, 195
    and n.
Loncke, — (Captain), ii, 147;
    vi, 157; capt. of the Faam,
    ii, 193
Looe, v, 405
Losecaet, Frederick (Commissioner), ii, 364
Lourens, — (Captain), capt. of
    Eenhoorn, ii, 343
Lourenszoon, Symon (skipper),
    ii, 343, 352
Louwenz (*or* Louwerensz, *or*
    Laurens), Cornelis (Captain),
    battle of the Gabbard, v, 23,
    74, 242
Love, —, i, 287; ii, 157, 167
Lovingland, Isle of, ii, 12
Low, Jeremiah, i, 357
Lowestoft, v, 142 *n.*, 174, 275,
    293, 375; battle of, i, 46 *n.*
Lowson, William, iii, 419
Lübeck, iv, 334, 388; v, 253;
    vi, 42, 253. *See also* Contraband; 'Free Ships, Free
    goods'
Lucas, Nicholas (Captain), iv,
    280; v, 16, 202; capt. of the
    Society, iii, 382
Lucas, Thomas (Deputy Clerk
    of the Check), iii, 441
Luken, Michael van (Master),
    master of the Morning Star,
    iv, 137
Lummen, Gerrit van, i, 262
Lundy, v, 296; vi, 6, 247, 250
Luther, Jeremiah, ii, 17
Lymbaye, Edward (seaman), iii,
    173

Lym, vi, 234
Lynn, iii, 313, 432, 441; iv,
    160, 357; v, 345; vi, 57
Lyons, Richard (Captain), letter from, v, 82; capt. of the
    Resolution, v, 85; battle of
    the Gabbard, v, 82 *sqq.*;
    capt. of the Taunton, vi, 200

MACLINE, Matthew (seaman),
    vi, 108
Maddison, Henry (Captain),
    v, 17; vi, 51, 201
    Capt. of the Mary Prize, iv,
    278
Maerdon, vi, 62 *and n.*, 109,
    119 *sq.*, 123, 144 *sq.*, 148
Maertensen, Cornelis, bo'sun of
    St. Mary, i, 221
Maes (*or* Maas, *or* Maze), i, 236,
    382, 394; v, 128, 383,
    385
    Dutch rendezvous, i, 399
    Blake's fleet sighted off, ii,
    338
    See also Meuse
Maeslantssluijs, v, 387
Maidstone, vi, 217
Maidwell, — (Mr.), i, 142
Maine, Stephen, iv, 256
Major, Mr., v, 50
Malaga, iv, 187; vi, 227
Malcontent, Gijsbert (Captain),
    i, 262, 351, 393; ii, 363; iii,
    225, 240; iv, 178
    battle of Portland: his ship
    taken, iv, 182
Maltman, John (trumpeter),
    iv, 124
Man, Isle of, pressed men from,
    iv, 324
Mandal, vi, 62 *n.*, 119
Mandeville, Lord, vi, 253
Mangelaer, Cornelis, iii, 248;
    iv, 193
Mangelaer, Cryn (skipper), iv,
    193, 196

MANGELAER

Mangelaer, Fraus Prynssen (Captain), ii, 64 n., 111, 142, 145, 146, 163, 164, 188 sq.; iii, 228; v, 321, 418; vi, 118, 144, 156
    Capt. of the De Liefde, ii, 146
Manley, — (Major), ii, 286
Manning. See Seamen
Mantle, William (seaman), iii, 173
Manton, Nathaniel (merchant), iii, 327
Marbury (or Mearbury), Richard, iv, 365
    letter from, iv, 363
Marckham, Alexander, iv, 124
Marcusz, Lambert (Captain), ii, 363
Marcusz, Pieter (Captain), ii, 342; vi, 118
    Capt. of the Vaelenhaen, ii, 343
Mardrig, Francis (Captain), capt. of the Arms of Holland, v, 20
Marenszoon, Pieter (Captain), ii, 305
    Capt. of the Louisa, ii, 305
Margate, iv, 134, 322, 332, 387, 390; v, 21, 28, 52, 80; vi, 134
Mariner's Hall, Charter for, iii, 172, 289
Marrevelt (or Marvelt), Niclaes (Lieutenant Commodore), i, 261, 388, 393; ii, 336, 343; iii, 57, 62, 224, 240; v, 358
Marryott, Thomas, vi, 51, 199
    Capt. of the Discovery, i, 65
Marseveen, — (Amsterdam Delegate), v, 191
Marshall, Philip (Captain), iv, 59
    Capt. of the John and Elizabeth, iii, 382
    Capt. of the Marmaduke, iii, 382
Marston, —, iii, 103

MATYSEN

Martenszoon, Job (skipper), i, 345, 349
Marten (or Martin), Roger (Vice-Admiral), ii, 386; iii, 18, 50, 132, 377; iv, 217; vi, 44 sq., 50, 200; letter from, iii, 100; v, 278
    Capt. of the Diamond, i, 65; iii, 354; took Dutch ship, iii, 100
    Rear-Admiral of the White and capt. of the Diamond, iv, 20 n.; battle of Portland, iv, 95, 125 n.
    Capt. of the Speaker, iv, 279
    Capt. of the Bristol: to command ships for coast protection, v, 95, 107, 278, 334; vi, 181
Martin, John (Master), ii, 114
Martinson, Martin (skipper), skipper of the Old Man, ii, 244
Martsz, Pieter (Corporal), iv, 186
Martyn, Christopher (Commissioner of the Navy), iii, 307, 317
Masen, Jan (boatman), v, 136
Masham, Sir William (President of C.O.S.), ii, 158; iii, 26, 37, 65
Mason, Henry, to command fireship, i, 143
Masson, — (Captain), iii, 370
Master of Attendance (or Attendant), one appointed for Portsmouth, iv, 116, 155; vi, 232
Matham, — (Captain), vi, 205
Mathew, Thomas (Mayor of Barnstaple), iii, 435
Mathewson, John (Master), master of the Justice of Copenhagen, iii, 413
Matroos, Gerrit (Commander), iii, 233
Matysen, Jan (Captain), v, 127

INDEX 309

MAUDITT

Mauditt, Edward (chaplain), minister of the Lion, ii, 247
Mauregnaultz, I. v. Meijden de (Lord Commissioner), ii, 362
May, Isle of, i, 291 ; iii, 386
May, Thomas (midshipman), vi, 250
Mayes, Martin (Captain), iv, 164
Mayo, Richard (chaplain), minister of the Sovereign, ii, 105
Medenblick, iv, 185; v, 235, 394
   Commander of Directors' ship from, i, 263
   Commander of Vice-Admiral de With's squadron from, i, 265
Medendicht, v, 185
Mediterranean : Dutch :
   squadrons employed in, ii, 22, 26, 42, 44 ; iii, 16, 57, 79 ; iv, 308 ; vi, 97, 245
   merchantmen from the Straits, i, 197, 219, 282 ; v, 210
   ships relieved, iv, 222 sq.
   reinforcements intended, iii, 16, 57, 79 ; vi, 63
   20 men-of-war recalled, v, 111, 118, 119, 150
   a list of ships in, iv, 308
Mediterranean : English :
   squadrons employed in, i, 61 sqq., 66, 68 ; iii, 58, 61, 67, 73, 79, 166, 209 ; iv, 159, 216, 300 ; v, 59, 65 ; vi, 46
   reinforcements intended, iii, 58, 61, 67, 73, 79, 166, 209; iv, 159, 216, 273, 279 sq., 287
Meer, Symon Cornelissen van der (Captain), iii, 225 ; iv, 388
Meerman, — (Delegate), iii, 69 ; v, 239, 306
Meertens, Bartholomees (Captain), i, 278

MIDDELCOOP

Meeusen, Egbert (Master), v, 239 ; vi, 118 sq., 123, 150 and n.
   Master of the Brederode, i, 278 (afterwards known as Cortenaer)
Meijer, E., vi, 76
Meirpoort, —, iii, 69
Menicus, Harmon, ii, 162
Merkus, Pieter (Captain), v, 418
   Capt. of the Conyng, ii, 211
Meuse, i, 196 ; iv, 248, 354, 359, 367, 375 sq., 380, 383 sq., 388 sq. ; v, 28, 41, 45, 59, 110, 121, 127 sq., 133, 142, 144 sq., 172, 190, 193, 195, 199, 201, 210, 222 sqq., 234, 244, 288, 336, 346, 368 sq., 418, 420 sqq. ; vi, 28, 29 n., 154, 160, 163
   Dutch rendezvous, iv, 371 sq., 377
   English fleet off, v, 94, 101, 118
   Dutch fleet off, v, 347
Michell, Benjamin (boatswain), v, 276
Michiels (or Michielszoon), Joannes, i, 263 ; iii, 248
   took English ship off Dover, i, 339
   sent westward to Ostend and Nieuport, i, 425
   battle of Portland : reported dead, iv, 189
Michiels, Sacharias (Master), master of the Hercules, iii, 192
Middelburg, iv, 190, 258, 286, 370 ; v, 44, 108, 126 sq., 133, 219, 287
   Commanders of Directors' ships from, i, 263
   Commanders of East Indiamen from, ii, 342
Middelcoop, Johan van (Commissary), iii, 199

MILDMAY

Mildmay, John (Captain), ii, 238 sq., 285; iii, 126, 168; letter from, ii, 268
  Capt. of the Nonsuch, i, 7, 67; capture of Dutch northern fishing guard, i, 386; battle of Kentish Knock, ii, 268–290; proposals by, iii, 373 sq.
  Capt. of the Vanguard, iv, 20; battle of Portland, iv, 80, 84, 101
Mill, Lieutenant-Colonel, iv, 304
Mill, Richard, letters from, v, 333, 405
Mill, Robert, letter from, vi, 251
Mill, Robert (Captain), iv, 149; vi, 6
  Capt. of the Advantage, iv, 21
  Capt. of the Falmouth, vi, 202; action with French Newfoundland fleet, vi, 251
Miller, Thomas (seaman), iii, 366
Milton, Robert, iii, 368
Minehead, v, 39
Mol, Sijbrant Janss (Captain), capt. of the Witten Oliphant, iv, 308
Molins, William, iii, 368
Monck, George (Admiral and General at Sea), i, 14, 15 and n., 138; iii, 102, 110, 290, 318, 366, 435; iv, 33, 38, 172, 260, 262, 273, 275 sq., 284, 353; v, 16, 112, 115, 129, 148, 259, 310, 340, 373, 390, 401, 408, 411; vi, 1 sq., 5, 16 sq., 31 sq., 44 n., 99, 101, 104, 114, 116, 128, 136, 176, 186, 219 sq., 231, 247, 250
  Letters to, i, 138; iii, 344; v, 278; vi, 32

MORLAIX

Letters from, iii, 353; iv, 163, 245, 252, 295, 299, 305, 319, 347, 361, 385, 386, 389; v, 31, 35, 53, 64, 72, 81, 94, 103, 111, 186, 208, 214, 228, 248, 255 sq., 261 sq., 267, 271, 275, 299, 313, 328, 347, 351, 374, 380, 391, 398, 406, 413; vi, 73, 176, 180, 183, 187, 189, 195, 203, 209, 218
  Admiral of the White, i, 14; General at Sea, iii, 110, 178, 317; vi, 189; Navy Commissioner, vi, 189
  Battle of Portland, i, 14; iv, 101, 125, 163 sqq.
  Battle of the Gabbard, v, 122; reported killed, v, 102, 110, 118, 121
  Battle of the Texel, v, 163 sqq., 176, 347 sqq., 378
  Commander-in-Chief in Scotland, vi, 228
  See also Squadrons Employed; Instructions
Monickendam, i, 263, iv, 136
Monroe, Sir George, iv, 107
Monster, v, 419
Montague, Colonel, v, 373
Mootham (or Motham), Peter (Captain), ii, 365; iv, 356 sq; letters from, iv, 317, 329, 331
  Capt. of the Bear, iv, 259
  Capt. of the Pelican, vi, 50
  (See also Mortham, Peter)
Mordcock, Edward (Captain), capt. of the Elias, vi, 52
Morgan, — (Captain), capt. of the John and Katherine, v, 196
Moriacq, Lieutenant-Colonel de, v, 287
Morlaix, iv, 41, 65; petition of English merchants of, iii, 327–331

MORLEY

Morley, H. (Colonel), i, 222, 294; ii, 18, 90, 169, 264; iii, 37, 96, 121, 122, 132, 148
Letter from, i, 341; ii, 180
To hasten ships into Downs, i, 334, 346
Morley, Thomas (Master), master of the Jonathan and Abigail, merchant, i, 153
Morris, Humphry (Captain), vi, 52; capt. of the Fortune, v, 16
Morris, Mr., iv, 86; wounded at Portland, iv, 175
Mortham, Peter (Captain), capt. of the Pelican, v, 16
Moscovy Roads, vi, 24
Mostart, John, v, 186
Moulton, Robert, jun. (Captain), i, 356; ii, 139
 Capt. of the Sapphire, i, 65; action off Dover, account of, i, 227, 228
Moulton, Robert (Navy Commissioner at Portsmouth), i, 54, 216, 268, 358; ii, 176
 Letters to, ii, 183; vi, 79
 Orders to, i, 215, 247, 267
 Money for Plymouth, i, 288
 Dead: his successor appointed, ii, 267
Mounts Bay, Dutch fleet off, iv, 148
Mouron, — (Captain), i, 123
Moy, Hillebrandt Jeroensz de (Captain), battle of the Texel; killed, v, 361
Moyer, Mr., v, 398
Moyle, Justice, v, 405 sq.
Mumincx, Hermes (Captain), iii, 225
Munnekes, — (Captain), capt. of the Wapen van Hollandt, iv, 314
Munnich (or Munnicnk or Munnick), Hendrick de (Captain), i, 261; iii, 156, 196, 224, 245
VI.

NAVY

Battle of Portland, iv, 69, 88 and n., 123, 195
Reported death, iv, 189
Munnich, Sr. Jansz, de, i, 351
Münster, Treaty of Peace at, iv, 351
Munth, Gerrit (Captain), i, 264
 Capt. of the Huijs van Nassau, iv, 313
 Capt. of the Ganapan, v, 185
Musgrave, John, boatswain of the Briar, iv, 129
Muster Books, v, 96
Mynertsz, Albert, iv, 186
Myngs, Sir Christopher (Captain), vi, 7, 50, 201, 214; letters from, vi, 104, 208
 Formerly coxswain to Captain Goodsonn, i, 13
 Capt. of the Elizabeth, i, 12; took three Dutch ships, i, 12

NAEN, Cornelis (Captain), iii, 224
Naenoogh (or Nanooch), Cornelis, i, 218, 262, 416; iv, 25; court-martialled, v, 192
Nantes, iv, 26, 90, 92, 98, 137; v, 136, 266; vi, 204, 221, 237
Narrow. See Dover, Straits of
Naval Affairs, Committee of the States-General for, v, 183
Naval Law, English, advocate appointed, iii, 425
Navy, Dutch:
 Strength and distribution of, i, 260, 350, 363, 368, 370, 375, 388, 398, 400, 410; ii, 233, 237, 306, 341; iii, 42, 47, 60, 71, 78, 94, 107, 136, 223, 233, 238, 255, 281, 332, 402; iv, 23 sq., 27, 30 sq., 48, 60, 64 sq.,

U

INDEX

NAVY

67, 72, 79, 88, 109, 118, 132, 148, 165, 178, 191, 192 *and n.*, 207 sq., 228, 259, 322, 328, 330, 334, 341 sq., 346, 354, 356, 367 sq., 388; v, 25 sqq., 30, 40, 54, 56, 69, 86, 101, 109 sqq., 116 sq., 124, 139, 144, 162 sq., 193, 197 sq., 220, 238, 253, 264, 290, 304, 306 sqq., 312 sq., 321 sq., 330, 347 sqq., 350 sq., 354, 365, 367, 369, 371 sq., 378, 384, 397, 417, 422; vi, 35, 120, 134 sq.
Five Boards of Admiralty, i, 55, 104, 106, 120
36 ships added to fleet, 1651, i, 57
Proposed to add 150 ships, 1652, i, 51, 57-8, 85, 88, 94, 100, 103; The first 50 of the 150 ships, i, 85, 90; The remaining 100 of the 150 ships, i, 104, 106; specification for them, i, 120; Provision of 132 ships, iv, 222
Committee of Directors, members of, i, 97; Directors' ships, i, 56, 261 sqq., 368; ii, 248, 250
Admiralty of North Quarter, ships of, i, 154, 275; iv, 313
Admiralty of Amsterdam, ships of, i, 271
Naval and military preparations, i, 97 sq.; v, 201 sqq.
Ruyter's squadron, ii, 59, 61, 79, 87 sq., 99, 166, 253
Complaints as to ships, by Ruyter, ii, 182, 186; by De With, ii, 237; by Tromp, iii, 20; iv, 207, 377
Tromp asks for Deputies to inspect fleet, iv, 378; v, 190 sq.

NAVY

Assembling of fleet, v, 189 sqq., 193 sq., 198 sq., 203, 222, 234 sq., 238, 244 sq., 265 sq., 288, 290, 297, 308, 322 sq., 411
Hastening of reinforcements desired, v, 341 sq.
A Fiscal to accompany the fleet, v, 289, 402
State of fleet after Portland, iv, 162; before Texel, v, 202; after Texel, vi, 3, 18
Proposed to lay up the fleet for winter, vi, 2
De With's squadron suffers from gale, vi, 4, 154 sqq., 158, 160, 162, 165, 175, 216
Navy, English:
Strength and distribution of, ii, 60, 68, 79, 88, 189, 306, 360; iii, 43, 94, 107, 116, 120, 130, 166, 251, 428, 433, 451; iv, 24, 118, 188, 193, 203, 206, 216, 228, 251, 322, 324, 350 sqq., 367, 384; v, 21, 25, 28, 43, 60, 64, 69, 86, 88 *n*., 92, 101, 116, 118, 124, 129, 133, 136 sq., 198, 224, 226, 232, 237, 285 sq., 290, 297, 318, 327, 336, 341, 348, 357, 369, 382, 385, 408, 419; vi, 31, 39, 113, 202 sq.
Organisation of, i, 53
40 more ships required, 30 to be merchants, i, 224, 233, 247, 268, 280, 304, 322, 362
to be hastened out, i, 316
reorganisation after Dungeness, iii, 98; vi, 16
condition of fleet after Texel, vi, 1 sq.
superiority over Dutch fleet, vi, 10
See also Victualling; Ships; Instructions

INDEX 313

NAVY

Navy, French:
  at Brest, ii, 54
  New Fleet to be formed, ii, 366
  to be sent to Blaye, iv, 24
Navy Chaplains, Dutch, vi, 126
Navy Chaplains, English, ii, 53, 105
Navy Commissioners:
  enlarged powers, i, 146
  victualling of fleet transferred to, i, 306.
  See also Commissioners
Naylor, — (Captain), ii, 116
Naze, v, 40, 42 *sqq.*, 130, 132; vi, 55, 119, 138, 149
Neale, — (Captain), iii, 35
Neales, Richard, iii, 172
Neck, Jan van, ii, 38
Neeringh, Claes (Master), master of the Phœnix, iii, 193
Neeve, Robert (Master), iii, 34
Nes, A. J. van, vi, 76
Nes, Jan Jacobsz van (Captain), i, 261, 351, 393; ii, 62, 221, 336, 338, 341
  at battle of Kentish Knock, ii, 358
Ness, The. *See* Dungeness, *and* Orfordness
Netherlands: foreign relations:
  Denmark: report of a treaty with, ii, 368; v, 115, 118, 194; report of closer alliance, ii, 384; suggested exchange of ships, v, 244 *sqq.*, 254, 281, 283, 290, 313, 386
  France, ships to join Van Galen's fleet, iii, 61; reported treaty with, v, 115
  Spain, iii, 150; treaty with (1650), i, 165; iii, 60, 170; frontiers strengthened by, iii, 61; Dutch fear breach with, iii, 181
  Sweden, ii, 368; v, 313

NEWPORT

Netherlands: Internal politics:
  Political differences between the States, ii, 224; v, 265
  Opposition of States-General to the Prince of Orange, ii, 365; v, 233
  Recall of the Stadtholder expected, iii, 181
Neville, —, i, 200
New England. *See* Stores, Naval
Newbery, Richard (Captain), v, 20, 250; vi, 200
  Capt. of the Swan, i, 65; ii, 179; of the Entrance, iv, 278; of the Laurel, vi, 49
Newbury (*or* Newbery), Thomas, i, 119; iv, 364; vi, 241
Newcastle, i, 203, 224, 269, 295, 331, 380; ii, 227; iv, 50, 160, 173, 235, 259, 291 *sq.*, 303, 318, 336, 346, 348, 361, 369, 373, 375, 381; v, 32, 98, 105, 346; vi, 102, 229, 255
  Blake's fleet off, i, 407
  Deane and Monck off, v, 35
Newfoundland, i, 224, 268, 286, 290, 316, 324; iii, 386; iv, 149, 305; vi, 251
  petition for convoy for fishing fleet, iii, 387
  protection of seamen against impress, v, 36
Newhaven, iv, 170; *See also* Havre
Newly, Richard, Master's mate of the Briar, iv, 129
Newman, — (Captain), battle of the Texel: his death, v, 353, 390 *n.*
  Capt. of the Mayflower, v, 390 *n.*
Newport, — (Lord Deputy), vi, 217

NICHOLAS

Nicholas, Sir Edward (Secretary of State to Charles II), ii, 225-31; v, 102
Nickson (or Nixon), Robert (Captain), iv, 278; v, 17; vi, 50
    Capt. of the Adventure, iv, 20
    Capt. of the Centurion, vi, 201
Nieuburch, — van der, ii, 321
Nieuhuijs, vi, 167
Nieuport, i, 196, 218; iv, 196; v, 31, 69, 86, 136
Nieuport, Willem (Commissioner to England), i, 217, 244, 314; iv, 353; v, 118, 197, 213, 389; vi, 225
    letter from, vi, 29
Noades, Butler (Captain), capt. of the Success, i, 65
Nobel, Gerrit (Captain), i, 264, 393; ii, 343, 345 sq.
    at battle of Kentish Knock, ii, 358; capt. of the Burgh van Alckmaer, iv, 313 and n.
Noble, Mr., vi, 84
Noblet, — (Captain), capt. of the Landt van Beloften, iv, 314
Noblitt, John, ii, 162
Noose, Jan, vi, 124
Nore, iv, 345; account of ships and ordnance at, iii, 314, 315
Noret, John, i, 409
Norman, — (Captain), capt. of the Lady, i, 66; of the Arms of Medemblick, ii, 280
Norris, John, i, 74
North Foreland, i, 370; iv, 261, 283, 289, 321 sq., 332, 372, 379, 387, 395; v, 26, 28, 56 sq., 76, 80, 134, 136 sq.
    Dutch fleet sighted, iii, 75
North Quarter. See Friesland and Admiralties: Dutch
Northam, iii, 416

OFFICERS

Northern Guard. See Squadrons Employed
Northsands Head, i, 373
Norton, — Colonel, iii, 127, 422
Norway, i, 367; iii, 371, 413; iv, 311, 370; v, 29, 40, 42 sqq., 121, 130 sq., 193, 210, 224 sq., 245, 308, 340, 409; vi, 37, 60, 62, 81, 84, 134, 138, 145 sq., 153, 161, 165, 214. See also Denmark
Nottill, William, iii, 435
Nutt, Richard, iii, 423; v, 310
Nutton, Michael (Captain), capt. of the Satisfaction, vi, 52
Nyhoff (or Niehoff or Neeuhoff), Willem van, iii, 156, 242; iv, 308; capt. of the Archangel, iii, 160

Octon, Mr. (Clerk of the Cheque), v, 98
Odey (or Oddy), — (Captain), i, 414; v, 63; vi, 99; capt. of the Nonsuch ketch, iv, 293
Odway, Arthur, iv, 217
Officers, Dutch:
    List of, 1652, i, 260 sqq.
    Resolutions passed by De With's officers, iv, 336 sqq.
    Officer as executioner to sail with fleet, v, 205, 221
    Petition for leave of absence, v, 387
    Payments to officers and wives to be stopped, vi, 64
Officers, Administrative, English:
    In need of reform, iii, 180; Deputy Checks, at the outports, iii, 441
Officers, Sea, English:
    Authority given to communicate with Navy Board, iii, 28

INDEX 315

OGEL

Merchant captains in hired ships, their failure, iii, 92, 105; to be appointed by the State, iii, 168, 179; iv, 295, 343; vi, 9

Encouragements for, iii, 394, 397, 431

Captains, proposal for choosing, iii, 292; Master and Commander, iii, 445; Midshipmen, iii, 417, 437; Reformado, iii, 428; Warrant Officers, iii, 428; iv, 160

Petition from, as to care of wounded, iv, 211, 301

See also Flag Officers; Generals at Sea

Ogel, Dirck (Captain), capt. of the Orangie, i, 391, 397

Okey, John, vi, 235

Oldenburg, iv, 186; v, 265

Olivierszoon, Jan (Captain), i, 264; iii, 222 *sq.*; iv, 193; v, 127, 418; his instructions, v, 320

Ommeren, — van (Deputy), i, 89; iii, 185

Ooms, Jan Egbertsen (Captain), i, 388; iii, 224, 242; iv, 323; vi, 157

Capt. of the Gouda, iv, 310 *and n.*; took merchantman off Dover, v, 58; battle of the Texel, v, 359; his ship lost in storm off the Texel, vi, 160

Ooren, Adrien der (Captain), battle of the Gabbard, v, 74 *n.*

Oostergoo, Cornelis Ales (Captain), capt. of yacht De Waterhont, iii, 187

Oosteroon, — (Captain), (capt. of the Waterdog, v, 186

Oosterwout, Meijndert Theuniss (Captain), capt. of the Salomons Oordeel, iv, 308

OPERATIONS

Opdam, Lord ? (Admiral), v, 412; vi, 46, 112, 134 *sq.*

Operations and Movements, Dutch:

Northern voyage, i, 339, 345, 350, 387, 400–406, 410

Fleet dispersed by storm, i, 391, 396, 403, 430

Tromp's attempt on Ayscue in Downs, i, 363, 369, 401; vi, 16

De Ruyter in Channel, ii, 59, 61, 68, 77, 105 *sq.*, 146, 182; De Ruyter joins de With, ii, 210

Tromp's plans for assembling his fleet, iii, 47, 48, 70, 79

Tromp near the Downs, iii, 84, 204, 229; follows Blake to Dungeness, iii, 91, 205, 229; his movements after the battle, iii, 92, 118, 208 *sq.*, 252 *sq.*; off Dover, iii, 159, 162, 236 *sq.*, 252, 255; at Ushant, iii, 220

Evertsen's squadron separated from Tromp by storm, iii, 242 *sq.*; off the Start, iii, 244; Ile de Rhé, iii, 247

De Ruyter's squadron off Guernsey, iii, 261; Ile de Rhé, iii, 266

Tromp off Dover, iii, 332; v, 135; arrives at St. Martins, iv, 23; sailing of fleet and convoy, iv, 65, 90; v, 126–139; movements after battle of Portland, iv, 115, 117, 122, 142, 167, 183, 191 *sqq.*

De With off Gravelines, iv, 132; threatens coal fleet, iv, 335

OPERATIONS

Before the battle of the Gabbard, v, 40 sqq., 52, 56 sq., 66, 134, 137 sq.: battle of the Gabbard, v, 72, 82 sqq.
After battle of the Gabbard, v, 24, 74 sq., 94, 96, 98 sqq., 108 sqq., 117, 121, 125, 183, 189
Before the battle of the Texel, v, 162 sqq., 297, 316, 325, 336, 338 sq., 340 sq., 348 sq., 354, 365, 367, 371
After the Texel, v, 351 sq., 368 sq., 418 sqq.
De With's squadron to the Sound, vi, 2 sq., 45, 49, 53, 109, 118, 124, 136 sqq.; strength of, vi, 27, 45, 53, 55, 77, 118 sqq., 123, 137, 148, 150 sq., 155, 164; caught in storm off the Texel, vi, 4 sq., 155 sq., 158
12 men-of-war to lie in wait for English convoy, vi, 78, 99, 112, 182
Reinforcements for De With, vi, 79, 112, 119, 123, 149 sq.
Report of 6 English merchantmen taken by privateer, vi, 112
30 ships of war to proceed to Ostend, vi, 161
See also Navy: Dutch Squadrons Employed
Operations and Movements, English:
Northern voyage, i, 299, 385, 407; vi, 16
Ayscue in the Downs, i, 363, 369
Blake's fleet dispersed by storm, i, 405
Ayscue in the Channel, ii, 17
Blake ordered to seek Ayscue, ii, 100; off Torbay, ii, 184; to return to watch Tromp, ii, 120

OPERATIONS

Blake anchored in Downs, iii, 68, 84, 125, 209, 251; sailed from, iii, 229; his movements after Dungeness, iii, 105, 114, 150, 232
Blake's fleet in Thames, iii, 155, 161, 167, 234, 235, 254, 332; it sails to intercept Dutch convoy, iii, 452; anchors in Dover Road, iv, 47, 49; west of Beachy Head, iv, 60; off Isle of Wight, iv, 62, 65; after battle of Portland, iv, 115, 168
Penn to assistance of Colliers' fleet, iv, 319, 321 sq., 332 sq., 340 sq.; to join Deane, iv, 368
The main fleet before battle of the Gabbard, v, 25 sq., 30 sq., 60 sqq., 66 *and n.*, 71, 129, 139-146; in the battle, v, 82 sqq.; after it, v, 91, 93 sq., 98, 101 sq., 104, 106, 118, 125, 192 sq.
To intercept merchant fleet, v, 140, 142, 207, 210, 217, 232 sq., 301, 395; vi, 17 sq., 21, 196, 203 sq.
Blockade of Dutch coast, v, 147 sqq., 161 sq., 180, 195 sq., 226, 231 sq., 237, 266, 290, 327, 335, 337, 367, 416; vi, 1, 31, 39, 72, 77, 216
Before the battle of the Texel, v, 224, 226, 228 sq., 249, 271, 285, 302, 313, 330, 354, 364, 367, 370, 419, 426
After the battle of the Texel, v, 368, 374, 385, 392, 395, 408, 413, 425
Decision to lay up fleet for winter, vi, 1, 6, 71
See also Actions; Fleets and Squadrons

INDEX

ORANGE

Orange, Prince of, ii, 365;
v, 233, 265, 290, 402 sq.
Orders and Instructions, Dutch:
States-General to Tromp,
i, 155, 219, 325
Admiralty of Amsterdam: to
Captains, ii, 49; to Tromp,
iii, 23, 68; v, 112 sq.; to
Verbuch, v, 56
By Ruyter, ii, 58, 62 sqq.,
80, 90, 140 sq., 374; v,
319 sqq.
By Tromp, i, 164-69, 321,
345, 393; iii, 38 sq.; v,
199 sq.
By De With, vi, 58 sq.
Orders and Instructions,
English:
By C.O.S.: to Blake, i, 301;
to Admiralty Commissioners, iv, 216 sq.; to
Ayscue, ii, 29; to Ball,
ii, 155; to Capts. Locke
and Quixley, ii, 30; to
Capt. Reed, ii, 118; to
Col. Thompson, i, 302,
308 sq., 314, 318, 356
Admiralty Committee to
Capts. Hosier and Wyard,
iv, 173 sq.
By Generals at Sea: to
officers, vi, 191 sqq., 197
sq.; fighting instructions,
iv, 209, 262–266, 394;
sailing instructions, iv, 210,
266–273; to Vice-Admiral
Penn, iv, 34 sq., 260 sq.,
273, 275; to Jordan, iv,
276; to Capts. Strong and
Pestall, v, 53
Commissioners of Navy to
Warrant Officers, iii, 403;
By Blake to Penn, i, 336;
By Monck to Capt. Wm.
Hill, vi, 44
See also Prize Goods, Commissioners of; Sick and
Hurt

ORDNANCE

Ordnance, Office of, and
Establishments:
Committee of, i, 137, 164,
199, 200, 204, 241, 259,
328; ii, 12
Lieut. of, i, 151; iii, 326;
office taken away, i, 152;
compensation to, i, 152, 153
Gun wharves and storehouses, i, 146; stores to
be sent to Blake, i, 215
Salaries of officers, etc., iii,
326
See also Ordnance and Stores
Ordnance and Ordnance Stores,
Dutch:
Ammunition: received, i,
349, 427; v, 118, 234;
wanted, v, 28, 70, 75,
113, 125, 190, 203, 205,
218, 285; vi, 28, 40
Cartridges, ii, 22, 303, 330;
Powder, ii, 144; iv, 120,
191 sq.; v, 121, 138,
358 sqq.; Shot, ii, 144;
iv, 120, 191 sq.; v, 358 sqq.
Return of stores ordered,
v, 189
Guns: description of, i, 90;
contract for, for ships
building, iii, 83; captured,
v, 145; size of, in battle
of the Gabbard, v, 194;
brass guns for fleet, v,
234; from Denmark, vi,
182; from Sweden, v,
216, 233, 235, 238, 266
See also Inventions
Ordnance: English
ii, 91, 177; iii, 40, 103, 132,
163; iv, 364; v, 216, 266,
409; vi, 196
Buying of guns, i, 108, 130,
141, 281, 335
To be sent to the Tower
of London from: Portsmouth, i, 109; Hull, i,
109 n.; York, county of,

ORDNANCE

i, 109 n.; Clifford's Tower, i, 109 n.; Landguard Fort, i, 109 n.; Dumbarton, Stirling and Leith, i, 114; Scotland, i, 114; Wallingford, i, 119; Bristol and all western garrisons, i, 119; from several garrisons, i, 130; from Gresham College, i, 132; from City of London, i, 137; from ships in the Thames, i, 304, 306; from Berwick, Tynemouth and Newcastle, i, 267

Guns for Weymouth harbour, i, 328; for Portsmouth, iii, 141; for Inch Keith, i, 403; for frigates building, i, 131; iii, 67, 325; badness of new iron guns, i, 241; privateers to carry twenty, i, 358; of Dutch prizes not to be sold, ii, 61, 117; v, 145, 230; at Tower, to be recast, iii, 365; want of, iv, 344; survey of, vi, 241

Ordnance Stores: English i, 201; ii, 13, 61; iii, 67; iv, 364, 386, 390; v, 80, 209, 269, 299, 400

Stores, want of, iv, 344, 346, 363 sq.; v, 52, 72, 380

Cartridges, v, 215, 230, 250, 255, 262, 329, 375, 392

Powder, i, 200, 203, 204, 222-5, 242, 246, 259, 269, 281, 295, 307; iii, 122, 314 sq., 326, 360; iv, 116, 282, 284, 299, 307, 318, 368, 385; v, 32, 94, 103, 112, 187, 193, 195 sq., 209, 215, 230, 269, 275, 329, 391, 399, 407, 413, 234; vi, 41, 78 sq.

OUTLOOKS

from Hamburg, iv, 157; v, 329, 426; vi, 99, 113; from Carlisle, iv, 290 sqq.; from Norfolk, v, 401, 414

Powder mills, iv, 158

Saltpetre, manufacture of, i, 287, 335; iii, 149, 326

Shot, i, 204, 259, 281, 319, 336; iv, 280, 284, 307, 363, 386; v, 94 sq., 103, 112, 188, 209, 215, 230, 262, 269, 275, 300, 329, 391, 399, 407, 413 sq., 424; vi, 42

Orfordness, iv, 393; v, 34, 59, 68 n., 106; vi, 254

Orkney and Shetland:
further forces to be sent to, i, 223
nature of harbours to be ascertained, i, 223
English fleet off, i, 386; v, 140
Tromp's fleet near, i, 395

Orlton, Thomas (Clerk of Cheque), letter from, v, 378

Orton, Simon (Captain), capt. of the Charity: petition of, ii, 180; capt. of the Sun, victualler, vi, 53

Ostend, i, 196, 337; iv, 137, 193, 197, 370, 375 sq.; v, 23, 74, 82, 86, 92 sq., 99, 125 sq., 197, 223, 225; vi, 161

Ostend, privateers of:
Brewer, Erasmus, i, 25
Duyts, Jan, iii, 231

Ostenders: iv, 71; v, 251; action with the Greyhound, i, 5; action with the Briar, i, 28

Otford, v, 410

Ouens, — den (Captain), iii, 241

Ousley Bay. *See* Hollesley Bay

Outlooks, The, v, 132

INDEX

OVEN

Oven, Adriaen Jansz den (Commander), i, 263; ii, 58, 68, 189 sq., 352; v, 130; battle of the Gabbard, v, 242
Overbeeck, Hendrich, ii, 354
Overbeecke, Jan (Captain), capt. of the Amsterdam, ii, 65, 198
Overen, iv, 374
Overissel, v, 233; states of, unable to raise funds, vi, 183
Overkerck, Jan Hendricksen (Captain,) ii, 256
Over-masting, of English ships, i, 44
Overton, Robert, letter from, v, 62
Overwater, P. I., letter from, v, 337
Ovescamp (or Overcamp), — (Captain), capt. of the Pelican, v, 185; battle of the Texel, v, 359
Oxenbridge, Clement (Checkmaster to Collector of Prizes), ii, 114; pay of, iii, 441
Oxö, vi, 62

Paar, van de (Ambassador), v, 118
Pack, John (carpenter), vi, 250
Packe, Henry (Captain), vi, 50; letter from, vi, 225 Capt. of the Amity, ii, 123; v, 20; of the Great President, iv, 279
Packe, Michael (Rear-Admiral), i, 343
Capt. of the Amity, i, 67; Rear-Admiral to Ayscue, ii, 19, 29; wounded in action off Plymouth, ii, 106, 117; death, ii, 173

PATTEN

Paddison, — (Captain), capt. of the Francis privateer, i, 80; took Orangieboom, i, 80
Paine, Richard (Captain), capt. of the King Ferdinando, v, 20
Palmer, John (merchant), letter from, iii, 322
Pampus, v, 286, 311
Papillon, Thomas (merchant), iii, 327
Par (or Perre), Rombout Van der (Captain), ii, 63, 111, 142, 147, 163, 164, 187, 188 sq., 305, 354; vi, 157; capt. of the Albertina, ii, 147
Paris, Jacob (Master), v, 136
Park, Francis (Captain), vi, 50, 202, 257; capt. of the Great President, v, 19
Parker, Nicholas (Captain), capt. of the Briar, i, 26; took Ostend privateer, i, 27; consul at Algiers, i, 26
Parliament, Acts of:
 Navigation Act, 1651, i, 48, 51, 329
 Act of 1650 prohibiting trade with certain colonies, i, 49, 76, 80 n.
 for calling home seamen, i, 337; ii, 18, 97, 125 154, 167, 169, 177; iii, 28, 52
 forbidding correspondence with Dutch, ii, 21, 94, 97, 169
 for impress of seamen, iii, 129, 145
Parliament, Joan. See Alkin, Elizabeth
Parrish, William, letter from, i, 139
Partingale. See Portugal
Pater, Dirck (Captain), i, 262; iii, 190, 192; battle of the Texel, v, 363
Patten, vi, 153

320 INDEX

PAULET

Paulet, Robert, letters of reprisal, i, 74, 75
Paulet, William, i, 75
Pauluzzi, Lorenzo (Venetian Secretary), ii, 194
Pauw, Adrian, i, 322, 332
Pauw, Leo de, ii, 25, 38
Pauwelsen, Jan (Captain), iv, 193
Pawelszoon, Jacob, iii, 156
Pay, Dutch:
  For officers and men, scale of, i, 104 sq.; payments for, by Rotterdam Admiralty, iii, 195 sq.; abuses, ii, 221, 330; iii, 62; gratuities, ii, 124
  Senior officers, additional allowance proposed, vi, 126; of officers court-martialled, v, 192; of musketeers, v, 247; vi, 67; of seamen, i, 155; ii, 61, 338, 380; iii, 16, 20, 44, 134; iv, 317, 363; v, 219, 223, 234, 264; vi, 67
  Amsterdam Board's inability to pay wages, vi, 65; proposal for officers and seamen to be paid off for three months, vi, 97 sq.
Pay and Pensions, English:
  ii, 158, 162, 167, 257; iii, 30, 37, 96 sq., 166, 385; vi, 102
  Increase of, to officers, iii, 278, 283; to seamen, iii, 274, 284, 318 sq.; merchant captains ask for, iii, 394
  Revised table of, iii, 285, 319, 396
  Flag officers, iii, 374 sq., 436; iv, 56; vi, 106
  Judge Advocate, iii, 425; vi, 106
  Midshipmen, iii, 417; shipwrights, ii, 372; dockyard artificers, iii, 326

PEACE

Seamen, iii, 134, 175, 394; vi, 43, 74, 83, 102, 114 sq., 129 sq., 169; allowance to, for losses, iv, 61
Soldiers, iii, 424; iv, 253; to be paid by the Navy, iii, 432
Pay withheld, ii, 126, 133, 136; iii, 14, 73, 164, 279, 312, 365, 377, 382; iv, 131, 202, 287, 391; v, 276 sq.; vi, 8, 128
Payment by ticket, iii, 438; iv, 252, 255, 284, 286, 305 sq., 320; v, 97
Payment of ships, i, 128; ii, 20; iii, 45, 87, 309 sq., 317, 342, 353; iv, 162; v, 236; vi, 79, 102, 168, 173, 176
Widows to be paid wages due, iii, 141, 146, 307; pensions to, iii, 409; iv, 212 sqq.; v, 236, 261, 374, 381; vi, 91, 211
Full pay to captains of ships fitting, v, 332
Petty warrant, vi, 220
Payler, George (Ordnance Officer), iii, 314, 316
Peace, Negotiations for:
  Dutch ambassadors to be protected, i, 191, 200, 240, 245; their proposition to Council of State, i, 228–232, 243, 270; letters from, i, 237, 243; letters to, i, 281; v, 412
  Answer of English Parliament to, i, 278–80
  Departure of, i, 327, 331; vi, 217, 225
  proposals after Portland, iv, 233, 250
  negotiations re-opened after the Gabbard, v, 111, 213, 232 sq., 264, 266, 304, 386

PEACOCK

after the battle of Texel, v, 389, 403; vi, 47, 188
acceptance of by Deputies, vi, 217; delay of settlement, vi, 231, 247, 250
Peace declared, vi, 11, 259 sq. Causes of English success, vi, 11 sqq.
Peacock, James (Vice-Admiral), ii, 365; iii, 28, 30, 65, 81, 111, 168; iv, 215, 245, 293; v, 17, 92; letter from, ii, 373
Capt. of the Tiger, i, 4, 65; took Portuguese ship, i, 4 and n.; to repair to Downs, i, 215; month's provisions for ships commanded by him, i, 216; Vice-Admiral of the Red, in Triumph, i, 6; commended, i, 292; Vice-Admiral of the White and capt. of the Rainbow, iv, 20 and n; battle of Portland, iv, 125; battle of the Texel, slain, i, 6; v, 390 n.
Peacocke, Robert, ii, 162
Pearce, John (Captain), v, 17; capt. of the Providence, iv, 85; battle of the Texel, v, 369
Peck, Francis (Captain), iv, 279; capt. of the Amity, iv, 21
Peeke, Thomas (Mayor of Colchester), vi, 169; letter from, vi, 132; asks for funds for relief of seamen and English prisoners, vi, 132, 136
Peerboom (or Peerboonz or Pereboom), Thys Tymersz (Captain), i, 264; ii, 363; iii, 225; capt. of the Pereboom, iv, 316 and n.
Peirepoint, — (Captain), capt. of the Peter, iv, 293

PENN

Pembroke and Montgomery, Earl of (President of C.O.S.), i, 315, 319; letter to, i, 341
Pendennis, iv, 307
Penington, — (Alderman), i, 222
Penn, Sir William (Admiral and General at Sea), i, 7 sq., 14 sq., 17, 66, 68, 70, 129, 162, 336; iii, 308, 436; iv, 33, 56, 216 sq., 219, 259 sq., 278, 282, 289, 294 sq., 300, 302, 319, 321 sq., 332 sq., 355 n., 391, 396; v, 18, 311; vi, 49, 104, 234
Letters to, i, 154, 161, 290, 374, 406; ii, 95, 135, 139, 311; iv, 303, 382; v, 266
Orders to, from Blake, i, 154, 323, 326, 374, 406; ii, 95, 135, 139
Letters from, ii, 276; iv, 298, 299, 304, 333, 340, 369, 378; vi, 203, 209, 218, 219, 221, 226, 230, 235, 241, 243, 246, 247, 249
Report from, ii, 238 sqq.
Seized Dutch shipping at Barbados, i, 49 n.; capt. of the Fairfax, in command of Mediterranean squadron, i, 67; capt. of the Speaker and Admiral of the Blue, i, 14; iv, 20 n.; battle off Portland, i, 15, 102, 125; iv, 171; capt. of the Triumph, i, 161; Vice-Admiral, i, 185–189, 202; capt. of the James, i, 318
Sights Dutch off Torbay, ii, 184, 238
Battle of Kentish Knock ii, 276
Vice-Admiral of the Fleet, iii, 406, 408; iv, 20 n.

PENNINCK

to assist collier fleet, iv, 319, 321 sq., 332 sq., 340 sqq., 351, 355, 373, 381, 394 sq. to join Deane, iv, 368, 385 sq., 389; v, 129 *and n*.
General at Sea, v, 73 *and n* ; vi, 6, 189
Battle of the Texel, v, 409
Navy Commissioner, vi, 189
See also Instructions
Penninck, Cornelis Lyevensen, iii, 233
Pennington, Sir John (Admiral), i, 87 *n*.
Pennoyers, Mr., iv, 364
Penny, Jon., letter from, v, 35
Penrose, Thomas (Captain), iii, 34; iv, 279; v, 19; vi, 50, 200; capt. of the Concord, i, 65; capt. of the Nonsuch, iv, 20
Pensel (*or* Pense *or* Pensen), Jacob Ariensz (Captain), i, 263, 351, 393; ii, 337, 343; iii, 156, 224, 228; iv, 192; v, 127, 239; vi, 118; capt. of the Golden Lion, vi, 175
Pensier, Lourens (Captain). *See* Dispensier
Perre, Paulus van de (Dutch Ambassador), letters to, vi, 112; letters from, i, 239, 245, 271; v, 408; vi, 31, 70, 72; arrival of, i, 48
Perry, John (waterman), iv, 51
Pesse, Rombout van der (Rear Admiral), iii, 225
Pestle (*or* Pestall), William (Captain), letter to, v, 53; capt. of the Satisfaction, i, 65; instructions from Deane and Monck, v, 53, 63
Peters, Hugh, i, 217 *n*.; ii, 266 *n*.
Petersen, Cornelius (Master), master of the Arms of Riga, vi, 237

PHILIPS

Petersfield, iv, 256, 302
Peterson, J., letters from, v, 200, 263
Peterson, John (Master), master of the Nightingale merchant, i, 116
Petitions, Dutch: merchants, to the Admiralty of Amsterdam, iii, 35
Petitions, English:
Alkin, Elizabeth, iv, 104
Arkinstall, Thomas, iii, 352
Barnes, Rebecca, ii, 95
Dare, Jeffery, iii, 400
Dartmouth, the inhabitants of, iii, 387
Lambe, Thomas, iii, 327
Officers of the fleet, iv, 211
Taylor, Mary, ii, 160
Todd, Judith, vi, 232
Truelove, Henry, iii, 86
Wells, Thomas, iii, 368
Widows of ship's company of the John, ii, 112
Worcester, ship's company of the, i, 249
Young, John, i, 290
Pett, Peter (Navy Commissioner, Chatham), i, 54; iii, 147, 356, 398, 426; iv, 136; v, 260, 262, 274, 294; letters from, iii, 157, 357, 383, 404, 451; iv, 221, 257, 288; v, 65, 77, 269; vi, 93, 107
Pett, Peter (Master Shipwright, Deptford), ii, 10; two frigates to be built, i, 140
Pett, Phineas (Captain), iv, 76
Pett, Phineas (Assistant Master Shipwright, Chatham), letters from, iv, 237; v, 76; building frigate, i, 338; iii, 427; iv, 231
Pettingale, Robert, i, 75
Philips, — (Captain), iii, 154
Philips, Isaac, letters of reprisal on behalf of, i, 72

Philipsen, — (Captain), iii, 235, 238. *See also* Flyps
Philpott, — (Captain), capt. of the William and John, i, 191
Phipps, John (Commissary), i, 119
Pickering, Robert (merchant), letter from, iii, 321
Pickering, William, i, 409
Pidner, John (Captain), capt. of the Providence, vi, 50
Pierce, John (Captain), iv, 278 ; capt. of the Sapphire, i, 45 *n.*; capt. of the Providence, i, 65
Pierson, Joseph (Master), iii, 34 ; master of the Thomason, iii, 34
Pieter, Swart (skipper), battle of Portland, iv, 123, 189 ; taken by the English, 195 and *n.*
Pieters, Hendrick (Captain), battle of the Gabbard, v, 23, 74, 242
Pieterson, Ivert (Master), master of the Black Buss, iv, 136
Pieterszoon, Cornelis (skipper), ii, 349
Pieterszoon, Jan (skipper), i, 379
Pieterszoon, Lambert (Captain), i, 262, 351 ; ii, 351 *sq.* ; iii, 224, 245 ; left fleet without leave, i, 369
Pietersz., Reijer, v, 40
Piggen, Joannes (Fiscal), ii, 142
Pile, William (Captain), v, 17 ; capt. of the Ann and Joyce, iv, 22
Piltersz., R., v, 43 *n.*
Pinto, Jan (Captain), ii, 293
Pirates :
    Algiers, ii, 299
    Brest, iii, 328 ; vi, 6, 55, 250
    Channel, iii, 35, 90 ; v, 298 ; vi, 6, 55, 228

Downs, ii, 19
Jersey, i, 330
Lands End, v, 296
Western coast, i, 304, 308
See also Privateers, Royalist
Pitson, J., letter from, iv, 113
Pitteck, Richard (Captain), vi, 51 ; capt. of Hare, i, 66
Plact, Jan van der (Captain), capt. of Wapen van Rotterdam, fireship, i, 265
Plans, Dutch :
    Tromp proposes to attack Blake in the Thames, iii, 155, 160, 236
    project to block channel to London, iii, 332, 390, 399 ; iv, 192 ; vi, 4, 6, 134
    for campaign of 1653, January, iii, 390 *sq.* ; iv, 27
    for campaign of 1653, May, v, 56 *sqq.*
    See also Operations and Movements ; Strategy and Disposition
Plate fleet, taken by General Blake, i, 25
Pley, John, iii, 387
Plisted, William, carpenter of Worcester, i, 250
Plumleigh, Robert (Captain), iv, 148, 293 and *n.* ; vi, 52, 202 ; letter from, v, 298
    nominated capt. of the Sampson, iv, 41 ; appointed, iv, 50
    to command new frigate, vi, 185
Plunder, iii, 100, 276. *See also* Prizes and Prize Goods
Plymouth, iii, 360, 386, 441 ; iv, 67, 80, 103, 163, 177, 216 ; v, 334 ; vi, 176, 227, 250 *sq.*, 252
    Re-fitting station at, i, 26, 268 ; ii, 159

INDEX

POINTER

Victualling stores at, i, 181 ; ii, 20, 164, 183
spare powder from Arundel Castle to be sent to, i, 222
money for, i, 288
Ayscue's fleet off, ii, 56, 79 ; action off, ii, 105–108, 116, 121, 142, 158, 195, 222, 300
Danish ships at, to be stayed, iii, 58
list of English ships at, vi, 202
See also Actions ; Fleets and Squadrons
Pointer, Thomas, vi, 218 ; letters from, v, 192 ; vi, 60
Pol, Jan (Captain), ii, 59, 190 *sq.* ; iii, 235, 238, 256
Poland, Vice-Chancellor of, vi, 104
Polders, The, iv, 183, 196 ; v, 136
Poole, iii, 441
Poole, William, Orders to, i, 326
Poort (*or* Poert), Cornelis Jansz. (Captain), i, 262 ; ii, 331 ; iii, 46, 156, 224 *sq.*, 233, 250 ; Orders to, ii, 375, 383 ; battle of Portland, iv, 123, 181, 189 ; reported death, iv, 189
Poort, Tennis (skipper), iv, 192
Poortmans, Edmund (clerk to Treasurer of the Navy), iii, 324
Poortmans, John, iii, 280, 395 ; iv, 42, 54, 58, 76, 152, 391 ; v, 188 ; vi, 184 *sq.*, 190 ; letters from, iii, 381 ; iv, 42, 54, 86, 153, 156 ; v, 25, 30, 50, 54, 89, 98, 106, 195, 303 ; vi, 196, 220 ; battle of the Gabbard, v, 90
Popham, Edward (Admiral and General at Sea), i, 54
Porbrock, v, 39 *and n.*

PORTSMOUTH

Porchester Castle, proposed as hospital, iv, 220, 241, 256, 296
Porlock. *See* Porbrock
Port à Port, iv, 138
Porter, Anthony, letter from, vi, 239
Portland, iv, 153, 164, 172, 180, 187, 235, 348
new frigate at, iii, 427
Dutch rendezvous off, ii, 58
Battle of, i, 14, 15 *n.* ; iv, 68, 72, 78 *sqq.*, 88 *sqq.*, 93 *sqq.*, 100 *sqq.*, 108 *sqq.*, 118 *sqq.*, 163 *sqq.*, 180 *sqq.*, 188 *sqq.*, 194 *sq.*, 227 *sqq.* ; vi, 17
Dutch losses, iv, 81, 83, 170, 171
English losses, iv, 79 *sq.*, 83, 250
Porter, Roger, v, 333
Portman, —, ii, 372
Porto Longone, iii, 61
Ports, fit for cleaning ships, i, 42, 43, 134 ; ordered to stay all Dutch ships, i, 190
Portsmouth, i, 199 ; iii, 127, 360, 441 ; iv, 31, 64, 81, 87, 94, 101, 104, 112, 125, 130, 136 *sq.*, 139 *sq.*, 147 *sq.*, 170, 176, 216, 218, 220, 231, 273, 289, 298 *sq.*, 317, 324, 334, 355, 369, 373, 381, 383 *sq.*, 386, 390, 392, 395 ; v, 66 *and n.*, 70 *sq.*, 115, 208, 278, 298 *sq.*, 334, 370, 373 ; vi, 53, 73, 83, 166, 176, 179, 190, 209 *sq.*, 216, 219, 229, 236, 238, 241, 246, 253
Guns to be removed to Tower of London, i, 109 ; ships fitting at, i, 118, 287 ; rendezvous, i, 154
Victualling stores at, ii, 20, 164, 169, 183 ; ships at, to join Ayscue, ii, 101 ;

INDEX 325

PORTUGAL
reported Dutch attempt on, iii, 333
Defence of, iii, 141
Postmasters to hasten despatches, iv, 140
Post between Dover and, iv, 158
List of ships at, vi, 199
Portugal, iv, 388; v, 128; vi, 34 *n.*, 166
Post, Antheunis (skipper), i, 393; iii, 240
Potter, Richard (Captain), vi, 50, 186, 201; capt. of the Constant Warwick, i, 25; took the Sorlings, i, 25
Pouwelszoon, Jan (Captain), ii, 146, 187, 188 *sq.*, 336, 342, 345 *sq.*; iii, 222 *sq.*, 229, 231, 239; vi, 156; capt. of the Neptune, ii, 146
Pouwelzy, Jan, vi, 76
Preice, Richard (Victualler of the Navy), letters from, vi, 29, 69
Preparations for War, Dutch, i, 97
Prescott, Edward, letter from, v, 211
Pressentur, Claes (Master), master of the Golden Hawk, iii, 192
Pride, — (Colonel), iii, 421; iv, 236 *sq.*; v, 257, 262, 280, 291, 393
Priestly, —, ii, 110
Prince, Peter, iii, 282
Prior, Thomas (seaman), iii, 173
Prisoners of War, Dutch: Ill-treatment of, i, 81; vi, 71; by privateers, iii, 40; ill-treatment to be punished, i, 82; examination of, i, 211 *sqq.*; officers to be sent up from Dover Castle, i, 294; disposal of, i, 268, 294, 315, 317, 327,

PRIVATEERS
331, 374, 380; ii, 12, 70, 162, 169; iv, 74, 85, 116, 157, 176; v, 31, 98, 106, 393; vi, 87, 92, 94; exchange of, i, 413; ii, 325; vi, 71; maintenance of, ii, 128, 168, 177; iv, 126, 134, 157; vi, 71, 92, 116, 242
Discharged, ii, 39, 178, 265, 292, 325; iii, 169; taken at battle of Gabbard, v, 87 *sq.*, 94, 102, 105, 110, 118, 121, 145, 198; at battle of Texel, v, 176 *sq.*, 352, 372, 381, 397; vi, 47
Escape of, v, 381; vi, 70, 72
Navy Committee asks to be freed from responsibility for, v, 236
See also Sick and Hurt
Prisoners of War, English, ii, 292; iii, 49, 52, 360, 400 *sq.*; iv, 24; vi, 132, 136; exchange of, iii, 59; put ashore in France, iii, 227 *sqq.*, 321; iv, 24; transport of, iii, 407; maintenance, iv, 226; taken at the battle of the Gabbard, v, 87; taken at the battle of the Texel, v, 390 *n.*, 391; orders concerning, vi, 89
Privateers, Dutch, ii, 92, 131; iii, 88, 340, 432; iv, 160; v, 140, 278, 290, 405; vi, 55, 112, 212
of Flushing, iii, 241, 412, 420, 437; v, 34, 45, 60
of Middelburg, iii, 132; v, 58
of Rotterdam, v, 129
Privateers, English, ii, 73; iii, 7, 97, 107, 211, 289, 309, 311, 433; iv, 48, 67, 160, 367, 375 *sq.*; v, 296, 343 *n.*; vi, 104, 247
Power to impress men, iii, 96
Cruelty to prisoners, iii, 40

PRIVATEERS

A cause of lack of men for the fleet, iii, 7, 92, 159; iv, 39, 65, 163, 231; vi, 9, 253
Action of Helena with Royalist Privateers, iii, 188 sq.
Lack of discipline, iv, 163
Granting of commissions to be stopped, iv, 231
Permission to impress men from, iv, 231
Abuses by, vi, 253 sq.
See also Abuses and Complaints
Privateers, French, v, 285, 405; vi, 6, 55, 113
Privateers, Royalist:
 Richard Beach, i, 23, 25; vi, 227 sq., 235 sq., 243
 Capture of, vi, 7, 250
 From Brest, ii, 131; iii, 188; from Calais, v, 49
 Grants of Letters of Marque to Dutch, ii, 313
 Free entry into Dutch ports, iii, 61, 171
 Action with Helena, privateer, iii, 188 sq.
See also Pirates
Prize Courts, ii, 177-178
 Cases in: Salamander, Three Golden Herrings, Golden Buss, Hope, Prince, Peter, i, 140; St. Anthony, ii, 40
Prize Goods, Commissioners for or Collectors of, ii, 11, 40, 61, 63, 109, 158, 170, 171, 258, 260, 261, 376; iii, 51, 59, 72, 178, 338, 441; v, 268; vi, 254
 To send Dutch passengers home, i, 267; expenditure, i, 111; ii, 114
 To sell perishable goods, i, 347
 Instructions to, ii, 51
 Appointment of, ii, 108
 To supply money for sick and hurt, v, 375

PRIZES

To supply sail cloth from prize goods, vi, 179
Prize Money, ii, 21; iii, 275, 286; iv, 210; vi, 184, 190; the Admiral's tenths, ii, 178; iii, 277, 288; iv, 233; bounty, iii, 275, 287
Prizes and Prize Goods, Dutch, ii, 32, 86; v, 214, 287; vi, 171, 205
 sale of prizes, i, 414; iii, 44
 proposal for immediate destruction of those taken in fleet actions, v, 48
 taken in the East Indies, vi, 24
Prizes and Prize Goods, English, i, 346 sq., 354, 356; ii, 12; iii, 290; iv, 112 sq., 144; v, 195, 210, 216, 228, 235, 251, 266, 275, 292 sq., 300, 347, 423 sq.; vi, 34, 55 sq., 89, 99, 108, 180, 204, 212, 224, 228, 230, 237, 240, 251, 258
 Their safe keeping, i, 310, 312; sent in by Blake, i, 311; sent into Thames, i, 267 sq.; ii, 11; iv, 273 sq., 303, 373; v, 98, 106, 187, 258; sent to Dover, i, 343, 352; iv, 52, 98, 136; disposal of, ii, 19, 33, 39, 51, 61; iii, 132, 282; iv, 127 sq.; v, 293; proceeds of sale advanced to victuallers, ii, 74; advanced for seamen's pay, ii, 167
 Fit for Winter and Summer Guard, ii, 173
 Instructions concerning, iii, 361 sq.
 Embezzlement of stores in, iv, 145 sq.
 Proposal to use proceeds for sick and hurt, iv, 214, 221; v, 345

INDEX

PROCTOR

Abuses by prize crews, iv, 146
Taken at the battle of the Gabbard, v, 87 sq., 94, 98, 105, 145
Homeward bound merchantmen, v, 148 sq.
Taken at the battle of the Texel, v, 176
See also Ships, fitting out
Proctor, Richard (Commissioner), iii, 432
Proud, — (Captain), capt. of the Resolution, iv, 245
Pruican, Dr., iv, 241
Pruyssenaen, Jan (skipper), iii, 246
Prynne, Thomas (seaman), iv, 91
Purefoy, William (President of C.O.S.), ii, 98
Purefoy, William (Captain), iii, 77, 88; capt. of the Peter, ii, 97
Purser's Necessaries, v, 64, 96, 187, 215, 230, 329
Purvis, — (Lieutenant-Captain), ii, 274
Putten, —, v, 422
Pyggen, Joanes (Fiscal), ii, 201
Pyle, Thomas (Captain), capt. of the Anne and Joyce, iv, 293
Pyne, William, letter to, iii, 321

QUABOER (or Qua Coer), Aldert Pietersen (Captain), ii, 64 n., 147, 187, 188 sq., 305, 354; vi, 157; capt. of the Schaapherder, ii, 147
Quaeff, — (Captain), battle of the Texel, v, 361
Queenborough (or Quinborow), iv, 237, 306; vi, 29, 93; ships to assemble in the Downs, iv, 31
Quern, i, 351
VI.

READER

Quinsborough. See Königsbergen
Quixley, Thomas (Captain), capt. of the Bachelor (ketch), ii, 30

RAAT, Claas, iv, 223
Rabuet, — (Master), v, 303; master of the Sovereign, ii, 21
Raedt, Hendrick de, i, 262; vi, 76
Rael, Henry de (Captain), i, 411
Raet, Hendrich de (Captain), capt. of the Black Lion, vi, 159
Raet, Jan de (Captain), i, 409
Ramhead, vi, 252
Rammekens, v, 75, 189, 200, 202 sqq., 287
Ramsgate, v, 137
Rand, Andrew (Captain), iv, 280; v, 18; vi, 200; capt. of the Thomas and Lucy, iv, 22
Randers, D— (Victualler of the Navy), ii, 76
Ratcliffe, iv, 55; v, 115
Ré, Isle of, iv, 98, 136, 301; v, 40; vi, 204, 253
Rendezvous for merchantmen awaiting convoy, iii, 23, 39, 220; iv, 23, 26, 30
Arrival of Evertsen's squadron, iii, 247
Arrival of Florissen's squadron, iii, 216
Arrival of De Ruyter's squadron, iii, 266
Arrival of Tromp's fleet, iv, 23
List of ships off, iv, 309
Read, Roger, iv, 342
Reade, George, iii, 310
Reader, Mr. (Master-gunner), v, 52

X

REAEL

Reael, Govert (Captain), i, 261; iv, 338; capt. of the Leeuwaerden, iv, 309 *and n.*

Redgacke (*or* Redjack), William (Captain), iv, 42, 294; letter from, iii, 84; capt. of the Katherine, iii, 84; iv, 21

Redwood, John, action off Dover: account of, i, 227, 228

Reed (*or* Read), — (Captain), ii, 91, 120; vi, 206; capt. of the Sovereign, ii, 53; orders to, ii, 118; battle of Kentish Knock, ii, 279

Reede, Johan van, iv, 286

Reeves, Jonas (Captain), capt. of the Elizabeth, i, 18, 68

Reformado, i, 11

Regemorter (*or* Regenmortel *or* Regenmorten), Joannes van (Captain), i, 263, 393, 417; ii, 337, 343; iii, 224, 228, 234; iv, 193; battle of Portland, iv, 123, 188; reported dead, iv, 189, 192

Renaren, Jan Pietersz. (Captain), i, 363

Reprisal, Acts of, twenty-seven ships taken under the Act of 1650, i, 76; Orangieboom taken by Francis, i, 80

Revel, — (Captain), i, 388

Rewards, to Dutch officers, iv, 251; for each English ship taken, v, 319, 335; for English officers, v, 398; proposed for prizes destroyed, v, 48

Reyerszoon, Jan (skipper), i, 266, 424

Reynolds, Commissary, iv, 283

Reynolds, Jacob (Captain), ii, 244; iii, 59; vi, 49; capt. of the Nightingale, i, 68; Young's action off the Start,

ROCHELLE

i, 180; battle of Kentish Knock, ii, 276; capt. of the Kentish, iv, 293

Reynolds, James (Captain), letter from, v, 253; capt. of the Kentish, iv, 20

Reynolds, Joe (Captain), capt. of the Kentish, v, 19

Riael, Govert (Captain), capt. of the Leeuwerden, v, 363; battle of the Texel, v, 363

Rich, Colonel, i, 371; iii, 112, 135; iv, 176

Rich, Nathaniel, vi, 107; letter from, vi, 72

Rich, Robert (merchant), owner of ship Negro, iii, 290

Richewyn (*or* Richwijn), Jan (Captain), i, 388; ii, 49; vi, 171; capt. of the Goes, iv, 308

Rickby, Mr., iv, 318

Ridder, D. de, iv, 223

Ridder, Nic. de, iv, 360

Ridley, Thomas, vi, 254 *sq.*

Rietberch, — (Captain), battle of the Gabbard, v, 74 *n.*

Riff, The, v, 141, 217; vi, 184, 186 *sq.*, 239, 256

Riga, i, 329; vi, 39, 81, 237

Ring, David, iv, 343

Ringh, Rem Janssen, iv, 186

Roach, — (Mast Master), iv, 52

Robbeknuyt, vi, 144

Robin Hood's Bay, iv, 317, 327

Robinson, — (Captain), capt. of the Plover, iv, 293

Robinson, John, letter to, i, 119

Roch, — (Master), master of the Remembrance of Maidstone, iv, 50

Rochelle, i, 21; iv, 26, 374; vi, 171, 221; rendezvous, iii, 240, 257; reported blocked by Dutch, iii, 332; report of Tromp's plans from, iv, 24

INDEX 329

ROCHENSSEN

Rochenssen, Cornelis (Captain), iii, 223, 224, 228
Rochester, iii, 436; iv, 76, 125; vi, 71, 248
Rockwell, — (Lieutenant), to be appointed to new 3rd rate, vi, 218
Rodenhaes, Adriaen (Captain), capt. of the Rodenhaes, iv, 308
Roebergen, Burgomaster, v, 287
Roelantsz, Abel (Captain), capt. of Brederode, i, 278; battle of the Texel, v, 357
Roeteringh, Jan (Captain), i, 388; ii, 49
Rogaart, — (Captain), i, 389
Rohan, iv, 142
Roitters, Heinrich (Amsterdam Director), v, 191
Rolle, Henry (President of C.O.S.), iii, 341, 342, 343, 353
Roocher, Jacob Janss. (Captain), capt. of the Venetia, iv, 308
Roothooft, D., letters from, v, 317, 325, 337
Rootjes (*or* Rootiers), John (Captain), capt. of the Radebold, v, 185; his ship lost off the Texel, vi, 160, 175
Rose, John (Master Mate), iv, 345
Rose, Stephen (Captain), ii, 11, 157, 365; iii, 88; capt. of the Convert, ii, 21
Ross, David (Colonel), iii, 337, 338 *n.*; iv, 106
Rosse, Willeboort (Captain), iii, 241
Rothwell, James, iv, 365; letter from, iv, 363
Rotterdam, v, 118, 127, 129, 207, 219, 231; vi, 165
Captains of Directors' ships from, i, 261; ii, 336, 342

RUYTER

Commanders of V.-A. de With's squadron from, i, 265
Commanders of fireships from, i, 265
Commanders of Admiralty ships, ii, 336, 341
List of ships from, vi, 157
Rouen, iv, 374
Rous, Colonel, letter from, iv, 163
Rouse, — (Captain), capt. of the Love, ii, 137. *See also* Row
Row, — (Captain), battle of the Texel, v, 390 *n.*; capt. of the Portland, v, 390 *n.*
Rowe, William, i, 130; iii, 131 *n.*, 431; letter to, iii, 131
Rowles, Mr., iv, 256
Roy, Niclaes, iv, 186
Royalists, English, plots against Commonwealth, ii, 225–231, 312; agent at Brest, ii, 225 *n. See also* Privateers
Roys, Frans (skipper), orders from De Ruyter, ii, 72, 123
Royston, iv, 106
Ruddock, George (Master), master of the Unity, ii, 174
Ruijsch, N., iv, 286
Rupert, Prince, i, 4 *and n.*, 5, 291, 316, 324, 341; ii, 54; iii, 136; encounter with Blake, i, 13; in St. Christopher's Sound, ii, 135
Russell, — (Captain), capt. of Catherine, i, 191
Russell, B., vi, 76
Russell, James (Captain), i, 138
Rusthall, v, 410
Ruyter, Michiel de (Vice-Admiral of Zeeland), ii, 57 *sq.*, 62 *sq.*, 79 *sq.*, 86, 90, 111, 146, 157, 163, 176, 181, 341, 343; iii, 10 *sq.*, 33, 54, 69, 78, 109, 135 *sq.*, 154, 156, 222 *sq.*, 248, 250;

INDEX

RUYTER

iv, 179, 248, 251, 370 *sq.*; v, 56, 114, 130, 134, 200, 223, 239, 377, 403 *sq.*; vi, 17 *sq.*, 25, 29, 118, 134, 159 *sq.*, 162, 171, 182
Letters to, ii, 53, 174, 382; letters from, ii, 59, 61, 68, 78, 86, 93, 142, 185; iv, 370; v, 42; vi, 122, 190
His journal, ii, 188–211, 293–298; iii, 248 *sqq.*; iv, 194 *sqq.*; v, 126–138, 417–422
His squadron in the Channel, i, 410; ii, 59, 61, 68, 77, 146, 188 *sqq.*; commission as Vice-Commodore, ii, 27; instructions to, ii, 53; action off Plymouth, ii, 105 *sqq.*
His general orders, ii, 141; learns Blake's position, ii, 145; follows Ayscue, ii, 152, 196; resolves to join main fleet, ii, 182, 186; report of proceedings, ii, 185; receives orders from De With, ii, 187, 209; joins De With, ii, 187, 210, 253, 352; receives news of Ayscue's squadron, ii, 189; of Blake's fleet, ii, 202, 205, 208; want of victuals and men, ii, 232; battle of Kentish Knock, ii, 268 *sqq.*
Statement of services, ii, 299 *sqq.*; ill-feeling against, iii, 51; supersedes De With, iii, 77; battle off Dungeness, iii, 102, 106, 143
His squadron separated by storm, iii, 261 *sq.*; battle of Portland, iv, 68 *sq.*, 89, 118, 183, 188 *sqq.*; his report on the battle, iv, 123 *sqq.*; capture of the Prosperous, iv, 188

SAILS

Commission as 'Vice-Commander,' iv, 285; joins De With, iv, 367 *sq.*; battle of the Gabbard, v, 70, 83, 110, 122
His orders, v, 319 *sqq.*; battle of the Texel, v, 166 *sqq.*, 177, 351, 355, 383 *sq.*, 412; vi, 47
Refusal to serve under De With, vi, 25; with De With's convoy to the Sound, vi, 26 *sq.*, 46; commander for Zealand, vi, 156; offered Vice-Admiralship of Amsterdam, vi, 191
See also Instructions, Dutch; Complaints
Ruyter, — de (the Younger), his journal, vi, 136–156
Ryde Bay, vi, 236
Rye, iv, 51, 135, 280, 284, 307; vi, 253
Rye Bay, i, 194
Ryves, Richard, i, 291

SAARDAM, ii, 224; v, 237
Sable de Grace, iv, 122
Sacheverell, Theophilus, letter from, v, 371; vi, 252; battle of the Texel, his account, v, 371 *sqq.*
Sadler, Mr., vi, 189
Sael, Claes (Captain), ii, 49, 147, 353; vi, 157; capt. of the Maria, iv, 310
Saen, Balck van (Captain), iv, 354
Sage, Jas le (*or* Jan), (Captain), i, 263; iii, 222 *sqq.*, 240, 247; battle of Portland, iv, 120, 124, 195 *and n.*; convoy duty, iv, 179, 187 *sq.*; killed, iv, 190
Sails, studding, i, 10

INDEX 331

St. Abustynes, v, 251
St. Alban's Head, iv, 194 n.
St. Germains, ii, 231
St. Handryes, iv, 194 and n.
St. Helens (or St. Ellen's), iv, 168 ; vi, 6, 184, 196, 210, 221, 224, 246; Blake's rendezvous at, iv, 65, 154 ; list of ships at, vi, 199
St. Ives, v, 296
St. John's Roads, v, 58
St. Lucas, iv, 137
St. Malo, iii, 340 ; iv, 179, 187 ; vi, 251 ; petition of English merchants of, iii, 321 ; Dutch rendezvous at, ii, 234
St. Martins. See Ré, Isle of
St. Ubes, iv, 334 ; v, 43, 266
St. Uves. See Setabul
St. Valerico, iv, 97
St. Vincent, Cape, Silver fleet sighted, ii, 15
Salinge (or Zalingen), Anthonis van (Captain), i, 388 ; capt. of the Son, iv, 308
Salingen, Cramer van (Captain), iii, 190 sq.
Salingen, Pieter van, i, 389 ; iv, 309 and n.; capt. of the Brack, i, 112
Salings (or Salinx), Emanuel (Captain), ii, 49, 147 ; vi, 157 ; capt. of the Aartsengel Michael, ii, 147, 323
Salmon, — (Lieutenant - Colonel), i, 246 ; governor of Hull, ii, 325
Salmon, Benjamin (Captain), capt. of the Industry, v, 19
Salmon, Edward (Admiralty Commissioner), letter from, vi, 72
Salmon, James (Captain), vi, 52 ; capt. of the Renown, v, 16
Salmon, Thomas (Captain), iv, 280 ; v, 20 ; capt. of the Gift, iv, 21

Salomonszoon, Jan (master carpenter), ii, 363 ; iii, 120, 137
Salomonszoon, Pieter (Captain), ii, 147, 353 sq.; vi, 157, 160 ; capt. of the De Vreede, ii, 147
Salter, Isaack (seaman), v, 397
Saltonstall, Charles (Captain), ii, 238 ; capt. of the Lion, i, 64 ; trial of, iii, 163, 164, 412, 445
Salutes, Dutch, by Dutch to English, i, 134 ; by Dutch to foreign ship of war, i, 168 ; forbidden under penalty, ii, 339
Salwey, R—, Major (Admiralty Committee), i, 354 ; iii, 318, 407, 415, 426 ; iv, 67, 136, 139, 160, 295 ; v, 33, 81 ; letter to, iii, 450 ; iv, 368 ; v, 49 ; letter from, iii, 429 ; iv, 175
Sanders, — (Captain), ii, 241
Sanders (or Saunders), Gabriel (Captain), v, 17 ; vi, 50, 200 ; capt. of the Weymouth Pink, i, 66 ; capt. of the Tiger, iv, 279
Sanders, Robert (Captain), vi, 50 ; capt. of the Ruby, v, 18
Sanders, William (Master), master of the Briar, i, 28
Sandgate Castle, i, 210 ; ii, 245
Sandilands, Andrew iv, 105 sq.; letter from, iii, 369
Sandridge, v, 90
Sandwich, i, 46 ; iii, 441 ; iv, 130, 134, 175 ; v, 66 ; defence of, i, 190 ; letter of commendation to, i, 241, 245
Sanen, Dirck Dirckxz. van (Captain), capt. of the Orangieboom, taken by the Francis, i, 80
Sanger, Claes Jansz. (Captain), i, 263 ; ii, 63, 90, 146, 187,

SANGER

188 *sq.*, 354; iii, 217; vi, 157; to cruise off Ostend, i, 425; capt. of the Galeas van Middelburg, ii, 146

Sanger, Hendrich (Leendert) Arensen (Captain), ii, 256, 354

Sansum (*or* Samson), Robert (Captain), iii, 444; iv, 293; vi, 52, 200; capt. of the Briar, i, 65; selling stores out of States ships, iii, 419; took Dutch privateer, iii, 420, 423; capt. of the Adventure, vi, 237 *and n.*

Saunders, Robert (Captain), i, 7, 67; iii, 73; vi, 34 *sq.*; capt. of the Star, i, 7; capt. of the Assurance, i, 15 *n.*; iv, 21; capt. of the Ruby, iv, 293; capt. of the Essex, vi, 200

Say, —, iii, 441

Scarborough, i, 384; ii, 19; iv, 317 *sq.*, 328 *sq.*, 331, 333, 335 *sq.*, 342, 346, 350 *sq.*, 355 *sqq.*, 375, 394; v, 32, 290, 424; strength and situation of, iv, 337, 339; vi, 99, 113; Blake's fleet off, i, 407

Schaeff, Boelius (Captain), v, 220, 281

Schaeff, Marten (Captain), i, 389; iv, 338; orders to, ii, 374, 383; capt. of the Engel, iv, 310. See also Troucquois

Schaep, Egbert Jansz, iv, 338

Schaep, Gerard (Dutch Ambassador), arrival of, i, 48; letter from, i, 239, 245, 271

Schatter, Gerbrant (Captain), i, 261, 388; iii, 190; iv, 338; capt. of the Dolphijn, iv, 309 *and n.*

Scheele, — (Delegate), v, 237

SCHRAEN

Scheldt, iv, 193 *n.*; v, 142, 238, 318, 337; vi, 24

Scheletje, Teunis Vechterssen op (Captain), iv, 316

Schelling, Island of, v, 60, 142

Schellingen, —, letter from, v, 337

Schellinger, Jacob (Captain), capt. of the Venetia, iv, 308; his ship captured, v, 23, 138

Schellinger, Pieter (Commodore), i, 264, 251, 393; ii, 345, 374, 383; iv, 323; capt. of the Stadt van Medemblick, iv, 315; battle of the Gabbard, v, 74

Scheltinga, — (Delegate), v, 358, 393

Scheth, K. H. (Lord Commissioner), ii, 362

Scheveningen (*or* Scheveling), i, 213, 364, 404; iv, 142, 186, 376; v, 60 *sq.*, 110, 224, 226, 317, 322, 338, 340, 421; vi, 134; place of rendezvous for Dutch fleet, i, 260, 275; v, 47

Schey, Dirck (Captain), i, 389; ii, 336, 342; iii, 224; battle of Portland: reported dead, iv, 189

Schiedam, v, 43

Schilt, vi, 159 *and n.*

Scholte, Hendrick (Master), vi, 76

Schoock, Arent (Delegate), iv, 311

Schoonevelt, i, 424; iv, 282, 371, 375; v, 316, 417; De With's fleet at, ii, 233; iv, 335, 354 *sq.*, 367; v, 126

Schoonevelt, — (Captain), capt. of the Hoop, ii, 343; capt. of the Gouden Reael, vi, 160

Schouwen, v, 127, 223, 244

Schraen, Adriaensen (Captain), iii, 245

INDEX   333

SCHUYT

Schuyt Gerrit, i, 262; iii, 190; iv, 338
Scilly Islands, i, 336, 377; vi, 181, 227; cruising station off, i, 12; iv, 216, 300; proposal of Dutch to buy from Charles II, i, 41; Dutch fleet off, ii, 165; iv, 177 *sq.*; four Dutch ships off, v, 296; Lizard and —, ships plying between, vi, 200
Scobell, Henry, i, 335; iii, 319; vi, 134
Sconeling, vi, 26 *and n.*
Scotland, iv, 353, 361; v, 29, 33, 210; vi, 81, 228
  Army in, provisions for use of, i, 234
  Provision ships for, to be exempted from embargo, i, 248; iii, 323; victualling of ships on coast of, i, 319; ships to be called home and replaced, iv, 216
  Powder from, v, 32
  List of ships on coast, vi, 201
Scot, Thomas (Commissioner for Ireland and Scotland), iii, 337; letter from, iii, 431
Scott, Thomas (Master), master of the Sovereign, ii, 46, 91 *and n.*
Scott, Thomas (Master Attendant), i, 356; ii, 69, 105, 169; iv, 176 *sq.*; vi, 88; letter from, iii, 417; to hasten ships into Downs, i, 346
Scotter, Gerbian (Captain), battle of the Texel, taken prisoner, v, 390 *n.*
Scrael, Jan (skipper), iii, 220
Scroope, — (Colonel), letter to, i, 119
Seafield, Richard (Captain), capt. of the Duchess, v, 19
Seaman, John (Captain), iv, 293; v, 20; vi, 50, 201;

SEAMEN

capt. of the Fox, i, 65; capt. of the Tiger, iii, 408; capt. of the Dragon, iv, 20; battle of the Texel, v, 390 *n.*
Seamen, Dutch:
  Forbidden to take service in foreign ships, i, 84; fear of their joining English ships, vi, 65; foreigners in Dutch fleet, ii, 224
  Manning of the fifty ships, i, 98; of Ruyter's squadron, ii, 61; of fleet at Helvoetsluys, ii, 326; iii, 19; of De With's fleet, iv, 64; vi, 245; of Tromp's fleet, v, 117, 134, 199, 219, 234, 285, 307, 387
  Discontent of, ii, 220, 223; vi, 131; desertion, ii, 329; iii, 27, 43 *sq.*, 60; v, 201; leave to, v, 189, 387; vi, 24; mutiny, ii, 235; iii, 60; v, 223; general muster of, v, 201; ships ill-manned, v, 138; want of men, ii, 223, 232; iii, 10, 60; iv, 64, 257, 363; v, 219, 247, 287, 290, 313; vi, 10, 67 *sq.*
  See also Discipline; Prisoners of War
Seamen, English:
  Manning of the fleet, i, 374; ii, 11, 28, 107, 133, 137; iii, 86, 111, 127, 157, 408; iv, 148, 157, 201, 218, 284, 295, 305, 381; v, 67, 76, 80, 91, 192, 249, 256 *sq.*, 259, 345, 396, 399; vi, 218
  Volunteers, i, 9, 241, 371, 374; v, 37; landsmen, i, 352 *sq.*; iv, 201, 253; v, 33; continuous service proposed, iv, 201, 253
  Desertion, iii, 125, 382, 385; iv, 147, 234; v, 259, 310, 409; vi, 83, 169, 241;

SEATON

discharge tickets, v, 259; dissatisfaction of, causes delay, v, 274
Encouragement of, iii, 273 sq., 283 sq., 318 sq.; fishermen forced to serve in Dutch fleet, i, 379 sq., 384, 399; leave tickets, v, 79; privateers, preference for service in, iii, 92, 159; iv, 39, 65; unruly ashore, iv, 55; v, 295; vi, 8, 83
In Dutch service, iv, 149, 177; for Summer Guard, vi, 68 sqq.; for Winter Guard, v, 414; vi, 68 sqq.
Want of, i, 216, 267, 362; iii, 74, 281, 372, 398 sqq., 423, 425, 434, 439, 447 sq.; iv, 42, 200 sq., 284, 298 sq., 321 sq., 324, 352; v, 313, 329, 366, 374, 410; vi, 243; want of, due to raising of embargo, vi, 190, 218, 241
See also Complaints; Discipline; Impress; Pay; Soldiers; Stores, General
Seaton, — (Captain), iii, 359
Seaverne, — (Boatswain), v, 303
Seelts (*or* Seelst *or* Zeelst), Bruyn van (Commander). iii, 212 sq., 216, 221, 224, 233; battle of Portland, iv, 120, 124; his ship taken, iv, 182, 190
Sehey, Dirck (Captain), capt. of the Achillis, iv, 309
Seine Head, iv, 164; v, 252; Dutch rendezvous at, ii, 58
Sekema, Reynier (Captain), ii, 147; vi, 157; capt. of the Hector of Troy, ii, 79
Semalo, Jan van (Captain), ii, 145, 199
Sempsen, Jan (Master), iv, 370
Sempson, Bastjaen (Captain), ii, 343

SHIPBUILDING

Semssen, Gerrit (Captain), capt. of the Wapen van Enchuijsen, iv, 315 *and n.*
Senior, J— (Captain), capt. of the Tiger, iv, 20
Sentsey, Jan (Captain), v, 126
Scrooskercke, Tuyll De, iv, 223
Setabul, vi, 34 *n.*
Sevenhuysen, Rens Cornelisz. (Captain), ii, 383; v, 218; capt. of the Rode Leeu, iv, 313
Seward, John, to command fireship, i, 143
Shadwell, — (seaman), iii, 449
Sharpley, —, steward of the James, i, 11
Shelley, Giles (Captain), iv, 279; v, 19; vi, 52; capt. of the Waterhound, iv, 21
Sherwin, John (Captain), vi, 50, 201; capt. of the Primrose, i, 65; capt. of the Richard and Benjamin, i, 191
Shetland, v, 30, 46, 50, 98, 121 *n.*; English fleet off, i, 385, 396, 405; v, 45, 140 sq.; Tromp's fleet off, i, 389; v, 29 sq., 40, 43; fifty-one ships take refuge after storm, i, 404, 411, 412, 430; hookers to warn Dutch ships off, iv, 360; Dutch trading fleet expected off, iv, 375 sq., 381; v, 29, 40, 42 sqq., 131, 246, 254
Shewell, Mr. (Collector of Customs), v, 36, 38
Shinner, Christopher (Captain), capt. of the Negro, privateer, iii, 290
Shipbuilding, Dutch, ii, 224; iii, 72, 391; v, 404
Thirty frigates to be built, iii, 82, 120, 152 sq.; to be hastened, iii, 402; sixty frigates to be built, iv, 143; ship for Genoa to

INDEX   335

SHIPBUILDING

be sent De With, v, 191, 222, 237, 286, 297, 308, 402; new ships building, v, 326, 402; vi, 183
Shipbuilding, English, ii, 177; iii, 98, 335; v, 232, 250, 275, 302, 414; vi, 31, 86, 88, 115, 176, 218
   Eleven ships to be built, i, 141; frigates to be built, i, 140, 338; ii, 156; iii, 65, 335, 427; iv, 231; v, 292, 329; vi, 185, 236; thirty frigates to be built, ii, 285; iii, 64, 146, 308; frigates built for flagships, v, 315; forecastles built on frigates, iv, 204, 255; timber for building, iii, 290, 369 sq.
Ships, Danish, to be stayed, iii, 31, 58
Ships (Men-of-War), Dutch: Complements, i, 104; condition, after Texel, v, 358 sqq.; East India Co. to provide six ships, iv, 143; v, 120, 203, 222, 264, 282; Directors' ships, suggestion to form squadron of, v, 288
Ships (Men-of-War), English: To be divided into ranks or rates, iii, 179, 279, 285, 319, 396, 417; protection of, against musketry, vi, 32; lost in storm, vi, 72
Ships (Merchantmen), Dutch: Release of ship stayed, i, 130; stayed, i, 200 sq., 239, 246, 274; ii, 172, 176; iii, 272; to remain in port, iv, 252; v, 120; vi, 135
   See also Convoys
Ships (Merchantmen), English: Taken up by the State, i, 112, 200; ii, 13; forty to be taken up, iii, 426 sqq., 452;

SHIPS

iv, 218, 343; thirty to be taken up, vi, 229; ships in port surveyed, i, 115; guarantee for loss of ships hired, iii, 394; payment of imprests for, iv, 287; the State to man and store them, iii, 428; iv, 364; contract for hire of, iv, 238; crews of time-expired ships turned over, v, 257; hired ships returned to owners, vi, 9, 31
Not to be restrained, i, 120, 127; to sail to Downs, i, 192; ships stayed to be released, v, 112 sq.; loss of, in storm, vi, 72
See also Embargo
Ship's bell, its position, i, 27
Ships, fitting out of, Dutch, i, 85, 120, 275, 388 sq.; ii, 85, 246; iii, 17, 82; iv, 354, 362, 377 sq.; v, 47, 51, 181, 189, 201 sqq., 218, 227, 247, 358 sqq., 386; vi, 23, 26, 40, 121, 167, 183, 245
Delay in, iv, 281; v, 189 sq.; vi, 40, 66, 77; fitting out to be stopped, vi, 64; E.I.C. to provide six men-of-war, iv, 143
Ships, fitting out of, English, i, 118, 287, 306; ii, 125, 386; iii, 32, 142, 149, 316, 427; iv, 161, 216; v, 95, 103, 156, 180, 253, 256, 272, 292 sqq., 301, 344 sq., 380, 391 sq., 400, 409 sq., 428; vi, 1, 56, 73 sq., 83, 85 sq., 101, 115 sq., 169, 172, 187 sq., 216, 236
of prizes, i, 317 sqq.; ii, 16, 20 sq., 34, 63, 125, 154, 162, 179; iii, 147; iv, 127 sq., 144; v, 208,

336 INDEX

SHIPS

300; of squadron for the Straits, iii, 58, 61, 67; iv, 216; of flagships for Winter Guard, v, 268
Delayed by slackness of officers, v, 330; by dissatisfaction of seamen, v, 274; badness of chain-plates, vi, 88; full pay for captains of ship's fitting, v, 332
Ships, force of, Danish, v, 111, 254; a very large three decker, iii, 448
Ships, force of, Dutch, iv, 328; v, 52, 92, 187
Ships, force of, English, iii, 168, 179, 279, 427; v, 273
Ships, hastening out of, i, 23, 110, 201, 249, 335; ii, 118; iii, 114, 147, 157, 356 sq., 383, 398, 404, 414, 440, 447 sq.; iv, 157, 216, 219, 317; v, 28, 41, 68, 76, 110, 390, 392
Of the Summer Fleet, iii, 406; iv, 159; vi, 188; order countermanded, iii, 418; of ships in the river, iv, 326 sq.; v, 111, 250, 272, 375, 398 sq.; vi, 177
Ships, Lists of, Dutch:
Fireships from Rotterdam and Zeeland, i, 265; Ruyter's squadron, ii, 146, 353; fleet commanded by De With, ii, 336, 341; iv, 323
Admiralty ships, ii, 353; to be refitted, ii, 354; fleet commanded by Tromp, iii, 224; Zeeland ships, iv, 192; Amsterdam ships, iv, 308 sqq.
The 'hundred' ships, iv, 313; the 'thirty-six' ships, iv, 314; for convoy, iv, 316; at the Texel, v,

SHIPS

184; lost off the Texel, vi, 175; list of September, 1653, vi, 156 sq.
Ships, Lists of, English:
From Trinity House, i, 108, 112, 204; ordered to sail into Downs, i, 191; anchored in Downs, i, 289; iv, 293
Taken by Blake in North Sea, i, 383; fleet off the Nore, iii, 315 sq.; ships ready to sail, iii, 333 sqq.; iv, 44 n.; between London and the Hope, iii, 378 sq.; fitting out, iii, 427; in the river, iii, 440
in battle of Portland, iv, 20 sq.; Vice-Admiral Penn's squadron, iv, 33, 278, 294; to be victualled for six months, iv, 66; prizes, iv, 98, 136; Blake's squadron, iv, 100; for the Straits, iv, 279 sq.; to attend the Generals, iv, 293; for convoy, iv, 293; to be hastened out, iv, 327
for Summer Fleet, iv, 365 sq.; the Commonwealth Navy at Sea, May, 1653, v, 16 sqq.; to join Monck, v, 315; Lawson's squadron, v, 415 sq.; list of September, 1653, vi, 49 sqq.; in the Hope, vi, 177; Winter Guard, vi, 199 sqq.
Ships and Vessels, Types of:
Buss, v, 32
Coble, i, 384; iv, 318, 328
Dogger boat, i, 409; ii, 96
Frigate, *passim, and see* Ships
Flute, i, 266, 379; iv, 195, 388; v, 43, 128, 208; vi, 34, 118
Fly-boat, i, 65, 319; v, 87, 253
Galley, v, 190

SHIPWRIGHTS

Galliot, i, 266; iv, 328; v, 29, 43
Galliot hoy, i, 66; v, 83, 143
Hooker, iii, 226; iv, 360
Hoy, iii, 75; iv, 236, 386; v, 87
Ketch, i, 9, 66, 253, 289, 314, 342, 344 *and passim*
Light horseman, iii, 367 *and n.*; iv, 55
Pickeroons, iv, 159
Pink, i, 153, 289 *and passim*
Pinnace, i, 289
Shallop, i, 66, 130, 246, 289
Smacks, used as scouts, i, 342
Shipwrights. *See* Artificers
Shirter, John Fananssen (Captain), battle of the Gabbard, v, 74 *n.*
Shish, Jonas (shipwright), ii, 156, 169
Shoeburyness, v, 67
Shorcham, frigate building at, vi, 185
Sichels (*or* Sichalsen), Jacob (Captain), ii, 146, 305; vi, 156; capt. of the Wafen van Sweden, ii, 146
Sick and Hurt, Dutch, v, 41, 113, 117 *sq.*
   Dutch losses, ii, 313; iv, 186; wounded sent to Zeeland, ii, 355; to Hoorn, iv, 185; provision for widows, iv, 251
   Lack of medical stores, iv, 380
   Report after battle of Texel, v, 358 *sqq.*
Sick and hurt: English, i, 344; ii, 13, 168, 285; iii, 139, 320; iv, 104, 107, 138, 154 *sq.*, 161, 231 *sq.*, 240 *sq.*, 288, 299, 306, 386; v, 88, 94, 105, 173 *sq.*, 190, 216 *sq.*, 247 *sq.*, 270 *sq.*, 310, 352, 374, 390, 408, 410

SICKENAR

Care of, iii, 171, 273, 276, 288, 338; iv, 177, 200, 212 *sqq.*, 223 *sqq.*, 320; vi, 89 *sqq.*; Porchester Castle proposed as hospital, iv, 220, 241, 256
Relief to, iii, 397; gratuities to dependents, iv, 213, 225; vi, 91; provisions for, iii, 276, 288, 320, 338; v, 215; payments to, iii, 358, 444; vi, 90 *sq.*; maintenance allowance, iv, 213, 220, 224; v, 268 *sq.*, 271; vi, 90, 180, 210; allowance to surgeons, iv, 288; v, 212, 293; surgeons to be hastened v, 76, 81, 206, 218, 263
Harwich unsuitable, v, 206 *sq.*; landed at Solebay, v, 158; great sickness in the Fleet, v, 249, 257, 260, 268, 291, 304; vi, 180
Essex, Norfolk and Suffolk commended for their care of wounded, v, 374; surgeons request fresh medical supplies, v, 388 *sq.*; unfit for future service sent to London hospitals, v, 411; vi, 57; subscription for seamen and widows, v, 398
Sickness amongst Dutch prisoners, vi, 71 *sq.*; to be sent to hospitals, vi, 93; list of wounded and slain to be sent to Commissioners, vi, 92; those recovered to be returned to ships, vi, 92; lack of quarters for, vi, 179; want of surgeons, vi, 220
See also Alkin, Elizabeth; Finance; Pay
Sickenar, — (Captain), ii, 353, 363

SIDERICKSZ

Sidericksz, Jan (Master), iv, 370, 372
Siggelszoon, Jacob, ii, 354
Signals, Dutch :
  Tromp's signal for fighting, i, 167, 193 ; iii, 206 ; iv, 263
  weft, i, 211 ; iv, 262
  on sighting an enemy, ii, 64, 81
  to speak a ship, ii, 72
  of recognition, ii, 141 ; v, 339
  for council of war, ii, 193 ; iv, 346
  for sailing, ii, 268 ; iii, 200, 208, 251, 257 ; v, 129, 137, 417 ; vi, 58 sq.
  for captains, ii, 297, 339 ; iii, 200 sq. ; iv, 181, 184, 192, 195 sq. ; v, 126, 128, 134, 136, 227, 286, 383 ; vi, 140, 146, 149
  Admiral's little flag, iii, 250 ; iv, 179 ; v, 129, 417 ; vi, 142, 154
  for bearing up, iii, 216
  other signals, iv, 178, 183, 328, 330, 331 ; v, 324
Signals, English :
  pass-words, i, 407 ; signal for attack, iv, 124
  code for fighting instructions, iv, 262 sqq.
  code for sailing instructions, iv, 266 sqq. ; v, 93 n.
  on sighting the enemy, v, 83, 93, 143
  vessels passing through fleet, v, 140
  to weigh, v, 143 ; vi, 223
  on sighting a ship, v, 423, 426
  for surrender, v, 367
  for council of war, vi, 195
  night signals, vi, 254
Sijdracken, Jan (Captain), v, 126

SMITH

Silvergieter, Cornelis Engelen, i, 260
Silvius, —, ii, 225
Simpson, Mr., v, 411
Siriacksea. See Zierikzee
Skagen (or Schagen), v, 46 ; vi, 28, 61, 109, 122, 139, 143 sq.
Skagen, Hook of, vi, 61, 139
Skaw, v, 246 ; vi, 62, 84 sq., 139, 144 n., 209, 213
Skaw Riff, rendezvous, vi, 54 sq., 62, 76
Skelly, Mr., iv, 103
Skeveling. See Scheveling
Skipp, — (Captain), acquitted of cowardice, vi, 46
Skutt, George, jun. (Mayor of Poole), iii, 306, 324
Slaak, Symon van der (Captain), ii, 147
Slordt, Cornelis Barentss. (Captain), capt. of the Jonge Prins, iv, 315 ; capt. of the Utrecht, vi, 171
Sluys, v, 100
Smith, Edmund (Captain), capt. of the Duchess, vi, 201
Smith, Edward (Captain), capt. of the Dragoneare, v, 20
Smith, Edward (merchant), letter from, iii, 322
Smith, Eustace (or Hughson) (Captain), i, 116 ; iii, 87 ; iv, 221, 280 ; v, 18 ; vi, 200, 259 ; capt. of the Richard and Martha, i, 191 ; ii, 292 ; iv, 22 ; captures Dutch East Indiaman, vi, 7, 255 ; capt. of the Worcester, vi, 184
Smith, George (Master), master of the Prosperous, ii, 174 ; master of a smack, iii, 127
Smith (or Smyth), Jer., vi, 50 ; letter from, vi, 256 ; capt. of the Advice, v, 16
Smith, John (Captain), vi, 200 ; capt. of the Hector, vi, 52

INDEX

SMITH

Smith (*or* Smyth), Thomas (Navy Commissioner), i, 54, 268; ii, 130, 133; 156, 170; iii, 96, 279, 376, 397, 430, 450; iv, 99, 221, 256, 288, 382 *n.*; v, 333; letter to, iii, 124, 164, 279; letter from, iv, 382; orders to repair to Blake, iii, 123 *sq.*
Smithson, William (Captain), capt. of the Horsely Down, vi, 51
Smyth, Anthony (Captain), capt. of the Drake, i, 66
Smyth, Elizabeth, to be paid wages due to husband, iii, 146
Smyth, Sir Jeremiah, i, 45 *n.*
Snouck, Dirck, supercargo of Salamander, i, 397
Soenen, — van (Captain), iii, 118
Soldiers, Dutch, i, 367; iii, 180, 182; v, 194, 233 *sq.*, 282; vi, 49, 213 complaint of, ii, 234; v, 387 for service in fleet, ii, 322, 327, 329; iii, 19, 199; iv, 194; v, 133, 247, 312 lack of musketeers, v, 48, 55, 204; vi, 67 *sq.* to be pressed, v, 119, 287
Soldiers, English: For service in the fleet, i, 185, 358, 370; ii, 10, 120; iii, 76, 398, 422 *sq.*, 425 *sq.*, 431; iv, 75, 175, 201, 231, 252, 300, 302, 304, 307, 333, 385, 390; v, 33, 66 *sq.*, 79, 187, 197, 208, 210, 216, 314, 329, 340, 376, 393; vi, 21, 247 For Chatham, vi, 107 *sq.*; for Dover and coast counties, i, 190; iii, 97, 110, 112; for Dunkirk, iv, 274; v, 251; for Harwich, vi, 83, 100, 103; for Ipswich, vi,

SOUTHERNE

129; for London, v, 410; for ships in the river, i, 337, 344 *and n.*; iv, 325; report of large body embarked in English fleet, i, 426; soldiers embarked, pay of, i, 337, 355; provisions for, iv, 236 *sq.*; orders concerning, iii, 424; iv, 216; recruiting, i, 337, 355; discharged, ii, 292
Soldiers, Irish, iii, 231; to be sent to Dunkirk, iv, 138 *and n.*, 283 *and n.*, 372 *n.*
Solebay, v, 228 *sq.*, 249, 255, 257, 291, 367, 408, 424, 428 *sq.*
Blake off, ii, 102; Deane and Monck, v, 82; Jordan, v, 143; Penn, iv, 321 *sq.*, 332 *sq.*, 340 *sq.*, 393, 395
The fleet at, v, 156, 373; vi, 72
Somerset House, v, 114
Somme, River, iv, 117, 167, 193
Sonne, Harman (Captain), capt. of the Madona de la Vique, iv, 308
Soonwater, vi, 62
Souck, Pouwelis Egbertsz. (Captain), battle of the Texel, v, 363
Sound, The, iv, 143, 370, 375, 382; v, 121, 141, 244, 246, 254, 290, 308, 395, 404; vi, 3, 26, 34 *sq.*, 48, 77, 79, 117, 141 *sq.*, 187, 212, 215, 245, 258. *See also* Stores, Naval
South Foreland, i, 196, 219 *n.*, 370; iv, 396; v, 135
South Sand's Head, iv, 379
Southampton, iii, 441; iv, 114, 229, 236, 353
Southerne, — (Captain), capt. of the Red Hart, pink, vi, 202

SOUTHSEA

Southsea Castle, i, 281
Southwold, i, 364, 387; iv, 53, 395; v, 259 sq., 263, 268 sqq., 271, 275, 313, 343, 346, 351, 374, 391, 428; vi, 58, 114
  Dutch fleet took two ships, i, 368
  Rendezvous for English fleet, i, 407
  Blake's fleet near, ii, 96
  Sick to be accommodated, v, 399; lack of money for, vi, 114
Southwood, Henry (Captain), iii, 168, 368; vi, 51; letter from, iv, 329; capt. of Greyhound, i, 65; capt. of the Violet, v, 17
Sovder, Barren Tiniens (Captain), battle of the Gabbard, v, 74 n.
Spain, iv, 388; v, 128; vi, 247
Spain, foreign relations:
  Netherlands, treaty of 1650, i, 165; iii, 60; army on frontier and garrisons strengthened, iii, 61
Spanheym, Jacob Pietersen (Captain), iii, 225; iv, 178
Spaniard's Shallow, v, 325, 339; vi, 137
Spanseyins, Jacob Syverszv. (Captain), i, 262
Sparks, Robert (Captain), capt. of the Benjamin, v, 20
Sparling, Thomas (Captain), ii, 131; vi, 50, 200; letters from, ii, 130; v, 295; capt. of the Little President, i, 65
Sparrow, Drue (Secretary to Blake), letter from, iv, 63; battle of Portland, iv, 80, 83
Sparrow, John (Treasurer and Collector of Prize Goods), i, 111

SQUADRONS

Spatchurst, Anthony (Captain), v, 20; vi, 51, 199; capt. of the Fortune, to repair to Downs, i, 187; capt. of the Paul, iv, 278
Speck, Cornelis, iv, 186
Speed, Thomas (Deputy Clerk of the Check), iii, 441
Spierdyck, Barend Claessen, i, 362
Spillman, George (Bailiff of Yarmouth), i, 378, 384
Spithead, iv, 152, 369, 392; vi, 73, 221
Spitsbergen, Jacob Stevens (skipper), skipper of the Spitsbergen, ii, 127
Spoens, Jan, iv, 186
Spragge, Sir Edward (Captain), i, 23; French commission, i, 20; action with Captain Heaton, i, 22; action at Bugia, i, 29
Spurn Head, iv, 341 n.
Spurwaie, Edward (Mayor of Dartmouth), iii, 325, 415
Squadrons employed, Dutch:
  Channel, i, 77, 377, 410; ii, 16, 32, 38, 44; iv, 23; with Ruyter in, ii, 59, 61, 68, 77, 146, 182
  North Sea, ii, 24; iv, 259; fishing guard captured, i, 385 sq., 399
  Schevingen, with De With, i, 265
  to the Sound, ii, 250, 332, 334; iii, 47; vi, 2, 27, 53; captures ship carrying contraband, iii, 190 sq.
  Wielings, i, 236, 410; ii, 37, 41 sqq., 55
  See also Commerce, Protection of; Convoys; Mediterranean; Operations and Movements
Squadrons employed, English:
  Barbados, i, 67

INDEX 341

STADHOLDERS

Channel, ii, 17, 29, 68; iv, 172, 300, 348; vi, 6, 223, 226 *sq.*
Dover, Straits of, iv, 261
Downs, i, 350, 363, 369
Heligoland, vi, 44 *sq.*
Ireland, iv, 300; vi, 247
Lands End, iv, 216; vi, 57, 243
North Guard, ii, 12; iii, 67, 445; iv, 145, 390; v, 346
North Sea, vi, 1, 7
Virginia, i, 67
West Guard, i, 178; v, 95; vi, 188 *sqq.*
with Blake, iv, 100; v, 20, 42
with Bourne, ii, 249, 275, 315
with Penn, iv, 33, 216, 321 *sq.*, 368, 385 *sq.*
See also Convoys; Summer Guard; Winter Guard; Mediterranean
Stadholders, with supreme control over naval affairs, abolished 1650, i, 55
Stadtlandet, v, 308
Stanton, — (Captain), to repair to Downs, i, 215
Stanton, Robert (seaman), iii, 173
Stapley, — (Colonel), ii, 101; iii, 38
Start, iv, 153, 178, 187, 334; vi, 55, 228; Young's action off, i, 179; Dutch rendezvous at, ii, 256
Stayner, Richard (Captain), iv, 293; v, 18; vi, 50, 200, 256; letters from, v, 105; vi, 258; capt. of the Mermaid, i, 68; capt. of the Foresight, iv, 20; captures Dutch East Indiaman, vi, 7, 257
Steen, — van der (Delegate), iii, 69; v, 237
Steenbergen, —, ii, 328

STORES

Steengracht, J—, ii, 25, 38; iv, 223
Stege (*or* Stegen), Jan der (Captain), i, 261, 388; capt. of the Æmilia, iv, 309 *and n.*; capt. of the Keyser, iv, 310 *and n.*; battle of the Gabbard, v, 242
Steinfield, v, 410
Stellinswerf, — (Captain), his death, vi, 72
Stephens, — (Doctor of Law), i, 247
Stephens, William (Commissioner of the Navy), iii, 307
Stevens, — (Surgeon), iii, 320
Stevens, Thomas (Lieutenant), appointment cancelled, ii, 61; capt. of the London, ii, 131
Steventon, John, Clerk of the Cheque at Portsmouth, iv, 139
Steward, a warrant officer, i, 17; proposals concerning, iii, 373
Steward, Francis (Captain), capt. of the Sarah, v, 18
Steyner, — (Captain), ii, 162
Stoakes (*or* Stokes), John (Captain), iv, 279; v, 302; capt. of the Dragon, i, 65; capt. of the Pelican, iv, 20; battle of Portland, iv, 81; capt. of the Laurel, v, 17; battle of the Texel, v, 390 *n.*; capt. of the Victory, vi, 49
Stockholm, vi, 211, 215
Stokes Bay, iv, 152, 155, 168, 363; vi, 73, 204, 220, 248
Stoodwick, Mr., iv, 364
Stores. *See* Ordnance, Stores; Stores, General; Stores, Naval
Stores, General: Dutch, ii, 22, 254, 303, 327; v, 203 *sq.*; want of, vi, 65; clothes for seamen, vi, 121, 126

STORES

Stores, General: English, ii, 374; iii, 326, 395; v, 115, 193, 208 sq., 214, 217, 258, 261; vi, 88
Security required from storekeeping officers, iii, 25; required at Chatham, iii, 147; private sale of stores from States' ship, iii, 419
For soldiers serving in the fleet, iii, 431; v, 197
Clothes for seamen, v, 80; vi, 179
Rosin, v, 90; vi, 179
See also Purser's Necessaries
Stores, Naval: Dutch, ii, 187; vi, 27
Anchors and cables, i, 236, 381; ii, 22
Sails, i, 381; ii, 22
De With complains of lack of, iv, 380
From the Baltic, v, 128
See also Ordnance, Dutch; Contraband
Stores, Naval: English, i, 314 sq., 318; iii, 149, 175, 291; iv, 161; v, 235, 375, 380, 392; vi, 80 sq.
From the Baltic, iii, 133, 280, 446; iv, 143; v, 27; vi, 7
From Brittany, iii, 133
From Norway, iii, 413; iv, 41; v, 409
From Scotland, iii, 369 sq.
Cables and anchors, v, 90; lack of, iv, 386, 389; v, 214, 230, 258, 262
Cordage, i, 204; ii, 138; iii, 46, 377; iv, 115, 145, 153; v, 78, 275; vi, 80, 178; from St. Malo, iii, 355; iv, 40, 161
Hemp, i, 328; iii, 280, 377; vi, 80 sq., 115, 178; growing of, iii, 434; from

STRATEGY

Brittany, iii, 355; from Hamburg, vi, 113
Masts, i, 354; ii, 138; iii, 281; iv, 115, 153; v, 380, 392, 399; vi, 84 sq., 101; from Hamburg, v, 329; vi, 41 sq., 99, 113; from Jersey, iii, 387; from New England, iii, 50, 64, 405; iv, 51; vi, 81, 205; from Scotland, iii, 331, 337; iv, 52, 105 sqq.; vi, 81
Sail-cloth, vi, 178 sq.
Tar and pitch, ii, 55; iii, 65, 234, 280, 377; from New England, iii, 50, 64; iv, 51; from Scotland, iii, 337; iv, 52, 105 sqq.
Embezzlement of, iv, 145; to be sent to fleet for repairs, v, 380; vi, 78; want of, iii, 68, 150, 180; iv, 234, 245; v, 76, 95; vi, 80 sqq.
See also Ordnance
Story, Robert (Captain), vi, 201; capt. of the Cardiff, vi, 52
Straeten, Moan der, iv, 117
Straits. *See* Mediterranean
Stratagems of War, i, 4, 19, 28
Strategy and Disposition, Dutch:
Anchorage and position for the fleet, i, 100 sq.; Tromp's plan of July 5, 1652, i, 350, 376; Dutch fear English landing, i, 425 sq.; advice of Boards of Admiralty to States General, ii, 71; Ruyter's plans, ii, 111; concentration of the fleet, ii, 119; Tromp's criticism of instructions, iii, 24; defensive measures, v, 63, 71; Tromp's pro-

INDEX 343

STRATEGY

posal for attacking English communications, v, 152 sq., 224; proposal to lay up fleet for winter, vi, 95, 166, 182 sq.
  See also Commerce, Protection of; Instructions; Operations and Movements; Squadrons; Tromp, etc., letters from
Strategy and Disposition, English:
  Decision to seek Dutch on their coast, v, 25; to intercept Tromp and merchant fleet, v, 142, 207, 210, 217, 232; policy after the Texel, vi, 1 sqq., 6; decision not to divide fleet, v, 140
  See also Commerce, Protection of; Instructions; Operations and Movements
Strelly, George, ii, 157; letter from, iv, 67
Strickland, Lady, vi, 225
Strickland, Walter, iii, 446; v, 393; letter to, v, 85
Strijp, Jan Pietersz. van (Captain), iv, 338; his instructions, v, 321
Strong, Peter (Captain), iv, 245, 296, 319; v, 32 sq., 62, 96, 143; letter to, v, 53; capt. of the George, iv, 93; capt. of the Unicorn, v, 32 n.; his instructions from Deane and Monck, v, 53, 63; capt. of the Rainbow, vi, 49
Stroo, Dick (Captain), battle of the Gabbard, v, 74 n.
Stros, Jacob Dirckz (Commander), battle of the Gabbard, v, 23
Strudshavn, vi, 161
Sturteene, vi, 257
VI.

SWART

Sudan, Bartimaeus (Captain), battle of the Gabbard, v, 145
Suffeild (or Suffill), Richard (Captain), iv, 21, 278; vi, 51; his commission as capt. of the Duchess, iii, 353
Summer Guard, i, 64, 109, 110, 117, 126, 130, 132, 240; iii, 37, 175, 308, 335; vi, 242
  List of ships, i, 64; Blake ordered to hasten forth fleet, i, 110; victualling of, i, 117, 118; additional ships, i, 118; additional men, i, 125; strengthened by ships taken from convoy duty, i, 128
  Number of men for, vi, 68 sq., 73
Sunderland, i, 331; ii, 93; iv, 290
Sussex:
  De Ruyter's squadron off coast, ii, 90, 99
  Dutch fleet off, iii, 109
  Dutch landing repulsed, iii, 106, 108
  Ships, prohibited sailing, from coast of, iii, 177
Suycken, —, vi, 29
Svinshad, vi, 62
Swaen, Laurens (Master), master of the Angel Michael, iii, 191
Swan, Richard (seaman), iii, 382 n., 449
Swan, Thomas (gunner), vi, 250
Swanley, George (Captain), i, 316; iv, 294; capt. of the Providence, i, 153, 191
Swart, Evert (Captain), v, 421; capt. of the Gerechtigheijt, iv, 323; his instructions, v, 321
Swart, Hendrick (Captain), i, 388

Y

SWART

Swart (*or* Svart), Jacob (Captain), i, 234, 262, 393; ii, 337, 342 *sq.*; vi, 118, 149; capt. of the Swarte Arent, iii, 187; his instructions, v, 321; his ship lost off the Texel, vi, 160

Swart, — de (Captain), capt. of the Faem, iv, 324

Swarts, — (Captain), capt. of the Justice, vi, 175

Sweden. *See* Contraband; Stores: Naval; Commerce

Sweden: Foreign Relations, with Netherlands, ii, 368; breach with Denmark, v, 211. *See also* Contraband

Sweden, Thomas van, iv, 186

Sweers, Isaak (Captain), i, 388; ii, 49, 147, 353; iii, 224; iv, 25, 310; vi, 157; battle of Portland, iv, 123, 189 *n.*; reported dead, iv, 182

Swetnam, John (Mayor of Weymouth), iv, 139

Swindon, Toby, ii, 230

Swinn, The, iv, 42, 63, 86, 259, 274, 283, 289, 294 *sqq.*, 298 *sqq.*, 345; v, 143; vi, 87; rendezvous, iii, 447; v, 195; victualling station, v, 95, 209, 214; re-inforcements to be sent to, v, 95, 103

Sydenham, Colonel (Vice-Admiral of Hampshire), ii, 168; iii, 111, 148, 302; iv, 385; letter from, iii, 142

Sydney (*or* Sidney), — (Colonel), iii, 332, 422, 446; appointed on committee to prepare Articles of War, iii, 272

Sylbrantz, Andries (Captain), capt. of the Purmerlant, vi, 159

Symball, —, iii, 112

TAEN

Symons (*or* Simonds), John (Captain), vi, 199; capt. of the Pelican, vi, 52

Symons, Richard (Minister), ii, 162

Symonsz, Claes (Captain), iv, 372

Syricks, Reynder (Master), master of the Abigail, iv, 98

Sydrachszoon, Jan (Captain), capt. of the Dolphyn, i, 380

TACTICS, Dutch:
Tromp's fighting instructions, i, 321, 345
division of De Ruyter's squadron into three, ii, 57, 148
a reserve squadron formed, ii, 294
division of Tromp's fleet into four, iii, 224
sub-division of Evertsen's squadron, iii, 228
at Portland, iv, 180
at the Gabbard, v, 21, 73, 83
division of fleet into five squadrons, v, 130
to attack ships in Downs, v, 134 *sq.*
at battle of the Texel, v, 167 *sq.*, 382, 420
use by Tromp of line formation, vi, 20

Tactics, English:
division of fleet into squadrons, i, 177, 300; iii, 375; iv, 394; vi, 106
at battle of the Gabbard, v, 109; vi, 16
disposition of scouts, v, 142
at the battle of the Texel, v, 167 *sq.*, 372; vi, 16
origin of line-of-battle, v, 178

Taen, Joris van der (Captain), capt. of the Campen, iv, 310 *and n.*

INDEX 345

TAEN

Taen, Willem van der (Captain), ii, 334
Taenman, Cornelis Pietersz. (Captain), i, 264; ii, 340, 343, 345 sq.; iii, 225, 246; iv, 338; capt. of the Prins Maurits, iv, 314
Talbot, James (Master), contract for hire of ship, iv, 238
Tallar, — (Captain), battle of the Texel: his death, v, 353
Tamess, Allert (Captain), capt. of the Wapen van Hoorn, iv, 313
Tammisen (or Taemsem), Th. (Delegate), iv, 248, 258; v, 285, 307, 358, 393; vi, 158; letter from, v, 337
Tanneman, — (Captain), v, 421
Tantallon, v, 35
Tarbartness, iv, 106 sq.
Tarrant, John, letter from, v, 396; battle of Texel, v, 397
Tatnell, Francis (Captain), ii, 28, 100; iv, 96; capt. of the Fortune, battle of Portland, iv, 80, 84
Tatnell, Valentine, jun. (Captain), iii, 173; capt. of the Rosebush, vi, 52, 199
Tatum, — (Captain), capt. of Hannibal, i, 191; death of, i, 269
Taullerye, Joris der (Captain), capt. of the Hoop, iv, 310
Taverner, Samuel (Governor of Deal Castle), iii, 419
Tayler, Mr., v, 50
Taylor, John (Master Shipwright), ii, 156; iv, 231; letter from, v, 272
Taylor, John (Captain), ii, 241; iii, 368; iv, 127; vi, 234; capt. of the Laurel, i, 64; order to repair to Downs, i, 187; censure of,

TEXEL

by Council of State, i, 292; capture of Dutch northern fishing guard, i, 386; to be tried for misconduct, iii, 364, 406, 412, 437; capt. of the Prudent Mary, v, 18; capt. of the William, slain at the battle of the Texel, ii, 160, 161; v, 373, 390 n.
Taylor, Joseph (Captain), capt. of the Adventure, merchant, vi, 202
Taylor, Mary, petition of, ii, 160
Taylor, Robert (Captain), iv, 279; v, 18; vi, 51, 200; capt. of the Raven, iii, 408; iv, 21
Taylor, Thomas (gunner), his petition, vi, 206 sq.
Taylor, William, iv, 290
Tearne, Henry, iv, 217
Tearne, Nathaniel (Clerk of the Check), i, 226; iii, 104
Teby, Cornelius (Captain), ii, 32; prisoner of war, examination of, i, 212
Teignmouth, burnt by French, i, 41
Teincen, Cornelis Rocusenz. (Captain), i, 264
Temsen, Gerrit (Captain), ii, 343; vi, 159
Tenby, iv, 92
Teneriffe, taking of Plate Fleet at Santa Cruz, i, 25
Terhaye, English fleet off, v, 101
Terry, James (Captain), vi, 199; capt. of the Great Charity, vi, 52
Texel, i, 213, 382, 394; ii, 45, 69, 78; iv, 142, 185, 247, 259, 309 sq., 316, 322, 350, 354, 359, 367, 371, 375, 378, 380, 384; v, 25, 27 sq., 31, 39 sqq., 45, 58, 61, 82, 93 sq., 98, 100, 103, 106, 110, 118

THAMES

sq., 128 *sq.*, 133, 139, 141 *sq.*, 145 *sq.*, 190 *sq.*, 195, 198 *sq.*, 200 *sqq.*, 204 *sq.*, 210, 220, 222, 233 *sqq.*, 237, 243 *sqq.*, 253, 264 *sq.*, 266, 271, 275, 283 *sqq.*, 288 *sq.*, 290, 302, 305, 307 *sq.*, 312 *sq.*, 315 *sqq.*, 322 *sqq.*, 326 *sq.*, 330, 340 *sq.*, 351 *sq.*, 354, 357, 364, 367 *sqq.*, 370, 384 *sq.*, 387, 393, 395, 403 *sq.*, 411 *sq.*, 419 *sqq.*, 423, 425 *sqq.*; vi, 4, 24 *sqq.*, 27, 29, 35 *sq.*, 38 *sq.*, 42, 45, 53 *sq.*, 60, 62 *sq.*, 76, 97, 99, 118, 120, 125 *sq.*, 131, 134 *sq.*, 145, 150 *sqq.*, 158 *sq.*, 162 *sq.*, 167, 171, 186, 216, 245, 256, 258 Squadron from, to join de Ruyter in Channel, ii, 84, 90, 93; List of ships off, iv, 309; Dutch rendezvous, iv, 383, 388; v, 128; English fleet off, 136, 193; vi, 72 Battle of, losses: Dutch, v, 350 *sq.*, 356 *sq.*, 369, 372 *sq.*, 383 *sq.*, 389 *sq.*, 390 *n.*, 397, 402, 404; vi, 25, 47; English, v, 348 *sq.*, 353, 366, 373, 380, 383, 390 *and n.*, 404, 409; vi, 25, 31, 47 Fortification of, v, 194; Dutch ships lying in, v, 204, 335 *sq.*, 338 *sq.*; vi, 67, 77; English rendezvous, vi, 72; arrival of De With and convoy, vi, 153 *sqq.*; list of ships from, vi, 157
See *also* Actions, Fleets and Squadrons
Thames, blockade of, proposed, iv, 192; vi, 4, 6, 134 *sq.*; lists of ships in, iv, 327; v, 315; vi, 200
Thanet, v, 66

THOMSON

Thenuszoon (*or* Teuniszoon, *or* Tourmissen, *or* Theunissen), Gabriel (Captain), ii, 353; iii, 156, 225; iv, 314; battle of Portland, iv, 182
Theodorus, letters from, v, 197, 213
Theunisse, Isaac (Boatswain's mate), bo'sun's mate of the Brederode, i, 278
Theuniszoon, Jan (skipper), i, 266; iii, 226
Thomas, George (Admiralty Committee), iii, 318
Thompson, Edmund (Captain), letter from, v, 352; battle of the Texel, v, 353
Thompson, Edward (Captain), vi, 201; capt. of the Ruth, i, 67; capt. of the Advantage, vi, 51
Thompson, F. (Captain), capt. of the Crown, v, 19
Thompson, George (Colonel) (Admiralty Committee), i, 356; ii, 173, 258; iii, 98, 334, 340, 403, 407, 417, 427, 447; iv, 67, 136, 230, 295; letter from, i, 341; iv, 289; to hasten ships into Downs, i, 334, 346
Thom(p)son, Robert (Navy Commissioner), i, 54, 61, 62, 141, 268, 293, 301 *sq.*, 308, 314; ii, 133, 156, 170, 292; iii, 74, 96, 376, 397, 430; iv, 99, 131, 176, 217, 297; v, 96, 236; to hasten ships into Downs, i, 346. See *also* Instructions
Thompson, Thomas (Captain), capt. of the Mary Flower, i, 66; capt. of the Crow, vi, 51
Thomson, — (Captain), vi, 128
Thomson, Jonas (Master), master of the Supply, iii, 34
Thomson, Maurice, iii, 368

Thorowgood, Charles (Captain), i, 69, 70, 240, 257, 274; capt. of the Worcester, and in command convoy squadron Mediterranean, i, 68; ship's company petition for him, i, 249, 250
Thorowgood, Thomas (Captain), iii, 279; v, 20; letter from, iii, 164, 279; capt. of the Crescent, iv, 280
Thorpe, v, 410
Thorpe, Robert (Captain),capt. of the Redheart, vi, 52
Thurloe, Jo. (Clerk of the Council), i, 222, 249, 344; ii, 39, 101, 261; iii, 149, 178, 331, 399; iv, 102, 104, 128, 176, 217, 326; vi, 44, 260; letters to, vi, 39, 41; letter from, iii, 425
Thuydecoper, Joan, iv, 223
Thylse, Jan (Captain), iii, 233
Thyssen, — (Councillor of Flushing), ii, 84
Thyssen (or Tyson), John (Commodore), i, 196, 198, 251, 264, 351; iii, 222 sq., 248; v, 282; ordered to ply into Downs, i, 219
Tiddeman, Henry (Captain), ii, 91 n.; iv, 136, 280, 284; v, 18; capt. of the Exchange, iv, 22
Tide-waiters, appointment of, iii, 272
Tijbij, Cor. (Captain), v, 418
Tijssen, Jan, iv, 186
Tilbury Hope, iv, 58, 76, 86, 244, 345, 356, 371; v, 33, 68, 76, 273, 292, 329; vi, 6, 107 sq., 177, 180 sq., 188, 195, 211, 217; ships not to be brought above, i, 184; merchant ships at, i, 337, 369, 372; to be hastened out, i, 346; list of ships in, vi, 201

Tiler, —, iii, 337
Timmerman, Ariaen, iv, 186
Tippets, —, iii, 337
Titchfield, iv, 256
Tobiesen, Cornelius (Master), master of the Black Elephant, iv, 98
Todd, Judith, her petition, vi, 232 sqq.
Todd, Thomas (Master), vi, 232 sqq.
Tol, — (Captain), capt. of the Moerian, vi, 175
Tola, Cornelis, i, 261
Tolhurst,Jeremiah,letters from, iv, 290; v, 49
Tomassen, Jan (Skipper), iii, 236
Tomasz, Tomas, iv, 186
Toope, Henry (Captain), ii, 281; iv, 293; v, 31; capt. of the Giles, i, 191; to repair to Downs, i, 202
Torbay, vi, 55 sq.
Tower of London, i, 288, 331; iv, 51, 344; shortage of powder at, i, 222; lieut. of, iii, 364; order against private ships lying at wharf, iii, 364; pressed men sent to, iv, 352. *See also* Ordnance
Trade. *See* Commerce
Treaty. *See* Peace, Negotiations for
Tregony, v, 405
Trehearne, John (Deputy Clerk of the Check), iii, 441
Trevill, Mr., v, 333
Trinity House, i, 108, 112, 200, 204, 216, 224, 291; ii, 11; iii, 172; iv, 38, 129; directed to borrow guns and ordnance stores, i, 304, 306
Trommel, Jacob Jansz (skipper), i, 266; master of the Tromslager: to repair to Shetland, i, 394

INDEX

TROMP

Tromp, Cornelis (Captain), i, 388; v, 193; vi, 150, 168, 171
  Took the Phœnix, i, 19; the Phœnix re-taken by English, i, 20; v, 150; capt. of the Maecht van Enckhuijsen, iv, 308
Tromp, Marten Harpertzoon (Lieutenant-Admiral of Holland), i, 121, 218, 260, 313, 351, 371, 375, 384, 386, 391, 393, 400; ii, 32, 58, 96, 182, 223, 302, 351; iii, 24, 26, 33, 136, 195, 220, 259, 402; iv, 24 sq., 97, 142, 251, 258, 360; v, 25 sq., 30, 51, 54, 99, 102, 116, 120 sq., 125, 128, 130, 133 sqq., 141 sqq., 200 sq., 234, 239, 253, 264 sq., 284, 290, 312 sq., 325, 327, 337, 382, 417, 426; vi, 16 sqq.
  Letters to, i, 237, 257, 325, 345, 347; iii, 125, 165; iv, 381; v, 207, 231, 317
  Letters from, i, 196, 216, 234, 243, 281, 338, 348, 352, 365, 379, 395, 407, 409, 415; iii, 19, 47, 56, 62, 65, 70, 72, 78, 116, 137, 159, 186; iv, 23, 25, 28, 118, 358, 362, 377, 383 sq., 388; v, 27, 39, 44, 55, 69, 73, 112, 188, 198, 202, 218, 224, 227, 243, 254, 281, 297, 304, 307, 315, 321, 334, 338 sq., 340
  Action off Dover, i, 9 sq., 192 sqq., 281 sqq., 423; his comment on his instructions, i, 159; his fleet dispersed by storm, i, 391, 396, 403, 430; return from Northern Voyage, i, 410; his dismissal reported, i, 411, 414

TRUELOVE

  To command new fleet, ii, 311; iii, 10 sq.; fears partizan criticism, iii, 21; his preparations, iii, 75; battle of Dungeness, iii, 102, 106, 116 sq., 143, 151, 230, 252; receives report of English fleet, iii, 125; his plans, iii, 138 sq.; asks for pilots for the Thames, iii, 185
  Battle of Portland, iv, 68, 89, 94, 101, 164 sqq., 188; demands twenty-four more fire-ships, iv, 362; asks for deputies to inspect the fleet, iv, 378
  Battle of the Gabbard, v, 21 sqq., 69 sq., 73 sqq., 83 sq., 85 n., 88 and n., 101 sq., 107, 109 sq., 117 sq., 144 sq., 177
  Battle of the Texel, v, 162 sqq., 349 sqq., 354 sqq., 372, 382 sq.; vi, 47
  His death, v, 171, 177, 351, 355, 358, 383, 401 sqq., 412; vi, 32
  His character, v, 178; vi, 32
  His successor, vi, 25 sq.
  See also Complaints; Instructions; Operations and Movements
Tromp's broom, iv, 174
Tronquoys, — (Captain), i, 388
Trotter, Clement (Master), iii, 34
Troucquois, Jacob (Captain), capt. of the Omlandia, iv, 309 and n.
Truelove, Henry (Master), petition for command of frigate, iii, 86
Truelove, Samuel (Master), master of the Adventurer, merchant, i, 153

INDEX 349

Tubb, Roberthay (Captain), capt. of the Recovery, vi, 201
Tucker, Robert (Captain), capt. of the Entrance, vi, 50
Tuere, Corn., v, 44 and n.
Tullibardine, Lord, iv, 105 sq.
Tulsing, — (Amsterdam Delegate), v, 220
Tuick, Jan Cornelis, vi, 124
Turner, John, quarter-master of the Briar, iv, 129
Turner, Methuselah (Commissioner for Sick and Hurt), instructions to, vi, 89
Turner, Thomas (Navy Office), iii, 365 ; letter to, ii, 285
Turner, William, v, 62
Turpin, Robert (Commissioner of Prizes), ii, 108
Tursch, — (Delegate), v, 239
Tutty, Thomas (Captain), iii, 445
Tuynemans, Bastiaen (Captain), i, 199, 217, 263, 284 ; capt. of the St. Laurence, i, 207 n. ; prisoner of war, examination of, i, 211, 212
Tybe, Cornelis, capt. of the Oostende, fireship, i, 265
Tynemouth, ii, 230 ; iv, 129, 259, 292, 317, 329, 356 ; vi, 230 ; Dutch fleet off, i, 384
Tyson, —, ii, 262
Tyssen, Gillis (Captain), appointed Rear-Admiral, v, 318. See also Campes and Campen

UDAL, Sir William, iv, 256
Upnor Castle, i, 269 ; vi, 94
Upsall, vi, 215
Urk, v, 311
Ushant, iv, 72, 300 ; v, 278 ; vi, 96, 231, 251 ; Tromp's fleet off, iii, 220 ; iv, 48 ;

Dutch rendezvous off, ii, 58, 141, 157
Uyttenhout, Jan (Captain), i, 388

VALCK, Jan Jansen van der (Captain), ii, 60, 64 n., 147, 189 sq., 353 ; vi, 157 ; capt. of the St. Pieter, ii, 147
Vallis (or Vollis) Thomas (Captain), v, 18 ; vi, 50, 200 ; capt. of the Expedition, iv, 278
Vane, Sir Henry, i, 189, 202, 232, 288, 308 ; ii, 180, 265, 287 ; iii, 38, 272, 334, 403, 407, 417, 427, 444, 446 ; iv, 104, 127, 139, 295 ; letters to, ii, 268 ; iii, 415, 425 ; iv, 45, 240, 304 ; chairman of Admiralty Committee, i, 53
Vane, Sir Walter, letter to, vi, 247
Varvell, Thomas (Captain), capt. of the Increase of London, i, 67
Vechterszoon (or Vechterts), Teunis (Captain), i, 265, 393 ; iii, 225
Veere, v, 61, 203, 219, 287 ; commanders of Director's ships from, i, 264
Veere, Kempen van der (Captain), i, 396 ; iv, 354
Veghters, Symon (Captain), ii, 352
Velsen, Cornelis van (Captain), i, 388 ; ii, 64 n., 111, 142, 147, 163, 164, 353 ; iii, 208, 210, 233 ; iv, 310 and n., 324 n.; vi, 157 ; capt. of the Gelderland, ii, 147 ; battle of the Gabbard, v, 22, 69 n., 121, 137
Velsen, Johan van (Commissioner), ii, 364

VENDÔME

Vendôme, Duc de (Admiral of France), at Rochelle, iii, 219
Venn, John (Colonel), iii, 325
Venne, v, 311
Verburgh (or Verburcht), Jan Gideon (Commodore), i, 410; ii, 49, 83, 93, 142, 147, 163, 164, 193, 353; iii, 225, 233; iv, 309 and *n.*; vi, 118, 157
Rear-Commodore, ii, 111
Capt. of the Graaf Willem, ii, 147; action with Fairfax, iii, 237
Battle of the Gabbard, v, 23. See also Instructions
Vereycks, Jan Jansen (skipper), ii, 63, 146; orders from Ruyter, ii, 90
Verhaeff (or Verhaven), Jan Arentsen (Rear-Commodore), ii, 142, 146, 187, 188 *sq.*, 305, 354–355; iii, 224; vi, 157; Rear-Commodore, ii, 57; Vice-Commodore, ii, 111; capt. of the Rotterdam, ii, 146
Verhaeff, Peter, ii, 111, 163, 164, 197
Verhoeff, Jongen, iii, 240
Vermees, Laurens (Captain), capt. of Flushing privateer, v, 60
Vermoes, J. J. (Captain), iv, 338
Verveen, Dirck Qurynen (Captain), i, 388; capt. of the Haerlem, iv, 308
Vesey (or Vessey), John (Captain), iv, 293; v, 16; vi, 50; capt. of the Martin, iv, 21; his death, v, 216, 381 and *n.*
Vesey, Mrs., v, 381
L'Vesque, iii, 125
Vessen, Cornelis van (Captain), iii, 225

VICTUALLING

Vessey, Robert (Captain), vi, 51; capt. of the Truelove, i, 66; capt. of the Fox, vi, 201
Vessey, William (Captain), capt. of the Merlin, i, 66; battle of Portland, iv, 80
Vet, Mägenys Arent (Governor of Vlecken), vi, 147
Veth, Adriaen, ii, 319; letter from, v, 107, 183
Vett, Adriaen, v, 108
Vice-Admirals of the Coast: orders to impress men, i, 225; to embargo ships, i, 248
Victualling, Dutch:
scale of, i, 92
of the fleet, i, 366, 381; ii, 323, 327, 378; v, 28, 114, 118, 203, 221, 234; vi, 135
of Mediterranean squadron, ii, 22; iii, 16, 17, 57, 160
Shortness of provisions, i, 367, 380, 395, 408; ii, 164, 232; iii, 10, 135; iv, 23, 64, 192; v, 47, 285; vi, 119, 123 *sqq.*, 131, 150
Water, v, 28, 47, 190, 205, 285, 312; vi, 121, 159
Victualling money, allowance per head, iii, 62
Cost of, for officers and men of Rotterdam Admiralty, iii, 195 *sq.*
Beer, v, 190, 312
of De With's squadron, vi, 62, 109 *sqq.*, 142, 146 *sq.*, 150, 162
Rations to be reduced, vi, 111, 117, 119
Victualling, English, i, 201, 222, 242, 287, 292, 294, 306, 328, 340; ii, 11 *sq.*, 21, 33, 35 *sqq.*, 39, 70, 73, 75, 95, 97, 109, 132, 137, 154, 157, 261; iii, 112, 141, 174, 176, 341, 343; iv, 66,

INDEX 351

VICTUALLING
141, 219 *sq.*, 287 *sqq.*, 294 *sqq.*, 300, 370, 379, 382 *sq.*, 389 *sq.*; v, 26, 32, 35, 73, 95, 103 *sq.*, 112, 115, 186, 195 *sq.*, 209, 214, 217, 229, 232, 249 *sq.*, 262, 267, 293, 398, 422; vi, 29 *sq.*, 85 *sq.*, 188, 238
Of Summer Guard, i, 117 *sq.*; ii, 179, 183; vi, 68 *sqq.*, 72 *sq.*; of ships off Dover, i, 242; of ships on coast of Scotland, i, 319; v, 231; of Winter Guard, ii, 164, 169, 370; iii, 28, 49; vi, 30, 68 *sqq.*, 72
Returns called for, i, 184, 290; hastening of, v, 78; payment for, ii, 73 *sqq.*; iii, 175; want of money for, ii, 267; iii, 74; iv, 320; v, 64; proportion to be provided at several ports, iii, 175
Proposals as to the system on board ship, iii, 373 *sq.*; transport of, v, 208, 210, 215, 279, 295; list of ships, vi, 52
Want of, i, 280; ii, 115, 365; iii, 30; iv, 203, 387; v, 215; vi, 236
Beer, iii, 384, 386, 395, 397, 403, 405; iv, 255 *sq.*, 287, 385; v, 115, 157, 215, 256, 258, 267, 270, 274, 279 *sqq.*, 299, 314, 328, 342 *sq.*, 345, 375, 391, 400, 407, 413 *sqq.*; vi, 30, 57, 114
Water, iii, 414, 423, 425, 430; iv, 62, 387; v, 26, 33, 35, 140, 186, 229, 255, 258, 262, 269, 279 *sqq.*, 303, 314, 328, 391, 407, 413; vi, 57
See also Complaints; Sick and Hurt

VRIES
Vijch, Dirck (Captain), iv, 338, 384; vi, 76
Vintners, Company of, iv, 141
Virginia, i, 67
Visit and Search, Tromp instructs captains to defend ships against, i, 165, 166
Visser (*or* Vysser), Jacob Hermann (Captain), capt. of the Gecroonde Liefde, ii, 65, 206 *n*.
Vleckery. *See* Fleckken
Vleckfort. *See* Flekkefiord
Vlicter, vi, 167
Vlie, iv, 259, 309 *n*.; v, 21, 25, 40, 43, 50, 60 *sq.*, 94, 98, 103, 106, 119, 190, 194 *sq.*, 199, 201, 210, 216, 222, 229, 235 *sq.*, 237, 244 *sqq.*, 264 *sqq.*, 271, 283 *sqq.*, 289, 297, 306 *sq.*, 315, 324, 369, 395, 423, 425; vi, 33 *n*., 35 *n*., 39, 49, 53, 63, 118, 120, 125 *sq.*, 130 *sq.*, 137, 153, 167, 171, 182, 247
report of Dutch squadron at, ii, 104; arrival of Muscovy fleet, ii, 334; arrival of homeward trading fleet, v, 44; English fleet off, v, 136, 142, 193; Dutch ships lying in, v, 335 *sq.*
Vlieland, v, 44
Vlieland, East, v, 60
Vlietant, Cornelis de, v, 186
Vogelsang, — (Captain), capt. of the King David, vi, 175
Volderij, — (Captain), battle of the Texel, v, 359
Vorlecht, Abraham (Captain), battle of the Gabbard, v 74 *n*.
Vos, Jan Jacobsen de (Captain), iii, 223, 226, 233
Vos, Loureys de, ii, 59
Vries, Frederick de (Resident at Copenhagen), ii, 333, 375, 381; v, 386; vi, 182

VRIES

Vries, Pieter Janss de (Captain), capt. of the Susanna, iv, 308
Vrijter, v, 311
Vygh (*or* Vych), Derrick (Captain), ii, 162 ; iii, 139, 224, 240 ; v, 128 ; took English ship, iii, 186, 239, 256

Waad, Thomas (Deputy Clerk of the Check), iii, 441
Wadsworth, John (Captain), capt. of the Phœnix, i, 68
Wagenaer, Jan Reynderszen (Captain), ii, 80, 147, 187, 188 *sq.*, 305 ; iii, 224, 240 ; v, 186 ; vi, 118, 141, 157, 175 ; capt. of the Graaf Henrik, ii, 147 ; his ship lost off the Texel, vi, 160
Wager, Charles (Captain), boatswain's mate of the Tiger, i, 6 ; capt. of the Yarmouth, i, 6
Wager, George (Captain), boatswain of the Tiger, i, 5 ; capt. of the Greyhound, i, 5 ; blown up in action with Ostenders, i, 6
Walcheren, iv, 282, 354, 375 ; v, 82, 136, 200, 387
Walderswick, v, 258, 263
Wale, Thomas (shipwright), i, 354
Wales, iv, 234
Walfershoon, 190 *and n.*
Walker, — Dr. (Advocate for Commonwealth), i, 136, 338 ; ii, 40, 257, 259 ; iii, 34, 38, 149, 163, 173, 175, 338, 364 ; iv, 128, 242
Wall, Peter (Master), master of the Sampson of Weymouth, ii, 109
Wallis, Hugh (seaman), iii, 382 *n.*

WAUTON

Wallis, Thomas (Captain), capt. of the Expedition, i, 65
Walters, John (Captain), capt. of the Eastland Merchant, v, 19
Waltham, Henry, iv, 139
Ward, Samuell (Commissioner for Sick and Hurt), instructions to, vi, 89
Wardmondt, William Arents : battle of the Texel, v, 350 *sq.*, 355 *sq.*
Warnaertszoon, Johan, i, 264
Warrants. *See* Commissions and Warrants
Warre, William, iii, 360
Warremon, — (Captain), vi, 154
Warren, Eleanor, to be paid wages due to Capt. Peter Warren, iii, 37
Warren, Peter (Captain), capt. of the Merlin, to be sent for trial, ii, 262, 266 ; executed, iii, 37
Warrener, —, iii, 386
Washett, v, 39
Wassenaer, J. van, letters from, vi, 158, 166, 170
Watermen, Company of, petition for allowance for services, v, 309 *sq.*
Watermen's Hall, iv, 39, 40, 130
Waterner, Adriaen (skipper), iii, 234
Waters, Joseph (Master), ii, 174
Waterton, John (—), vi, 235
Watson, — (Colonel), i, 294
Watten, The, v, 265
Watts, Thomas, recommended for commission in the Portsmouth, iii, 372
Wauton (*or* Walton), Valentine (Colonel), iii, 64, 96, 121, 122, 148, 318, 408, 446 ; appointed on committee to prepare Articles of War, iii, 272

WAVEREN

Waveren, P. — van, ii, 38, 72
Waynflett, — Mr., i, 139
Webb, Sackville (Lieutenant), lieut. of the Hampton Court, i, 46
Weight, Thomas (Captain), capt. of the Heart's Ease, v, 17
Welch, — (Captain), capt. of privateer, vi, 253 *sq.*
Welch, William, letter from, vi, 37
Wells, iii, 359; English fleet reported near, i, 349; letter from, i, 408
Wells, Thomas (gunner), petition of, iii, 368
Welsh, William (Master), iii, 386
Wentworth, Lord, letter to, v, 109 *and n.*
Werff, Jan Adriaenss van de (Captain), iv, 323 *and n.*
Werff, T. van der, vi, 118
Wescomb, Richard, i, 291
Weser, v, 265
West, Henry (merchant), letter from, iii, 322
West Capel, iv, 193
Westerryse, vi, 149
Westhiel, iv, 186
Wettewang (*or* Whitwang, *or* Wetwang), John (Captain), vi, 51, 202; letter from, vi, 229; master and commander of the Sparrow, iii, 445; vi, 7
Weymouth, iii, 437, 441; iv, 235; sixty Dutch ships sighted off, i, 246; defence of, i, 328
Whaley, — (Commissary General), i, 200, 245
Wheeler, Abraham (Captain), capt. of the Triumph, i, 64
Wheeler, Edward (merchant), iii, 330
Whetham, Nathaniel (Colonel) (Governor of Portsmouth),

WIELINGS

ii, 162; letters to, i, 108; iv, 113; letter from, i, 281
Whistler, Daniel, M.D., iv, 200, 288; v, 81, 249, 259, 263, 381, 399; letter from, iv, 231, 240; v, 206, 410
Whitby, i, 384; Dutch fleet sighted near, i, 378
White, — (Colonel), ii, 13; vi, 196
White, John, to command fireship, i, 143
White, Joseph (Ordnance Officer), iii, 314, 316
White, Thomas, i, 205 *n.*; ii, 311; letter from, i, 205; action off Dover, account of, i, 205–209
White, Thomas, capt. of the Mathias, vi, 200
Whitehorne, William (Captain), recommended for commission in the President, iii, 372; capt. of the Little Charity, vi, 52; capt. of the Pelican, vi, 199
Whitelocke, — (Ambassador for Sweden), vi, 7, 166, 208, 211, 215
Whitelocke, B. (President C.O.S.), ii, 97, 124, 376; iii, 105, 112, 113, 114, 124, 283
Whiting, Joseph, letter from, v, 96
Whitton, Thomas, vi, 248 *sq.*
Wickelma, — (Captain), iii, 224
Wickham, iv, 256
Wielings, i, 377; ii, 78; iv, 184; v, 24, 28, 45, 59 *sq.*, 70, 75, 80, 82, 91, 94, 98, 101, 103, 106, 108 *sq.*, 114, 117, 121, 125, 142, 144 *sq.*, 183, 191, 197, 220, 253, 330, 348, 367; vi, 97, 172; Dutch rendezvous, iv, 248, 281, 285, 316, 334, 350, 358, 361

Wieringen, iv, 185 ; vi, 158 and n., 159
Wiggelina, — (Captain), ii, 343
Wigglema, Schelte (Captain), battle of Portland, iv, 123, 189. See also Wickelma
Wight, Isle of, i, 336 ; iii, 127, 130, 157, 441 ; iv, 79, 82, 90 sq., 95, 112, 121, 135, 144, 164 sqq., 228, 352, 386, 396 ; v, 251, 298 ; vi, 56, 176, 196, 210, 223 ; defences at, i, 107 ; iii, 111 ; rendezvous, iv, 60, 62, 65 ; ships plying between Cape Barfleur and, vi, 200, 204, 219, 221
Wilck, Pieter (Master), master of St. Martin, iii, 194
Wild, John (Master), master of Fortune, ii, 126
Wilde, Davt. de (Amsterdam Delegate), v, 191 ; letter from, v, 393
Wilde (or Wylde or Wildt), Gideon de (Commodore), i, 261, 351, 388, 390, 391, 393, 397, 430 ; ii, 336, 342 ; iii, 57, 62, 156, 224, 245, 247, 256 ; iv, 248, 281, 323, 354 ; v, 40, 130, 239
  Battle of Kentish Knock, ii, 294, 301 ; iii, 238 ; to cruise in Straits, iii, 239 sq., 257
  Battle of Portland, iv, 119, 181 sqq., 187 sqq. ; capt. of the Vrede, iv, 309 and n.
  Battle of the Texel, v, 361
Wilde, Thomas (Major), letter from, iii, 442
Wilderwick. See Walderswick
Wildey, — (Captain), iv, 346
Wilds, July (Light Keeper, Dungeness), iii, 303 n.
Wildt, Davt. de, ii, 25 ; iii, 389, 392 ; iv, 360 ; letter from, v, 396

Wildy (or Wildey), William (Captain), iii, 414, 427, 452 ; iv, 39, 305 ; letter from, v, 66
Wilkes, Thomas (Captain), vi, 202 ; letter from, v, 104 ; capt. of the Elizabeth, i, 66 ; capt. of the Swan, vi, 50
Wilkinson, Robert (Captain), letter from, v, 34 ; capt. of the Weymouth, vi, 51
Willebore, Daniel (Captain), capt. of the Walcheren, vi, 228
Willekens, Admiral (Danish), vi, 122, 143
Willemsen, Thomas, iii, 226
Willemszoon, Hendrick, iv, 186
Willemszoon, Pieter (skipper), ii, 349
William, Count of Nassau, ii, 225
Williams, John (Captain), capt. of the Helena, privateer, iii, 188
Willings. See Wielings
Willoughby, Francis (Navy Commissioner), iii, 31, 59, 73 n., 82, 113, 141 sq., 163, 169, 289, 350, 385, 387, 407 ; iv, 104, 139, 153, 221, 257, 288, 390 ; v, 236, 298, 333 ; vi, 183 sqq., 190, 210 ; letters to, iii, 113 ; vi, 73 ; letters from, ii, 372 ; iii, 30, 45, 301, 309, 311, 320, 336, 365, 372, 438 ; iv, 62, 72, 73, 78, 84, 115, 155, 161 ; vi, 238 ; appointed to succeed Robert Moulton, ii, 267
Wilson, —, ii, 286
Wilson, Samuel (Commissioner of Prizes), ii, 108
Wilson, Thomas, letter from, v, 52, 92
Winds, Mr. (Surgeon), v, 207
Windsor Castle, 150 barrels of powder from, to be delivered to Ordnance, i, 259

WINSLOW

Winslow, —, iii, 50
Winter Guard, ii, 370; iii, 28, 29, 37, 87, 90, 109, 175, 326; v, 268, 300, 407, 414; vi, 30, 43
ships for, ii, 125; to be hastened, vi, 94, 108;
number of, vi, 44
mutiny in, iii, 74
number of men for, vi, 68 *sq*, 73
list of, 1653, vi, 199 *sqq*.
Winterton, i, 364; iv, 342; v, 424; vi, 209
With, Nicolaes de (Captain), i, 262; capt. of the Prins Mauritius, iii, 57
With, Witte Corneliszoon de (Vice-Admiral), i, 351, 353, 376, 390, 393, 414, 428; ii, 42, 176, 183, 187, 188 *sq*., 223, 260, 293 *sq*., 302 *sq*., 327, 336, 341; iii, 10 *sq*., 26, 33, 69, 77, 160, 196, 224, 228; iv, 132, 251, 253, 259, 301, 316 *sq*., 338, 358, 361, 368, 377, 388; v, 25, 28, 39, 56, 113, 126, 128 *sqq*., 134, 147, 191, 200, 285 *sq*., 297, 306, 312, 318, 322, 324, 337, 358, 385, 395, 402 *sq*., 412; vi, 25 *sq*., 29, 35, 48, 60, 67, 118, 122, 134, 140, 142 *sq*., 145 *sq*., 148, 150, 154, 160, 164 *sq*., 215
Letters to, iv, 373 *sq*.; vi, 166
Letters from, i, 379, 395; ii, 220, 222, 231, 233, 236, 246, 252, 286, 329, 369; iii, 14, 53; iv, 246, 257, 281, 334, 354, 366, 370, 374, 379; v, 237, 311, 322, 326, 350, 354, 377; vi, 23, 27, 39, 53, 61, 76, 109, 119, 124, 130, 161, 165
His journals, ii, 336 *sqq*.; v, 354 *sqq*.

WITHERIDGE

Vice-Admiral, i, 349; Commander-in-Chief, ii, 119; joined by Ruyter, ii, 187, 210, 253; his fleet off Dover, ii, 214, 245; receives orders from Zeeland Admiralty, ii, 234; receives news of Blake, ii, 236; his plans, ii, 255; his fleet off the Goodwins, ii, 263; battle of Kentish Knock, ii, 268 *sqq*.
Proceedings of his fleet, ii, 302 *sqq*.; battle of Dungeness, iii, 102, 106, 143; to command new fleet, iv, 32, 247; seamen refuse to serve under him, iv, 248, 258
Attempt to intercept coal fleet, iv, 318 *sq*., 328 *sqq*., 335 *sqq*., 346, 350
Battle of the Gabbard, v, 70
Battle of the Texel, v, 163 *sqq*., 350 *sq*., 354 *sqq*., 382 *sq*., vi, 47
His unpopularity, v, 177
His protest on being superseded, v, 377
His squadron to the Sound as convoy, vi, 2, 46, 49, 53, 76, 109
In command of the fleet, vi, 24, 26
His instructions, vi, 117
Asks for leave, vi, 131
See also Complaints; Instructions
Witheridge, Edward (Captain), capt. of the Success, i, 67; wounded in action off Plymouth, ii, 121; capt. of the Marie, iii, 442; capt. of the Middleborough, iii, 442; capt. of the Kentish, vi, 200
Witheridge, John (Captain), capt. of Bonadventure, i, 68

INDEX

WITHERIDGE

Witheridge, Thomas (Captain), vi, 51; capt. of the Middleborough, iv, 278
Withernsea, iv, 341 n.
Withing, Thomas (Captain), capt. of the Middleborough, v, 18
Witt, C. de, ii, 38, 72; letter from, v, 386
Witt, John de, letters from, i, 51; v, 403
Wittesen, Witte, v, 264; vi, 134
Wolfersen, Jacob (Captain), iii, 222 sq.; iv, 193; battle of Portland, iv, 191; his instructions, v, 321
Wolfsen, — (Delegate), v, 239
Wollters, John, letter from, iii, 420
Wood, — (Mast Master), iv, 52
Wood, Walter (Captain), iv, 278; v, 18; vi, 50; letter from, iv, 60; capt. of the Centurion, iv, 20
Woodbridge, v, 259 sq.; vi, 86, 114 sq.
Woodward, Robert (Captain), letter from, iv, 327
Wood-Greene, Robert (seaman), iii, 173
Woolter, — (Captain), ii, 177; capt. of the Mayflower, i, 191
Woolwich, i, 110, 139, 329; ii, 133, 170; iv, 44 n., 238; v, 106, 215, 301; vi, 70, 177, 218, 250; state ships not to be brought to, i, 184
Worledge, Thomas (Master), master of the Hopewell of Maidstone, iv, 50
Worm, — (Captain), ii, 175
Wounded. See Sick and Hurt
Wright, —, i, 344; capt. of the John and Elizabeth, i, 343; overtook and burnt Dutch ship, i, 343

YARMOUTH

Wright, Thomas, vi, 199; capt. of the Heartsease, vi, 51
Wyard, Robert (Captain), iii, 14, 88; iv, 43, 59, 86, 150; letter from, ii, 175; iii, 359; capt. of the Adventure, complaint of ship's company against, iii, 16; instructions for convoy duty, iv, 174 n.
Wyckel, Hans van, iii, 399
Wyckersloot, Ghysb de, ii, 25, 38, 72
Wyk, v, 354, 356 sq.
Wytheridge, Judah, to be paid wages due to husband, iii, 146
Wyttenhout, Jan (Captain), capt. of the Zutphen, iv, 308

Yarmouth, i, 6, 316, 331, 364; ii, 12; iii, 340, 344, 359, 429, 441, 443; iv, 160, 303, 319, 340 sq., 346, 394 sq.; v, 32, 34, 53 sq., 62 sq., 71, 95, 104, 142, 187 sq., 206, 225 sq., 228 sq.; 249, 270, 285, 290 sq., 342 sq., 344 sqq., 379, 409, 412, 414, 424, 428; vi, 38, 60, 71, 85, 89, 114, 169 sq., 174, 187 sq., 257, 259; letters from, i, 375, 387, 413
Ships to repair to, i, 186; victualling station, ii, 75, 98, 164; v, 73; English ships warned to avoid Dutch fleet, iii, 123; petitions for a resident commissioner, iii, 346 sq.; English rendezvous, v, 62 sqq., 103; English fleet off, vi, 72; sick and hurt to be accommodated, v, 300, 375, 397, 399, 408, 411; vi, 114, 240; prisoners at, vi, 115

INDEX 357

Yates, Bartholomew (Captain), vi, 199; capt. of the Falcon, vi, 52
Yeankes, Jacob (Master), master of the St. David, vi, 237
York, Edmund (Master), master of the Hopeful, merchant, i, 224
Young, Anthony (Captain), ii, 183, 242; iii, 74; iv, 127; vi, 79 *and n.*; letter from, i, 178; capt. of the Great President, i, 65; capt. of the Worcester, i, 257; action off the Start, i, 179; to be tried for misconduct, iii, 364, 406, 412, 437
Young, John (Master), master of the Exchange, petition of, i, 290
Younger, William (Captain), master's mate of the Tiger, i, 5; capt. of the Tenth Whelp, i, 5

ZAAL, Claas (Captain), i, 388
Zaan, W. D., vi, 76
Zaanen (*or* Saen *or* Saenen *or* Zaan *or* Zaunen), Joris van der (Captain), i, 179 *n.*, 261, 282, 388, 393; ii, 336, 342; iii, 139, 156, 220, 224, 229, 242; convoy to merchantmen from Straits, i, 197, 219, 235, 418; took English ship, iii, 231, 234, 252; battle of Portland, reported dead, iv, 182, 189
Zaanen (*or* Zaen, *or* Saen), Willem van der (Captain), i, 389; iv, 324 *and n.*; vi, 118 *sq.*, 123, 149 *sq.*; capt. of the Æmilia, iv, 309 *n.*; battle of the Gabbard, v, 22; battle of Texel, v, 360

Zalinge, Pieter van, ii, 332
Zalingen, Emanuel (Captain), ii, 353
Zalingen, Pieter van (Lieutenant), orders to, ii, 375, 383
Zalinghs, — (Captain), i, 388
Zanger, Julaus Janszoon (Captain), ii, 305; battle of the Texel: taken prisoner, v, 390 *n.*
Zee, — de, vi, 160
Zeeland, iv, 142, 248, 286, 350, 354, 367, 375, 380; v, 70, 76, 86, 101, 113, 118 *sq.*, 125, 129, 133, 234, 265, 362, 387, 412, 422; vi, 160, 165, 171, 182, 191, 221, 224, 237
  Commanders of Admiralty ships from, i, 263; ii, 337, 342
  Commander of Vice-Admiral de With's squadron from, i, 265
  Commanders of fireships from, i, 265
  English fleet reported making for, i, 425
  Commanders of Directors' ships from, ii, 337, 343
  List of ships from, iv, 192; vi, 156
  Musketeers from, v, 287
  See also Admiralties, Dutch
Zeeuw, Adriaen de, i, 261
Zeiftland, vi, 237
Zierikzee, iv, 193; v, 45, 137; vi, 240; Commander of Directors' ship from, i, 264; fishing boats from, vi, 152
Zouteland, v, 417
Zuyder Zee, v, 235
Zween, Isaac (Captain), battle of Portland, iv, 189 *and n.*
  See also Sweers
Zwieten, — van, iii, 85

SHIPS

[Foreign ships are distinguished by capital letters after their names :—(D.), Dutch ; (Dan.), Danish ; (G.), German ; (S.), Spanish. Ships with no distinguishing letter are English.

It has been found impossible to take notice of all the variant spellings of names, especially of Dutch ships ; also confusion sometimes occurs owing to two or more ships of the same name having been serving at the same time.]

ABIGAIL

ABIGAIL of Emden (D. prize), iv, 98
Abrahams Offerhande (D.), i, 79, 347
Achillis (D.), iv, 309
Acorn (hired ship), iii, 308, 316
Adam and Eve (D. prize), i, 383 ; iii, 147, 356 ; iv, 314 and n. ; v, 218, 258 ; vi, 52
Advantage (D. prize), ii, 16, 29, 157 ; iii, 315, 333 ; iv, 21, 365 ; vi, 51, 201
Advantage, frigate, iv, 97, 149 sq. ; v, 76, 79, 293, 315 ; vi, 169 sq., 174
Battle of the Texel, v, 353
Adventure, frigate (3rd r.), iii, 163, 333, 379 ; iv, 100, 173, 174 n., 278, 365 ; v, 17, 416 ; vi, 50, 116, 181, 202, 226, 237
Adventure (hired ship), i, 7, 67, 128, 129, 289 ; ii, 115 ; iii, 334, 360 ; iv, 20, 86, 327 ; v, 19, 206 ; vi, 202
Took French ship, i, 2 ; took Algerine ships of war, i, 29 ; to be given sixteen months' pay, i,

AMITY

243 ; action off Dover, i, 251 ; men paid off, ii, 129 ; petition of ship's company, iii, 16 ; for Northern Guard, iii, 445
Adventurer (merchant), i, 153
Advice (4th r.), i, 65, 289 ; ii, 139, 243, 267 ; iii, 333, 404 ; iv, 20, 33, 74, 84, 219, 293, 364 ; v, 16 ; vi, 50, 87, 102, 115, 130, 172 sq., 184, 187, 201, 237
Fight off Portland, i, 16 ; iv, 73, 80 sq. ; took the Ostender, i, 25
Advisor, pink, v, 344
African (merchant), ii, 76
Albertina (D.), ii, 147 ; vi, 157
Alckmaer (D.), iv, 315 and n.
Aldborough, vi, 255
Aleppo Merchant (E.I.Co.), ii, 55
Amelia (D.), iv, 309, 310 n., 324 n.
Amity (4th r.), i, 67 ; iii, 147, 157, 158, 333, 380 ; iv, 21, 31, 279 ; v, 20, 345 sq., 391, 399, 416 ; vi, 50, 102, 116, 217, 225

Battle of Portland, iv, 101;
   battle of the Gabbard,
   v, 98 *n.*; takes Dutch
   ship, vi, 239 *sq.*
Amsterdam (D.), iv, 310; v,
   318; battle of the Texel,
   v, 362; lost off the Texel,
   vi, 175
Amsterdam (D. Admiralty
   yacht), iv, 249, 259
Amsterdam (D. fireship), ii,
   65, 200, 343
Amsterdam (D. merchant,
   prize), ii, 117
Andrew (2nd r.), i, 64, 212,
   289; iii, 63, 130, 310, 320,
   335, 427; iv, 66, 85, 219,
   230, 278, 284; v, 303, 416;
   vi, 49, 94, 170, 200
   Action off Dover, i, 251;
   battle of Kentish Knock,
   ii, 275, 282; vi, 233 *sqq.*
   Flag of R.A. Graves, v, 19;
   battle of the Texel, v, 373,
   390 *n.*, 409
Angel (hired ship), iv, 22, 100
Angel (merchant), i, 268
Ann of Newcastle, iv, 291
Ann Cleer (E.I. Co.), ii, 55
Ann Peircy (hired ship), iii,
   334, 381; iv, 22 *and n.*, 136,
   221, 280; v, 18, 206
Anne, pink (merchant), i, 153
Anne and Joyce (hired ship),
   iii, 308, 334, 378; iv, 22,
   34, 293; v, 17, 211
Anne of Maidstone (transport),
   iv, 50
Antelope (2nd r.), i, 64 *and n.*;
   ii, 19, 34, 101, 118, 129,
   131, 153; iii, 309
   Guns for, i, 130; Manning,
   ii, 46, 127; Loss of, ii, 365,
   374; iii, 13, 41; petition of
   ship's company, iii, 49
Archangel (D.), iii, 160
Arms of Amsterdam (D.), v,
   402

Arms of Holland (D. prize),
   i, 383; ii, 183, 257; iii,
   315, 333, 395; iv, 21, 279;
   v, 20, 344; vi, 51, 79, 94,
   202
Taken by the Assurance,
   i, 18
Arms of Riga (D. merchant,
   prize), vi, 237
Assistance (4th r.), i, 65;
   ii, 239; iii, 147, 157, 158,
   333, 367; iv, 33, 78, 84,
   90, 293; v, 18, 206, 424;
   vi, 50, 178 *n.*, 179 *sq.*, 200,
   237
   Fight off Portland, i, 16;
   iv, 73 *sq.*, 81, 125; flag
   of R. A. Bourne, iv, 20 *n.*
Assurance (4th r.), i, 14, 31,
   67, 128, 129, 289; ii, 96,
   113, 241; iii, 73, 157, 333,
   357, 384; iv, 21, 33, 279;
   365; v, 19, 195 *n.*, 293, 343,
   416; vi, 50, 87 *sq.*, 128,
   168 *sq.*, 172 *sq.*, 184, 186 *sq.*,
   201, 239
   Took Portuguese ship of war,
   i, 6; action off Dover,
   i, 11, 251; fight off Portland, i, 15 *n.*, 17; iv,
   100, 166; took the Arms
   of Holland, i, 18; took
   Dutch merchant, ii, 166;
   battle of the Texel, v,
   390 *n.*
Augustine, v, 236; victualler,
   vi, 53

BACHELOR, ketch, ii, 30, 98
Beane of Tragoose (D. merchant, prize), vi, 237
Bear (3rd r.), iii, 334; 380,
   427; iv, 66, 259, 318, 329,
   332; v, 17; vi, 51
Benjamin (hired ship), iv, 327,
   345; v, 20

INDEX

BERCK

Berck Howter Church, of Saerdam (D. prize), iv, 136
Betty (hired ship), iv, 244
Black Buss, of Medemblick (D. prize), iv, 136
Black Eagle (G. merchant), iii, 192
Black Elephant, of Flushing (D. prize), iv, 98
Black Lion (D.), v, 326, 337; vi, 159 *n.*
Black Raven (D. prize), iv, 137; v, 229, 298, 415; vi, 52, 200
Blaeuwen Arent. *See* Blue Eagle
Block (D. yacht), battle of the Texel, v, 357
Blossom (hired ship), iv, 327, 345; v, 20
Blue Eagle (D.), vi, 159 *n.*; battle of the Texel, v, 357
Bommel (D.), iv, 309, 323 *and n.*; battle of the Texel, v, 360
Bonaventure (3rd r.), i, 68
Bonaventure (*or* Anthony Bonaventure) (hired ship), iii, 136, 146, 289, 409; iv, 24, 45, 365; v, 219, 287 *n.*
   In the action off Plymouth, ii, 107, 122
   Taken by Dutch in battle off Dungeness, iii, 95, 117, 144, 149, 151, 230
   Petition of ship's company, iii, 342
   Destroyed by English in battle of Texel, v, 176, 372
Brack (*or* Brach) (D.), i, 112; iv, 309; v, 185
Bracke (D. yacht), battle of the Texel, v, 362
Brazil (hired ship), i, 67; iii, 379, 396, 440; iv, 22 *and n.*, 31, 44 *n.*, 54, 60, 279; v, 19, 257, 294

CATHARINA

Breda (D.), i, 397; wrecked, i, 390
Brede (D.), v, 186; battle of the Texel, v, 357
Brederode (D.), i, 199, 218, 237, 350, 367; iii, 53; iv, 24, 383; v, 41, 56 *sq.*, 114, 191, 234, 254, 336, 358, 387; vi, 123, 150, 154
   Declaration by officers of, i, 276; battle of Kentish Knock, ii, 277; repairs to, iii, 137; immediate equipment asked, iv, 362 *sq.*, 377 *sq.*; battle of the Gabbard, v, 24, 75; court martial held, v, 239; battle of the Texel, v, 341
Briar (5th r.), i, 65; ii, 245; iii, 419, 444; iv, 128, 173, 253, 289, 293; v, 188, 229; vi, 52, 200, 237, 254 *sq.*
   Took Ostend privateer, i, 27, 28; took Flushing privateer, iii, 411
Bristol (3rd r.), iv, 231; v, 95, 181, 278, 301, 334, 416; vi, 44, 50, 102, 181, 200, 222, 238
Bromel (D.), v, 185
Bull (D.), mutiny of ship's crew, v, 223; battle of the Texel, v, 357
Burgh van Alckmaer (D.), iv, 313 *and n.*

CALVER SLITTLE (D. prize), i, 383
Campen (D.), iv, 310; battle of the Texel, v, 360
Cardiff (4th r.), vi, 52, 201
Casteel van Medemblick (D.), ii, 69, 190; iv, 314, 324 *and n.*
Castle of Medemblik (D.). *See* Casteel van Medemblick
Catharina (D.), iv, 310

INDEX

CATRINA

Catrina (D.), iv, 323 *and n.*
Centurion (4th r.), i, 7, 67, 128, 129, 289; ii, 115, 129; iii, 334, 379, 417, 440; iv, 20, 31, 33, 44 *n.*, 54, 55, 278; v, 18, 206, 416; vi, 33 *sqq.*, 36, 50, 82 *sq.*, 85, 87, 130, 170, 172 *sq.*, 187, 201, 219, 237
  Action off Dover, i, 208, 251; to be given sixteen months' pay, i, 243; winter guard, ii, 125
Charity (fireship), ii, 180. *See also* Crowned Charity; Great Charity; Little Charity
Charles (hired ship), i, 191; iii, 334, 379; iv, 22, 34, 294, 365
Charles Knox, iii, 380
Chase (hired ship), iii, 334, 380; iv, 22, 34, 279 *and n.*
Christopher of Flushing (D.), battle of Dungeness, iii, 130, 144
Christopher Whelp, iii, 310 *n.*, 335
Church Prize, vi, 52
Cleyne (D.), v, 186
Cock (D. prize), v, 188, 416; vi, 52, 178, 180 *sq.*, 200. *See also* Golden Cock
Concord (D. prize), renamed Advantage [*q.v.*]
Concord (5th r.), i, 65; iii, 333; v, 345; vi, 82
  Victualler, vi, 52; hulk, vi, 174
Coning David (D.fireship), i, 265
Coning David (D. storeship), i, 397, 404
Consent (hired ship), v, 67
Constant I (privateer), i, 73
Constant II (privateer), i, 73
Constant Anne (ketch), ii, 30, 98
Constant Reformation (King's), i, 13

CYGNET

Constant Warwick (4th r.), i, 68; iv, 366; v, 105, 150, 229, 252, 263; vi, 50, 82, 130, 170, 172 *sq.*, 184, 186 *sq.*, 201, 227, 250
  Action off Isle of Elba, i, 18; took the Sorlings, i, 25; took the Royal James, vi, 7
Convert (prize), i, 191, 247; ii, 21, 28, 134, 154, 157, 178; iii, 25, 333; iv, 21, 33, 278; v, 20; vi, 52, 200, 232, 237
  Battle of the Gabbard, v, 98 *n.*
Convertine (3rd r.), i, 65, 289; ii, 134; iii, 315, 316, 334, 357; iv, 20, 33, 279; v, 20, 273, 405, 413 *sq.*; vi, 51, 82, 169, 172 *sq.*, 201, 224
  Battle of Portland, iv, 100; battle of the Gabbard, v, 98 *n.*
Conyng (D.), Ruyter transfers flag to, ii, 187
Count Henry (D.). *See* Graaf Henrik
Count William. *See* Graaf Willem
Crescent (hired ship), iii, 312, 335; iv, 280, 365; v, 20, 315, 343, 415
Crow, iii, 335; iv, 65, 134, 150 *sq.*, 279; vi, 51, 94
Crown (3rd r.), v, 19
Crowned Charity (prize), iv, 52
Crowned Love (D.), vi, 175. *See also* Gecroende Lyfde
Cullen (hired ship), iii, 308, 316, 334, 440; iv, 22 *and n.*, 44 *n.*, 54, 60, 294
Culpepper (hired ship), iii, 308, 316; v, 415
Cygnet (5th r.), i, 65, 187, 289; iii, 333, 440; iv, 21, 43, 44 *n.*, 54; vi, 50, 201
  Battle of Portland, iv, 101

INDEX

DART

Dart (merchant), ii, 76
David (*or* Talbot) (hoy), loss of, v, 215, 250
Defence (hired ship), iv, 327
Deptford, shallop, i, 289; vi, 51
Diamond (4th r.), i, 65, 289; ii, 96, 113, 241; iii, 18, 140, 166, 335, 350, 354, 377; iv, 62, 98, 278; v, 16, 104, 315, 416; vi, 50, 87, 116, 200, 221, 224, 238
    Battle of Kentish Knock, ii, 289; took Dutch ship, iii, 100; flag of R.A. Martin, iv, 20 *n.*; battle of Portland, iv, 81, 100, 125 *n.*; battle of the Texel, v, 353
Discovery (5th r.), i, 65; iv, 21, 128, 391; v, 415; vi, 51, 199
    Battle of Portland, iv, 100
Dolphijn (D.), iv, 309; v, 219
Dolphyn (D. merchant, prize), i, 379; ii, 183, 257; iii, 315, 334, 395, 427, 452; iv, 21, 60, 278, 365; v, 20, 415; vi, 36, 51, 56, 79, 199
Dorset (privateer), iv, 48
Dove I (privateer), i, 247; took Portuguese ship, i, 74; taken by Dutch, i, 74
Dove II (6th r.), iv, 365
Dover Merchant (hired ship), discharged, i, 268
Dragon (4th r.), i, 65, 289; ii, 134; iii, 315, 316, 334, 404, 452; iv, 20, 33, 293, 364 *sq.*; v, 20, 195 *n.*, 293, 315, 416, 426; vi, 50, 201, 226, 237
    Took Dutch ship, ii, 134; battle of Portland, iv, 81; battle of the Texel, v, 390 *n.*
Dragoneer (hired ship), iv, 327, 344 *sq.*; v, 20, 415

ENDEAVOUR

Drake (6th r.), i, 64 *n.*, 66, 289; ii, 139; iii, 334; v, 252; vi, 50, 246, 248 *sq.*, 252 *sq.*
    Guns for, i, 130; action with privateer, v, 49
Drum (D.), v, 186
Drye Coningen (*or* Konyngen) (D. merchant), i, 234; ii, 205; iv, 309
Duchess (French prize) (5th r.), ii, 172; iii, 335, 353, 354, 435; iv, 21, 41, 62, 278; v, 19, 315, 343; vi, 51, 94, 201
Duke, vi, 202

Eagle (E.I. Co.), ii, 55
Eagle (shallop), iv, 366
Eagle (6th r.), i, 66; iv, 22, 100; v, 415
    hulk for careening, vi, 53
Eastland Merchant, v, 19
Edan (D.), iv, 309
Eendraght (D.), ii, 147, 149; iv, 315; vi, 157
Eenhorn (D.), i, 265; iv, 313
    Rated as a fireship, ii, 343
Egmont, v, 340, 367, 422, 425
Elector (D.), v, 185
Elias, v, 415; vi, 52, 178 *n.*, 179, 200, 238
Eliza, v, 78
Elizabeth (hired ship), iii, 334, 446; iv, 366
Elizabeth (prize) (4th r.), i, 12, 18 *n.*, 66, 68; ii, 373; iv, 144, 365; v, 229, 258, 263; vi, 7, 50, 104, 113, 201, 211, 214 *sq.*, 219, 224, 238
Elizabeth (sloop), i, 364
Elizabeth and Ann (hired ship), iv, 22, 34, 294
Endeavour (hired ship), from Barbados, iii, 302, 312, 320, 336

INDEX 363

ENDEAVOUR

Endeavour, hoy, v, 258, 261
Engel (D. hired ship), iv, 310
Engel (D. privateer), i, 362
Engel Gabriel (D.), iv, 310;
   v, 185; battle of the Texel,
   v, 360
Entrance (3rd r.), i, 64, 128,
   129, 289; ii, 115, 129;
   iii, 49, 173, 315, 333, 408;
   iv, 21, 278, 365; v, 20,
   250, 416; vi, 50, 94, 108
   Action off Dover, i, 208,
   251; battle of Dungeness,
   iii, 144; to be given sixteen months' pay, i, 243;
   Winter Guard, ii, 125;
   battle of Portland, iv, 101,
   125; battle of the Gabbard, v, 92
Ertsengel Michiel (D.), ii, 147,
   323; iv, 308
Essex (3rd r.), iii, 45; iv, 231;
   v, 67, 69, 181, 211, 415;
   vi, 49, 176, 200, 222 *sq.*, 237
   Battle of the Gabbard, v, 145
Exchange (hired ship), iii, 308,
   316, 334, 378, 440; iv,
   22, 44 *n.*, 54, 136, 280, 284,
   327, 366; v, 18, 415
   To be taken for service if
   fit, i, 288, 290
Exeter Merchant (hired ship),
   v, 67; battle of the Texel,
   v, 174, 380
Expedition (4th r.), i, 65; iii,
   335, 354, 377; iv, 33 *and
   n.*, 62, 85, 278, 365; v,
   18, 293, 315, 415; vi, 50,
   82, 169, 172 *sq.*, 187, 200,
   224, 238
   Battle of Portland, iv, 100

FAAM (*or* Fama) (D.), ii, 147,
   193; iv, 324 *and n.*; vi, 157
Fair Sisters (hired ship), v, 17
Fairfax (2nd r.), i, 7, 14, 67,
   128, 129, 154, 289; ii, 115,

FORESTER

   129; iii, 50, 72, 166, 315,
   333; iv, 31, 92, 100, 112,
   127, 133 *sq.*, 144, 147;
   v, 273, 302; vi, 49, 94,
   107, 176 *sq.*, 199, 250
Fight off Portland, i, 15 *n.*;
   iv, 111, 124, 165; action
   off Dover, i, 208, 251; to
   be given sixteen months'
   pay, i, 243; Winter Guard,
   ii, 125; flag of V. A.
   Lawson, iv, 20
Destruction by fire, iv, 203,
   234, 237, 242 *sqq.*
Falcon (*or* Falcion), fireship,
   iii, 418; v, 18; vi, 52
Falcon, fly boat, v, 210; vi,
   52
Falcon, frigate, iv, 107; vi,
   199
Falcon, shallop, i, 405, 408;
   iv, 366
Falmouth (D. prize), ii, 20, 28,
   125, 127, 129, 157, 241;
   iii, 32, 143, 302, 310, 335,
   372, 377, 436; iv, 21, 62,
   293; v, 17, 424; vi, 6, 52,
   202
Fellowship (5th r.), iv, 365;
   hulk for careening, vi, 53
Ferdinand (hired ship), iv,
   327, 386 *and n.*, 389
Fleece (hired ship), iii, 334,
   380; iv, 280
Flushing (D.), lost off the
   Texel, vi, 175
Fly, shallop, iv, 366
Foresight (4th r.), i, 7, 67,
   186, 289; ii, 96, 113, 136,
   239 *sq.*; iii, 315, 333, 395;
   iv, 20, 293; v, 18, 106,
   258, 315, 405, 415; vi,
   34, 50, 87, 93, 116, 200,
   237
   Battle of Portland, iv, 100;
   battle of the Gabbard,
   v, 98 *n.*
Forester, frigate, v, 249

FORTUNE

Fortune (5th r.), i, 289; taken by the Dutch, ii, 96, 105, 126; petition from, ii, 171
Fortune (D. prize), ii, 157; iii, 315, 333; iv, 99, 128, 131; vi, 51, 201; at battle of Portland, iv, 80
Fortune, fireship, i, 164; iii, 336 *n.*; iv, 62; v, 16; vi, 52
Fortune (G. merchant), iii, 191
Fortuyn I (D. buss.), taken by English, but retaken, i, 123
Fortuyn II (D. merchant), i, 124
Fortuyn III (D. fireship), v, 186
Four Sisters (hired ship), iv, 327; v, 272
Fox, (5th r.), i, 65; v, 345; vi, 52, 201
　Taken by the Briar, i, 28
Fox, fireship, v, 16; vi, 52
Francis (privateer), i, 358
　Took Orangieboom, i, 80
Freedom (D.), v, 359
　Battle of the Texel, v, 357
Friendship (merchant), i, 191, 286
Frisia (D.), vi, 167

GALEAS VAN MIDDLEBURG (D.), ii, 146; vi, 157
Ganapan (D.), v, 185
Garden of Holland (D.). *See* Garland of Holland
Garland (3rd r.), i, 9, 64, 289; ii, 136, 239; iii, 120, 135, 136, 162, 179; iv, 24, 45, 365
　Action off Dover, i, 208; battle of Kentish Knock, ii, 291; battle of Dungeness: taken by Dutch, iii, 91, 95, 102 *and n.*, 117, 130, 144, 149, 151,

GILLIFLOWER

230; petition of ship's company, iii, 353, 360
Battle of the Texel, v, 173, 176, 365, 369, 372
Re-taken from Dutch, v, 353, 378
See also Rosencrans
Garland of Holland (D.), battle of the Texel, v, 357; vi, 46
Gecroende Haes (D.), v, 282
Gecroende Liefde (D.), flag of Ruyter, v, 126
Gecroende Liefde (D. fireship), ii, 65, 206 *n.*
Gelderland (D.), ii, 147; iv, 310, 324, 384, 388; vi, 157
George (2nd r.), i, 200; iii, 147, 157, 272, 316, 334, 427; iv, 66, 93, 125 *n.*, 230, 319, 366, 394; v, 415; vi, 36, 49, 94, 181, 184, 200, 232
　Action off Plymouth, ii, 107; flag of R.A. Lawson, v, 19
　Battle of the Gabbard, v, 83
George (fireship), i, 164, 289
George of Medemblick (D. prize), iv, 137
George Bonaventure (hired ship), iii, 312, 335
　Discharged, iii, 385, 386
Gerechtigheijt (D.), iv, 323 *and n.*; v, 421
Gideon (G. merchant), iii, 191
Gift, major (4th r., prize), iii, 335, 354, 435; iv, 21, 33 *and n.*, 41, 62, 280, 284 *n.*; v, 20, 293, 343; vi, 101, 201
Gift, pink (hired ship), ii, 136; v, 329
Giles (hired ship), i, 191, 202, 289; ii, 154; iii, 290, 334, 381; iv, 22, 34, 293; v, 31
Gilliflower (D. prize), i, 65, 289; ii, 115 *n.*; iii, 81, 315, 333, 395, 452; iv,

GIMNA

21, 293, 299, 305; v, 18, 399, 415; vi, 33, 51, 224
Battle of the Gabbard, v, 98 *n.*
Gimna. *See* Guinea
Globe (hired ship), iv, 327; v, 18
Gloeyenden Oven (D. yacht), i, 339; iv, 194 *and n.*
Glowing Furnace. *See* Gloeyenden Oven
Goes (D.), ii, 146; iv, 308; vi, 157, 171
Lost off the Texel, vi, 175 *n.*
Golden Buss (D. merchant), i, 140
Golden Castle, pink, v, 345 *and n.*
Golden Cock of Medemblick (D. prize), iv, 98
Battle of the Texel, v, 390 *n.*
Golden Dove, i, 191; ii, 134
Golden Fleece (D. merchant, prize), ii, 117; iii, 73, 87; v, 16, 415
Golden Hawk (G. merchant), iii, 192
Golden Katherine (merchant), iii, 368
Golden Lily (D. merchant), i, 356
Golden Lion (D.), ii, 379
Lost off the Texel, vi, 175
See also Goude Leeuw
Golden Lion (D. merchant, prize), ii, 33
Golden Pelican (D. prize), vi, 52, 199
Taken in the battle of the Gabbard, v, 145
Gouda (D.), ii, 147; iv, 310, 323 *and n.*; vi, 157
Battle of the Texel, v, 359
Lost off the Texel, vi, 175
Goude Leeuw (D.), iv, 310
Goude Saele (D. fireship), ii, 64
Gouwe Rijael (D.), battle of the Texel, v, 361
Lost off the Texel, vi, 160

HAMBURG

Graaf Henrik (D.), ii, 147; v, 186; vi, 157
Lost off the Texel, vi, 175 *and n.*
Graaf Sonderlandt (D. fireship), ii, 343
Graaf Willem (D.), ii, 147; iv, 309
Battle of the Texel, v, 357
Taken by the English, v, 257; vi, 112
Great Charity (prize), v, 229, 251, 298, 415 *sq.*; vi, 52, 176, 199
Great President (4th r.), i, 65; iii, 335; iv, 279; v, 19, 315, 416; vi, 50, 116, 202, 210, 222, 237
Greyhound (6th r.), i, 5, 65, 287, 289; iii, 12, 315, 334, 427; iv, 66, 237, 244, 340, 366; vi, 50, 169, 174, 201
Action off Dover, i, 208, 251; battle of Kentish Knock, ii, 289
Groeningen (D.), iv, 309; v, 185, 318
Battle of the Texel, v, 359
Guinea (4th r.), i, 67; iii, 302, 310, 335, 337, 400; iv, 21, 279; v, 17, 195 *n.*, 415; vi, 50, 82, 199
Battle of Kentish Knock, ii, 275
Guinny F. *See* Guinea
Gulden Beer (D.), v, 41

HAAS IN'T VELD (D.), ii, 146; vi, 157
Haerlem (D.), iv, 308
Half Moon (D. prize), v, 273, 415; vi, 52, 87, 199
Halve Maen (D.), iv, 324. *See* Half Moon
Hamburg Merchant (hired ship), iii, 308, 316; iv, 327, 344 *sq.*; v, 17, 272, 415

HAMMEKEN

Hammeken (D. fireship), v, 27 *and n.*, 43, 127, 130
She founders, v, 130 *sq.*
Hammetic. *See* Hammeken
Hampshire (4th r.), iii, 45; iv, 231; v, 416; vi, 50, 178 *n.*, 179 *sq.*, 200
Hannibal (hired ship), i, 191, 269, 289; ii, 115 *n.*; iii, 50, 334, 380; iv, 22, 280; v, 17, 315, 397; vi, 56, 82, 176 *sq.*, 199
Happy Entrance. *See* Entrance
Harder (D.), v, 318
Hare, ketch, i, 66; iv, 75, 151; vi, 51
Hare, pink, iv, 87, 151; v, 252; vi, 231
Hart (6th r.), i, 66
Northern Guard, i, 241; taken by Dutch, i, 414; ii, 96, 126; petition of, ii, 154; iii, 407; iv, 61
Heart Frigate (Royalist), iv, 366
Heartsease (4th r.), iii, 335, 380, 427; iv, 66, 319, 340; v, 17, 272; vi, 51, 199, 238
Hector (privateer), ii, 38
Hector (5th r.), i, 65; iv, 280, 365; v, 405; vi, 52, 178 *n.*, 200
Hector of Troy (D.), ii, 79, 147; vi, 157
Helena (privateer), action with two Royalist privateers, iii, 188
Henrietta, pinnace, vi, 51
Henrietta Maria (3rd r.), iv, 366
Henriette Louise (D.E.I.C.), v, 219, 286, 321. *See also* Louyse
Henry the Fourth (D. prize), iv, 52
Hercules (hired ship), i, 191, 289; ii, 136, 154; iii, 49, 73 *n.*, 121, 338

HUIJS

Taken by Dutch, iii, 109, 116, 118, 130, 149; petition and examination of ship's company, iii, 322, 323; battle of Dungeness, iii, 144
Hercules (G. merchant), iii, 192
Herder (D.), vi, 167 *and n.*
Hind (hired ship), iv, 366
Hoeijgen (D.), v, 135
Hof van Seelant (D.), vi, 153
Holland of Amsterdam, (D.), v, 185
Holland of Rotterdam (D.), battle of Portland, iv, 88
Hollandia (D.), i, 87; ii, 89; iii, 222; iv, 187 *n.*, 309
Flagship of Evertsen, i, 87
See also Holland
Hollantsche Tuijn (D.), iv, 309, 324 *and n.*
Battle of the Texel, v, 364
Hoop (D.), battle of the Texel, v, 363
Hoope (*or* Great Hope) (D. fireship), ii, 65, 343; iv, 310; v, 186
Hope (D. merchant), i, 140
Hope of Camphire, vi, 221
Hope (victualler), iii, 356; vi, 52
Hope of Rotterdam, battle of Dungeness, iii, 144
Hopeful (merchant), i, 224, 234
Hopefull Luke, vi, 56
Hopewell (merchant), iii, 34
Hopewell of Maidstone (transport), iv, 50
Hopewell, pink, v, 252, 296; vi, 178 *n.*, 179 *sq.*, 200
Horsely Down, shallop, i, 289; v, 252; vi, 51
Hound (D. prize), ii, 157, 241, 243; iii, 315; iv, 279; v, 17, 195 *n.*, 260, 293, 343; vi, 51, 199
Huijs te Creuningen (D.), v, 337; vi, 121, 124, 136

HUIJS

Huijs te Swieten (D.), v, 326;
  vi, 24, 121, 163
Huijs van Nassau (D. hired
  ship), iv, 313
Battle of the Texel, v, 357
Hunter, fireship, v, 19
Battle of the Texel, v, 373

INDUSTRY (hired ship), iv,
  327, 345, 348; v, 19; vi,
  199, 237
Increase, iv, 365
Increase of London (hired ship),
  i, 67; iv, 366

JAERSVELT (D.), iv, 310
James (2nd r.), i, 141, 289, 318,
  322; ii, 310; iii, 310,
  320, 332, 335, 427; iv,
  66, 85, 125, 230, 278, 298,
  333, 340, 366, 370, 391
  Blake's flag, i, 8; action
  off Dover, i, 8 and n., 9,
  10, 11, 195; to be added
  to Summer Guard, i, 118;
  battle of Kentish Knock,
  ii, 274; battle of Portland, iv, 100; Penn's flag,
  iv, 219
James (hired ship), v, 67,
  229
John (hired ship), i, 67, 191,
  289; ii, 112, 115 n., 180;
  iii, 334, 445; iv, 58, 86,
  132, 144, 147, 151, 294, 365
John Baptist (D. prize), i,
  383
John and Elizabeth (hired
  ship), iii, 334, 381, 382;
  iv, 59, 86 sq., 132, 147,
  173, 245
  To be refitted, i, 343
John and Katherine (hired
  ship), iv, 327; v, 187 sq.,
  196, 396
  Battle of the Texel, v, 397

LANDRELL

John and Sara (merchant),
  captured by Dutch, iii, 186,
  239, 256, 280
Jonas (merchant, impressed),
  iv, 366
  Battle of the Texel, v, 359
Jonathan (hired ship), iii, 334,
  381; iv, 280; v, 20
Jonathan and Abigail (merchant), i, 153
Jonge Prins (D.), iv, 315 and n.
Joshua (hired ship), iii, 103;
  v, 68, 77
Jupitar (D.), iv, 308
Justice (D.), lost off the Texel,
  vi, 175
Justice of Copenhagen (Dan.),
  iii, 413

KATHERINE I, (hired ship) iii,
  334; iv, 294; v, 405
Katherine II, iii, 334
Katherine (D. prize), i, 191,
  289, 383; ii, 115 n.; iii,
  84; iv, 21, 42; vi, 52, 85,
  177, 199
  For Northern Guard, iii,
  444
Kent, iv, 347
Kentish, frigate (3rd r.), iii,
  45, 67, 333, 382; iv, 20, 33,
  293, 364; v, 19, 206, 254,
  416; vi, 49, 94, 107 sq., 177,
  200, 204, 218, 222 sq., 237
Keyser (D.), iv, 310
King David (D.), lost off the
  Texel, vi, 175
King Ferdinando, v, 20, 407,
  415
Kirke of Grame (D. prize), iv,
  137 and n.

LADY, ketch, i, 66
Lady, pinnace, i, 289
Lam (D.), iii, 248; iv, 194 n.
Landrell. See Laurel

LANDT

Landt van Beloften (D. hired ship), iv, 314
Land of Promise (D. prize), i, 383
Lastdrager (D.E.I. Co.), i, 390, 397, 404
Laurel (3rd r.), i, 64, 187, 289, 292; ii, 96, 113, 115 n., 241; iii, 315, 333, 395, 406; iv, 278; v, 17, 206, 275, 292, 302, 416, 425; vi, 49, 80, 93 n., 107 sq., 177, 183, 200, 223, 238
Flag of R. A. Howett, iv, 20 and n.; battle of Portland, iv, 124
Battle of the Texel, v, 390 n.
Leeuwaerden (D.), iv, 309
Battle of the Texel, v, 363
Leijden (D.), iv, 309
Battle of the Texel, v, 363
Leopard (4th r.), i, 19, 68; iv, 282, 336, 356, 365, 367; v, 250; vi, 46, 171 n.
Lieutenant of, killed, i, 20; capture by Dutch, v, 150
Leopold, ii, 114
Leuinne (D.), v, 133
Liberty (D.), lost off the Texel, vi, 175
Liefde (D. merchant), taken by Phœnix, i, 124
Liefde, of Rotterdam (D. fire-ship), iii, 245, 246, 264
Liefde, of Zeeland (D. pinnace), i, 265
Liefde I (D.), ii, 146; vi, 156
Liefde II (D.), ii, 146; vi, 156
Lillyflower, vi, 100
Lily (6th r.), i, 66; ii, 131; iii, 146; iv, 366; v, 296; vi, 51
Action with Brest privateer, vi, 55
Lily (hired ship), iv, 294
Lion (3rd r.), i, 64, 107; ii, 12, 118, 238, 247; iii, 315,

MAEN

316, 334, 357, 385, 393, 396; iv, 20, 278, 319, 365; v, 18, 416; vi, 49, 94, 200
Battle of Portland, iv, 81, 100, 125
Lion of Amsterdam (D.), battle of Dungeness, iii, 144
Lioness (hired ship), iv, 366
Lisbon (or Lixbone) Merchant (hired ship), iii, 308, 316, 334, 380, 440; iv, 22 and n., 44 n., 54, 55, 59, 279 and n.; v, 18, 416
Little Charity (prize), v, 196, 210; vi, 52, 200, 236. See also Crowned Charity
Little Katherine (hired ship). See Katherine
Little President, fire-ship (5th r.) i, 65; ii, 101, 118, 153; iii, 335; v, 296; vi, 50, 178 n., 200
London (hired ship), ii, 65, 73, 118, 131, 153; iii, 308, 316, 334, 380, 382, 427, 449; iv, 66, 327, 349, 386 and n., 389; v, 17, 415
Lonk, flute (D.), battle of Portland, iv, 195 and n.
Louyse (D.E.I.Co.), ii, 85, 234, 341, 352 sq.; iii, 47; v, 418
Flagship of De With, ii, 223; of De Ruyter, ii, 305. See also Henriette Louise; Princess Louysa
Love (hired ship), i, 289; ii, 125, 137, 139; v, 301
Loyalty (hired ship), i, 191, 289; ii, 115 n.; iii, 50, 334; iv, 280; v, 16, 416

Madona de la Vique (D.), iv, 308
Maecht van Enckhuijsen (D.), iv, 308
Maen (D.), iv, 308

INDEX

MAGDALEN

Magdalen (hired ship), i, 289; iii, 34, 381; iv, 86 sq., 290, 366
Appointed for convoy duty, iv, 173
Maiden, iii, 440
Maidenhead (hired ship), ii, 101; iii, 73, 380; iv, 294
Malacca (D. merchant), vi, 109, 118, 120, 123, 144 sqq.
Malaga Merchant (hired ship), i, 67; iii, 381; iv, 280; v, 16, 315, 328; vi, 102, 172 sq., 201
Malligo (hired ship), iii, 334
Marcuerjus (D.), iv, 323 and n.
Marcus Curtius (D.), iv, 310
Maria (D.), iv, 310
Marigold (5th r.), i, 65; v, 415; vi, 52
   Appointed convoy to the Hopeful, i, 224
Marigold (fisher-boat), i, 378
Marmaduke (4th r.), i, 280; ii, 21, 28, 125, 128, 129, 157, 170; iii, 335, 361, 377, 382; iv, 67, 103, 147 sq., 293, 307; v, 16, 206, 250, 415; vi, 51, 116, 200
   To be fitted out at Portsmouth, i, 287; took Dutch merchantmen, iii, 18
Mars (D.), v, 289
Marston Moor, vi, 199, 218, 222 sq., 237
Martha (hired ship), iii, 316
Martin (6th r.), i, 64 n., 66, 289; iii, 315, 334, 418, 427; iv, 21, 43, 44 n., 84 sq., 87, 293; v, 16, 195 n., 216, 293, 416; vi, 50, 60, 102, 183, 202, 246, 248 sqq.
   Took Ostender, i, 25, 26; guns for, i, 130; action off Dover, i, 209
Mary, hoy, v, 258, 261

MERLIN

Mary (prize), i, 289; iii, 147, 157, 158, 333, 442; iv, 278; v, 17, 236, 258, 315, 407; vi, 51, 56 sq., 82, 101, 201
   To be fitted out at Portsmouth, i, 287; battle of the Gabbard, v, 98 n.
Mary (hired ship), iv, 366
Mary, fly-boat (5th r.), i, 65, 319; ii, 245; iii, 315, 334, 395
   Victualler, vi, 53
Mary, ketch, i, 289; ii, 96; iv, 22, 137; v, 62, 416
Mary and William (hired ship), i, 224
Mary Flower (5th r.), i, 66
Mary of Antrim, iv, 365
Mary Rose (5th r.), i, 11; iv, 365; vi, 200, 219
Master, iv, 125 and n.
Matthew (hired ship), iii, 308
Matthias (D. prize), v, 273, 415; vi, 52, 116, 177, 183 sq., 200, 238
Mayflower (hired ship), i, 191; ii, 177; iii, 333; iv, 86, 219, 327; vi, 51, 201
   Discharged, i, 268; for Northern Guard, iii, 445; battle of the Texel, v, 390 n.
Medemblick (D. prize), ii, 147; vi, 157
   Taken in battle of Kentish Knock, ii, 280
Merchant Adventure (hired ship), iv, 327, 345, 348
Merchant's Delight, v, 415
Merlin (6th r.), i, 64 n., 66; ii, 139, 258–9, 262; iii, 37, 92, 116, 333; iv, 21, 33, 84, 87, 219, 279; v, 18, 195 n., 293, 315, 346, 415; vi, 50, 246, 248 sq., 252
   Guns for, i, 130; battle of Portland, iv, 80, 188 n.

MERMAID

Mermaid (5th r.), i, 289; ii, 96, 113; iii, 146, 157, 333, 452; iv, 278; v, 16, 195 *n.*, 293, 416; vi, 50, 82, 128, 168, 172, 184, 186 *sq.*, 201, 239
    Appointed for the Straits, i, 61, 62; action off Dover, i, 209
Middleburg (D. prize), iii, 132, 395, 442, 452; iv, 76, 144, 152, 278; v, 18, 206, 415; vi, 51, 82, 169, 172 *sq.*, 187, 199, 251, 252
Middleburgh (D.), iv, 310
Moerian (D.), lost off the Texel, vi, 175
Monnich (D.), iv, 314
Monickendam (D.), iv, 315 and *n.*
    Her journal, iii, 199 *sq.*; iv, 24 *n.*, 177 *sqq.*
Moor (D.), v, 286
    Battle of the Texel, v, 357
Morgenstart (D.), battle of the Texel, v, 361
Morning Star (D. prize), ii, 373; iii, 28; iv, 137. See also Plover
Mousenest, fireship, i, 164, 289

NACHTEGAEL (D.), i, 124
Nantes of Rotterdam (D. prize), iv, 98
Negro (privateer), to give warning to ships off Scilly, iii, 291
Neptune (D.), ii, 58, 146, 188, 305; vi, 156
    Flagship of De Ruyter, ii, 58; action off Plymouth, ii, 142–146, 195, 300
New Flushing (D.E.I.Co.), v, 219, 286
Newcastle (3rd r.), iv, 231; v, 272, 415; vi, 50, 60, 82 *sq.*, 85, 87, 169, 172 *sq.*, 184, 186 *sq.*, 201, 239

OAK

Nicodemus, iii, 132, 335, 377; iv, 22, 279, 341, 366; v, 20, 251, 413; vi, 51
    Battle of Portland, iv, 101
Nieucasteel (D. hired ship), iv, 314
Nightingale (5th r.), i, 68, 289; ii, 96, 113, 131, 136, 244; iii, 334, 378, 440; iv, 21, 33, 43, 44 *n.*, 54, 219; v, 296; vi, 50, 201, 219, 228, 237
    Battle of Kentish Knock, ii, 276; battle of Portland, iv, 91
Nightingale (merchant), i, 116
Noah's Ark (D. prize), i, 383
Nonsuch (4th r.), i, 7, 67, 289; ii, 136, 139, 239; iii, 32, 157, 333, 357, 384; iv, 20, 279, 365; v, 19, 405; vi, 50, 99, 178, 180, 200, 219, 222 *sq.*, 238, 246, 248 *sq.*, 252
    Battle of Kentish Knock, ii, 269 *sq.*; battle of Portland, iv, 100; battle of the Gabbard, v, 98 *n.*; convoy for prizes, v, 145
Nonsuch, ketch (hired ship), i, 66, 191; ii, 96; iv, 293; v, 195, 293, 301; vi, 202
    Guard to mackerel fishery, i, 153
Nonsuch (merchant), iii, 350
Norwich, frigate, v, 426

OAK (D. prize), ii, 157; iii, 81, 103, 315, 333; iv, 22, 84, 279; v, 19
    Took the Ostrich, i, 16; battle of Portland, iv, 73, 82, 166
    Lost in the battle of the Texel, v, 169, 350, 368 *sq.*, 373, 397

INDEX

OLD JAMES

Old James. *See* James
Old Man (D. prize), ii, 244
Old President. *See* President
Old Warwick. *See* Warwick
Omlandia (D.), iv, 309
Oostende (D. fireship), i, 265
Orangen (D.E.I.Co.), v, 129
Orangie (D.E.I. Co.), i, 390, 397
Orangieboom (*or* Orange Tree) (D. prize), iii, 387
    Taken by the Francis, i, 80
Oranienboom (D. fireship), ii, 65
Ostrich (D.), vi, 53
    Captured in Portland fight, i, 16
    See also Struisvogel
Outward, ii, 328
Overijssel (D.), iv, 310, 323 and *n*.; v, 185
    Battle of the Texel, v, 362

PARADOX (6th r.), i, 66, 289; ii, 136, 241; iii, 379, iv, 22, 33, 219; vi, 51, 201
Paragon (2nd r.), i, 68; vi, 49, 94, 201, 217, 224
    Action off Isle of Elba, i, 18
Parrot-tree (*or* Papageyboom) (merchant of Dantzig), iii, 192
Patientia (D.), iv, 310
Paul (D. prize), i, 383; ii, 115 *n*., 170; iii, 81, 315, 333, 385, 393; iv, 22, 278; v, 20, 415; vi, 33, 51, 177, 199
Peacock (D. prize), iv, 98
Pearl (5th r.), i, 65; ii, 243; iii, 143, 302, 310, 335, 337, 366, 395, 439; iv, 21, 253, 293; v, 19, 301; vi, 50, 246, 254
    Battle of the Gabbard, v, 98 *n*.
Pear-tree (D.), battle of the Texel, v, 357

PLANTER

Pelican (4th r.), i, 7, 67, 202 *n*.; ii, 121, 241; iii, 315, 404; iv, 20, 279; v, 16, 276, 315, 416, 426; vi, 36, 50, 116, 199, 238, 246
    To be hastened out, i, 328
    Battle of Kentish Knock, ii, 272 *sq.*; battle of Portland, iv, 100; battle of the Gabbard, v, 98 *n*.
    See also Golden Pelican
Pelican (D. privateer), v, 185
    Taken by the Tiger, iii, 437
    Battle of the Texel, v, 359
Pereboom (D. hired ship), iv, 316
Perrell, v, 278
Peter (D. merchant, prize), i, 140; ii, 33, 63, 97, 125, 129, 157; iii, 335, 427; iv, 66, 93, 293; v, 18, 415; vi, 51
Peter of Hamburg (I), iv, 137
Peter of Hamburg (II), iv, 138
Phesant (D.), iv, 309
    Battle of the Texel, v, 364
Phœnix (4th r.), i, 18, 31, 68; iv, 327, 345, 365; v, 17, 78, 229, 252, 263, 301, 343, 346, 424; vi, 7, 50, 116, 201, 209, 211, 216, 257
    Took French ship of war, i, 8; taken by Dutch, i, 18; retaken by Capt. Cox, i, 19, 20; took Dutch merchant ship, i, 124; action with Dutch men-of-war, vi, 212 *sqq.*; battle of the Texel, v, 174, 366, 390 *n*.
Phœnix (merchant), v, 415
Phœnix (G. merchant), iii, 193; v, 343
Pieter (D.), took Dove, i, 74
Planter van Medemblik (D. merchant), ii, 210

372 INDEX

PLOVER

Plover (D. prize), iii, 28, 333, 379; iv, 21, 33, 293; v, 229; vi, 51, 202
Plymouth, took D.E. Indiaman, vi, 7, 256
Portland (3rd r.), iv, 231; v, 64, 195 *n.*, 416; vi, 50, 102, 178, 202, 222 *sq.*, 237
Battle of the Texel, v, 390 *n.*
Portsmouth (4th r.), i, 65, 289; ii, 136, 238; iii, 30, 73 *n.*, 131, 134, 140, 143, 301, 309, 311, 335, 439; iv, 62, 153 *n.*, 157, 278; v, 18, 196, 293 *and n.*, 310, 315, 416; vi, 50, 87, 116, 200, 222, 227, 250 *sqq.*
Action off Dover, i, 209; action with Dutch man-of-war, iii, 349, 351
Battle of the Texel, v, 174, 373
Post Horse (D.), v, 286
Postpaert (D.), iv, 323 *and n.*
President (4th r.), i, 181, 257, 289; ii, 134, 239 *sq.*; iii, 143, 301, 310, 311, 337, 372, 378, 439; iv, 20, 90, 365; v, 206, 253, 293, 329, 334; vi, 93
Took Ostender, i, 25; battle of Portland, iv, 101, 115
Primrose (5th r.), i, 65; vi, 50, 201
Prince (2nd r.). *See* Resolution
Prince (D. merchant, prize), i, 140; ii, 170
Prince William (D. prize), ii, 170
Prince William (*or* Prins Willem) (D.E.I.Co.), ii, 254, 308, 341, 352; iv, 309; v, 129; vi, 175
Flagship of De With, battle of Kentish Knock, ii, 295 *sq.*, 357; condition of crew in, iii, 53; battle of Texel, v, 358

PURMERLANT

Princess Louise (D.), iv, 383; v, 41, 220, 281
Princess Maria (3rd r.), ii, 183, 257; iii, 315, 316, 334, 357, 385, 404; iv, 21, 279; v, 19, 304; vi, 51, 79, 94, 184, 210, 237
Princess of Rotterdam (D. prize), iv, 137
Princesse Royaele (D.), iv, 314
Prins (D.), iv, 383; v, 41, 56 *sq.*
Prins Mauritius (D.), wreck of, iii, 57, 71
Prins Maurits (D.), iv, 314
Prins Willem (D.). *See* Prince William
Promised Land (G. merchant), iii, 193
Prophet Samuel (D.), v, 289
Propperyteijt. *See* Prosperous
Prosperous (hired ship), i, 191, 289; ii, 115 *n.*, 365; iii, 334; iv, 20, 85, 87, 124, 246, 294
Battle of Portland, iv, 79 *sq.*, 83, 92, 142, 166; taken by Dutch, iv, 188 *and n.*, 195 *and n.*; battle of the Texel, v, 390 *n.*
Prosperous (merchant), ii, 174
Provence Rose (fisher-boat), i, 383
Providence (4th r.), i, 65, 191; ii, 115 *n.*; iii, 143, 310, 335, 337; iv, 278, 365; v, 17, 416; vi, 50
Employed as convoy, i, 153; Northern Guard, i, 241
Providence (hired ship), iii, 334; iv, 22, 34, 62, 85, 294
Battle of Portland, iv, 101
Providence (transport), iv, 50
Prudent Mary (hired ship), iii, 308, 316; iv, 327, 344 *sq.*; v, 18, 416
Purmerlant (D.), vi, 159

INDEX

RADEBOLD (D.), v, 185
Rainbow (2nd r.), i, 67; iii, 147, 157, 316, 334, 404, 452; iv, 245, 288, 293, 347, 366; vi, 49, 94
 Flag of Ayscue, i, 343; flag of V. A. Peacock, iv, 20 n.; battle of Portland, iv, 100, 125; flag of Goodson, v, 20; battle of the Texel, v, 174, 370
Raven (4th r.), iii, 333, 379, 408, 440; iv, 21, 44 n., 54, 60, 279, 395; v, 18, 251, 293, 315, 415; vi, 51, 82, 116, 200
 Officers tried for misdemeanour, v, 141
Real of Gold (D.), v, 185
Recovery (hired ship), i, 65, 289; ii, 129, 373; iii, 335, 427; iv, 66, 365; v, 68, 76 sq., 79 sq., 230, 379 sq., 415; vi, 52, 170, 172 sq., 201, 210, 232
 Young's action off the Start, i, 180; discharged, i, 268; Winter Guard, ii, 125
 Battle of the Texel, v, 174
Recovery (E.I. Co.), ii, 55
Redheart, pink, vi, 52, 202, 229
Reformation (hired ship), i, 191, 202 n., 242, 289; ii, 154; iii, 73, 86, 334, 381; iv, 22, 34, 280; v, 19, 105
Reformation (merchant), iii, 377
Remembrance, of Maidstone (transport), iv, 50
Renown, fireship, ii, 118, 153; iii, 336 n.; v, 16, 315; vi, 52
Reserve (4th r.), i, 65; iv, 364; v, 78, 209, 214 sq., 255 sqq., 416; vi, 50, 87, 93, 116, 199, 237
Resolution (1st r.), i, 269, 322, 331, 336; ii, 69, 320; iii,

335, 427; iv, 66, 125 and n., 219, 230, 245 sq., 288, 293, 363, 369, 383, 386 sq., 391; v, 73, 90, 188, 192, 230, 260, 276, 281, 373, 400, 416; vi, 49, 61, 74, 94
 Added to Summer Guard, i, 118
 Blake's flagship, i, 331
 Battle of Kentish Knock, ii, 274 sq., 289, etc.
 Flag of Generals Deane and Monck, v, 16
 Battle of the Gabbard, v, 85 and n., 88 n., 102; battle of the Texel, v, 174, 350, 368
Reuben (hired ship), action off Dover, i, 208
Richard and Benjamin (hired ship), i, 191, 289
Richard and Martha (hired ship), i, 191, 289; ii, 136, 154, 292; iii, 334, 381; iv, 22, 34, 221, 280; v, 18; vi, 56, 82, 179 sq., 200, 237
Robert (hired ship), iv, 365
Robert and Richard (merchant), i, 286, 289
Rode Leeu (D., hired ship), iv, 313 and n.
Rodenhaes (D.), iv, 308
Roebuck (hired ship), iv, 22, 327; v, 20, 415
 Battle of Portland, iv, 101
Rose of Amsterdam (D.E.I.Co. prize), vi, 256 sq.
Rosebush (D. prize), v, 276; vi, 52, 199
Rosemary Tree (D. prize), v, 257
Rosencrans (D.), iv, 363, 383; v, 41, 220, 281
 Battle of the Texel, v, 350
 See also Garland
Rotterdam (D.), ii, 146; vi, 157
Rotterdam (D. prize), renamed Falmouth [q.v.]

ROYAL

Royal of Calais (privateer), action with Drake, v, 49
Royal Defence, vi, 56
Royal James (King's), i, 25 *n.* Taken by Constant Warwick, vi, 7, 250
Royal Princess (D.), battle of Dungeness, iii, 144
Ruby (4th r.), i, 14, 65 *and n.*, 289; ii, 96, 113, 239; iii, 73 *n.*, 109, 133, 140, 143, 166, 302, 310, 335, 340; iv, 20, 33, 97 *sq.*, 293; v, 18, 210, 329, 345 *sq.*, 399, 415; vi, 34 *sqq.*, 50, 199, 221, 237 *sq.*
  Flag of Houlding, i, 14; action off Dover, i, 209; battle of Kentish Knock, ii, 270 *sq.*; battle of Dungeness, iii, 144; action with Dutch man-of-war, iii, 349, 351; iv, 135
Ruth (hired ship), i, 67; iv, 22
  Battle of Portland, iv, 101

St. Andrew (2nd r.), iv, 125, 365
  Action off Dover, i, 8
St. Anthony (D. merchant, prize), ii, 40
St. David of Horne, pink (D. prize), vi, 237
St. George. *See* George
St. Jacob (D. fireship), i, 265
St. Jan (D.), ii, 147; vi, 157
St. Jeronimus (D.), to be paid off, iii, 47
St. John of Fredrickstadt (Dan.), iii, 413
St. John (G. merchant), iii, 193
St. Julian Castle, i, 4
St. Laurence (D. merchant), i, 213
  Action off Dover, i, 207 *and n.*

SAMPSON

St. Lucas (hired ship), discharged, i, 268
St. Maria (fireship), ii, 65
St. Martin (G. merchant), iii, 194
St. Mary (D.), action off Dover, i, 207 *and n.*
St. Matheeuwes van Nauwoogh (D.), iv, 324 *and n.*
St. Matthew (G. merchant), iii, 194
St. Nicolaes (D.), vi, 157
St. Paul (merchant), captured by French, i, 72
St. Pieter (D.), ii, 147; iv, 308; vi, 157
St. Vincent (D.), lost off the Texel, vi, 175
Salamander (D.E. I. Co.), i, 390, 404; ii, 299; v, 286
Salamander (D. merchant), i, 140
Salomon's Ordeel (D.), iv, 308
Salvador, iii, 272
Samaritan (hired ship), iv, 327, 344 *sq.*; v, 19, 415
Sampson of Enkhuisen (D. prize), iii, 272; iv, 41, 50, 293; vi, 52, 185, 202
  Taken during Northern Voyage, i, 383
  Fitting out, iii, 354; iv, 103, 147 *sq.*
  Convoy and cruising, iv, 307, 320; v, 229, 251, 299, 407, 416
Sampson of Hoorn (D. prize), ii, 134; iii, 310, 315, 333, 380; iv, 21, 33, 66, 310
  Taken during the Northern Voyage, i, 383
  Destroyed at Battle off Portland, iv, 21 *n.*, 73, 79, 83, 102, 114, 162, 166, 171, 229, 316
Sampson, of Weymouth (merchant), ii, 109

INDEX

SAMUEL

Samuel I (hired ship), iii, 308, 316
Samuel II (hired ship), iii, 308, 316; v, 187
Samuel III, iv, 344 *sq*.
  Contract for hire of, iv, 238
Samuel, shallop, iv, 366
Samuel Talbot, v, 20, 415
Sandenbergh (D.), vi, 240
Sandwich, pink (hired ship), i, 289
Sapphire (4th r.), i, 23, 26, 28, 65 *and n*., 289; ii, 136, 183, 241; iii, 75, 87 *n*., 109, 290, 315, 333, 379, 395; iv, 20, 60, 137, 153 *n*., 173, 279, 391; v, 16, 32; vi, 50, 79, 178 *n*., 179 *sq*., 199, 222
  Action with privateers, i, 21, 22; lost off coast of Sicily, i, 45 *and n*.; action off Dover, i, 209; battle of Dungeness, iii, 95, 144; battle of Portland, iv, 81; took Dutch man-of-war, vi, 228
Sara (D.), ii, 147; v, 186; vi, 157
Sarah (hired ship), iv, 327; v, 18
Satisfaction (5th r.), i, 65; iv, 21, 365; v, 258, 263, 415; vi, 52, 199
  Battle of Portland, iv, 101
Saudados, took French ship of war, i, 30
Saudados Prize, i, 30
Schaapherder (D.), ii, 147; vi, 157
Seabird (hired ship), iii, 435
Seven Brothers (hired ship), i, 289; v, 68, 196, 210, 315, 343, 415; vi, 33
  Action off Dover, i, 251
Sevenwoolden (D.), v, 186
Shepperd (D.), v, 185
Shepherdess (D.), v, 185
VI.

SPEAKER'S

Smyrna Merchant, v, 278
Society (hired ship), iii, 334, 380, 382; iv, 280; v, 16, 206, 416; vi, 202, 237
Son (D.), iv, 308, 323 *and n*.
Sophia, of Amsterdam (D. prize), iii, 103, 427; iv, 66, 357; v, 17, 98; vi, 52, 200
  Battle of the Texel, v, 174, 378
Sorlings (King's), taken by Constant Warwick, i, 25
Southwold, vi, 255
Sovereign (1st r.), i, 70, 107, 141, 322; ii, 21, 34, 53, 61, 105, 120, 129, 166; iii, 136, 335, 405, 427; iv, 66, 125, 230; v, 71, 257, 303; vi, 49, 206, 218, 238, 248, 250
  To be added to Summer Guard, i, 118; to be hastened out, i, 330, 337 *and n*.; ii, 10, 11, 17, 118
  Guns for, i, 331; ii, 19; vi, 241, 243
  Manning, ii, 28, 46, 101
  Battle of Kentish Knock, ii, 271 *sq*., 283
Sparrow (D. prize), iii, 445; vi, 7, 51, 202, 255; took Dutch man-of-war, vi, 230
Speaker (2nd r.), i, 14, 18, 64, 289; ii, 96, 113, 136, 239; iii, 50, 82, 115, 136, 166, 315, 333, 373; iv, 33, 219, 279, 364; vi, 49; 176, 199, 238
  Fight off Portland, i, 15 *n*.; iv, 100, 125, 165; took Dutch ships, i, 17; action off Dover, i, 208; battle of Kentish Knock, ii, 289; battle of Dungeness, iii, 90, 102; flag of Admiral Penn, iv, 20 *n*.; flag of R.A. Howett, v, 17
Speaker's prize, iii, 379, 382, 408; iv, 22, 23

2 A

SPITSBERGEN

Spitsbergen (D. merchant), ii, 127
Stadt van Medemblick (D.), iv, 315 and n., 323 and n.
Star (6th r.), i, 7, 67, 289; ii, 374; iv, 366
  Action off Dover, i, 209
  To be given 16 months' pay, i, 243
Star (D.), iii, 44; iv, 308 sq.
Star of Hoorn (D. prize), iv, 98
State of Elbing (D. merchant), ii, 274
Stork (4th r.), iii, 335, 379, 427; iv, 66; vi, 51
Struisvogel (D.E.I.Co.), ii, 147, 295, 358 sq.; iii, 47, 210; iv, 87 and n.
  With De Ruyter, ii, 147, 149
  Battle of Portland, iv, 81 and n., 89 and n., 119, 123
  Taken by English, iv, 189, 195
  See also Ostrich
"Stump-Nose," taken by the Martin, i, 25, 26
Success (prize) (4th r.), i, 65, 67; iii, 143, 302, 310, 335, 372, 377, 435; iv, 21, 31, 33 and n., 41, 62, 278; v, 19, 258, 273 sq., 376, 415; vi, 35, 51
  Taken by Blake, i, 7; to be hastened out, i, 328
  Battle of Portland, iv, 100, 169; battle of the Gabbard, v, 98 n.
Sun I (prize), iv, 280; vi, 201
  To be added to Summer Guard, i, 118
  Victualler, vi, 53
Sun II (D.), captured in battle of the Gabbard, v, 23
Sun III (D.), v, 186
Supply (merchant), iii, 34

THOMAS

Susan (merchant), taken by Dutch, iii, 400 sq.
Susanna (D.), iv, 308
Sussex (3rd r.), iii, 45, 333, 379, 382; iv, 20, 293, 347, 364; v, 17, 206, 416; vi, 49
  Battle of the Gabbard, v, 97
Swallow, i, 23
Swan (5th r.), i, 65, 289; ii, 245; iii, 72, 315, 333; iv, 86, 132, 150 sq., 173, 245; v, 105; vi, 50, 202
  To be paid off, ii, 248
  Rebuilding, ii, 126, 179, 248; Northern Guard, iii, 445
Swan, of Amsterdam (D. prize), i, 383
Swarte Arent (D.), iii, 187; iv, 308
Swarte Bull (D.), iv, 324 and n.
  Battle of the Texel, v, 361
Swarten Leeuw. *See* Black Lion
Swiftsure (2nd r.), i, 46; ii, 154; iii, 427; iv, 66, 230, 245, 254, 296, 366; vi, 49, 176 sq., 181, 185 sq., 188, 199, 250
  Launched (rebuilt), vi, 114
Swift (D. prize), vi, 51, 56 sq., 82

TALBOT, hoy, loss of, v, 250. *See also* David
Tarrenton, vi, 258
  Took D.E. Indiaman, vi, 7, 255, 258 sq.
Taunton, vi, 200, 210, 222, 237
Tenby (D. prize), iv, 93
Tenth Whelp (6th r.), i, 4, 5, 66; iii, 143, 310 and n., 337; iv, 21 and n., 33 and n., 62, 85, 151, 173, 366; v, 104 sq.; vi, 50, 202
Thomas, hoy, v, 258

Thomas and Lillie, iii, 440
Thomas and Lucy (hired ship), iii, 334, 378; iv, 22, 44 n., 54, 60, 280; v, 18; vi, 200, 238
Thomas and William (hired ship), i, 191, 289; ii, 115 n.; iii, 334, 452; iv, 22, 34, 280; v, 17, 236; vi, 56
Thomason (merchant), iii, 34
Three Golden Herrings (D. merchant), i, 140
Tiger (4th r.), i, 4, 5, 6, 65, 186, 202 n., 289; ii, 374; iii, 333, 408; iv, 20, 279, 365; v, 17, 293, 315, 415, vi, 36, 50, 116, 200, 210, 226, 237
　Took Portuguese ship, i, 4; took Dutch ship of war, i, 29; iii, 437; battle of Portland, iv, 100
Tobyas (D. hired ship), iv, 313
Town and Country (D.), sunk at battle of the Gabbard, v, 22
Tresco (King's), i, 25 and n.
Trinity (G. merchant), iii, 194
Triumph (2nd r.), i, 4, 6, 8, 14, 15 and n., 23, 64 and n., 189, 289; ii, 239; iii, 148, 158, 315, 316, 334, 357, 367, 384, 395, 439, 451; iv, 138, 245, 284, 288, 293, 347, 365; v, 17, 92, 416; vi, 49, 94, 181, 184, 200
　Flag of Generals Blake and Deane, i, 14; iv, 20 n.; fight off Portland, i, 15; iv, 79 sq., 83, 93, 100 sq., 124, 165, 172
　Flag of Vice-Admiral Penn, i, 202; private ship in action off Dover, i, 207, 251; battle of Dungeness, iii, 93, 95 sq.

Flag of V. A. Peacock, v, 17; battle of the Gabbard, v, 87; battle of the Texel, v, 390 n., 409
Tromslager (D. galliot), i, 394
Truelove, i, 66; iv, 365; vi, 51
Tulip (4th r.), iii, 333, 380, 382, 408; iv, 21; v, 20; vi, 51, 201, 210
　Battle of the Texel, v, 168, 366, 390 n.

Uijtrecht (D.), iv, 308; vi, 171
Unicorn (2nd r.), iii, 147, 157, 316, 335, 427; iv, 66, 125, 230, 237, 245, 296, 298, 301, 319, 366, 391; v, 64, 143, 185, 345, 415; vi, 36, 49, 94, 107 sq., 177, 181, 184, 199
Unity (hired ship), iv, 327
Unity, of Hull (merchant), ii, 174

Vaelenhaen (D. fireship), ii, 343
Vanguard (2nd r.), i, 14, 269, 322; ii, 17, 239; iii, 148, 315, 316, 334, 357, 384, 395; iv, 245, 278, 284, 366, 392; v, 139–146, 422–429; vi, 49, 94, 253
　Fight off Portland, i, 15 n.; iv, 80, 84, 101, 125; to be hastened out, i, 316, 328; battle of Dungeness, iii, 91, 94 sq.; flag of Monck, iv, 20 n.; flag of V. A. Jordan, v, 20
Vanity, vi, 201
Veere (D. merchant), ii, 79
Venetia (D.), iv, 308
Vercken (D. fireship), i, 265
Vereeniche Provintien (D.), iv, 308

VERGULDE

Vergulde Buys (D. fireship), ii, 343
Victory (2nd r.), i, 64, 289; iii, 148, 315, 316, 334, 357, 404; iv, 33, 293, 347, 365; v, 18, 415; vi, 36, 49, 94
    Action off Dover, i, 208; battle of Dungeness, iii, 91, 94; flag of V.A. Lane, iv, 20; battle of Portland, iv, 125; battle of the Texel, v, 368
Victory (merchant), v, 415
Violet, iii, 334, 379, 427; iv, 66, 330; v, 17, 97; vi, 51
Vlissingen (D.), ii, 146; vi, 157
Vogelstruys (D.E.I. Co.). *See* Struisvogel
Vos (D. fireship), ii, 343
Vreede (D.), ii, 147; iv, 309, 323 *and n.*; v, 55
    With De Ruyter, ii, 147; battle of the Texel, v, 361
Vryheyt (D.), ii, 334; iv, 310, 324 *n.*, 335 *n.*
    Flagship of Balck, ii, 334; battle of the Texel, v, 351, 358
Vurow Anthony Solay (D. prize), iv, 137

'T WAFEN VAN SWEDEN (D.), ii, 146; vi, 156
Walcheren of Middleburg (D.), vi, 228
Wapen van Enchuijsen (D.), iv, 315
Wapen van Hollandt (D. hired ship), iv, 314
Wapen van Hoorn (D.), iv, 313; vi, 167
Wapen van Rotterdam (D. fireship), i, 265
Warwick (5th r.), i, 65, 289, 319; ii, 240; iii, 315, 333, 395; iv, 21, 56, 58,

WILLIAM

152, 280, 284, 366; v, 78, 251 *sq.*, 278, 334; vi, 50, 246
Northern Guard, iii, 445; took Dutch frigate, iii, 446; battle of Portland, iv, 101
Wassende Maen (D. flute), i, 379
Waterdog (D.), v, 186
Waterhound (D. prize), i, 383; iii, 315, 333, 395; iv, 21, 33, 88, 151, 279, 364; v, 19, 195 *n.*, 416; vi, 52
    Takes Dutch ship, iv, 150
Waterhout (D. yacht), iii, 187
Welcome (E.I. Co.), ii, 55
Welcome (4th r.), iii, 333, 379, 440; iv, 21, 44 *n.*, 279; v, 19, 250, 258, 273, 415; vi, 51, 178 *sqq.*, 200, 238
    Battle of the Gabbard, v, 98 *n.*
Wellmen, vi, 255
Westergate (D. prize), v, 415; vi, 52, 200, 238
Westergo (D.), ii, 146; iii, 187; v, 240, 242, 376, 399; vi, 157
    Captured at battle of the Gabbard, v, 23, 74
Westvrieslandt (D.), iv, 309, 323 *and n.*
    Battle of the Texel, v, 362
Weymouth, pink, i, 66, 289; iii, 315, 333, 395; iv, 87, 151, 173, 290, 366; vi, 51, 255
Northern guard, i, 241; iii, 445
Whale (D.), battle of the Texel, v, 357
White Unicorn (D.E.I. Co.), v, 282, 288
Wildman, fireship, iii, 418; v, 345; vi, 52, 174
William, ii, 160; v, 415
    Battle of the Texel, v, 390 *n.*

INDEX

WILLIAM

William Watts (merchant), taken by Dutch, iii, 231, 234
William and John, i, 191 ; iii, 334 ; iv, 22, 293 ; v, 20
Battle of the Gabbard, v, 98 *n*.
Winthont (*or* Windhondt) (D.), iv, 309 ; v, 185
Battle of the Texel, v, 363
Witten Oliphant (D.), iv, 308
Wonder (D.), battle of Dungeness, iii, 144
Worcester (3rd r.), i, 68, 249, 257, 289 ; ii, 136, 183, 241 *sq.* ; iii, 315, 333, 406 ; iv, 20, 138, 293, 364 ; v, 16, 273, 343, 416 ; vi, 44 *n.*, 49, 78 *sq.*, 87, 93, 116, 176, 181, 184, 199, 219, 221, 238

ZUTPHEN

Appointed for the Straits, i, 61, 62 ; action off Dover, i, 208 ; petition of the ship's company, i, 249, 250 ; battle of the Texel, v, 350 ; reported lost, v, 173
Wren (prize), iv, 245 ; vi, 51

YOUNG Prince, v, 210

ZEELANDT (D.), battle of the Texel, v, 358
Zeelandia (D.), iv, 310, 324 *and n.*
Zutphen (D.), iv, 308 *sq.*, 323 *and n.*
Battle of the Texel, v, 361

THE NAVY RECORDS SOCIETY

THE NAVY RECORDS SOCIETY was established for the purpose of printing rare or unpublished works of naval interest, thereby rendering accessible the sources of our naval history, and assisting in the elucidation of questions of naval archæology, construction, administration, organisation and social life.

Any person wishing to become a Member of the Society is requested to apply to the Secretary (W. G. Perrin, Admiralty, S.W.), who will submit his name to the Council. The Annual Subscription is One Guinea. the payment of which entitles the Member to receive one copy of each work issued by the Society for that year.

Messrs. William Clowes & Sons, Ltd., of 94 Jermyn Street, London, S.W. 1, are the sole agents for the sale of publications to NON-MEMBERS. A list of the volumes available for sale to the public, and their prices, may be obtained from them.

MEMBERS requiring copies of any volume, at the prices marked herein, should apply to the Secretary.

The stock of Vols. III., V., IX., XIV., and XXIX. is now exhausted, and that of several other volumes, notably Vols. XXII., XXIII., and XXXV., is very low. It is, therefore, no longer possible to offer complete sets to new members, and having regard to this fact, the Council have decided to offer to all members selections of 20 volumes and upwards from such of the first 56 volumes as are in print (except Vols. XXII., XXIII., and XXXV.) on the following terms :—

  Any 40 or more at 10s. each
  ,, 30 ,, ,, 10s. 3d. ,,
  ,, 20 ,, ,, 10s. 6d. ,,

subject to the restriction that *Great Sea Fights*, Vol. I., will only be sold with Vol. II.

Some of the volumes can only be supplied 'cut'; others only 'uncut,' but the latter can be rebound 'cut,' at the expense of the purchaser. The uncut volumes are about half an inch taller than those with cut edges.

The Society has already issued :—

For 1894 : Vols. I. and II. *State Papers relating to the Defeat of the Spanish Armada, Anno* 1588. Edited by Professor J. K. Laughton. (30s.)

For 1895 : Vol. III. *Letters of Lord Hood,* 1781–82. Edited by Mr. David Hannay. (*Out of Print.*)

Vol. IV. *Index to James's Naval History,* by Mr. C. G. Toogood. Edited by the Hon. T. A. Brassey. (12s. 6d.)

Vol. V. *Life of Captain Stephen Martin,* 1666–1740. Edited by Sir Clements R. Markham. (*Out of Print.*)

For 1896 : Vol. VI. *Journal of Rear-Admiral Bartholomew James,* 1752–1828. Edited by Professor J. K. Laughton and Commander J. Y. F. Sulivan. (10s. 6d.)

Vol. VII. *Hollond's Discourses of the Navy,* 1638 and 1658. Edited by Mr. J. R. Tanner. (12s. 6d.)

Vol. VIII. *Naval Accounts and Inventories in the Reign of Henry VII.* Edited by Mr. M. Oppenheim. (10s. 6d.)

For 1897 : Vol. IX. *Journal of Sir George Rooke.* Edited by Mr. Oscar Browning. (*Out of Print.*)

Vol. X. *Letters and Papers relating to the War with France,* 1512–13. Edited by M. Alfred Spont. (10s. 6d.)

Vol. XI. *Papers relating to the Spanish War,* 1585–87. Edited by Mr. Julian S. Corbett. (10s. 6d.)

For 1898 : Vol. XII. *Journals and Letters of Admiral of the Fleet Sir Thomas Byam Martin,* 1773–1854 (Vol. II.). Edited by Admiral Sir R. Vesey Hamilton. (*See* XXIV.)

Vol. XIII. *Papers relating to the First Dutch War*, 1652-54 (Vol. I.). Edited by Dr. S. R. Gardiner. (10s. 6d.)

Vol. XIV. *Papers relating to the Blockade of Brest*, 1803-5 (Vol. I.). Edited by Mr. J. Leyland. (*Out of Print.*)

For 1899 : Vol. XV. *History of the Russian Fleet during the Reign of Peter the Great. By a Contemporary Englishman.* Edited by Admiral Sir Cyprian Bridge. (10s. 6d.)

Vol. XVI. *Logs of the Great Sea Fights*, 1794-1805 (Vol. I.). Edited by Vice-Admiral Sir T. Sturges Jackson. (*See* XVIII.)

Vol. XVII. *Papers relating to the First Dutch War*, 1652-54 (Vol. II.). Edited by Dr. S. R. Gardiner. (10s. 6d.)

For 1900 : Vol. XVIII. *Logs of the Great Sea Fights* (Vol. II.). Edited by Vice-Admiral Sir T. Sturges Jackson. (*Two vols.* 25s.)

Vol. XIX. *Journals and Letters of Sir T. Byam Martin* (Vol. III.). Edited by Admiral Sir R. Vesey Hamilton. (*See* XXIV.)

For 1901 : Vol. XX. *The Naval Miscellany* (Vol. I.). Edited by Professor J. K. Laughton. (15s.)

Vol. XXI. *Papers relating to the Blockade of Brest*, 1803-5 (Vol. II.). Edited by Mr. John Leyland. (12s. 6d.)

For 1902 : Vols. XXII. and XXIII. *The Naval Tracts of Sir William Monson* (Vols. I. and II.). Edited by Mr. M. Oppenheim. (40s.)

Vol. XXIV. *Journals and Letters of Sir T. Byam Martin* (Vol. I.). Edited by Admiral Sir R. Vesey Hamilton. (*Three vols.* 31s. 6d.)

For 1903 : Vol. XXV. *Nelson and the Neapolitan Jacobins.* Edited by Mr. H. C. Gutteridge. (12s. 6d.)

Vol. XXVI. *A Descriptive Catalogue of the Naval MSS. in the Pepysian Library* (Vol. I.). Edited by Mr. J. R. Tanner. (15s.)

For 1904 : Vol. XXVII. *A Descriptive Catalogue of the Naval MSS. in the Pepysian Library* (Vol. II.). Edited by Mr. J. R. Tanner. (12s. 6d.)

Vol. XXVIII. *The Correspondence of Admiral John Markham*, 1801–7. Edited by Sir Clements R. Markham. (12s. 6d.)

For 1905 : Vol. XXIX. *Fighting Instructions*, 1530–1816. Edited by Mr. Julian S. Corbett. (*Out of Print.*)

Vol. XXX. *Papers relating to the First Dutch War*, 1652–54 (Vol. III.). Edited by the late Dr. S. R. Gardiner and Mr. C. T. Atkinson. (12s. 6d.)

For 1906 : Vol. XXXI. *The Recollections of Commander James Anthony Gardner*, 1775–1814. Edited by Admiral Sir R. Vesey Hamilton and Professor J. K. Laughton. (12s. 6d.)

Vol. XXXII. *Letters and Papers of Charles, Lord Barham*, 1758–1813 (Vol. I.). Edited by Sir J. K. Laughton. (12s. 6d.)

For 1907 : Vol. XXXIII. *Naval Ballads and Songs.* Edited by Professor C. H. Firth. (12s. 6d.)

Vol. XXXIV. *Views of the Battles of the Third Dutch War.* Edited by Mr. Julian S. Corbett. (20s.)

For 1908 : Vol. XXXV. *Signals and Instructions*, 1776–94. Edited by Mr. Julian S. Corbett. (15s.)

Vol. XXXVI. *A Descriptive Catalogue of the Naval MSS. in the Pepysian Library* (Vol. III.). Edited by Dr. J. R. Tanner. (12s. 6d.)

For 1909: Vol. XXXVII. *Papers relating to the First Dutch War, 1652-54* (Vol. IV.). Edited by Mr. C. T. Atkinson. (12s. 6d.)

Vol. XXXVIII. *Letters and Papers of Charles, Lord Barham, 1758-1813* (Vol. II.). Edited by Sir J. K. Laughton. (12s. 6d.)

For 1910: Vol. XXXIX. *Letters and Papers of Charles, Lord Barham, 1758-1813* (Vol. III.). Edited by Sir J. K. Laughton. (12s. 6d.)

Vol. XL. *The Naval Miscellany* (Vol. II.). Edited by Sir J. K. Laughton. (12s. 6d.)

For 1911: Vol. XLI. *Papers relating to the First Dutch War, 1652-54* (Vol. V.). Edited by Mr. C. T. Atkinson. (12s. 6d.)

Vol. XLII. *Papers relating to the Loss of Minorca in 1756.* Edited by Capt. H. W. Richmond, R.N. (10s. 6d.)

For 1912: Vol. XLIII. *The Naval Tracts of Sir William Monson* (Vol. III.). Edited by Mr. M. Oppenheim. (12s. 6d.)

Vol. XLIV. *The Old Scots Navy, 1689-1710.* Edited by Mr. James Grant. (10s. 6d.)

For 1913: Vol. XLV. *The Naval Tracts of Sir William Monson* (Vol. IV.). Edited by Mr. M. Oppenheim. (12s. 6d.)

Vol. XLVI. *The Private Papers of George, second Earl Spencer* (Vol. I.). Edited by Mr. Julian S. Corbett. (12s. 6d.)

For 1914: Vol. XLVII. *The Naval Tracts of Sir William Monson* (Vol. V.). Edited by Mr. M. Oppenheim. (12s. 6d.)

Vol. XLVIII. *The Private Papers of George, second Earl Spencer* (Vol. II.). Edited by Mr. Julian S. Corbett. (12s. 6d.)

For 1915: Vol. XLIX. *Documents relating to Law and Custom of the Sea* (Vol. I.). Edited by Mr. R. G. Marsden. (17s. 6d.)

For 1916: Vol. L. *Documents relating to Law and Custom of the Sea* (Vol. II.). Edited by Mr. R. G. Marsden. (15s.)

For 1917: Vol. LI. *Autobiography of Phineas Pett.* Edited by Mr. W. G. Perrin. (12s.)

For 1918: Vol. LII. *The Life of Admiral Sir John Leake.* (Vol. I.). Edited by Mr. G. A. R. Callender. (15s.)

For 1919: Vol. LIII. *The Life of Admiral Sir John Leake* (Vol. II.). Edited by Mr. G. A. R. Callender. (15s.)

For 1920: Vol. LIV. *The Life and Works of Sir Henry Mainwaring* (Vol. I.). Edited by Mr. G. E. Manwaring. (15s.)

For 1921: Vol. LV. *The Letters of Lord St. Vincent,* 1801–1804 (Vol. I.). Edited by Mr. D. B. Smith. (15s.)

Vol. LVI. *The Life and Works of Sir Henry Mainwaring* (Vol. II.). Edited by Mr. G. E. Manwaring and Mr. W. G. Perrin. (12s. 6d.)

For 1922: Vol. LVII. *A Descriptive Catalogue of the Naval MSS. in the Pepysian Library* (Vol. IV.). Edited by Dr. J. R. Tanner. (24s.)

For 1923: Vol. LVIII. *The Private Papers of George, second Earl Spencer* (Vol. III.). Edited by Rear-Admiral H. W. Richmond. (16s.)

For 1924: Vol. LIX. *The Private Papers of George, second Earl Spencer* (Vol. IV.). Edited by Rear-Admiral H. W. Richmond. (15s.)

For 1925: Vol. LX. *Samuel Pepys's Naval Minutes.* Edited by Dr. J. R. Tanner. (21s.)

For 1926: Vol. LXI. *The Letters of Lord St. Vincent, 1801–1804* (Vol. II.). Edited by Mr. D. B. Smith. (20s.)

Vol. LXII. *Letters and Papers of Admiral Viscount Keith* (Vol. I.). Edited by Mr. W. G. Perrin. (17s.)

For 1927: Vol. LXIII. *The Naval Miscellany* (Vol. III.). Edited by Mr. W. G. Perrin. (20s.)

For 1928: Vol. LXIV. *The Journal of the First Earl of Sandwich*. Edited by Mr. R. C. Anderson. (17s.)

For 1929: Vol. LXV. *Boteler's Dialogues*. Edited by Mr. W. G. Perrin. (16s.)

For 1930: Vol. LXVI. *Papers relating to the First Dutch War, 1652–54* (Vol. VI.; with index). Edited by Mr. C. T. Atkinson. (15s.)

Vol. LXVII. *The Byng Papers* (Vol I.). Edited by Mr. W. C. B. Tunstall. (15s.)

Among other intended works are further volumes of *The Catalogue of the Pepysian MSS.*, *The Naval Miscellany*, the *Letters and Papers of Admiral Viscount Keith* and *The Byng Papers*; and selections from the papers of *The Fourth Earl of Sandwich*.

www.ingramcontent.com/pod-product-compliance
Lightning Source LLC
Chambersburg PA
CBHW051248300426
44114CB00011B/938